A NEW INTRODUCTION
TO MODAL LOGIC

A NEW INTRODUCTION
TO
MODAL LOGIC

G. E. Hughes

Late Professor of Philosophy
Victoria University of Wellington

M. J. Cresswell

Professor of Philosophy
Victoria University of Wellington

London and New York

First Published 1996
by Routledge
11 New Fetter Lane, London EC4P 4EE

Simultaneously published in the USA and Canada
by Routledge
29 West 35th Street, New York, NY 10001

Typeset in Times by M.J.Cresswell

Printed and bound in Great Britain by
T. J. Press (Padstow) Ltd.

British Library Cataloguing in Publication Data
A catalogue record for this book is available from the British Library.

Library of Congress Cataloguing in Publication Data
A catalogue record for this book has been requested.

ISBN 0-415-12599-5 (hbk)
ISBN 0-415-12600-2 (pbk)

CONTENTS

Part Two: *Normal Modal Systems*

Part Three: Modal Predicate Logic

PREFACE

Modal logic is the logic of necessity and possibility, of 'must be' and 'may be'. By this is meant that it considers not only truth and falsity applied to what is or is not so as things actually stand, but considers what would be so if things were different. If we think of how things are as the actual world then we may think of how things might have been as how things are in an alternative, non-actual but possible, state of affairs – or possible world. Logic is concerned with truth and falsity. In modal logic we are concerned with truth or falsity in other possible worlds as well as the real one. In this sense a proposition will be necessary in a world if it is true in all worlds which are possible relative to that world, and possible in a world if it is true in at least one world possible relative to that world. All this is explained in the first chapter of this book.

Our aim in this book is to introduce readers to modal logic, and we assume that to begin with the reader knows nothing of modal logic. We have attempted to make the book self contained so that it could even be tackled by someone who had not studied any logic at all. However, we anticipate that most readers will already know a little about the (non-modal) propositional and predicate calculi, and will be able to use this knowledge as a foundation for understanding modal logic.

This book is intended as a replacement for our earlier two books *An Introduction to Modal Logic* (Hughes and Cresswell, 1968, IML) and *A Companion to Modal Logic* (Hughes and Cresswell, 1984, CML) and we shall here say a little about the relation between it and the earlier books. Part I covers most of the ground covered in IML with two important changes. First, as in CML, we take the system K as basic rather than T. Second, as also in CML, we have (in Chapter 6) used the method of canonical models to prove completeness. We have retained (in Chapter 5) the method of modal conjunctive normal forms to prove the completeness of S5, but while (in Chapter 4) we have retained from IML the method of semantic diagrams for testing formulae, we have omitted the completeness proofs based on this method.

Part II covers a range of topics in modal propositional logic, most of which are also discussed in CML. In the present work we have attempted to be particularly sensitive to its role as an introduction. Thus, to take one example, our approach to finite models is one that we believe is easier to follow than the more standard method of filtrations which we used in CML. Although this part of the book may be seen as more of interest to specialists we have tried to present its topics in a way which should be easily accessible to the reader who has followed Part I. Part III of IML contained a survey of modal logic as it was in 1968. A comparable survey would be impossible today but we have attempted, in Chapter 11 of the present book, to give an outline of the more important developments in the earlier history of modal logic. Readers who need more may be referred to IML.

Part III was the most difficult to write. Modal predicate logic is rightly regarded as the most philosophically important branch of modal logic, and although this is a book on formal logic not philosophical logic, we have attempted to discuss topics which have a bearing on such important philosophical questions as what to say about things which exist in one world but not another or about things claimed to be identical but not necessarily so. Unfortunately, the semantics of modal predicate logic is extremely complicated, and while we have tried to make our discussions as approachable as we can, we are conscious of the burden imposed on the reader. All we can say is that we have attempted to set out all technical material so that with patience a reader should be able to follow every proof without requiring more than is in this book.

George Hughes died on 4 March 1994. At the time of his death we had completed the first five chapters. Chapter 6 and most of Part II has been adapted from CML, and we had discussed many issues in that area. In preparing the manuscript I have endeavoured, to the best of my ability, to write it as a joint work and present it in a style as close as I can to what would have emerged had George Hughes lived to see its completion. It is in Part III that I have felt the greatest lack of his collaboration, and I am grateful especially to Rob Goldblatt and Edwin Mares here in Wellington who have looked at and commented on many passages. We would also thank various readers, and colleagues from around the world, whose 'wish lists' we have not always been able to take as much note of as they would like.

Our department secretary, Debbie Luyinda, put the initial manuscript into the computer, so that we could then play with it, and we would thank her for this, at times frustrating, work.

Wellington, New Zealand
January 1995

Part I

BASIC MODAL
PROPOSITIONAL
LOGIC

1

THE BASIC NOTIONS

In this chapter we introduce the basic notions of modal propositional logic. Modal logic is based upon the 'ordinary' (two-valued) Propositional Calculus, and when we use the expression 'Propositional Calculus' (or the abbreviation 'PC') *simpliciter*, it is to this non-modal system of logic that we shall be referring.[1] The present chapter begins by outlining, in a very summary fashion, those elements of PC which we shall take for granted in what follows, and at the same time explains some of the terminology which we shall use throughout the book.

The language of PC
We take as *primitive* (or undefined) symbols of PC the following:

A set of *letters: p, q, r, ...* (with or without numerical subscripts). We suppose ourselves to have an unlimited number of these.

The following four symbols: $\sim$, $\vee$, (,).

Any symbol in the above list, or any sequence of such symbols, we call an *expression*. An expression is either a formula — more exactly a well-formed formula (wff) — or else it is not. We are concerned only with expressions which are well-formed formulae (wff). The following *formation rules* of PC specify which expressions are to count as wff:

FR1   A letter standing alone is a wff.
FR2   If α is a wff, so is $\sim\alpha$.
FR3   If α and β are wff, so is $(\alpha \vee \beta)$.

In these rules the symbols α and β are used to stand indifferently for any expressions. Thus the meaning of FR2 is: the result of prefixing $\sim$ to any

3

wff is itself a wff. Symbols used as α and β are used here are known as metalogical variables. They are not among the symbols of the system (PC in this case), but are used in talking about the system.

Examples of wff are: p, $\sim q$, $\sim \sim \sim q$, $(p \lor \sim q)$, $((p \lor r) \lor \sim (q \lor \sim (\sim r \lor p)))$. For convenience, however, we allow ourselves to omit the outermost brackets round any complete wff (though not any subordinate part thereof). No ambiguity in interpretation or unclarity about what is permitted by the rules will result from this notational simplification.

Interpretation

We interpret the letters as variables whose values are *propositions*. We shall usually call them *propositional variables*. We assume that the reader is familiar with the notion of a proposition, and shall not enter into the philosophical issues which this notion raises. Rough synonyms of 'proposition' are 'statement' and 'assertion', where these words are used to refer to *what is stated or asserted,* not to the *act of stating or asserting.* Every proposition is either true or false, and no proposition is both true and false. (Hence if something is neither true nor false, or is capable of being both true and false, it is not to count as a proposition in the present context.) Truth and falsity are said to be the *truth-values* of propositions.

Now it is possible to form more complex propositions out of simpler ones. E.g., out of the proposition that Brutus killed Caesar we can form the proposition that it is not the case that Brutus killed Caesar. This is a proposition which is true if the original proposition is false, and false otherwise. In general, putting 'it is not the case that' in front of a sentence will result in a sentence which expresses a proposition which is true if the original sentence expresses one which is false, and a false proposition if it does not.

Similarly, from the proposition that Brutus killed Caesar and the proposition that Cassius killed Caesar we may form the proposition that either Brutus killed Caesar or Cassius killed Caesar. This proposition will be true iff (if and only if) at least one of the original propositions is true, and therefore false iff both of these are false.

'It is not the case that' and 'either ... or ...', when used in the way we have just described, may be said to be *proposition-forming operators* on propositions, because they make new propositions out of old ones. The propositions on which such an operator operates are called its arguments.

If an operator requires only a single argument, as 'it is not the case that' does, it is said to be *monadic*; if, like 'either ... or ...', it requires two, it is said to be *dyadic*.

Our explanation of these operators, 'it is not the case that' and 'either... or ...', showed that the truth-value of a proposition formed by means of either of them depends in every case only on the truth-value of the operator's argument or arguments. In other words, whenever we are given the truth-value of the argument or arguments, we can deduce the truth-value of the complex proposition. An operator which has this property is said to be a *truth-functional* operator, and the propositions it forms are said to be *truth-functions* of its arguments. Not all proposition-forming operators are of this kind. For example, given merely the truth or falsity of the proposition that Brutus killed Caesar we cannot deduce the truth or falsity of the proposition that Napoleon believed that Brutus killed Caesar; and given merely that two propositions are both true we cannot deduce from this either the truth or the falsity of the proposition that the first follows logically from the second (though if we are given that one proposition is false and another true, we *can* deduce from this that it is false that the first follows logically from the second). Hence although 'Napoleon believed that' and 'follows logically from' are proposition-forming operators on propositions (monadic and dyadic respectively), they are not truth-functional operators.

We interpret $\sim$ and $\lor$ as 'it is not the case that' and 'either ... or ...' respectively, in the senses we have explained, and we usually read them simply as 'not' and 'or'. $\sim$ so interpreted is called the *negation sign*; $\sim p$ is said to be the *negation* of p. Using 1 and 0 for the truth-values truth and falsity respectively, we can express the meaning we attach to $\sim$ in the following *basic truth-table for negation*:

	$\sim$
1	0
0	1

Here the left-hand column tabulates the possible truth-values of a given proposition, and the right-hand column sets down the corresponding truth-values of the negation of that proposition. When interpreted in the way we have described, $\lor$ is known as the *disjunction sign* and its arguments are called *disjuncts*; $p \lor q$ is said to be the *disjunction* of p and q. The basic truth-table for disjunction is:

5

V	1	0
1	1	1
0	1	0

The possible truth-values of the first disjunct are tabulated in the leftmost vertical column and those of the second in the topmost horizontal row. The truth-value of their disjunction is found by reading across and down.

These basic truth-tables bring out clearly the truth-functional nature of the operators. In fact, not merely ~ and ∨, but all operators in PC, are truth-functional and for this reason PC is sometimes called the theory of truth-functions. We said earlier that we interpret p, q, r, ... as variables whose values are propositions; but in view of the fact that the only feature of the arguments of the operators which is relevant to the truth-value of the complex propositions they form is their truth-value, it is equally satisfactory from a formal point of view to regard the variables as having as their range of values, not the whole infinite set of propositions, but simply the two truth-values 1 and 0.

Further operators

A number of other operators can be defined in terms of the primitive ones. We introduce three new operators, ∧, ⊃ and ≡, though it would be possible to have several others as well. The definitions are:

[Def ∧] $(\alpha \wedge \beta) =_{df} \sim(\sim\alpha \vee \sim\beta)$
[Def ⊃] $(\alpha \supset \beta) =_{df} (\sim\alpha \vee \beta)$
[Def ≡] $(\alpha \equiv \beta) =_{df} ((\alpha \supset \beta) \wedge (\beta \supset \alpha))$

In these definitions α and β represent any wff of PC and the symbol '$=_{df}$' is read as 'is defined as'. The meaning of the first definition is that whenever we have a wff of the form ~(~— ∨ ~—), where the blanks are filled by any wff we please, we can replace this wff by an expression which consists of the wff which filled the first blank followed by a ∧ followed by the wff which filled the second blank, the whole being enclosed in brackets. Analogous explanations apply to the two other definitions. Similarly, we can expand any expression of the form on the left into the corresponding expression of the form on the right.

Expressions which can be transformed, by applying definitions, into wff as specified by the original formation rules, are themselves to count as wff. When a wff contains no symbols except primitive ones it is said to be written in *primitive notation*. The definitions enable us to write all wff in primitive notation if we wish to do so.

Interpretation of ∧, ⊃ and ≡

The interpretation we have already given to ∼ and ∨ will determine the interpretation we give to the operators defined in terms of them. Thus, we can calculate the truth-values of $p ∧ q$ for all possible truth-values of p and q by calculating the appropriate truth-values of the wff of which it is an abbreviation, viz. $∼(∼p ∨ ∼q)$, and the basic truth-tables for ∼ and ∨ enable us to do this. It turns out that $p ∧ q$ will be true when both p and q are true, but false in all other cases. The basic truth-table for ∧ will therefore be:

$$
\begin{array}{c|cc}
∧ & 1 & 0 \\
\hline
1 & 1 & 0 \\
0 & 0 & 0
\end{array}
$$

When ∧ is so interpreted, it is called the *conjunction sign*; it may be read as 'and'. A wff formed with ∧ is known as a *conjunction*, and the arguments are called *conjuncts*.

Similar considerations give the following basic truth-table for ⊃:

$$
\begin{array}{c|cc}
⊃ & 1 & 0 \\
\hline
1 & 1 & 0 \\
0 & 1 & 1
\end{array}
$$

I.e. a proposition formed with ⊃ is false when the first argument is true and the second false, but true in all other cases. When so interpreted, ⊃ is known as the *(material) implication sign*. It may be read as '(materially) implies' or as 'if [the first argument], then [the second argument]'. The first argument is known as the *antecedent*, the second as the *consequent*. The precise relation of material implication to the various uses of the word 'if' in English raises complex questions into which we shall not enter here. It may plausibly be claimed, however, that material implication represents the truth-functional component in the meaning of 'if' in at least a great many of its standard uses.

The basic truth-table for ≡ works out as:

7

$\equiv$	1	0
1	1	0
0	0	1

I.e. a proposition formed with $\equiv$ is true when both arguments have the same truth-value, false when they have different truth-values. When so interpreted, $\equiv$ is known as the *(material) equivalence sign*. It may be read as 'is (materially) equivalent to', or as 'if and only if'.

Clearly these new operators, like the primitive ones, are truth-functional.

(We could have chosen other operators than $\sim$ and $\vee$ as primitive. Some authors, for example, take $\sim$ and $\wedge$ as primitive and define $\vee$ in terms of these. But whatever primitives we use, provided that all the operators can consistently be given the basic truth-tables listed above, the system of PC so obtained will be exactly equivalent to the one we have set down here.)

Validity

If we regard the variables, p, q, r, ... as taking the whole range of propositions as their values, we can say that a wff of PC becomes a proposition when all its variables are replaced by propositions. A wff is said to be *valid* iff the result of *every* such replacement is a true proposition. (It is assumed that the replacement is carried out uniformly, i.e. that two or more occurrences of the same variable are always replaced by the same proposition.) If, however, we speak instead of the variables taking simply the two truth-values 1 and 0 as their values, we shall say that a wff is valid iff it always has the value 1, no matter what truth-values are (uniformly) assigned to its variables. We shall normally choose to speak in this second way; since all the operators in PC are truth-functional, exactly the same formulae will turn out to be valid in each case. Simple examples of valid wff are $p \vee \sim p$ and $(p \wedge q) \supset p$. (A valid wff of PC is often called a *tautology* or a *PC-tautology*.)

A wff is said to be *unsatisfiable* iff it always has the value 0, no matter what truth-values are (uniformly) assigned to its variables. A simple example of an unsatisfiable wff is $p \wedge \sim p$. Many wff, such as $p \supset q$, are of course neither valid nor unsatisfiable.

Later in this chapter we shall extend this definition of validity to cover the formulae of modal logic, and to make the extended definition more

8

easily comprehensible we shall express it in the form of a parlour game. As a preliminary to this let us now consider how we might devise a simple game based on the definition of PC-validity which we have just mentioned. The game could take this form. We give a player a sheet of paper on which we have previously written a number of letters of the alphabet (preferably taken from the series, p, q, r, ... etc.). We shall refer to the player and the sheet as a *setting* of the *PC game*, or more succinctly a *PC-setting*. PC-settings will differ only in the list of letters on the sheet of paper.

We then call out to the player wff of PC, to which the player is to respond by either raising his or her hand or keeping it down. But each call must be appropriately prepared for, in that before a wff α is called we must have previously called all the formulae which occur as parts of α, beginning with the variables. E.g., if $(\sim p \lor p)$ is to be called we must first call p, and then $\sim p$ and only then may we call $(\sim p \lor p)$. The player's instructions are as follows:

1. If a single letter (variable) is called, raise your hand if that letter is on the sheet; keep it down if it is not.
2. If $\sim \alpha$ is called (where α is a wff) raise your hand if you kept it down when α was called; keep it down if you raised it when α was called. (Remember that if $\sim \alpha$ has been appropriately prepared for, α must have already been called.)
3. If $(\alpha \lor \beta)$ is called, raise your hand if you raised it for α or for β; keep it down if you kept it down for both α and β.

Using the definitions of $\supset$, $\land$ and $\equiv$ we can easily derive rules for responding to formulae containing these operators. Alternatively we can transform all formulae into primitive notation before we begin. It might be worth stating the rule for $\supset$ explicitly:

3a. If $(\alpha \supset \beta)$ is called, raise your hand if you kept it down for α or raised it for β; keep it down if you raised it for α and kept it down for β.

It is not difficult to see that in any PC-setting the rules require the player to respond unambiguously to any PC formula, provided that it is appropriately prepared for. If the player in a PC-setting raises his or her

9

hand when a PC wff α is called, we shall say that α is *successful* in that setting. Many formulae will be successful in some settings but not in others (depending of course on which letters appear on the sheet for a given setting). But there will be some formulae which will be successful in every PC- setting (e.g. $p \lor \sim p$). These we call *PC-successful*.

To make explicit what must be becoming an obvious parallel, let us call the sheet of variables an assignment of truth-values with the idea that a variable has the value 1 if it is on the sheet and 0 otherwise. On this understanding, when the player's hand is raised when a wff α is called it will mean that α has the value 1, and when the player's hand is kept down when α is called it will mean that α has the value 0. The rules 1, 2 and 3 for responding to formulae when thus translated exactly reflect the basic truth-tables for $\sim$ and $\lor$. A formula will be successful in a PC-setting iff it has the value 1 for the corresponding assignment of truth-values to its variables. And a formula will be PC-successful iff it is has the value 1 for every PC-assignment. I.e., the PC-successful wff are precisely those which are PC-valid.

Since for any wff α containing n variables we need only consider sheets which contain a selection (possibly all or possibly none) of those n variables (for clearly the responses to variables not in α cannot affect the response to α), we can set out all the relevantly different PC-settings on 2^n sheets. So we could check whether α is valid by preparing such a set of sheets and calling α (with the appropriate preparatory calls) for each of them. This procedure can be codified by what is called the truth-table method of testing for PC-validity.

Testing for validity: (i) the truth-table method

In this method of testing a PC formula, α, for validity, all possible PC value-assignments, i.e. all assignments of truth-values to the propositional variables in α, are tabulated, and for each such value-assignment, the basic truth-tables for the operators are used to calculate the truth-value of α as 1 or 0. The result is a column of 1s and/or 0s. This column is known as the *truth-table* of the wff. If and only if it consists entirely of 1s, the wff is valid.

An example should make the procedure clear. Let α be $((p \supset q) \land r) \supset ((\sim r \lor p) \supset q)$. Here we have three distinct variables and therefore eight PC value-assignments. The construction of the truth-table proceeds as follows:

p q r	$((p \supset q)$	$\wedge$ $r)$	$\supset$	$((\sim r$	$\vee$ $p)$	$\supset$ $q)$
1 1 1	1	1	1	0	1	1
1 1 0	1	0	1	1	1	1
1 0 1	0	0	1	0	1	0
1 0 0	0	0	1	1	1	0
0 1 1	1	1	1	0	0	1
0 1 0	1	0	1	1	1	1
0 0 1	1	1	1	0	0	1
0 0 0	1	0	1	1	1	0
	(1)	(2)	(6)	(3)	(4)	(5)

The complete list of value-assignments is set down to the left of the vertical line. The columns to the right are numbered in the order in which they are obtained. Thus column (1), for $p \supset q$, is obtained from the columns under p and q by the basic truth-table for $\supset$; column (2) is obtained from (1) and the column under r, by the basic truth-table for $\wedge$; ... until finally column (6), the truth-table for the whole wff, is obtained from (2) and (5). Since (6) consists entirely of 1s α is PC-valid.

Testing for validity: (ii) the Reductio method

A formula can usually be tested more expeditiously by trying to find a falsifying value-assignment for it. The *Reductio* method enables us to find such a value-assignment if there is one.

We begin by supposing that there is such an assignment for which α has 0. We express this supposition by writing 0 under the main operator of α. From this supposition certain consequences follow, by the basic truth-tables, about the values which must be assigned to certain well-formed parts of α; e.g., if α is of the form $\beta \supset \gamma$, it can only have 0 if β has 1 and γ has 0. From these new values certain other consequences follow in the same way, and so on, until finally we either (i) reach a consistent value-assignment to all the variables in α (in which case α is invalid), or (ii) find that we cannot reach such a consistent value-assignment (in which case α is valid).

As an example, let α be the formula we used to illustrate the truth-table method, viz. $((p \supset q) \wedge r) \supset ((\sim r \vee p) \supset q)$. We set out the whole working immediately and then explain it.

11

$$((p \supset q) \wedge r) \supset ((\sim r \vee p) \supset q)$$

0	10	1\underline{1}		0	1 \underline{0}	10	00
9	4 8	2 5	1		11 12	6 10	3 7

The numerals under the truth-values indicate the order of the steps. Step 1 is the initial assignment of 0 to α. Since α is of the form $\beta \supset \gamma$ if α has 0, β must have 1 (step 2) and γ must have 0 (step 3). The 1s at steps 4 and 5 are required by the table for $\wedge$ since β is a conjunction and must have the value 1. The remaining steps should now be clear. We finally reach the conclusion (indicated by underlining) that if we are to have α with 0 r must have both the value 1 and the value 0. Hence α can never have 0, and is therefore valid.

Other cases are sometimes not so simple. Suppose that α is the converse of the previous formula, viz. $((\sim r \vee p) \supset q) \supset ((p \supset q) \wedge r)$. Steps 1, 2 and 3 can proceed as before, but the values at steps 2 and 3 do not determine further values uniquely. We can however list exhaustively the alternatives left open at step 2 by the assumption that $((\sim r \vee p) \supset q)$ has 1, as follows:

$$((\sim r \vee p) \supset q) \supset ((p \supset q) \wedge r)$$

		1	0		0
		2	1		3
(a)	1	1 1	0		0
(b)	0	1 1	0		0
(c)	0	1 0	0		0

(a), (b) and (c) represent all the value-assignments to $(\sim r \vee p)$ and q which are compatible with the truth of $((\sim r \vee p) \supset q)$. If each of these leads us to an inconsistency, α is valid; if even one of them is compatible with a consistent assignment to the variables, α is not valid. In fact (b) and (c) both lead to inconsistencies; but (a) does not – it is compatible with $q = 1$, $r = 0$ and $p = 1$ or 0. Hence the whole formula is not valid.

Provided we consider in this way all alternative value-assignments as the need arises, we can test the validity of any wff of PC whatever by the Reductio method. We shall make considerable use of this method in Chapter 4.

Each of the two methods we have described gives us an effective (i.e.

mechanical and finite) procedure for deciding of any given wff of PC whether it is valid or not. Another way of expressing this is by saying that each method gives us a *decision procedure* for PC.

Some valid wff of PC

We list here some valid PC wff which we shall use in the next few chapters. In some cases we give, in addition to a reference number, a name by which the formula is commonly known and an abbreviation by which we shall usually refer to it in this book.

PC1	$(p \wedge q) \supset p$	
PC2	$(p \wedge q) \supset q$	
PC3	$(p \supset q) \supset ((p \supset r) \supset (p \supset (q \wedge r)))$	
		[Law of Composition–Comp]
PC4	$p \supset (q \supset (p \wedge q))$	[Law of Adjunction–Adj]
PC5	$(p \supset q) \supset ((q \supset p) \supset (p \equiv q))$	
PC6	$(p \supset q) \supset ((q \supset r) \supset (p \supset r))$	[Law of Syllogism–Syll]
PC7	$(p \supset (q \supset r)) \supset ((p \wedge q) \supset r)$	[Law of Importation–Imp]
PC8	$(p \supset q) \supset ((q \supset (r \supset s)) \supset ((p \wedge r) \supset s))$	
PC9	$p \supset (p \vee q)$	
PC10	$q \supset (p \vee q)$	
PC11	$(p \supset q) \supset ((r \supset q) \supset ((p \vee r) \supset q))$	
PC12	$p \equiv \sim\sim p$	[Law of Double Negation–DN]
PC13	$(p \vee q) \equiv \sim(\sim p \wedge \sim q)$	[De Morgan Laws—DeM]
PC14	$(p \wedge q) \equiv \sim(\sim p \vee \sim q)$	
PC15	$(p \supset q) \equiv (\sim q \supset \sim p)$	[Law of Transposition–Transp]
PC16	$(p \vee q) \equiv (q \vee p)$	[Commutative Laws—Comm]
PC17	$(p \wedge q) \equiv (q \wedge p)$	
PC18	$((p \vee q) \vee r) \equiv (p \vee (q \vee r))$	[Associative Laws—Assoc]
PC19	$((p \wedge q) \wedge r) \equiv (p \wedge (q \wedge r))$	
PC20	$p \equiv (p \vee p)$	
PC21	$p \equiv (p \wedge p)$	

Basic modal notions

On p. 5 we called attention to the distinction between truth-functional and non-truth-functional operators, and we noted that all the operators which we use in PC are interpreted purely truth-functionally. In modal logic, however, we are going to be concerned in addition with a number of non-truth-functional concepts, and to express these we shall extend the language of PC by adding to it some new operators which we shall interpret in a non-truth-functional way.

To begin with, we shall add to the language of PC a new monadic operator, L, with the formation rule that if α is a wff, so is $L\alpha$. We shall call L the *necessity operator*, and our intended interpretation of it is that it is to express, in the form of a proposition-forming operator on propositions, the notion which is commonly expressed by English words or phrases such as 'necessarily', 'must be', 'is bound to be'. In ordinary English such expressions, like the truth-functional 'not', are frequently found in the middle of a sentence rather than at the beginning; but just as it is possible, at the cost of a little artificiality, to replace an embedded 'not' by the phrase 'it is not the case that' at the beginning of the sentence, and thereby bring out more clearly its nature as an operator on propositions, so we can, for example, re-cast a sentence of the form 'A is bound to be B' as 'It is bound to be the case that A is B'. Necessity is called a *modal* notion, presumably because being necessarily true has been thought of as a *mode* or manner in which a proposition can be true.

We shall usually read Lp as 'Necessarily p'. But in doing so we do not intend to claim that our use of L will reflect all the standard English uses of 'necessarily' and the other expressions we have mentioned, any more that we could claim that the basic truth-table for conjunction provides an adequate analysis of all standard English uses of 'and'. On the other hand, we do not want to restrict its meaning to a single narrowly conceived sense of 'necessarily', etc. Very often, for example, when we say that something *must* be so, we can be taken to be claiming that it *is* so; and if we take L to express 'must be' in this sense, we shall want to have it as a principle that whenever Lp is true, so is p itself. On the other hand there are uses of words such as 'must' and 'necessary' in which they express not what necessarily *is so* but rather what *morally ought to be so;* and if we interpret L in accordance with these uses we shall want to allow the possibility that Lp may be true but p itself false, since people do not always do what they ought to do. As we shall see in the next chapter, it will prove possible to devise systems of modal logic which contain 'If Lp then p' as a principle, and other systems which do not. In fact, one of the important features of modal logic is that out of the same basic material we can construct a variety of systems which reflect a variety of interpretations of L, within the range which can be indicated, somewhat loosely, by calling it a necessity operator. We shall even sometimes extend the interpretation of L a little beyond these limits; for fruitful systems of logic have been inspired by the idea of taking the necessity operator to mean, for example, 'It will always be the case that ...', 'It is known that ...' or 'It is provable that ...'. All this should become clearer as we proceed.

One thing that should be clear already, however, is that in any of the interpretations we have referred to, the necessity operator is not a truth-functional one: that is, the truth-value of p itself is not always sufficient to determine the truth-value of Lp. Hence we cannot define L in terms of any combination of the PC operators, and we therefore introduce it as a new primitive symbol.

Another notion which leads, in a parallel way, to a monadic non-truth-functional operator is one expressed by terms such as 'possibly', 'can be', 'may be'. We shall use M as an operator with this meaning, and we shall usually read Mp as 'possibly p'. If we already have L in our logical language, however, we do not need to have M as a new *primitive* symbol; for to say that it is possible that p is equivalent to saying that it is not necessary that not-p, and we can therefore define $M\alpha$, for any α, as $\sim L \sim \alpha$. Thus for every interpretation of L there will be a corresponding interpretation of M: if Lp means that p is necessarily true, Mp will mean that p is possibly true, if Lp means that it is morally obligatory that p, Mp will mean that it is morally permissible that p (not obligatory that not-p), if Lp means that it will always be the case that p, Mp will mean that it will sometime be the case that p, and so forth. (If we had chosen to take M as primitive we could have defined L as $\sim M \sim$. Whether to take L or M as primitive is a matter of taste. We shall continue to take L as primitive and M as defined.) Impossibility, along with necessity and possibility, is often also classified as a modal notion, but it does not call for special discussion here since there is no difficulty in expressing it by the operator $\sim M$ (or alternatively $L \sim$). Propositions which are neither necessary nor impossible are called *contingent*.[2]

A relation between propositions that we may easily express with the tools at our disposal is that of necessary implication. Necessary implication is sometimes called *strict*, in contrast to material, implication, and we shall have more to say about it in Chapter 11. It is important not to confuse $L(p \supset q)$, which means that the whole hypothetical 'if p then q' is a necessary truth, or that q follows logically from p, with $p \supset Lq$, which means that if p is true then q is a necessary truth. Unhappily, these are often confused in ordinary discourse, sometimes with disastrous results; and neglect of the distinction is made all the easier by the ambiguity of such common idioms as 'If ... then it must be (or is bound to be) the case that —'. To make things worse, the structure of such sentences is more closely analogous to that of $p \supset Lq$, but one suspects that most frequently what the speaker intends to assert (or at least all they are entitled to assert) is something of the form $L(p \supset q)$. Thus someone who says, 'If it rains throughout December it is bound to rain on Christmas Day' probably means to assert that 'it will rain on Christmas Day' follows from 'it will rain throughout December' (which is true, since Christmas Day is in December); but they could be taken to be asserting that if it rains throughout December then it is a necessary truth that it will rain on Christmas Day (which, at least if it does rain throughout December, is false because, come what may about the weather, 'it will rain on Christmas Day' expresses a contingent proposition, not a necessary one).

Perhaps no one, except in their dullest moments, would be taken in by this example. But people have, it appears, confused the necessary truth of 'If a thing is going to happen it is going to happen' with the view that whatever happens happens by logical necessity, or even argued for Fatalism by inferring illicitly from the former to the latter. And in epistemological discussions the fact (if it is a fact) that, of necessity, if someone knows that p then p is true has sometimes been held to show something which does not follow from it at all, viz. that only necessary truths can ever be known. This transition is facilitated if we express the premiss of the argument by the ambiguous but more colloquial 'If you know something, it must be true (can't be false)'. Even a little study of modal logic can protect us from pitfalls in philosophy and elsewhere.

The language of propositional modal logic
We are now in a position to be able to specify precisely the language we shall use for all the systems of propositional modal logic which we shall describe in later chapters. Its symbols and rules are:

Primitive symbols

$p, q, r, \ldots$	[propositional variables]
$\sim, L$	[monadic operators]
$\vee$	[dyadic operator]
$(,)$	[brackets]

Formation rules
FR1 A propositional variable is a wff.
FR2 If α is a wff, so are $\sim\alpha$ and $L\alpha$.

FR3 If α and β are wff, so is $(\alpha \lor \beta)$.

Definitions
Def $\land$, Def $\supset$, Def $\equiv$ as in PC (p. 6), plus

[Def M] $M\alpha =_{df} {\sim}L \sim\alpha$

As we did for PC, we adopt the convention that brackets enclosing a complete wff may be omitted.

Clearly every wff of PC is also a wff of modal logic. A few examples of wff of modal logic which are not wff of PC are: $Lp \supset p$; $MLp \supset p$; $L(L(p \lor q) \supset Mq)$; $(Lp \land Mq) \supset L(Lp \lor Mq)$; $(MLMp \land p) \equiv Lp$.

Validity in propositional modal logic

Which modal formulae are we to count as valid? It is easy to give a general, intuitive account of validity for modal formulae exactly as we initially did for PC formulae, by saying that a wff is valid iff it 'comes out true' for every uniform replacement of its variables by propositions. In PC, because of the truth-functional nature of all the operators, this initial account led directly to a quite simple formal definition of validity. In modal logic, however, things are not as straightforward; for modal operators are not truth-functional, and it is not at all clear at the outset under what conditions propositions containing them are to count as true or false. The method of defining validity for modal wff which has proved most fruitful and widely applicable is based on the following ideas, which we shall state informally at first but which we shall express more rigorously later on:[3]

(a) Whereas determining the truth-value of a non-modal proposition involves only a consideration of how things actually are, determining the truth-value of a proposition of the form 'Necessarily p' or 'Possibly p' involves a consideration of how things might have been, of the nature of conceivable states of affairs alternative to the actual one.

(b) For each conceivable state of affairs there is a range of states of affairs which are possible relative to that one. (This reflects the idea we sometimes express by saying that if things were different a new range of possibilities might be opened up, so that things that are not even possible as things stand might be possible then.)

(c) In any given conceivable state of affairs, 'Possibly p' counts as true iff p itself would be true in *at least one* state of affairs which is possible relative to that one, and 'Necessarily p' counts as true iff p itself would be true in *every* such state of affairs.

With these ideas in mind we shall now describe a more elaborate version of the PC game described on p. 9. We shall call this game the *modal game*. Whereas the PC game involved only one player, in the modal game there can be any number (provided that there is at least one). We are to envisage these players as being seated in some way which determines precisely which players, if any, each player is to be able to see during the course of the game. Screens or some other devices might be used for this purpose; but since in this context being able to see someone means no more than taking note of that person's responses, it will be sufficient to specify, for each player, which players are to be watched and which ignored. There are no restrictions whatsoever on what 'seeing arrangement' among the players may be made: thus we may decide that no one is to be able to see anyone at all, or at the opposite extreme that everyone can see everyone, or we may specify any intermediate arrangement; we may decide that some players shall be able to see themselves while others shall not; if player A can see player B, B may or may not be allowed to see A; and so forth. Finally, before the game begins, each player is provided, as the single player in the PC game was, with a sheet of letters.

We shall call the set of players together with the specification of who is to be able to see whom, a *seating arrangement*, and this together with the players' sheets a *setting* for the modal game, or simply a *setting*.

The game proceeds by calling, to the whole set of players at once, any wff of modal logic we choose, provided that, as in the PC game, its well-formed parts, beginning with the variables, are called first. (We can again assume that the wff are written in primitive notation, with all defined operators eliminated, though we shall, for clarity, state the rule for wff containing M explicitly.)

The instructions for each player are those numbered 1, 2 and 3 in the PC game, together with the following two for calls involving L and M:

4. If $L\alpha$ is called (where α is a wff of modal logic), raise your hand if *every player you can see* raised his or her hand when α was called; otherwise keep your hand down.

5. If $M\alpha$ is called, raise your hand if *at least one of the players you can see* raised his or her hand when α was called; otherwise keep your hand down.

As with the PC game, it should be clear that in each setting each wff of modal logic (when appropriately prepared for) will get, from each player, a unique response. In a given setting the call of a formula may of course lead some players but not others to raise their hands, but if it leads every player without exception to raise his or her hand we shall say that that formula is *successful* in that setting.

How then should we use these games to define validity in propositional modal logic? We have said that our underlying intuitive idea is that a wff should count as valid iff it is true for all values of its variables. In the case of the PC game what this means is that the wff must be successful no matter what sheet is given to the player. Now if we compare the PC game with the modal game, it is not hard to see that the PC game is simply the modal game played in a seating arrangement with just one player and with only PC wff being called. (Strictly speaking there are two possible seating arrangements with one player, according to whether that player can see himself or herself or not; but although these seating arrangements can lead to different results for wff containing L or M, they cannot do so for wff of PC.) This suggests that an appropriate generalization of our notion of validity to make it cover modal wff is that of being *valid in a seating arrangement*, in this sense: that a wff α is valid in a given seating arrangement iff in that seating arrangement all the players would raise their hands for α, *no matter what sheets were distributed to them* – or, to put this in another way, iff α would be successful in all settings based on that seating arrangement.

If validity is thought of in this way, one consequence is that there will be as many different kinds of validity for modal formulae as there are different seating arrangements, and hence that we can have no unique account of validity in modal logic. At first sight this may seem undesirable; yet on reflection a plurality of criteria of validity is just what our earlier discussion of modal notions would lead us to expect. If 'necessarily' and 'possibly' can be used in a variety of different senses, then it is quite reasonable to suppose that corresponding to each of these senses there will be a different range of acceptable seating arrangements. In fact the possibility of having different kinds of seating arrangements is part of what gives modal logic its richness.

A simple example of a wff which is valid in a certain seating arrangement is $Lp \supset p$. Imagine a seating arrangement in which there are only two players, A and B, and both can see themselves and each other. Take player A. If p is on A's sheet, A will raise his or her hand for p, and hence, by the rule for $\supset$, will also raise it for $Lp \supset p$. If p is not on A's sheet, A's hand will not be raised for p, and hence, since A can see A, by the rule for L it will not be raised for Lp either. So, by the rule for $\supset$, it must be raised for $Lp \supset p$ in this case also. This means that A must raise his or her hand for $Lp \supset p$, whether p is on A's sheet or not; and B must do likewise, for the same reason.

But although $Lp \supset p$ is valid in this seating arrangement, it is not valid in *every* seating arrangement. For imagine a seating arrangement just like the previous one except that A cannot see himself or herself, and consider a setting in this seating arrangement in which p is on B's list but not on A's. Since B is the only player A can see, A's hand will be raised for Lp, but it will not be raised for p. So it will not be raised for $Lp \supset p$, and this shows that this wff is not valid in this seating arrangement.

The case of $Lp \supset p$ illustrates some of the richness of modal logic. For it is not difficult to see that this wff is valid not only in the seating arrangement described two paragraphs back, where A and B can see themselves and each other, but also in *any* seating arrangement in which all players can see themselves. And this means that any sense of 'necessary' in which whatever is necessary is true can be reflected by restricting the seating arrangements to those in which all players can at least see themselves.

There are, however, some wff which are valid in *every* seating arrangement. For reasons to be given in the next chapter we shall say that these wff are *K-valid*. It is easy to see that all PC-valid wff are K-valid: for in responding to a PC wff a player in the modal game takes no notice of any other players, and a PC-valid wff is precisely one which any sheet of letters whatsoever would lead a player to raise his or her hand. An example of a specifically modal wff which is K-valid is one which is often called **K**:

K $L(p \supset q) \supset (Lp \supset Lq)$

The proof that this wff is K-valid is this: If it were not K-valid then, by the rules for $\supset$, there would have to be a setting in which some player, say A,

    (i) raises a hand for $L(p \supset q)$,
    (ii) raises a hand for Lp,

but

    (iii) does not raise a hand for Lq.

There cannot, however, be any such setting. For by (iii) there must be a player, say B, whom A can see and whose hand was kept down for q. By (ii), since A can see B, B's hand must have been raised for p. Hence since B's hand was raised for p but not for q, it must have been kept down for $p \supset q$. This, however, conflicts with (i); for since A can see B, (i) means that B's hand was *raised* for $p \supset q$.

We can think of the modal game in this way: In any setting the players represent conceivable states of affairs or, as they are often called, alternative *possible worlds*, as we spoke of these near the beginning of this section; the players each player is allowed to see represent the states of affairs which are possible relative to the state of affairs which that player represents; and the letters on a player's sheet represent the propositions that are true in that state of affairs. Raising a hand and keeping it down represent respectively truth and falsity in the state of affairs the player represents. Hence what the K-validity of a wff means is that that wff would turn out to be true in every conceivable state of affairs, no matter what propositions we were to replace its variables by, no matter what was true or false in that state of affairs, and no matter what states of affairs were possible relative to that one.

One might at this point raise the question of just what a possible world or conceivable state of affairs really is.[4] This is a matter of some importance and controversy in metaphysics and in the application of modal logic to theories of meaning for natural language. Luckily however, from the point of view of *logic* it makes no difference just what they are, as may be seen from our discussion of the modal game in which the 'worlds' are players. In this book therefore we shall take no position on the ontological status of possible worlds.

Exercises — 1

1.1   Show that the following wff are valid in every seating arrangement:

   (a) $L(p \supset p)$
   (b) $(Lp \vee Lq) \supset L(p \vee q)$
   (c) $L(p \wedge q) \equiv (Lp \wedge Lq)$
   (d) $Mp \supset (Lq \supset Mq)$
   (e) $M(p \supset q) \equiv (Lp \supset Mq)$

1.2   Show that in any seating arrangement in which there is a player who cannot see himself or herself $Lp \supset p$ is not valid.

1.3   For each of the following wff devise a seating arrangement in which it is not valid:

   (a) $L(p \vee q) \supset (Lp \vee Lq)$
   (b) $M(p \supset p)$
   (c) $(Lp \supset Lq) \supset L(p \supset q)$
   (d) $Lp \supset LLp$

1.4 (a)   Consider a seating arrangement in which every player A can see *at most one* player (who may be A or may be another player). Show that in such a seating arrangement $Mp \supset Lp$ is valid.

(b)   Consider a seating arrangement in which a player A can see more than one player. Show that in such a seating arrangement $Mp \supset Lp$ is *not* valid.

Notes

[1] Most current logic textbooks give an account of PC in more or less detail. Terminology and notation vary somewhat but this should not confuse the careful reader. Despite its age the fullest introduction to the propositional calculus is still probably found in Church 1956.

[2] The notation L and M for the necessity and possibility operators dates from Feys 1950 (for L) and Becker 1930 (for M). For a history of notation see appendix 4 of Hughes and Cresswell 1968 (pp. 347–349). The commonly used $\square$ for L is due to F.B.Fitch and first appears in Barcan 1946. $\lozenge$ for M dates from Lewis and Langford 1932. Other primitives have been studied. Halldén 1949b has a triadic operator in terms of which both the modal operators *and* all the truth-functional operators can be defined. Montgomery and Routley 1966 use contingency ▽ (or non-contingency, △) to define the modal operators, though their definitions are only applicable to some systems of modal logic. (See Cresswell 1988.)

[3] The ideas which underlie this account of validity appeared in the late 1950s and early 1960s in the works of Kanger 1957a, Bayart 1958, Kripke 1959 and 1963a, Montague 1960 and Hintikka 1961. Anticipations can be found in Wajsberg 1933, McKinsey 1945, Carnap 1946, Meredith 1956, Thomas 1962 and other works. An algebraic description of this notion of validity is found in Jónsson and Tarski 1951, though the connection with modal logic was not made in that article. Some remarks about the earlier history of modal logic are found in Chapter 11 below.

[4] Some interesting perspectives on this question may be found in the essays in Loux 1979.

2

THE SYSTEMS K, T AND D

Systems of modal logic

For the rest of Part I we shall be concerned with a number of systems of propositional modal logic. The present chapter will deal with the first three of these. Our way of expounding the systems will be by the axiomatic method. Historically, modal systems were presented in this way before the discovery of an appropriate way to define validity for modal logic, and that is one reason for proceeding as we do. But another, and perhaps more significant, reason is that the axiomatic method allows us to define a class of wff without any reference to their meanings.

An *axiomatic basis* for a logical system consists of (a) a specification of the *language* in which the formulae of the system will be expressed – i.e. a list of *primitive symbols,* together with any definitions that may be thought convenient, together with a set of *formation rules* specifying which strings of symbols are to count as wff; (b) a selected set of wff, known as *axioms;* and (c) a set of *transformation rules,* licensing various operations on the axioms, and also (normally) on wff obtained from the axioms by previous applications of the transformation rules. The wff obtained from the axioms in this way, together with the axioms themselves, are known as the *theorems* of the system. All the systems of propositional modal logic which we shall consider will have the same language, the one specified in the previous chapter on p. 16; so in stating their bases we shall merely list their axioms and transformation rules. An axiomatic basis must be formulated in such a way that we can determine effectively (i) of any arbitrary string of symbols whether or not it is a wff, (ii) of any wff whether or not it is an axiom, and (iii) of any purported application of a transformation rule whether or not it is a genuine application of that rule. We therefore take care that our formulation of formation and transformation rules, and indeed our specification of a system as a whole, can be understood without reference to the interpretation of the symbols; this is often a matter of considerable importance when we come to demonstrate that a system has certain properties. The approach of the last chapter *did*, by contrast, specify a class of formulae: the wff valid in a seating arrangement, in terms of their meaning, for, as we said on p. 20, the players in the games can represent possible worlds, and so the account of validity developed there concerns the relation between symbols and what they stand for. Such an approach is often called a *semantical* approach to logic. An axiomatic approach is then often referred to as a *syntactical* approach.

All this, however, does not mean that in choosing the axioms for a system we ought to keep all thought of interpretation out of our minds. For although we could in theory take any wff whatsoever as axioms, in practice our reason for choosing certain wff as axioms will usually be either that they are valid by some criterion of validity that we have in mind, or at least that they are plausible or interesting in some way which leads us to want to explore their consequences; and these are matters which involve the interpretation we give to our symbols and formulae. Analogously, when we are constructing a system with a certain criterion of validity in mind, we see to it that its transformation rules are such that when they are applied to valid wff the theorems they yield are always valid too. Such transformation rules are said to be *validity-preserving* (with respect to that account of validity).

It is convenient at this point to explain some more of the terminology we shall use in discussing logical systems. When a formula is a theorem of a given system we shall say that it *belongs to*, or is *contained in*, or simply is *in*, that system. If two axiomatic systems, S and S′, have different bases but contain exactly the same theorems, we shall say that S and S′ are *deductively equivalent*, or sometimes simply that they are *equivalent*. If every theorem of S is also a theorem of S′ (whether or not S′ contains other theorems as well) we shall say that S′ *contains* S; thus two systems are deductively equivalent iff each contains the other. If S′ contains all the theorems of S and other theorems as well, we say that it *properly contains* S, or is a *proper extension* of S, and that S′ is the *stronger* and S the *weaker* of the two systems.

The system K

On p. 20 we introduced the notion of what we called *K-validity*. The first system we shall consider is one which will turn out to have as its theorems precisely those modal formulae which are K-valid. This is usually known nowadays as the system K.[1] Its axioms consist of all valid

24

wff of PC, i.e. all the wff specified by the following axiom schema,

PC   If α is a valid wff of PC, then α is an axiom[2]

together with the single distinctively modal wff

K $L(p \supset q) \supset (Lp \supset Lq)$

and it has the following three primitive (i.e. initially given) transformation rules:

US (The *Rule of Uniform Substitution*): The result of uniformly replacing any variable or variables p_1, ... , p_n in a theorem by any wff β_1, ... , β_n respectively is itself a theorem.
MP (The *Rule of Modus Ponens,* sometimes also called the *Rule of Detachment*): If α and $\alpha \supset \beta$ are theorems, so is β.
N (The *Rule of Necessitation*): If α is a theorem, so is $L\alpha$.

Where convenient we shall in future use the following notation:

1. Where p_1, ... , p_n are some or all of the variables occurring in a wff α, and β_1, ... , β_n are any wff, we use the expression $\alpha[\beta_1/p_1, ... , \beta_n/p_n]$ to denote the wff which results from α by replacing p_1, ... , p_n uniformly by β_1, ... , β_n respectively.
2. Where α is a wff and S is an axiomatic system, we write $\vdash_S \alpha$ to mean that that α is a theorem of S. Where no ambiguity is likely to arise we often omit the subscript 'S'.
3. We express the derivability of one wff from one or more other wff by the symbol $\rightarrow$.

Using this notation we could express the transformation rules more succinctly in this way:

US: $\vdash \alpha \;\rightarrow\; \vdash \alpha[\beta_1/p_1, ... , \beta_n/p_n]$.
MP: $\vdash \alpha, \alpha \supset \beta \;\rightarrow\; \vdash \beta$.
N: $\vdash \alpha \;\rightarrow\; \vdash L\alpha$.

US and MP are not specifically modal rules. US in particular is a rule that it is plausible to require of *any* logical system with a class of symbols to be interpreted as propositional variables, and MP simply reflects the truth-functional meaning of $\supset$. It is easy to see that both these rules are validity-preserving with respect to K-validity, though we shall prove this formally later. N, which *is* a specifically modal rule, also preserves K-validity, for this reason: Suppose α is K-valid – i.e. in every setting every player would raise a hand for α; then every player that any player can see would raise a hand for α; so by the rule for L, every player would raise a hand for $L\alpha$ – i.e. $L\alpha$ is K-valid.

Proofs of theorems

We have said that the theorems of a system are those wff which can be derived from its axioms by applying its transformation rules. To prove a theorem is therefore to derive it in this way. More precisely, a proof of a theorem α in a system S consists of a finite sequence of wff, each of which is either (i) an axiom of S or (ii) a wff derived from one or more wff occurring earlier in the sequence, by one of the transformation rules or by applying a definition, α itself being the last wff in the sequence. (Note that by this account of what constitutes a proof of a theorem, every wff in a proof is itself a theorem; and also that one reason why we count the axioms themselves as theorems is that any axiom can be thought of as a one-line proof of itself.)

We shall set out proofs in the following way. At the outset we state the theorem to be proved and give it a reference number. Each line of the proof itself contains three items: (a) a wff; (b) a reference number for that wff, written immediately before it; and (c) a justification for writing the wff, written on the left. This justification must consist in showing that the wff satisfies either condition (i) or condition (ii) mentioned above. In case (i) the justification entry consists of the reference number or name of the axiom in question (in the case of an axiom falling under the schema **PC**, if it is listed on p. 13, we cite the name or number assigned to it there; otherwise we simply write 'PC'). In case (ii) the justification entry refers by number to the earlier wff being used and indicates which transformation rule or definition is being applied. The application of US will be indicated in accordance with the notation explained above, noting within square brackets each variable being replaced and the wff replacing it. The application of MP and N will be indicated by '× MP' and '× N' respectively.

We shall first prove two theorems in full detail, and then describe some methods of abbreviating proofs. Theorems will be numbered using the name of the relevant system; thus K1 will be the first theorem we prove in K, and so on.

K1 $L(p \wedge q) \supset (Lp \wedge Lq)$

PROOF

PC1	(1)	$(p \wedge q) \supset p$
(1) × N	(2)	$L((p \wedge q) \supset p)$
K	(3)	$L(p \supset q) \supset (Lp \supset Lq)$
(3)$[p \wedge q/p,\ p/q]$	(4)	$L((p \wedge q) \supset p) \supset (L(p \wedge q) \supset Lp)$
(2), (4) × MP	(5)	$L(p \wedge q) \supset Lp$
PC2	(6)	$(p \wedge q) \supset q$
(6) × N	(7)	$L((p \wedge q) \supset q)$
(3)$[p \wedge q/p]$	(8)	$L((p \wedge q) \supset q) \supset (L(p \wedge q) \supset Lq)$
(7), (8) × MP	(9)	$L(p \wedge q) \supset Lq$
PC3	(10)	$(p \supset q) \supset ((p \supset r) \supset (p \supset (q \wedge r)))$
(10)$[L(p \wedge q)/p,\ Lp/q, Lq/r]$		
	(11)	$(L(p \wedge q) \supset Lp) \supset ((L(p \wedge q) \supset Lq) \supset$ $(L(p \wedge q) \supset (Lp \wedge Lq)))$
(5), (11) × MP	(12)	$(L(p \wedge q) \supset Lq) \supset (L(p \wedge q)$ $\supset (Lp \wedge Lq))$
(9), (12) × MP	(13)	$(L(p \wedge q) \supset (Lp \wedge Lq))$ **Q.E.D.**

K2 $(Lp \wedge Lq) \supset L(p \wedge q)$

PROOF

PC4	(1)	$p \supset (q \supset (p \wedge q))$
(1) × N	(2)	$L(p \supset (q \supset (p \wedge q)))$
K	(3)	$L(p \supset q) \supset (Lp \supset Lq)$
(3)$[q \supset (p \wedge q)/q]$		
	(4)	$L(p \supset (q \supset (p \wedge q))) \supset$ $Lp \supset L(q \supset (p \wedge q)))$
(2), (4) × MP	(5)	$Lp \supset L(q \supset (p \wedge q))$
(3)$[q/p,\ p \wedge q/q]$	(6)	$L(q \supset (p \wedge q)) \supset (Lq \supset L(p \wedge q))$
PC8	(7)	$(p \supset q) \supset ((q \supset (r \supset s)) \supset ((p \wedge r) \supset s))$
(7)$[Lp/p, L(q \supset (p \wedge q))/q, Lq/r, L(p \wedge q)/s]$		
	(8)	$(Lp \supset L(q \supset (p \wedge q))) \supset ((L(q \supset (p \wedge q))$ $\supset Lq \supset L(p \wedge q))) \supset ((Lp \wedge Lq) \supset L(p \wedge q)))$
(5), (8) × MP	(9)	$(L(q \supset (p \wedge q)) \supset (Lq \supset L(p \wedge q)))$ $\supset ((Lp \wedge Lq) \supset L(p \wedge q))$
(6), (9) × MP	(10)	$(Lp \wedge Lq) \supset L(p \wedge q)$ **Q.E.D.**

The proofs of these theorems satisfy exactly the requirements we listed for a proof in K. Setting out proofs at such length, however, can be not only tedious but sometimes actually a hindrance to understanding the principles which underlie them. We shall therefore introduce a number of conventions which will enable us to state proofs more briefly, while still providing all the information from which a full and rigorously formulated proof could be constructed.

Note first that theorem K2 is the converse of K1. Now we have defined equivalence as mutual implication, so we might expect to be able to use K1 and K2 to obtain $L(p \land q) \equiv (Lp \land Lq)$ as a new theorem. And in fact PC5 will enable us to do this; for if we substitute $L(p \land q)$ for p and $(Lp \land Lq)$ for q in PC5, and then apply MP twice, using K1 the first time and K2 the second time, the result will be precisely $L(p \land q) \equiv (Lp \land Lq)$. How shall we set all this out as a proof? If we are to adhere strictly to our criteria for a proof, we cannot use K1 (or K2) until we have written it down, and we are not allowed to write it down until we have derived it from axioms and earlier wff in the sequence which forms the proof; but this means that our proof of our new theorem will have to incorporate complete proofs of K1 and K2 before we begin to use these theorems in combination with PC5. Setting out the proof like this, however, involves a quite wasteful repetition of work that we have already done in proving K1 and K2 themselves. We shall therefore adopt the convention that *after* we have proved any theorem, we may write that theorem as a line in any subsequent proof, simply citing its reference number as its justification. The proof of our new theorem will then look like this:

K3 $L(p \land q) \equiv (Lp \land Lq)$

PROOF

K1	(1)	$L(p \land q) \supset (Lp \land Lq)$
K2	(2)	$(Lp \land Lq) \supset L(p \land q)$
PC5	(3)	$(p \supset q) \supset ((q \supset p) \supset (p \equiv q))$

(3)$[L(p \land q)/p, Lp \land Lq/q]$

$\quad\quad\quad\quad$ (4) $(L(p \land q) \supset (Lp \land Lq)) \supset$
$\quad\quad\quad (((Lp \land Lq) \supset L(p \land q)) \supset (L(p \land q) \equiv (Lp \land Lq)))$

(1), (4) × MP   (5) $((Lp \land Lq) \supset L(p \land q)) \supset$
$\quad\quad\quad\quad\quad\quad\quad (L(p \land q) \equiv (Lp \land Lq))$

(2), (5) × MP   (6) $L(p \land q) \equiv (Lp \land Lq)$ **Q.E.D.**

K3 may be called the *Law of L-distribution*.

Consider next how we used PC5 in the above proof. What we did was to make substitutions in it which produced, at line (4), an implicative wff whose antecedent was an already proved wff (K1) and whose consequent had as *its* antecedent another already proved wff (K2). We then used MP twice to obtain the consequent of its consequent as a theorem. Now it should be clear that we can use PC5 in this way not only in the case of K1 and K2, but whenever we have already proved both a wff of the form $\alpha \supset \beta$ and its converse $\beta \supset \alpha$; i.e. by substituting α for p and β for q in PC5 and applying MP twice, we can obtain $\alpha \equiv \beta$. We thus have a rule which could be expressed in this way:

$$\vdash \alpha \supset \beta, \ \vdash \beta \supset \alpha \ \rightarrow \ \vdash \alpha \equiv \beta$$

This rule is not part of the axiomatic basis of K. Nevertheless it is what we call a *derived* rule of K, in the sense that we may always use it as a transformation rule in a proof, since anything we can prove by using it we could also prove, though at greater length, from the axiomatic basis alone. To establish that a rule is a derived rule of a system we simply show how we could always do without it. In the present case we can do this as follows:

Given:	(1)	$\alpha \supset \beta$
Given:	(2)	$\beta \supset \alpha$
PC5	(3)	$(p \supset q) \supset ((q \supset p) \supset (p \equiv q))$
(3)$[\alpha/p, \beta/q]$	(4)	$(\alpha \supset \beta) \supset ((\beta \supset \alpha) \supset (\alpha \equiv \beta))$
(1), (4) × MP	(5)	$(\beta \supset \alpha) \supset (\alpha \equiv \beta)$
(2), (5) × MP	(6)	$\alpha \equiv \beta$ Q.E.D.

Since all we have used in establishing this rule (apart from US and MP) is PC5, we shall signal its use in justification entries simply by writing ' × PC5'.

The procedure we have described for the use of PC5 will in fact enable us to derive a rule of K from any valid PC wff whose main operator is $\supset$. For if α is a valid PC wff, it is an axiom of K, and hence, by US, all its substitution-instances are theorems of K. So if we can make substitutions for the variables in α which will turn it into a wff whose antecedent is a wff we have already proved, we can use MP to detach its consequent and count that as a theorem too. (This is why MP is sometimes called *Detachment*.) In cases such as PC5 itself where the PC axiom has the overall form $A \supset (B \supset C)$, if we can make substitutions which will turn both A and B into already proved wff, we can then use MP twice to obtain the result of these substitutions in C. A specially useful PC axiom of this kind is PC6, to which we gave the name *Syll* on p. 13. This gives us the rule

$$\vdash \alpha \supset \beta, \ \vdash \beta \supset \gamma \ \rightarrow \ \vdash \alpha \supset \gamma$$

which says that when we have proved two implicative wff in which the consequent of one is the antecedent of the other, we can count as a theorem the implicative wff whose antecedent is the antecedent of the former and whose consequent is the consequent of the latter. We shall indicate the application of this rule by '× Syll', and give analogous indications, by name or number, of other rules similarly derived from PC axioms. In cases where the PC wff is not one we have listed we shall write simply × PC.

Another way of shortening the statement of proofs is this. Line (3) in the proof of K1 is simply the axiom **K** itself, and line (4) is derived from this by US. The presence of **K** (without substitutions) is required by our definition of what counts as a proof; but it would be more economical, and still give all the information from which a detailed proof could be constructed, to omit line (3) altogether and give **K** with the appropriate substitutions as the justification for line (4). Similarly, we could omit line (10) and give PC3 with the appropriate substitutions as the justification for line (11). Somewhat analogously, we could omit line (1) and give 'PC1 × N' as the justification for immediately writing the present line (2). So we shall adopt the convention that citing any axioms or previously proved theorems by name or number and indicating the application of a transformation rule to them will be a sufficient justification entry for the wff obtained thereby.

Finally, by using **K** together with N, US and MP, we can obtain a very useful derived rule. This is a specifically modal rule and we shall give it a special name as the first such rule we shall prove:

DR1 $\vdash \alpha \supset \beta \ \rightarrow \ \vdash L\alpha \supset L\beta$

PROOF

Given:	(1)	$\alpha \supset \beta$	
(1) × N	(2)	$L(\alpha \supset \beta)$	
K$[\alpha/p, \ \beta/q]$	(3)	$L(\alpha \supset \beta) \supset (L\alpha \supset L\beta)$	
(2), (3) × MP	(4)	$L\alpha \supset L\beta$	**Q.E.D.**

In the light of all this let us see how we can set out the proofs of K1–K3 in the abbreviated style which we shall use from now on:

K1 $L(p \wedge q) \supset (Lp \wedge Lq)$

PROOF

PC1 × DR1	(1)	$L(p \wedge q) \supset Lp$	
PC2 × DR1	(2)	$L(p \wedge q) \supset Lq$	
(1), (2) × PC3	(3)	$L(p \wedge q) \supset (Lp \wedge Lq)$	**Q.E.D.**

K2 $(Lp \wedge Lq) \supset L(p \wedge q)$

PROOF

PC4 × DR1	(1)	$Lp \supset L(q \supset (p \wedge q))$	
K[q/p, $p \wedge q/q$]	(2)	$L(q \supset (p \wedge q)) \supset (Lq \supset L(p \wedge q))$	
(1), (2) × PC8	(3)	$(Lp \wedge Lq) \supset L(p \wedge q)$	**Q.E.D.**

K3 $L(p \wedge q) \equiv (Lp \wedge Lq)$

PROOF

| K1, K2 × PC5 | (1) | $L(p \wedge q) \equiv (Lp \wedge Lq)$ | **Q.E.D.** |

We shall now prove some more theorems and derived rules of K.

K4 $(Lp \vee Lq) \supset L(p \vee q)$

PROOF

PC9 × DR1	(1)	$Lp \supset L(p \vee q)$	
PC10 × DR1	(2)	$Lq \supset L(p \vee q)$	
(1), (2) × PC11	(3)	$(Lp \vee Lq) \supset L(p \vee q)$	**Q.E.D.**

Note that K4, unlike K3, is only an implication, not an equivalence. The converse of K4 is not a theorem of **K**, and in fact at the intuitive level is not a valid formula: it may be necessary that you are awake or asleep without its being necessary that you are awake or its being necessary that you are asleep.

We next prove two further derived rules. The first of these is:

DR2 $\vdash \alpha \equiv \beta \;\rightarrow\; \vdash L\alpha \equiv L\beta$

31

PROOF

Given:	(1)	$\alpha \equiv \beta$
(1) × PC	(2)	$\alpha \supset \beta$
(2) × DR1	(3)	$L\alpha \supset L\beta$
(1) × PC	(4)	$\beta \supset \alpha$
(4) × DR1	(5)	$L\beta \supset L\alpha$
(3), (5) × PC5	(6)	$L\alpha \equiv L\beta$

Q.E.D.

Note that in this proof we used purely PC principles to get from $\alpha \equiv \beta$ at line (1) to both $\alpha \supset \beta$ and $\beta \supset \alpha$ at lines (3) and (5). Clearly we could do this with any theorem which has the form of an equivalence, and for this reason whenever we have proved a wff of the form $\alpha \equiv \beta$ we shall assume that we have proved both $\alpha \supset \beta$ and $\beta \supset \alpha$; for example, if we have proved $\alpha \equiv \beta$ and α, we shall assume that β follows, and if we have proved $\alpha \equiv \beta$ and β, we shall assume that α follows, by MP in each case.

Our next derived rule is that of *Substitution of Equivalents,* which we shall usually call *Eq.* What this states is that if α is a theorem and β differs from α only in having some wff, δ, at one or more places where α has a wff, γ, then if $\gamma \equiv \delta$ is a theorem, β is a theorem. In other words, if we have proved $\gamma \equiv \delta$, we can replace γ by δ in any theorem (not necessarily uniformly), and the result will also be a theorem. We now want to show that this rule holds in K. To do so we first note that the following are valid wff of PC, and therefore axioms of K:

$$(p \equiv q) \supset (\sim p \equiv \sim q)$$
$$(p \equiv q) \supset ((p \vee r) \equiv (q \vee r))$$
$$(p \equiv q) \supset ((r \vee p) \equiv (r \vee q))$$

Suppose now that $\gamma \equiv \delta$ is a theorem of K. Then by substitution in these three axioms, and MP, it follows that the following are also theorems of K,

$$\sim \gamma \equiv \sim \delta$$
$$(\gamma \vee \zeta) \equiv (\delta \vee \zeta)$$
$$(\zeta \vee \gamma) \equiv (\zeta \vee \delta)$$

for any wff ζ. DR2, which we proved above, enables us to add to this list of consequences of $\gamma \equiv \delta$, $L\gamma \equiv L\delta$.

From this it follows that if α is any wff which is built up from γ using

32

$\sim$ and L as the only monadic operators and $\vee$ as the only dyadic one, and β is built up from δ in exactly the same way as α is from γ, then if $\gamma \equiv \delta$ is a theorem, so is $\alpha \equiv \beta$; and therefore, if α is a theorem, then by MP so is β. Since every modal wff can be written with $\sim$, L and $\vee$ as its only operators, what we have just shown is that we can apply Eq unrestrictedly in K; i.e. whenever we have a theorem of K of the form $\gamma \equiv \delta$, we can replace γ by δ in any theorem α, no matter where γ occurs in α, and the result will also be a theorem of K.

Where an equivalential wff has a name, e.g. K3, and we are using Eq to replace an instance of one side of the equivalence by an instance of the other side in some wff, we shall indicate the application of Eq by (in this example) '$\times$ K3 $\times$ Eq', and analogously in other cases. A rich source of equivalential wff is of course provided by valid PC equivalences.

L and M

Our next theorem, which will help us to establish another extremely useful derived rule, is:

K5 $\quad Lp \equiv \sim M \sim p$

PROOF

PC12 (DN)	(1)	$p \equiv \sim \sim p$
(1)[Lp/p]	(2)	$Lp \equiv \sim \sim Lp$
(2) $\times$ (1) $\times$ Eq:	(3)	$Lp \equiv \sim \sim L \sim \sim p$
(3) Def M	(4)	$Lp \equiv \sim M \sim p$

Q.E.D.

Clearly K5, by Eq, will entitle us to replace L by $\sim M \sim$ anywhere in a theorem; and by Def M we may replace M anywhere in a theorem by $\sim L \sim$. (By saying that we are 'entitled' to do these things, or 'may' do them we simply mean that the result of doing them is itself a theorem.) The rule we are about to state is a kind of generalization of these procedures. We shall call it the *Rule of L–M Interchange* ('LMI' for short), and what it states is that in any sequence of adjacent monadic modal operators (Ls and Ms) in a theorem, L may be replaced by M and M by L throughout, provided that a $\sim$ is either inserted or deleted both immediately before and immediately after the sequence. (Thus LM may be replaced by $\sim ML \sim$, $\sim LLL$ by $MMM \sim$, $MLLM \sim$ by $\sim LMML$, and so forth.)

We shall now establish that this rule holds in K. Let $A_1 \ldots A_n$ be a sequence of monadic modal operators (i.e. each A_i is either L or M). For each A_i, let A_i' be M if A_i is L, and L if A_i is M. We first show that

(*) $A_1 \ldots A_n p \equiv \; \sim A_1' \ldots A_n' \sim p$

is a theorem of K. To do so we begin with the following substitution-instance of the PC valid wff $p \equiv p$:

(1) $A_1 \ldots A_n p \equiv A_1 \ldots A_n p$

Next, in the right-hand side of (1) we replace each M by $\sim L \sim$ (by Def M) and each L by $\sim M \sim$ (by K5 and Eq). The result will be:

(2) $A_1 \ldots A_n p \equiv \; \sim A_1' \sim \; \sim A_2' \sim \ldots \sim A_{n-1}' \sim \; \sim A_n' \sim p$

We now use DN ($p \equiv \; \sim \sim p$) and Eq to delete all occurrences of $\sim$ in (2), and the result is (*) as required. Appropriate substitutions for p in (*), and Eq, will then entitle us to replace any sequence $A_1 \ldots A_n$ by $\sim A_1' \ldots A_n' \sim$ in any theorem. Finally, if the sequence before replacement was immediately preceded or followed by $\sim$, the result of the replacement will give us $\sim \sim$ at the beginning or the end of the new sequence, and this may be deleted by DN and Eq. We have thus shown that every application of LMI to a theorem of K results in a theorem of K – i.e. we have established LMI as a derived rule of K.

Note that the sequence to which we apply LMI may have only a single member. Applications of K5 and Def M are thus themselves applications of LMI, and when convenient we shall indicate them too by '$\times$ LMI'. Note too that there is nothing to prevent us applying LMI only to part of a sequence; e.g. we may apply LMI to the first three operators in $LMMLM$, leaving the last two unaltered, and thus obtain $\sim MLL \sim LM$.

K6 $M(p \lor q) \equiv (Mp \lor Mq)$

PROOF

K3 $[\sim p/p, \sim q/q]$	(1)	$L(\sim p \land \sim q) \equiv (L \sim p \land L \sim q)$	
(1) $\times$ LMI	(2)	$\sim M \sim (\sim p \land \sim q) \equiv (\sim Mp \land \sim Mq)$	
(2) $\times$ PC13 $\times$ Eq	(3)	$\sim M(p \lor q) \equiv (\sim Mp \land \sim Mq)$	
(3) $\times$ PC	(4)	$M(p \lor q) \equiv (Mp \lor Mq)$	Q.E.D.

K6 expresses the same kind of principle for possibility and disjunction as K3 does for necessity and conjunction; it may be called the *Law of M-*

distribution.

K7 $M(p \supset q) \equiv (Lp \supset Mq)$

PROOF

K6[~p/p]	(1)	$M(\sim p \lor q) \equiv (M\sim p \lor Mq)$	
(1) × LMI	(2)	$M(\sim p \lor q) \equiv (\sim Lp \lor Mq)$	
(2) Def ⊃	(3)	$M(p \supset q) \equiv (Lp \supset Mq)$	Q.E.D.

We now derive a rule which is like DR1 except that M takes the place of L.

DR3 $\vdash \alpha \supset \beta \rightarrow \vdash M\alpha \supset M\beta$

PROOF

Given:	(1)	$\alpha \supset \beta$	
(1) × PC15(Transp)	(2)	$\sim\beta \supset \sim\alpha$	
(2) × DR1	(3)	$L\sim\beta \supset L\sim\alpha$	
(3) × PC	(4)	$\sim L\sim\alpha \supset \sim L\sim\beta$	
(4) Def M	(5)	$M\alpha \supset M\beta$	Q.E.D.

Note that by repeated applications of DR1 and/or DR3 we can prefix any sequence of modal operators to both sides of an implicative theorem.

K8 $M(p \land q) \supset (Mp \land Mq)$

We shall give two ways of proving K8. The first uses DR3 in the way that the proof of K4 used DR1, and the second obtains K8 from K4 in the same manner as K6 was obtained from K3. Here is the first:

PROOF

PC1 × DR3	(1)	$M(p \land q) \supset Mp$	
PC2 × DR3	(2)	$M(p \land q) \supset Mq$	
(1), (2) × PC3	(3)	$M(p \land q) \supset (Mp \land Mq)$	Q.E.D.

Here is the second proof:

PROOF

K4[~p/p, ~q/q]	(1)	$(L\sim p \lor L\sim q) \supset L(p \lor q)$	
(1) × PC15 × Eq	(2)	$\sim L(\sim p \lor \sim q) \supset \sim(L\sim p \lor L\sim q)$	

| (2) × LMI | (3) | $M \sim (\sim p \lor \sim q) \supset \sim (\sim Mp \lor \sim Mq)$ |
| (3) × PC14 × Eq | (4) | $M(p \land q) \supset (Mp \land Mq)$ **Q.E.D.** |

As was the case with K4, but in contrast with K6, the converse of K8 is not a theorem of K. We do however have the following partial converse to K4:

K9 $L(p \lor q) \supset (Lp \lor Mq)$

PROOF

K[$\sim q/p, p/q$]	(1)	$L(\sim q \supset p) \supset (L \sim q \supset Lp)$
(1) Def $\supset$, × DN(PC12)	(2)	$L(q \lor p) \supset (\sim L \sim q \lor Lp)$
(2) Def M, × Comm(PC16)	(3)	$L(p \lor q) \supset (Lp \lor Mq)$ **Q.E.D.**

Validity and soundness

As we remarked earlier in this chapter, the theorems of the system K will turn out to be precisely those wff which are K-valid in the sense explained on p. 20. It is important to be quite clear that this is a substantive fact, and not something which is true by definition, as our use of the label 'K-valid' might at first suggest. To be a theorem of K is to be derivable from the axioms of K by the transformation rules of K; to be K-valid is to be successful in every setting of the modal game. We have here two distinct concepts, and the fact that a wff is a theorem of K iff it is K-valid is something we have to *prove*, not something we can assume. We shall in fact come across many cases in which we have an axiomatic modal system defined without any reference to an account of validity, and a definition of validity formulated without any reference to theoremhood in a system, and yet the theorems of that system are precisely the wff which are valid by that definition; but this is something which has to be proved in every case, and it should be obvious that giving the system and the validity-definition the same name (as we shall often do) does nothing to prove it but serves to remind us of the connection once it has been proved. To show that there is a match of this kind between a system and a validity definition we have to prove two things: (A) that every theorem of the system is valid by that definition, and (B) that every wff valid by that definition is a theorem of the system. If (A) holds, we say that the system is *sound*, and if (B) holds we say that it is *complete*, in each case with respect to the validity-definition in question. The completeness of a system is usually more difficult to establish than its soundness, and we shall defer the task of proving the completeness of K till Chapter 6. Here, however, we shall give a proof of its soundness with respect to K-validity.

In a sense we have done this already; for on p. 20 we gave a proof that all valid wff of PC and the wff **K** (i.e. all the axioms of K) are K-valid, and earlier in the present chapter we at least sketched an argument to show that the transformation rules of K preserve K-validity. We shall now, however, give a more rigorous definition of validity for modal formulae and in terms of it a more formally exact proof of the soundness of K.

Our account of the modal game on p. 18, though it was intended to make the idea of validity more immediately comprehensible, had both certain inessential features and also certain limitations, which we now want to remove. It ought not to be difficult to see that speaking of players at all, of some players being able or unable to see other players, and of the raising or non-raising of hands, is quite inessential to the logical structure of the test that is being applied to formulae. Instead of a set of human players we could have a collection of objects of any kind at all; but to reflect the idea, mentioned on p. 21, that the players represent alternative ways the world might be, these objects are sometimes called 'possible worlds', or simply 'worlds', and this is the terminology that we shall usually employ in this book. Similarly, it does not matter what takes the place of the seeing-relation among the players, so long as it is some kind of dyadic relation, R, defined over the objects in question, in the sense that it is specified for every pair of these objects, w and w', whether or not wRw'. Sometimes R is called the *accessibility-relation*, and when wRw', w' is said to be *accessible from* w, or to be *possible relative to* w. (In this book we shall sometimes use this terminology, but we shall also, when convenient, carry over a metaphor derived from the modal game and speak of one world being able to *see* another. The point to be clear about is that, whatever terminology we use, from a formal point of view R is no more than a relation which may or may not hold between any pair of worlds.)

In describing the modal game we called a set of players and a specification of which players could see which a *seating arrangement*. In our present more abstract account we call the pair $\langle W,R \rangle$, where W is a set of worlds and R is a specification of which of these is related to which, a *frame*.[3] We note here one limitation involved in our description of the modal game, which we can now remove. In any 'real life' attempt to play the modal game, the number of players involved would have to be finite, and in fact in practice fairly small; but we need place no limits to the number of worlds in a frame – there may be only one, there may be 17, there may be infinitely many.

Within each seating arrangement in the modal game we could have any number of *settings* by giving each player a list of variables. As we also remarked on p. 21, this corresponds to the idea that those variables are true, or are assigned the value 1, in the state of affairs represented by the player in question, with the other variable being false, or assigned the value 0. Again, there is a limitation here if we take the game literally, since in practice any list of variables would have to be finite; but we do not wish to have any such restriction in the formal definition of validity which we are now constructing. We shall refer to an assignment of values within a frame as V, and where p is any propositional variable and w is any world in the frame (i.e. $w \in$ W),[4] we shall write $V(p,w) = 1$ if V assigns the value 1 to p in w, and $V(p,w) = 0$ if it assigns the value 0 to it. Where $\langle W,R \rangle$ is a frame and V is a value-assignment within that frame, we call $\langle W,R,V \rangle$ a *model,* and more specifically a model *based on* the frame $\langle W,R \rangle$. Thus a model corresponds to a setting in the modal game.

We can set out all this as follows:

A *frame* is an ordered pair $\langle W,R \rangle$, where W is a non-empty set of objects (worlds), and R is a dyadic relation defined over the members of W, i.e. it is determinate for any (not necessarily distinct) w and w' in W whether or not wRw'.

A *model* is an ordered triple $\langle W,R,V \rangle$ where $\langle W,R \rangle$ is a frame and V is a value-assignment satisfying the following conditions:

1. For any propositional variable, p, and any $w \in$ W, either $V(p,w) = 1$ or $V(p,w) = 0$.

2. [V ~] For any wff, α, and any $w \in$ W, $V(\sim\alpha,w) = 1$ if $V(\alpha,w) = 0$; otherwise $V(\alpha,w) = 0$.

3. [V ∨] For any wff α and β, and for any $w \in$ W, $V((\alpha \lor \beta),w) = 1$ if either $V(\alpha,w) = 1$ or $V(\beta,w) = 1$; otherwise $V((\alpha \lor \beta),w) = 0$.

4. [VL] For any wff α and for any $w \in$ W, $V(L\alpha,w) = 1$ if for every $w' \in$ W such that wRw', $V(\alpha,w') = 1$; otherwise $V(L\alpha,w) = 0$.

Although the conditions for the other operators we have introduced are strictly unnecessary, since all wff can be written in primitive notation, we give them here for ease of reference:

[V ∧] For any wff α and β, and for any $w \in$ W, $V((\alpha \land \beta),w) = 1$ if both $V(\alpha,w) = 1$ and $V(\beta,w) = 1$; otherwise $V((\alpha \land \beta),w) = 0$.

[V ⊃] For any wff α and β, and for any $w \in$ W, $V((\alpha \supset \beta),w) = 1$ if either $V(\alpha,w) = 0$ or $V(\beta,w) = 1$; otherwise $V((\alpha \supset \beta),w) = 0$.

[V≡] For any wff α and β, and for any $w \in W$, $V((\alpha \equiv \beta),w) = 1$ if $V(\alpha,w) = V(\beta,w)$; otherwise $V((\alpha \equiv \beta),w) = 0$.

[VM] For any wff α and for any $w \in W$, $V(M\alpha,w) = 1$ if for some $w' \in W$ such that wRw', $V(\alpha,w') = 1$; otherwise $V(M\alpha,w) = 0$.

A model $\langle W,R,V \rangle$ is said to be *based on* the frame $\langle W,R \rangle$.

We now define validity on a frame by saying that a wff α is *valid on* a frame $\langle W,R \rangle$ iff, for every model $\langle W,R,V \rangle$ based on $\langle W,R \rangle$, and for every $w \in W$, $V(\alpha,w) = 1$. Finally we define K-validity by saying that a wff is *K-valid* iff it is valid on every frame.

We are now in a position to prove the soundness of K with respect to K-validity as we have just defined this. Our method of doing so will in fact yield a more general result which we shall be able to use to prove the soundness of many other systems.

THEOREM 2.1   Every theorem of K is K-valid.[5]

What we have to prove is that every wff derivable from the axioms of K by the transformation rules of K is valid on every frame. For this it is clearly sufficient to prove (1) that every axiom of K is valid on every frame, and (2) that the rules US, MP and N preserve validity on a frame – i.e. that if they are applied to wff which are valid on any given frame, the resulting wff are also valid on that frame. In stating the more general consequence which we mentioned above we shall use the following terminology: where Λ is any set of modal wff (which may have only one member or more than one – even infinitely many members), we let 'K + Λ' denote the axiomatic system obtained by adding to K, as extra axioms, all the wff in Λ (and retaining the transformation rules US, MP and N).[6] Our more general result is this:

THEOREM 2.2   If Λ is any set of modal wff and $\langle W,R \rangle$ is a frame on which each wff in Λ is valid, then every theorem of K + Λ is valid on $\langle W,R \rangle$.

As we have noted, the soundness of K with respect to K-validity (theorem 2.1) follows immediately from theorem 2.2. Theorem 2.2 follows from the following two lemmas:

LEMMA 2.3   If $\langle W,R \rangle$ is any frame, every valid PC wff is valid on $\langle W,R \rangle$, and so is the wff **K**.

LEMMA 2.4   Where $\langle W,R \rangle$ is any frame,

(i)   if α is valid on $\langle W,R \rangle$, so is $\alpha[\beta_1/p_1, \ldots ,\beta_n/p_n]$ (i.e. α with β_1, $\ldots$, β_n uniformly replacing $p_1, \ldots ,p_n$ respectively);

(ii)   if α and $\alpha \supset \beta$ are both valid on $\langle W,R \rangle$, so is β;

(iii)   if α is valid on $\langle W,R \rangle$, so is $L\alpha$.

We shall prove the lemmas in a moment, but before doing so we shall note that theorem 2.2 is an immediate consequence of lemmas 2.3 and 2.4, since by lemma 2.3 every axiom of K is valid on *every* frame, and by lemma 2.4 the transformation rules preserve validity on any frame whatsoever. The importance of theorem 2.2 can be indicated in this way. Apart from a few systems which we shall mention in Chapters 11 and 12, and which stand a little outside mainstream modal logic, K is the weakest of the modal systems we shall be discussing. Each of the other systems will be a proper extension of K (i.e. it will contain not only all the theorems of K but other theorems as well). Modal systems which contain K (including K itself) together with US, MP and N are commonly known as *normal* modal systems, and we shall usually present these other systems by adding one or more extra axioms to the basis of K. For each such system we shall also have (or at least we shall try to find) a definition of validity which matches it in the way that K-validity matches the system K; i.e., which is such that the theorems of the system are precisely the wff which are valid by that definition. Typically we shall produce such a definition by specifying a certain class $\mathscr{E}$ of frames, and saying that a wff is valid with respect to $\mathscr{E}$ ($\mathscr{E}$-valid) iff it is valid on every frame in $\mathscr{E}$. And when a system S is both sound and complete with respect to a class $\mathscr{E}$ of frames, so that the theorems of S consist of all and only those wff that are valid on every frame in $\mathscr{E}$, we say that S is *characterized by* $\mathscr{E}$. To come at last to the importance of theorem 2.2: what it tells us is that if we have a system K + Λ and a class of frames $\mathscr{E}$, then in order to prove that K + Λ is sound with respect to $\mathscr{E}$, all we have to do is to show that every wff in Λ is valid on every frame in $\mathscr{E}$.

We note here some of the terminology we shall use in discussing frames and models. If every theorem of a system S is valid on a frame $\langle W,R \rangle$, we say that $\langle W,R \rangle$ is a *frame for* S. If a wff α is not valid on a given frame we sometimes say that it *fails* on that frame, or that it can be *falsified* on that frame. A model in which α is false in at least one world is called a *falsifying model* for α.

So now what remains is to prove lemmas 2.3 and 2.4.

Proof of lemma 2.3: (A) In any model, a PC wff is evaluated in any world without reference to any other world. Therefore, since a valid PC wff has the value 1 for every value-assignment to the variables, it has the value 1 in every world in every model, i.e. it is valid on every frame. (B) If **K** were not valid on every frame, there would have to be a model $\langle W,R,V \rangle$ in which for some $w \in W$, (i) $V(L(p \supset q),w) = 1$, (ii) $V(Lp,w) = 1$, and (iii) $V(Lq,w) = 0$. There cannot, however, be any such model. For by (iii), there must be some $w' \in W$ such that wRw' and $V(q,w') = 0$; by (ii), since wRw', $V(p,w') = 1$; hence, by [V$\supset$], $V((p \supset q),w') = 0$; but then by [VL], since wRw', we have $V(L(p \supset q),w) = 0$, which contradicts (i).

Proof of lemma 2.4:

(i) Suppose that $\langle W,R \rangle$ is a frame and $\alpha[\beta_1/p_1, \ldots ,\beta_n/p_n]$ is not valid on $\langle W,R \rangle$. Then there is a model $\langle W,R,V \rangle$ based on $\langle W,R \rangle$ such that for some $w^* \in W$, $V(\alpha[\beta_1/p_1, \ldots ,\beta_n/p_n],w^*) = 0$. Let $\langle W,R,V^* \rangle$ be a model based on the same frame $\langle W,R \rangle$, in which V^* is just like V except that for any $w \in W$, and any $1 \leq i \leq n$, $V^*(p_i,w) = V(\beta_i,w)$. Then $V^*(\alpha,w^*) = 0$, and so α is not valid on $\langle W,R \rangle$. (What this amounts to is simply that whatever model falsifies $\alpha[\beta_1/p_1, \ldots ,\beta_n/p_n]$, if we had given the variables that have been replaced the same values as the wff that have replaced them, then we could have falsified the original α, showing that it wasn't valid in the first place.)

(ii) If both α and $\alpha \supset \beta$ are valid on $\langle W,R \rangle$, then in every world in every model based on $\langle W,R \rangle$, both α and $\alpha \supset \beta$ are true; hence by [V$\supset$] so is β; i.e., β is valid on $\langle W,R \rangle$.

(iii) If α is valid on $\langle W,R \rangle$, then in every world in every model based on $\langle W,R \rangle$, α is true; hence for every such world, α is true in every world which it can see; so $L\alpha$ is true in every such world – i.e., $L\alpha$ is valid on $\langle W,R \rangle$.

The system T
On p. 20 we showed that the wff $Lp \supset p$ is not K-valid. In the light of theorem 2.1, this means that it is not a theorem of K. We could, however, add it as an extra axiom to obtain a system stronger than K itself. Now what the formula means is that whatever is necessarily so is so, and we remarked on p. 14 that although there are some senses of 'necessarily' for which this does not hold, there are others for which it does; we therefore have a motive for constructing a system or systems which will reflect these latter senses. The system obtained by adding Lp

$\supset$ *p* as a single extra axiom to K has had a long history in modal logic dating from 1937, and is usually referred to simply as T.[7] We shall therefore give the name **T** to the formula itself. In other words, the system T is K +

T $Lp \supset p$

This axiom is sometimes called the *Axiom of Necessity*.

All the theorems of K are of course still theorems of T. The derived rules DR1–DR3 and Eq also hold in T. In fact if we look back at how these rules were proved in K, we can see that they are bound to hold in all systems which contain K, provided that they retain the rules US, MP and N. We prove a couple of theorems of T which are not in K.

T1 $p \supset Mp$

PROOF

T[$\sim p/p$]	(1)	$L\sim p \supset \sim p$	
(1) × PC	(2)	$p \supset \sim L\sim p$	
(2) Def *M*	(3)	$p \supset Mp$	**Q.E.D.**

T2 $M(p \supset Lp)$

PROOF

T1[Lp/p]	(1)	$Lp \supset MLp$	
K7[Lp/q]	(2)	$M(p \supset Lp) \equiv (Lp \supset MLp)$	
(1), (2) × Eq	(3)	$M(p \supset Lp)$	**Q.E.D.**

We leave it to the reader to show that neither T1 nor T2 is a theorem of K, by defining for each of them a model in which it is false in some world.

The fact that T2 is a theorem of T shows that the following rule, which is a kind of possibility counterpart of N, is not a rule of T:

P $\vdash M\alpha \;\rightarrow\; \vdash \alpha$

The reason is that if P were a rule of T, then from it and T2 we could derive $p \supset Lp$, but as we shall show in a moment, this is not a theorem of T.

A definition of validity for T

In discussing the modal game on p. 20 we showed that the wff $Lp \supset p$ is valid in every seating arrangement in which all players can see themselves. Transposed into our present frame-theory, this means that **T** is valid on every frame $\langle W,R \rangle$ in which R is *reflexive* – i.e. in which, for every $w \in W$, wRw. (We call such frames, for short, *reflexive frames*.) So by theorem 2.2, the system T is sound with respect to the class of all reflexive frames. We shall in fact be able to prove later that T is also complete with respect to this class of frames; so, anticipating this result, we shall say that a wff is *T-valid* iff it is valid on every reflexive frame, and we shall sometimes call a reflexive frame a *T-frame*.

We said a couple of paragraphs back that we would prove that $p \supset Lp$ is not a theorem of T. Now that we have shown that every theorem of T is valid on every reflexive frame, all that we need for this purpose is to find a reflexive frame in which $p \supset Lp$ is not valid. And this is not difficult: imagine a world in which p is true and which can see a world in which p is false, each world being able to see itself.

Since **T** is not K-valid, it is not a theorem of K, and this shows that K and T are distinct systems, with T being a *proper extension* of K.

The system D

We said on p. 20 that if we interpret L as expressing obligatoriness ('moral necessity') we shall be unlikely to want to regard $Lp \supset p$ as valid, since what it will then mean is that whatever ought to be the case is in fact the case. There is, however, a formula which, like $Lp \supset p$, is not a theorem of K but which with this interpretation it *is* plausible to regard as valid, and that is the wff $Lp \supset Mp$. For if Lp means that it is obligatory that p, then Mp will mean that it is permissible that p (not obligatory that not-p), and so $Lp \supset Mp$ will mean that whatever is obligatory is at least permissible, which sounds reasonable enough. This interpretation of L is known as a *deontic* interpretation, and for that reason $Lp \supset Mp$ is often called **D**, and the system obtained by adding it to K as an extra axiom is known as the system D;[8] i.e. D is defined as K +

D $Lp \supset Mp$

An easily derived theorem of D is

D1 $M(p \supset p)$

PROOF

PC	(1)	$p \supset p$
(1) × N	(2)	$L(p \supset p)$
$\mathbf{D}[p \supset p/p]$	(3)	$L(p \supset p) \supset M(p \supset p)$
(2), (3) × MP	(4)	$M(p \supset p)$	Q.E.D.

In fact D1 would provide an alternative axiom for D, since if we add it alone to K we can derive **D** in the following way:

K7[p/q]	(1)	$M(p \supset p) \equiv (Lp \supset Mp)$
D1, (1) × Eq	(2)	$Lp \supset Mp$	Q.E.D.

It is worth noting that if any wff α is a theorem of D, then so is $M\alpha$. For if α is a theorem, N gives $L\alpha$ as a theorem; and then by $\mathbf{D}[\alpha/p]$ and MP we obtain $M\alpha$.

It is also worth noting that if any system which is an extension of K has any theorems of the form $M\alpha$, that system contains D. To prove this it is clearly sufficient to derive D1 in such a system, and we can do this as follows:

Given:	(1) $M\alpha$
PC	(2) $q \supset (p \supset p)$
(2)[α/q]	(3) $\alpha \supset (p \supset p)$
(3) × DR3	(4) $M\alpha \supset M(p \supset p)$
(1), (4) × MP	(5) $M(p \supset p)$	Q.E.D.

In introducing the system D we mentioned that its axiom **D** is not a theorem of K. We shall prove this in a moment, and we shall also prove that **T** is not a theorem of D. **D**, however *is* a theorem of T, since it follows straightforwardly from **T** and T1 by Syll. What this means is that the system D is intermediate between K and T, in the sense that T is a proper extension of D, which in its turn is a proper extension of K.

To find a definition of validity which will match the system D, and also to clarify the difference between D and K, we shall draw attention to a feature of some frames on which we have not so far laid stress. We have observed that not all worlds in a frame need see themselves; but in fact there is nothing in our definition of 'frame' to prevent there being some worlds in a frame which cannot see *any world in that frame at all*. Krister Segerberg has called such worlds *dead ends*,[9] and we shall adopt this terminology in this book. Now the rule [V*L*] says that $L\alpha$ is true in a world w iff α is true in every world that w can see, and we interpret this to mean that if there is no world at all that w can see, then $L\alpha$ is (trivially) true in w, no matter what wff α may be (even if it is $p \wedge \sim p$). (It may be easier to see why we count $L\alpha$ always true in a dead end by seeing why its negation $\sim L\alpha$ is always false in such a world: for $\sim L\alpha$ is equivalent to $M \sim \alpha$, and by [VM] any wff of the form $M\beta$ can be true in w only if there *is* some world that w can see.) It should now be clear that if a frame contains any dead end w, then D is not valid on that frame, since in w Lp is true and Mp false, no matter what value is assigned to p there. Since there are such frames, D is not K-valid, and is therefore not a theorem of K. A more general consequence is that K has no theorems at all of the form $M\alpha$; for every wff of this form would be invalid on a frame containing any dead end.

Suppose we now consider the class of frames which contain no dead ends, i.e. frames in which each world can see at least one world (itself and/or some other or others). In such frames R is said to be a *serial* relation, and we shall call them *serial frames* for short. In other words, $\langle W,R \rangle$ is a serial frame iff for every $w \in W$, there is some $w' \in W$ such that wRw'. Now D must be valid on every serial frame: for if it were not, there would have to be a world w in a model based on a serial frame where (i) Lp is true and (ii) Mp is false; but since the frame is serial w must be related to some world w', and then by (i) and [VL] p must be true in w' and by (ii) and [VM] p must be false there, which is impossible. Since D is valid on every serial frame, theorem 2.2 assures us that every theorem of D is valid on every such frame, i.e. that D is sound with respect to the class of all serial frames. We shall be able to prove in Chapter 6 that D is also complete with respect to that class of frames; so, anticipating that result, we now define D-validity by saying that a wff is *D-valid* iff it is valid on every serial frame.

It is now easy to show that T is not a theorem of D, and therefore that the system T is a proper extension of D. All we need to do is to exhibit a serial frame on which T is not valid, and an example of such a frame is one consisting of two worlds, w and w', where w cannot see itself but can see w', and w' can see itself. T is not valid on this frame, for if p is false at w but true at w', then T is false at w.

A note on derived rules

Earlier in this chapter we introduced the notation $K + \Lambda$ to denote the result of adding all the wff in Λ to the basis of K. More generally, where S is any axiomatic modal system containing the transformation rules US,

MP and N and Λ is any set of wff, we shall let S $+$ Λ denote the system obtained by adding all the wff in Λ to the basis of S, while retaining the rules US, MP and N. It is a trivial fact that all theorems of S remain theorems of S $+$ Λ, for the *addition* of new axioms cannot result in the *loss* of any theorems. With derived rules, however, the position is more complicated. We noted earlier on that the rules DR1–DR3 and Eq which we derived in K still hold in all extensions of K. But consider the rule we discussed above and showed not to be a rule of T:

P $\vdash M\alpha \rightarrow \vdash \alpha$

Now K, as we observed, has no theorems at all of the form $M\alpha$; so P is (trivially) a rule of K. Less trivially, it is also a rule of D. So P is an example of a rule which holds in some systems but not in all their extensions, and this illustrates the care that must be taken with derived rules. If we look back at the way DR1–DR3 and Eq were proved to hold in K, we can easily see why *they* hold in all extensions of K: for they were derived by appealing only to elements in K (theorems and primitive transformation rules) which are still present in all its extensions. But P is a rule of K and D because of features of those systems which are *not* present in all their extensions – in the case of K because the system is too weak to have any theorem satisfying the antecedent of the rule.

So if we are given merely that some rule is a rule of S and that S$'$ is an extension of S, this does not by itself guarantee that it is also a rule of S$'$. This is just one of the pitfalls one may encounter in studying axiomatic systems and which should put us on our guard against jumping to conclusions too easily.

Consistency

We shall say that an axiomatic system is *consistent* iff not every wff is a theorem of that system. In other words, a system is *inconsistent* iff every wff is a theorem. Other definitions of consistency are sometimes given, but provided that the system contains the schema **PC** (or some other way of ensuring that every valid wff of PC is a theorem) and the rules US and MP, all the standard definitions of consistency are equivalent. One such definition is that a system is consistent iff no variable is a theorem. This is equivalent to our definition because (a) if a variable were a theorem, then by US every wff would be one, and (b) if every wff were a theorem, then since p is a wff it would be a theorem. Another definition is that a system is consistent iff no wff and its negation are both theorems. And this is also equivalent to the definition we have given because (a) if α and $\sim\alpha$ were both theorems, then by substituting α for p and any wff β for q in the PC-valid wff $p \supset (\sim p \supset q)$ we could obtain any wff whatsoever as a theorem, and (b) if *every* wff were a theorem, obviously a wff and its negation would both be theorems.

Now clearly the wff p (or any other variable) is not valid on *any* frame; so if a system is sound with respect to any (non-empty) class of frames whatsoever, p is not a theorem of that system, and so the system is consistent. Thus a proof of the soundness of a system is automatically a proof of its consistency.

In Chapter 1 we introduced the notion of an *unsatisfiable* PC wff – i.e. one which has the value 0 for every value-assignment to its variables. It should be obvious that the addition of any unsatisfiable PC wff to any system which contains all valid PC wff and has the rules US and MP would make the system inconsistent; for if α is unsatisfiable, $\sim\alpha$ is valid, and therefore a theorem of the system already, so we should have a wff and its own negation as theorems. But it is also worth noting that if any invalid PC wff at all were a theorem of such a system, the system would be inconsistent. To prove this it will be sufficient, in the light of what we have just said, to show that every invalid PC wff has a substitution-instance which is unsatisfiable, and we can do this as follows:

Let α be any invalid PC wff. The fact that α is invalid means that there is some assignment of truth-values to the variables occurring in it which will give the value 0 to α as a whole. Now let α' be α with $p \lor \sim p$ replacing each variable to which that assignment gives the value 1 and $p \land \sim p$ replacing each variable to which it gives the value 0. Then since these two wff have the values 1 and 0 respectively for *every* value-assignment, α' will have the value 0 for every value-assignment – i.e. will be unsatisfiable. But clearly α' is a substitution-instance of α.

Constant wff

In forming α' out of α in the previous paragraph we replaced every variable by a formula whose truth-value could be guaranteed to be 1 or 0 as the case might be, irrespective of any value-assignment made to the variables. A wff of this kind we shall call a *constant* wff. Since the truth-value of $p \land \sim p$ does not depend on the truth-value of p ($p \land \sim p$ is always false) we may write it as $\perp$ and interpret it as a 'constant false proposition'; and we then define a *constant* wff by saying that $\perp$ is a constant wff, that if α is a constant wff, so are $\sim\alpha$ and $L\alpha$, and that if α and β are constant wff, so is $\alpha \lor \beta$. Finally, for convenience, we define the symbol ⊤ as ~ ⊥, and hence interpret it as a constant true proposition, to be always assigned the value 1.

A constant wff may or may not contain modal operators. A constant PC wff (i.e. one which contains no modal operators but is built up from ⊤ and/or ⊥ by truth-functional ones only) must have the same truth-value for every value-assignment, and as a result every such wff will be either valid or unsatisfiable. In the case of a constant wff which contains modal operators, its truth-value in any world in a model will not depend on the value-assignment given to variables in that model, but only on how that world is related to other worlds (or to itself) in that model. We shall find further use for constant wff in later chapters.

Exercises - 2
2.1 Prove in K:
- (a) $(L(p \supset q) \wedge L(q \supset r)) \supset L(p \supset r)$
- (b) $L(p \supset q) \supset (Mp \supset Mq)$
- (c) $(L(p \supset q) \wedge M(p \wedge r)) \supset M(q \wedge r)$
- (d) $M(p \supset (q \wedge r)) \supset ((Lp \supset Mq) \wedge (Lp \supset Mr))$
- (e) $M(p \supset p) \supset (Lq \supset Mq)$
- (f) $(Lp \wedge M(q \supset r)) \supset (L(p \supset q) \supset M(p \wedge r))$
- (g) $(Lp \wedge Mq) \supset M(p \wedge q)$

2.2 (a) Let the axiomatic basis of K* be the same as for K except that N is replaced by the axiom $L\top$: $L(p \supset p)$), and the rule

R* $\vdash \alpha \supset \beta \rightarrow \vdash L\alpha \supset L\beta$ (R* is DR1 but taken as a primitive transformation rule). Show that K and K* have the same theorems.

   (b) Let K** be K but with N and **K** replaced by $L\top$, R* and

K2* $(Lp \wedge Lq) \supset L(p \wedge q)$ (K2* is K2 but taken as an axiom). Show that K and K** have the same theorems.

2.3 Let T* be the same as T except that in place of **K**, T* contains
   K* $L(L(p \supset q) \supset (Lp \supset Lq))$
and in place of N, T* contains R*. Show that T and T* have the same theorems.

2.4 Prove that K has no theorems of the form $LM\alpha$.

2.5 Where T' is exactly like T except that in place of **T** it has
   T' $p \supset Mp$,
prove that T and T' have the same theorems.

2.6 (a) Prove that the following is a rule of K:

$\vdash \alpha \lor \beta \to \vdash M\alpha \lor L\beta$

(b) Prove that the following is a rule of D but not of K:

$\vdash \alpha \lor \beta \to \vdash M\alpha \lor M\beta$

(c) Prove that the following is a rule of T but not D:

$\vdash \alpha \lor \beta \to \vdash M\alpha \lor \beta$

2.7 Prove in D

(a) $M{\sim}p \lor M{\sim}q \lor M(p \lor q)$

(b) ${\sim}L(Lp \land L{\sim}p)$

2.8 Show that T2 is not a theorem of D.

2.9 Show that if $M\alpha$ is D-valid then so is α.

2.10 Prove that $\vdash L\alpha \to \vdash \alpha$ is a rule of K and D. [Hint (Chellas 1980, p. 124): For any wff α let $\sigma(\alpha)$ be obtained from α by deleting every modal operator (L or M) which is *not* in the scope of another modal operator, and show that any proof of α in K (D) can be converted into a proof of $\sigma(\alpha)$ in the same system.]

2.11 Let $L^{\to}$ be the rule

$\vdash L\alpha \supset L\beta \to \vdash \alpha \supset \beta$

Show that $L^{\to}$ preserves validity in K and D but not in T.

Notes

[1] This name, which has now become standard, was given to the system in Lemmon and Scott 1977, p. 29, in honour of Saul Kripke, from whose work the way of defining validity for modal logic which we have begun to describe and will elaborate later is mainly derived. We give the same name to the system and to the formula which is its characteristic axiom, and shall do so for some other systems also. In such cases we shall use bold-face type when referring to the formula, but roman type when referring to the system.

[2] An *axiom* is a specific wff; an *axiom schema* is a statement to the effect that any wff satisfying certain conditions is an axiom. The fact that the axiom schema **PC** gives us infinitely many axioms does not conflict with our requirements for a satisfactory set of axioms, since we have (in the truth-table method, for example), an effective way of determining whether any given wff is a valid wff of PC or not. Although **PC** appeals to a notion of validity it is only PC-validity and makes no reference to the modal operators. It is of course possible to study PC itself as an axiomatic system with a finite number of axioms. See p. 210

below.

[3] The word 'frame' in this sense seems to have been first used in print in Segerberg 1968b, but Segerberg has informed us that the word was suggested to him by Dana Scott. Lemmon and Scott 1977 called frames 'world systems'. Kripke 1963a used the term 'model structure' in a related but not quite identical sense. At this point it might be worth stressing again that the nature of the 'worlds' does not affect the logic. In fact if we take any frame and make an isomorphic 'duplicate', in which the duplicate worlds are related exactly as the originals are, we clearly validate exactly the same formulae.

[4] The symbol $\in$ simply means 'is a member of'. This is a convenient use of set-theoretical notation which we shall employ in this book. Another piece of notation we have been using is the angle brackets $\langle$ and $\rangle$ as in $\langle W,R \rangle$ to indicate the ordered pair of W and R – W and R in that order – or an ordered triple as in $\langle W,R,V \rangle$ and so on. (This contrasts with the use of curly brackets as in $\{a,b\}$ to denote the *unordered* class whose members are precisely a and b without commitment to any order. Thus $\{a,b\}$ is the same class as $\{b,a\}$, $\{a,a\}$ is the same class as $\{a\}$, and so on.) We shall explain other set-theoretical terminology as we proceed.

[5] In calling theorem 2.1 a *theorem* we must be careful not to confuse it with a theorem of K. The theorems of K are the wff which can be derived from the axioms of K by the transformation rules. Theorem 2.1 states a fact *about* K and we prove it by ordinary reasoning. Some authors would call it a *metatheorem* but no confusion ought to arise over the difference in status between theorems like K1–K9 say, and theorems like theorem 2.1.

[6] Where Λ is finite K + Λ is said to be *finitely axiomatizable*. A system which is not finitely axiomatizable is discussed on p. 185. To call K + Λ *axiomatizable* it is often required that Λ be effectively specifiable.

[7] Feys 1937 (*vide* esp. pp. 533–535). Feys' own name for the system is 't' (it was first called 'T' by Sobociński 1953). Feys derived the system by dropping one of the axioms in a system devised by Gödel 1933 (p. 39), with whom the idea of axiomatizing modal logic by adding to PC originates. Sobociński (op. cit.) showed that T is equivalent to the system M of von Wright 1951; for this reason 'M' is often used as an alternative name for T. In this book we shall usually refer to systems by names which have become standard, but it might be worth referring, at this point, to an alternative naming system found in Chellas 1980 in the spirit of Lemmon and Scott 1977. This consists in simply listing the axioms in sequence. So T would strictly speaking be KT.

[8] This name is found on p. 50 of Lemmon and Scott 1977.

[9] Segerberg 1971, p. 93.

3

THE SYSTEMS S4, S5, B, TRIV AND VER

In the previous chapter T was the strongest of the systems we discussed. We saw that there are senses of 'necessary' and 'possible' for which some of its theorems seem unacceptable. Nevertheless it seems plausible to hold that there is also a perfectly good and standard sense of these terms in which all the theorems of T are non-controversial and formulae which are not among its theorems – for instance $Lp \supset LLp$ – are at least perplexing.

Iterated modalities

One feature of $Lp \supset LLp$ and of many other formulae which makes them hard to pronounce on from an intuitive point of view is that they contain consecutive sequences of modal operators; $Lp \supset LLp$, for example, contains the sequence LL. Such sequences are known as *iterated modalities*. Now not all formulae containing iterated modalities raise difficulties. If we accept the validity of $Lp \supset p$ (**T**), for instance, we are not likely to have any qualms about $LLp \supset Lp$ or $LMp \supset Mp$, since they are simply substitution-instances of it. But when we ask, informally, whether $Lp \supset LLp$ is valid, the issue we are raising is this: is whatever is necessary necessarily necessary? when something is necessarily so, is the fact that it is necessarily so always itself something that is necessarily so? Now this is both a disputed question and one of some obscurity, for it is not at all clear under what conditions we should say that something is necessarily necessary. It is, however, at least a reputable and plausible view that in certain well-established senses of 'necessary' it should be answered in the affirmative; it is, for example, plausible to maintain that whenever a proposition is *logically* necessary, this is never a matter of accident but is always something which is logically bound to be the case. We do not, however, need to try to settle the issue definitely here; for what we have just said about $Lp \supset LLp$ is enough to give us a motive for constructing a system stronger than T, in which that formula would be a theorem, and for seeing what such a system would be like.

We have already noted that $LLp \supset Lp$ is a substitution-instance of **T**, and is therefore a theorem of T and all its extensions; so the new system would have $Lp \equiv LLp$ as a theorem. An equivalential theorem such as this, which entitles us to replace some sequence of modal operators by a shorter sequence, we shall call a *reduction law* of any system of which it is a theorem. Taking the reduction law $Lp \equiv LLp$ as valid would be one way of resolving the perplexity about 'necessarily necessary', for we should then say that p is necessarily necessary whenever p is necessary, and not otherwise. An extension of T such as we are now contemplating would reflect, among other things, the decision to say just this.

Of the various equivalences which could act as reduction laws and have a certain plausibility under many of our intended interpretations of L and M, the most important are the following:

R1 $Mp \equiv LMp$
R2 $Lp \equiv MLp$
R3 $Mp \equiv MMp$
R4 $Lp \equiv LLp$

We shall prove a little later that none of these is a theorem of T; in fact one important feature of T is that it contains no reduction laws whatsoever.[1] If we want to have an extension of T in which R1–R4 are theorems, however, we do not need to go as far as adding them all as new axioms, for three reasons:

1. As we have already mentioned, $LLp \supset Lp$ and $LMp \supset Mp$ are theorems of T itself, and obvious substitutions in T1 will give $Lp \supset MLp$ and $Mp \supset MMp$. So one half of each equivalence is in T already, and it would therefore be sufficient to add the converses, viz.

R1a $Mp \supset LMp$
R2a $MLp \supset Lp$
R3a $MMp \supset Mp$
R4a $Lp \supset LLp$

2. Secondly, from R4a we could derive R3a and vice versa, and from R1a we could derive R2a and vice versa. (These derivations are given below.) So it would be sufficient to add as axioms one from each pair, say R1a and R4a.

3. Thirdly, R4a is derivable from R1a, though R1a is not derivable from R4a. (This derivation is also given below.) So we could obtain all four reduction laws by adding R1a to T, while by merely adding R4a we could obtain two of the reduction laws (R3 and R4) but not the other two.

All this suggests the construction of two axiomatic systems, each stronger than T and one of them stronger than the other. The first of these, obtained by adding $Lp \supset LLp$ (R4a) as a new axiom to T, is known as the system S4. The second, obtained by adding $Mp \supset LMp$ (R1a) to T, is known as the system S5.[2]

As in the previous chapter we number theorems using the name of the relevant system; but for theorems of S4 and S5, to avoid confusion, we enclose the theorem number in brackets, writing 'S4(1)' instead of 'S41' and so forth.

The system S4
The basis of S4 is that of T with the single extra axiom

4 $Lp \supset LLp$

We now prove some theorems.

S4(1) $MMp \supset Mp$

PROOF
4[$\sim p/p$]	(1)	$L\sim p \supset LL\sim p$
(1) × LMI	(2)	$\sim Mp \supset \sim MMp$
(2) × PC15(Transp)	(3)	$MMp \supset Mp$

Q.E.D.

S4(2) $Lp \equiv LLp$ **[R4]**

PROOF
T[Lp/p]	(1)	$LLp \supset Lp$
4, (1) × PC5	(2)	$Lp \equiv LLp$

Q.E.D.

S4(3) $Mp \equiv MMp$ **[R3]**

PROOF
T1[Mp/p]	(1)	$Mp \supset MMp$
(1), S4(1) × PC5	(2)	$Mp \equiv MMp$

      Q.E.D.

S4(4) $MLMp \supset Mp$

PROOF
T[Mp/p]	(1)	$LMp \supset Mp$
(1) × DR3	(2)	$MLMp \supset MMp$
(2), S4(1) × Syll	(3)	$MLMp \supset Mp$

      Q.E.D.

S4(5) $LMp \supset LMLMp$

PROOF
T1[LMp/p]	(1)	$LMp \supset MLMp$
(1) × DR1	(2)	$LLMp \supset LMLMp$
(2), S4(2) × Eq	(3)	$LMp \supset LMLMp$

      Q.E.D.

S4(6) $LMp \equiv LMLMp$

PROOF
S4(4) × DR1	(1)	$LMLMp \supset LMp$
S4(5), (1) × PC5	(2)	$LMp \equiv LMLMp$

      Q.E.D.

S4(7) $MLp \equiv MLMLp$

PROOF
S4(6)[$\sim p/p$]	(1)	$LM\sim p \equiv LMLM\sim p$
(1) × LMI	(2)	$\sim MLp \equiv \sim MLMLp$
(2) × PC	(3)	$MLp \equiv MLMLp$

      Q.E.D.

Modalities in S4

We define a *modality* as any unbroken sequence of zero or more monadic operators ($\sim$, L, M). We express the zero case by writing '—'. Examples of modalities are: —; $\sim$; L; $M\sim$; LL; $\sim ML \sim M$. It is clear, however, that in any system containing LMI every modality can be expressed either without any negation signs at all or else with only one, and that at the beginning. We shall say that a modality expressed in this way is in *standard form*, and from now on we shall assume that all modalities are expressed in standard form. A modality is said to be an *iterated modality* iff it contains two or more modal operators; thus *LL* and *~MLM* are iterated modalities, but ~ and *~L* are not. A modality is *affirmative* if it contains no negation signs and *negative* if it does contain one.

We say that two modalities, *A* and *B*, are *equivalent* in a given system iff the result of replacing *A* by *B* (or *B* by *A*) in any formula is always equivalent in that system to the original formula; otherwise we say that they are *non-equivalent*, or *distinct* in that system. In a system containing the rules US and Eq the modalities *A* and *B* are equivalent iff $(Ap \equiv Bp)$ is a theorem of that system. If *A* and *B* are equivalent in a certain system, and *A* contains fewer modal operators than *B*, then *B* is said to be *reducible* to *A* in that system. Clearly the formulae we have called reduction laws express the reducibility of certain modalities to others in systems of which they are theorems.

We are now in a position to prove an important result about S4, viz. that in it every modality is equivalent to one or other of the following or their negations:

(i) —; (ii) *L*; (iii) *M*; (iv) *LM*; (v) *ML*; (vi) *LML*; (vii) *MLM*

The proof is straightforward. We ignore the negative cases to begin with. Then clearly (ii) and (iii) are the only one-operator modalities. Now theorems S4(2) and S4(3) entitle us to replace *LL* by *L* and *MM* by *M*; so if we add a modal operator to (ii) or (iii) we shall obtain either a modality equivalent to the original or else (iv) or (v), which are therefore the only irreducible two-operator modalities. In just the same way, if we add a modal operator to (iv) or (v), the only three-operator modalities we can obtain are (vi) and (vii). If, however, we add a modal operator to (vi) or (vii), the result is always equivalent either to the original as before, or else to (iv) or (v) by S4(6) or S4(7); hence there cannot be any irreducible modalities with four or more operators.

Clearly the negative cases can be dealt with in the same way; so what we have shown is that there are at most fourteen distinct modalities in S4. In fact all fourteen are distinct from one another, though we are not yet in a position to prove this.

If we prefix a modality to a wff, α, the result is of course itself a wff. The implication relations which hold (in S4) among the formulae thus obtained from (i)–(vii) are set out in the following diagram.[3] (Implication is symbolized by an arrow for typographical convenience.)

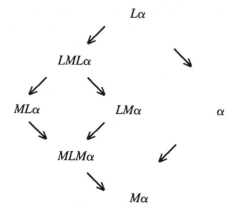

We can obtain an analogous diagram for the negative cases by negating all the formulae and reversing the direction of all the arrows.

The situation is strikingly different in T. The absence of any reduction laws in that system means that no matter how many modal operators a modality may contain, we can always construct a longer one which will not be equivalent to it. T therefore contains an infinite number of distinct modalities.

Validity for S4

We remarked earlier, though without proof, that the S4 axiom **4** ($Lp \supset LLp$) is not a theorem of T. We shall now prove this. We have already shown that every theorem of T is T-valid, i.e. valid on every reflexive frame; so in order to show that $Lp \supset LLp$ is not a theorem of T it is sufficient to describe a reflexive frame on which it is not valid. Here is one such frame: W consists of three worlds w_1, w_2 and w_3. Each world can see itself, w_1 can see w_2, w_2 can see w_3, but w_1 cannot see w_3. Now let p be true in w_1 and w_2 but false in w_3. Then since w_1 can see only itself and w_2, at both of which p is true, $V(Lp,w_1) = 1$. But since w_2 can see w_3, at which p is false, $V(Lp,w_2) = 0$. Hence, since w_1 can see w_2, $V(Lp \supset LLp,w_1) = 0$. So **4** is invalid on at least one reflexive frame, and therefore is not a theorem of T.

A feature of the frame we have just considered which was crucial to falsifying **4** on it was that although in it we had w_1Rw_2 and w_2Rw_3, we did *not* have w_1Rw_3; i.e. the frame was not a transitive one. (A frame $\langle W,R \rangle$

is *transitive* iff R is a transitive relation over W, i.e. iff for any three worlds w, w' and w'' in W (distinct or identical), if wRw' and $w'Rw''$, then wRw''.) And in fact it is impossible to falsify **4** on any transitive frame. The proof is this. Suppose there is some transitive frame $\langle W,R \rangle$ in which for some $w \in W$, $V(Lp \supset LLp,w) = 0$. Then by [V⊃],

(i) $V(Lp,w) = 1$

and

(ii) $V(LLp,w) = 0$.

From (ii), by [VL], there is some $w' \in W$ such that wRw' and

(iii) $V(Lp,w') = 0$

and from (iii) in turn there is some $w'' \in W$ such that $w'Rw''$ and

(iv) $V(p,w'') = 0$.

But since R is transitive, we have wRw'', and therefore, from (i),

(v) $V(p,w'') = 1$

which contradicts (iv). This proves that **4** is valid on every transitive frame.

Now the system S4 is K with the two additional axioms **T** and **4**. We showed earlier that **T** is valid on every reflexive frame, and we have now shown that **4** is valid on every transitive frame. So by theorem 2.2 on p. 39, it follows that every theorem of S4 is valid on every frame which is both reflexive and transitive, i.e. that S4 is sound with respect to the class of all such frames. We shall prove in Chapter 6 that S4 is also complete with respect to that class, so we shall define S4-validity as validity on all reflexive and transitive frames, and we shall call any reflexive transitive frame an *S4-frame*. In terms of the modal game, this means that we shall count a wff as S4-valid iff it is valid in every seating arrangement in which whenever any player A can see a player B and B can see a player C, then A must be able to see C.

The system S5
The basis of S5 is that of T plus the additional axiom

E $Mp \supset LMp$

This is the formula we previously called **R1a**.[4] The first three theorems of S5 are proved in the same way as S4(1)–S4(3), but using **E** instead of **4**, and we leave the proofs to the reader. These theorems are

S5(1)	$MLp \supset Lp$	
S5(2)	$Mp \equiv LMp$	[R1]
S5(3)	$Lp \equiv MLp$	[R2]

The S4 axiom $Lp \supset LLp$ is not an axiom of S5, but we now prove that it is a theorem of S5. Since the two systems have the rest of their bases in common, this constitutes a proof that S5 contains S4.

4 $Lp \supset LLp$

PROOF IN S5
T1[Lp/p]	(1)	$Lp \supset MLp$
S5(2)[Lp/p]	(2)	$MLp \equiv LMLp$
(1), (2) × Eq	(3)	$Lp \supset LMLp$
(3), S5(3) × Eq	(4)	$Lp \supset LLp$

Q.E.D.

S5(4) $L(p \vee Lq) \equiv (Lp \vee Lq)$

PROOF
K9[Lq/q]	(1)	$L(p \vee Lq) \supset (Lp \vee MLq)$
(1), **R2** × Eq	(2)	$L(p \vee Lq) \supset (Lp \vee Lq)$
K4[Lq/q]	(3)	$(Lp \vee LLq) \supset L(p \vee Lq)$
(3), **R4** × Eq	(4)	$(Lp \vee Lq) \supset L(p \vee Lq)$
(2), (4) × PC5	(5)	$L(p \vee Lq) \equiv (Lp \vee Lq)$

Q.E.D.

S5(5) $L(p \vee Mq) \equiv (Lp \vee Mq)$

PROOF
S5(4)[Mq/q]	(1)	$L(p \vee LMq) \equiv (Lp \vee LMq)$
(1), **R1** × Eq	(2)	$L(p \vee Mq) \equiv (Lp \vee Mq)$

Q.E.D.

S5(6) $M(p \land Mq) \equiv (Mp \land Mq)$

PROOF

S5(4)[$\sim p/p, \sim q/q$]	(1)	$L(\sim p \lor L\sim q) \equiv (L\sim p \lor L\sim q)$
PC	(2)	$(p \equiv q) \supset (\sim p \equiv \sim q)$
(1) × (2)	(3)	$\sim L(\sim p \lor L\sim q) \equiv \sim(L\sim p \lor L\sim q)$
(3) × LMI	(4)	$M\sim(\sim p \lor \sim Mq) \equiv \sim(\sim Mp \lor \sim Mq)$
(4), Def$\land$	(5)	$M(p \land Mq) \equiv (Mp \land Mq)$ **Q.E.D.**

S5(7) $M(p \land Lq) \equiv (Mp \land Lq)$

PROOF

S5(6)[Lq/q]	(1)	$M(p \land MLq) \equiv (Mp \land MLq)$
(1), **R2** × Eq	(2)	$M(p \land Lq) \equiv (Mp \land Lq)$ **Q.E.D.**

We can also show that **E** is not a theorem of S4, and therefore that S5 *properly* contains S4. To do this it is sufficient to produce a frame which is reflexive and transitive (and is therefore a frame for S4) on which **E** can be falsified. Such a frame is the frame $\langle W, R \rangle$ where W consists of two worlds, w_1 and w_2; each can see itself, w_1 can see w_2, but w_2 cannot see w_1. Now let V be a value-assignment which makes p true in w_1 but false in w_2. Then by [VM], since w_1 can see itself and p is true there, $V(Mp, w_1) = 1$. But since w_2 is the *only* world w_2 can see and p is false there, [VM] gives us $V(Mp, w_2) = 0$; so by [VL], since w_1 can see w_2, $V(LMp, w_1) = 0$. Thus at w_1 Mp is true but LMp is false, and hence $Mp \supset LMp$ is false. So **E** is not a theorem of S4.

Modalities in S5

We have shown that all the four reduction laws mentioned earlier are theorems of S5. We repeat them here for convenience:

R1 $Mp \equiv LMp$ [S5(2)]
R2 $Lp \equiv MLp$ [S5(3)]
R3 $Mp \equiv MMp$ [S4(3)]
R4 $Lp \equiv LLp$ [S4(2)]

A simple way of summarizing these laws is this: in any pair of adjacent modal operators we may delete the first. Since this procedure may be repeated indefinitely, we have the more comprehensive rule that in any sequence of modal operators we may (in S5) delete all but the last.

It is a straightforward consequence of this that S5 contains at most six distinct modalities, viz.

(i) —; (ii) L; (iii) M

and their negations. In fact these six modalities are all distinct from one another.

Validity for S5

If we look back at the frame we used a few paragraphs back to falsify **E**, we can see that although it is reflexive and transitive, it contains a world w_1 which can see a world w_2, where w_2 cannot see w_1. This means that the frame is not a *symmetrical* one, since a relation is said to be symmetrical iff whenever it holds in one direction it also holds in the other. I.e., a frame $\langle W,R \rangle$ is symmetrical iff, for any w and w' in W, if wRw' then w' Rw.

Now **E** cannot be falsified on any frame which is both transitive and symmetrical. For suppose there is a frame $\langle W,R \rangle$ of this kind on which **E** fails. This means that there is a model $\langle W,R,V \rangle$ based on this frame in which for some $w \in W$,

(i) $V(Mp,w) = 1$

and

(ii) $V(LMp,w) = 0$.

From (i), by [VM], there is some $w' \in W$ such that wRw' and

(iii) $V(p,w') = 1$

and from (ii), by [VL], there is some $w'' \in W$ such that wRw'' and

(iv) $V(Mp,w'') = 0$.

Now since wRw'' and R is symmetrical, we have $w''Rw$; and then, since wRw' and R is transitive, we have $w''Rw'$. Hence by (iv) and [VM], we have

(v) $V(p,w') = 0$

which contradicts (iii).

Now S5 is K with the two extra axioms **T** and **E**. Since we showed earlier that **T** is valid on every reflexive frame, and have now shown that **E** is valid on every transitive symmetrical frame, theorem 2.2 on p. 39 shows that S5 is sound with respect to the class of all frames which are reflexive, transitive and symmetrical. A relation which is reflexive, transitive and symmetrical is known as an *equivalence* relation. Since we shall be able to prove that S5 is also complete with respect to this class of frames, we define *S5-validity* as validity on every equivalence frame, and an *S5-frame* as a frame of this kind.

An everyday example of an equivalence relation is 'has the same height as', and this can be used to illustrate the fact that when such a relation is defined over a class of objects it divides them into a number (though perhaps only one) of self-contained 'equivalence classes'. Thus if 'has the same height as' is defined over a class of human beings, then for each height that any of them has there will be the 'equivalence class' of all and only those who have that height. Within each such equivalence class everyone will have the relevant relation to everyone, but no one will have that relation to anyone in any other equivalence class. To apply this to frames: if in a frame ⟨W,R⟩ R is an equivalence relation, this means that every world will be able to see every world in its own equivalence class but no world in any other equivalence class, and hence that we can equally well think of such a frame, not so much as a single frame but as a collection of separate frames, in each of which every world can see every world. And what this amounts to is that we could equally well, and equivalently, define S5-validity as validity on every frame in which R is a *universal* relation, i.e. one which holds between every pair (distinct or identical) of worlds in that frame.

(In terms of the modal game, what this means is that in order to produce a seating arrangement appropriate for S5, we must either let every player see every player without restriction, or else divide the players into segregated groups, in each of which everyone can see everyone but no one can see anyone outside the group. But if we do the latter, we might as well be playing a number of distinct games simultaneously, in each of which everyone can see everyone.)

In evaluating formulae in models based on frames of this kind, we could replace [VL] by the simpler rule

[VLS5] $V(L\alpha,w) = 1$ if $V(\alpha,w') = 1$ for every $w' \in W$; otherwise
$V(L\alpha,w) = 0$.

However, since this simplification can be undertaken only in the case of S5, we shall for the sake of uniformity stick to [VL] and assume that in S5 frames R is an equivalence relation but not necessarily a universal one.

The Brouwerian system

A special interest attaches to the following pair of theorems of S5:

S5(8) $p \supset LMp$

PROOF
T1, **E** × Syll

S5(9) $MLp \supset p$

PROOF

S5(8)[$\sim p/p$]	(1)	$\sim p \supset LM \sim p$
(1) × LMI	(2)	$\sim p \supset \sim MLp$
(2) × PC15(Transp)	(3)	$MLp \supset p$

Q.E.D.

Neither of these theorems is in S4. Indeed, if we were to add either as an extra axiom to S4 we should obtain a system at least as strong as S5. (In fact we should obtain exactly S5.) In the case of S5(8) we need only to substitute Mp for p and then apply **R3** to obtain the S5 axiom **E**, and the case of S5(9) is not much more complicated. If, however, we were to add either of them to T instead of to S4 we should obtain not S5 but a system which is weaker than S5 and which neither contains nor is contained in S4. This system has been called the *Brouwerian system*, and S5(8) the *Brouwerian axiom*.[5] We shall use 'B' to refer to the system and '**B**' (in bold face) to refer to the axiom.

The following is a derived rule of B (and also, of course, in view of the way in which it is derived) of S5:

DR4 $\vdash M\alpha \supset \beta \rightarrow \vdash \alpha \supset L\beta$

PROOF

Given:	(1)	$M\alpha \supset \beta$
(1) × DR1	(2)	$LM\alpha \supset L\beta$
B[α/p]	(3)	$\alpha \supset LM\alpha$
(3), (2) × Syll	(4)	$\alpha \supset L\beta$

Q.E.D.

Yet another way of obtaining S5 would be to add DR4 as a primitive transformation rule to S4, without any new axioms; for then, since $MMp \supset Mp$ (S4(1)) is a theorem of S4, DR4 would immediately give us $Mp \supset LMp$ (i.e. E).

Validity for B

We show first that **B** is valid on every frame in which R is symmetrical. Let $\langle W,R,V \rangle$ be any model based on any symmetrical frame. Suppose that for some $w \in W$, $V(p,w) = 1$. Now consider any w' such that wRw'. Since R is symmetrical, we also have $w'Rw$; and then, since $V(p,w) = 1$, [VM] gives us $V(Mp,w') = 1$. Since this is so for *every* w' such that wRw', $V(LMp,w) = 1$. Thus whenever p is true at any world, so is LMp, provided that R is symmetric; and therefore $p \supset LMp$ is valid on every symmetrical frame.

We already know that **T** is valid on every reflexive frame; so, since the system B is **K** + **T** + **B**, theorem 2.2 gives us the result that B is sound with respect to the class of all frames which are both reflexive and symmetrical. Such frames we shall call *B-frames*, and we define *B-validity* as validity on every B-frame.

Now we have seen that adding **B** to S4 gives S5, and we have also seen that S4 is weaker than S5; and from this it follows that **B** is not in S4, and hence that S4 does not contain the system B. (In fact the model we used to show that **E** is not in S4 can also easily be used to show that **B** is not in S4.) Furthermore, B does not contain S4 either, since **4** fails on the following reflexive and symmetrical (but non-transitive) frame $\langle W,R \rangle$: W consists of three worlds, w_1, w_2 and w_3. Each world can see itself, and in addition we have w_1Rw_2, w_2Rw_1, w_2Rw_3 and w_3Rw_2. It may help to visualize the frame like this:

$$w_1 \Leftrightarrow w_2 \Leftrightarrow w_3$$

– where the arrows represent the accessibility relation, and it is also assumed that each world is related to itself. If we now form a model on this frame by letting $V(p,w_1) = 1$, $V(p,w_2) = 1$ and $V(p,w_3) = 0$, then **4** fails in this model for just the same reasons as it fails in the model we used on p. 56 to show that **4** is not T-valid (Lp is true in w_1, but it is false in w_2 and so LLp is false in w_1). The only difference between the two cases is that our present frame is symmetrical as well as reflexive, and we have shown that every theorem of B is valid on every such frame.

So B and S4 are independent systems, in the sense that neither contains the other, and yet each lies between T and S5.

Some other systems

In later chapters we shall discuss other modal systems; we shall see that there are infinitely many of these, and we shall look at some of the general properties of modal systems. But even with the tools already at our disposal we can see how to define some other systems. For instance, instead of adding **4** to T to obtain S4, we could add it merely to K or to D. The resulting systems are often called K4 and KD4 respectively. If we define K4-*frames* as those which are transitive (whether or not they are reflexive), and *KD4-frames* as those which are both serial and transitive, then the results we have proved so far are sufficient to show that all the theorems of K4 are valid on all K4-frames and all the theorems of KD4 are valid on all KD4-frames. It is not difficult to produce a serial and transitive frame on which **T** fails: the frame we used on p. 45 to prove that **T** is not a theorem of D was in fact such a frame. (It was, of course, not reflexive.) This shows that KD4 does not contain T; *a fortiori*, K4 does not contain it either. We have also shown that **4** is not in T. Thus KD4 and T are independent of each other, and so are K4 and T. Moreover, KD4 is a *proper* extension of K4; for the frame which consists of a single dead end is (trivially) transitive and therefore a frame on which every theorem of K4 is valid; but as we saw on p. 45, **D** is not valid on any frame which contains a dead end.

We can similarly add **B** to K or to D instead of to T, to obtain the systems KB and KDB, which can easily be shown to be sound with respect to the classes of symmetrical frames and serial and symmetrical frames respectively. It can then be shown, by arguments of the kind used in the previous paragraph, that each of KB and KDB is independent of each of K4, KD4 and T; but we leave this task to the reader.[6]

Collapsing into PC

We shall now look at a system which can be obtained by adding even to D, and *a fortiori* to any of the stronger systems we have mentioned, the extra axiom $p \supset Lp$. This formula is not even S5-valid, since it can easily be falsified on a two-world frame in which each world can see both worlds (and which is therefore an S5-frame), by letting p be true in one world but false in the other. Nevertheless adding it even to S5 would not result in an inconsistent system, for the following reason. Consider a frame in which there is only one world, w, and it is related to itself. This is clearly an S5-frame, but $p \supset Lp$ is valid on it; for if $V(p,w) = 1$, then

V(p,w') $=$ 1 for every w' such that wRw', since there is only one such w', namely w itself, and so V(Lp,w) $=$ 1. Every theorem of S5 $+$ p $\supset$ Lp is therefore valid on this frame; but p is not, since there is obviously a value-assignment which makes p false at w. So not every wff is a theorem of S5 $+$ p $\supset$ Lp ; i.e. the system is consistent.

In this system the new axiom, together with **D**, immediately yields p $\supset$ Mp (by Syll); from this (by [$\sim p/p$], Transp and LMI) we can obtain Lp $\supset$ p, and then, by simple steps, Lp $\equiv$ p and Mp $\equiv$ p. By the rules US and Eq every formula would be then equivalent to the result of deleting all its modal operators; so in any formula we could delete or insert Ls and Ms to our heart's content (provided we preserved well-formedness), and the result would be equivalent to the original. In such a system, therefore, the modal operators would merely 'idle'; in interpreting the system we could draw no significant distinction between necessity, possibility and truth, and for all practical purposes it could be regarded simply as the Propositional Calculus itself, encrusted with Ls and Ms as mere typographical embellishments. The PC wff which results from deleting all the modal operators in a modal wff α is said to be the *PC-transform* of α. A system such as the one we have just described, in which every wff is equivalent to its own PC-transform, may be said to *collapse into PC*.

It is worth noting that although in the previous paragraph we appealed to the rule Eq, we could have obtained all our results from the new axiom and **D** alone (together with the axiom schema **PC**). We did not even need to have **K** as an axiom, nor did we need the rule of Necessitation. Moreover, the system would clearly contain S5, since the results of deleting all the modal operators in **T** and in **E** are PC theorems.

If we add the stronger axiom p $\equiv$ Lp even to K the resulting system similarly collapses into PC. The system D $+$ p $\supset$ Lp (or K $+$ p $\equiv$ Lp) is known as the *Trivial* system (*Triv* for short), because in it the modal operators are trivial in the sense we explained earlier. The wff p $\equiv$ Lp is itself sometimes called **Triv**.

It is only in the very strong system Triv that every wff is equivalent to its PC-transform. Even in the much weaker system D, however (and in all systems containing it), there is a somewhat analogous relation between a certain class of wff and their PC-transforms. These are the wff which at the end of the previous chapter we called constant wff - wff constructed out of the constant true and false propositions $\top$ and $\perp$ by truth-functional and modal operators. The PC-transform of any constant wff is of course itself a constant PC wff, and we noted on p. 48 that every such wff is either PC-valid or PC-unsatisfiable. The relation is this: If α is any constant wff, then if its PC-transform is PC-valid, α itself is a theorem of D; otherwise (i.e. if its PC-transform is unsatisfiable) $\sim\alpha$ is a theorem of D. Let us denote the PC-transform of any wff α by $\tau(\alpha)$; then we can state the result as the following lemma:

LEMMA 3.1 Let α be any constant wff. Then if $\tau(\alpha)$ is PC-valid, $\vdash_D \alpha$; otherwise $\vdash_D \sim\alpha$.

Since every constant wff can be constructed from $\perp$ by $\sim$, $\vee$ and L, in order to prove the lemma it is sufficient to show (i) that it holds for $\perp$, (ii) that if it holds for a wff α it also holds for $\sim\alpha$, (iii) that if it holds for α it also holds for $L\alpha$, and (iv) that if it holds for α and for β it also holds for $\alpha \vee \beta$.

To show (i) we need only remark that the PC-transform of $\perp$ is $\perp$ itself, and that since $\perp$ is unsatisfiable its negation, $\sim\perp$, is PC-valid and therefore a theorem of D. (ii) and (iv) hold by purely PC principles, and we omit the details of their proofs here. (They rely on the fact mentioned above that if α is a constant wff then $\tau(\alpha)$ is either PC-valid or PC-unsatisfiable.) For (iii) the proof is this: (A) Suppose that $\tau(L\alpha)$ is PC-valid. Clearly $\tau(L\alpha)$ is the same wff as $\tau(\alpha)$; so, since the lemma is assumed to hold for α, $\vdash_D \alpha$; hence by N, $\vdash_D L\alpha$. (B) Suppose that $\tau(L\alpha)$ is not PC-valid. As before, $\tau(L\alpha)$ is the same wff as $\tau(\alpha)$, and the lemma is assumed to hold for α. Hence $\vdash_D \sim\alpha$; hence (by N) $\vdash_D L\sim\alpha$; hence (by D) $\vdash_D M\sim\alpha$; hence (by LMI) $\vdash_D \sim L\alpha$.

We shall have a use for lemma 3.1 shortly. In the meantime, however, we shall consider another way in which a system can collapse into PC.

We produced the system Triv by adding $p \supset Lp$ to D. Adding it to K would not have been enough. For consider the frame which consists of a single dead end. It is easy to check that on this frame $p \supset Lp$ is valid but $Lp \supset p$ is not, so the latter is not a theorem of K + $p \supset Lp$. In that system, therefore, unlike Triv, $p \supset Lp$ and $Lp \supset p$ are not equivalent, even though they have the same PC-transform.

The system we are about to consider, however, is not K + $p \supset Lp$ but the even stronger system produced by adding the axiom Lp to K. From this axiom we can of course obtain by US every wff of the form $L\alpha$ as a theorem – even $L\perp$. This system is known as the *Verum* system (*Ver* for short). It no doubt appears bizarre in many ways, and certainly seems to impose some strain on the attempt to interpret L as meaning 'necessarily'. It is nevertheless a consistent system because Lp, and therefore every theorem of the system, is valid on the one-world dead end frame we have just referred to, but p is not. In Ver any wff will be equivalent not, as in Triv, to its own PC-transform, but to the wff which results from replacing every well-formed expression of the form $L\alpha$ in it by $\top$, and every one of the form $M\alpha$ by $\bot$. Since the formula thus obtained will always be a PC wff, we could regard the Verum system as providing a different form of collapsing into PC.

The reason for calling K $+$ Lp the *Verum* system is that in interpreting it we think of $L\alpha$ as always true. The wff Lp is sometimes itself called **Ver**.

Triv and Ver are incompatible systems; i.e. the system K $+$ **Triv** $+$ **Ver** is inconsistent. For if both Lp and $p \equiv Lp$ are theorems, so is p, and therefore by US every wff is a theorem. Hence Triv is not contained in Ver, nor is Ver in Triv.

Two other results which can be proved about these two systems are:

(1) Every normal modal system, in the sense explained on p. 40 (i.e. every consistent extension of K which retains the rules US, MP and N), is contained either in Triv or in Ver. (Some systems, of course, like K itself or K4 or KB, are contained in both.)

(2) Each of Triv and Ver is a maximal system, in the sense that in the case of each of them, if *any* wff which is not already a theorem were added to it, the resulting system would be inconsistent.[7]

The second of these results follows from the first. To show this, let us suppose that we have proved (1). Then to prove that Triv is a maximal system we take any wff α which is not a theorem of Triv. In that case, the system Triv $+$ α is not contained in Triv, and so by (1) it must either be inconsistent or else be contained in Ver; but the latter would mean that Triv itself is contained in Ver, and we saw above that it is not. That Ver is also a maximal system follows from (1) in an exactly analogous way. So in order to prove both (1) and (2) it will be sufficient to prove (1).

Our strategy for proving (1) will be to prove the following two lemmas, from which (1) clearly follows immediately:

LEMMA 3.2   Every consistent extension of K which is not contained in Ver contains D.

LEMMA 3.3   Every consistent system which contains D is contained in Triv.

The proof of lemma 3.2 will be made easier by some techniques we shall introduce on p. 108, so we shall postpone it till then. Lemma 3.3, however, can be proved with our presently available resources, as follows:

Proof of lemma 3.3: It is sufficient to show that if S is any system which contains D and has some theorem α which is not a theorem of Triv, then S is inconsistent. We show this as follows. Since α is not a theorem of Triv, its PC-transform $\tau(\alpha)$ is not PC-valid. Now precisely the same procedure which we used on p. 47 to show that every invalid wff of PC has a substitution-instance which is an unsatisfiable constant wff will also produce for any wff with an invalid PC-transform a substitution-instance which is a constant proposition whose PC-transform is an unsatisfiable wff. Let α' be such a substitution-instance of α. Then (1) by US, α' is a theorem of S. But by lemma 3.1, $\sim\alpha'$ is a theorem of D, and hence, since S contains D, it is also a theorem of S. Thus both α' and $\sim\alpha'$ are theorems of S, and S is therefore inconsistent.

Exercises — 3

3.1 Prove in S4:
   (a) $L(p \supset q) \supset L(Lp \supset Lq)$
   (b) $(Lp \lor Lq) \equiv L(Lp \lor Lq)$
   (c) $ML(p \supset LMp)$
   (d) $M(Lp \supset Mq) \supset M(p \supset q)$

3.2 Where A is any affirmative modality (i.e. a string of Ls and Ms) show that $L(p \supset q) \supset L(Ap \supset Aq)$ is a theorem of S4.

3.3 Show that T with $L(p \supset q) \supset L(Lp \supset Lq)$ in place of **K** is deductively equivalent to S4.

3.4 Prove that the modalities listed on p. 55 are non-equivalent in S4.

3.5 Prove that where $L^n p$ is p with n Ls in front of it then for n $\neq$ m, $L^n p \equiv L^m p$ is not a theorem of T.

3.6 S4.2 is S4 + the axiom
   G1 $MLp \supset LMp$
Prove that S4.2 has only four proper (i.e. non-empty) affirmative modalities, L, ML, LM, and M and that in terms of strength they can be

linearly ordered in the order listed here.

3.7 Prove the following in S5:
   (a) $L(Lp \supset Lq) \lor L(Lq \supset Lp)$
   (b) $L(Mp \supset q) \equiv L(p \supset Lq)$
   (c) $MLp \supset (Mq \supset L(p \land Mq))$

3.8 Show that S5 can be axiomatized as
   (a) $D + E$
   (b) $S4 + \mathbf{B}$
or as
   (c) $K +$
       E_1 $LMLp \supset p$
       E_2 $MLp \supset LMLLp$
   (d)   Show that neither $K + A$ nor $K + B$ on its own gives T, KB (K
          $+ p \supset LMp$) or K4 (K $+ Lp \supset LLp$). (Hughes 1980).

3.9 Show that S5 can be axiomatized as **PC**, US, MP, **T** and
$\vdash \alpha \supset \beta \rightarrow \alpha \supset L\beta$, provided α is fully modalized, i.e. every
variable in α is in the scope of a modal operator. (Prior 1955a, Lemmon
1956).

3.10 Show that adding $L(p \lor Lq) \supset (Lp \lor Lq)$ to T gives a system
deductively equivalent to S5.

3.11 Prove that $K + E$ is sound with respect to the class of frames in
which if wRw' and wRw'' then $w'Rw''$.

3.12 Prove in B
   (a) $(MLp \land MLq) \supset LM(p \land q)$
   (b) $MLp \supset LMp$

3.13 Show that B can be axiomatized by dropping N and **K** and adding
B and
   R* $\vdash \alpha \supset \beta \rightarrow \vdash L\alpha \supset L\beta$ (Jennings 1981)

3.14 Show that $\vdash L\alpha \rightarrow \vdash \alpha$ is not a rule of KB (i.e. K $+$
$p \supset MLp$).

3.15   Show that if **K** is strengthened to an equivalence ($L(p \supset q) \equiv$ $(Lp \supset Lq)$) then T would collapse into PC.

3.16   Prove that the addition to S5 of the axiom $LMp \supset MLp$ would make the resulting system collapse into PC.

3.17   Show that K $+\ p \supset Lp$ is sound with respect to any class consisting of just two frames, each containing just one world. In one frame this world can see itself. In the other it is a dead end.

3.18   Set out fully the inductive steps for cases (ii) and (iii) in the proof of lemma 3.1 on p. 66.

Notes

[1] See Bellissima 1989. Thomas 1964 cites as an unpublished result by Sobociński the fact that for each n the system $S4_n$, obtained by adding $L^n p \supset L^{n+1}p$ (where $L^n p$ is p preceded by n Ls) properly contains $S4_m$ when n $<$ m. The result is easy to obtain using the obvious definition of validity for these systems (Exercise 3.5). Sugihara 1962 proves that $T + LLp \supset LLLp$ contains infinitely many distinct modalities.

[2] The names 'S4' and 'S5', which have now for long been standard, derive from Lewis and Langford 1932 (p. 501), where systems deductively equivalent to these are the fourth and fifth in a series of modal systems. (For more on this see Chapter 11.) In the naming system referred to in note 7 on p. 50 S4 would be KT4, S5 would be KTE, and so on.

[3] This diagram is given in Prior 1957, p. 124. The results were originally obtained by Becker 1930 and Parry 1939.

[4] The name **E** for this wff is found on p. 50 of Lemmon and Scott 1977. It corresponds with a condition they call the *euclidian* condition. (See exercise 3.11.) Chellas 1980, p. 6 calls it **5**, and thus refers to S5 as KT5.

[5] This formula derives from Becker 1930, p. 509. An alternative version of **B** is of course $\sim p \supset L \sim Lp$. Some authors have called **B** the *Brouwersche* axiom, and the system the *Brouwersche* system, perhaps because in Lewis and Langford 1932, p. 497, Becker's German phrase 'Brouwersche Axiom' is quoted untranslated. The name derives from L.E.J. Brouwer, the founder of the intuitionist school of mathematics. In the intuitionist propositional calculus the law of double negation is not valid as an equivalence. More precisely, $p \supset \sim\sim p$ is valid but $\sim\sim p \supset p$ is not. One way of making this sound reasonable has been to suppose that in this calculus $\sim$ means something like 'it is not possible that', i.e. that it means what we usually mean by $L\sim$. Now if we replace $\sim$ by $L\sim$ then $\sim\sim p \supset p$ becomes $L\sim L\sim p \supset p$, i.e. $LMp \supset p$, and $p \supset \sim\sim p$ becomes $p \supset LMp$, i.e. **B**. On this view **B** therefore represents the intuitionistically

acceptable direction of the double negation law, and so has a connection, albeit somewhat tenuous, with Brouwer. (For a discussion of the intuitionistic propositional calculus see pp. 224–225.)

[6] These systems have some interesting properties in the matter of derived rules. We mentioned on p. 45 that a derived rule may hold in a system but not always in a stronger system. Some interesting examples of this are provided on p. 181f. of Chellas 1980. Thus the rule $\vdash L\alpha \to \vdash \alpha$ is a rule of K, D and KDB but not a rule of KB. (It is trivially a rule of every extension of T). Another example is what is called the 'rule of disjunction' that if $\vdash L\alpha \lor L\beta$ then either $\vdash \alpha$ or $\vdash \beta$. This is a rule of K, D, T and S4 but not a rule of B or S5. (See Chellas 1980, p. 181 and Hughes and Cresswell 1984, pp. 96–100. A weaker version of DR4 on p. 62, viz. $\vdash M\alpha \supset \alpha \to \vdash \alpha \supset L\alpha$, is studied in Chellas and Segerberg 1994 and Williamson 1994. Other studies of the effects of rules in systems of modal logic may be found in Williamson 1988 and 1992, where various philosophical interpretations of L are argued to fit certain rules.

[7] These results are obtained algebraically in Makinson 1971. See also Segerberg 1972. For some early results of this kind see McKinsey 1944.

4

TESTING FOR VALIDITY

A wff α of modal logic is valid (with respect to a class $\mathscr{E}$ of frames) iff, for every $\langle W,R \rangle \in \mathscr{E}$, and every model $\langle W,R.V \rangle$ based on $\langle W,R \rangle$, $V(\alpha,w) = 1$ for every $w \in W$. In this chapter we shall show how to test wff for validity in K, D, T, S4 and S5, when the relevant classes of frames are the following: For K, $\mathscr{E}$ is the class of all frames without restriction. For D, $\mathscr{E}$ is the class of all serial frames; for T, all reflexive frames; for S4, all reflexive and transitive frames and finally for S5, all equivalence frames, i.e. all frames which are reflexive, transitive and symmetrical. So let S be one of these systems, and let $\mathscr{E}$ be the appropriate class of frames. In what follows, by an S-model we shall mean a model based on a frame in the class of frames appropriate for S.

In testing a PC formula for validity by the truth-table method outlined in Chapter 1 we list all the distinct PC-assignments with respect to the variables in the formula, and then check whether the formula is true for each of them. This method can in theory be applied to any PC formula whatsoever; and even for moderately complicated formulae it is a practical method since for a formula containing n variables there are only 2^n distinct value-assignments. The corresponding method for a system S would be to list all the relevantly different S-models for the formula with which we were concerned, and then check whether the formula was true in every world in each of them. Now, as we shall show in Chapter 8, for the systems we have just mentioned, though not for all modal systems, this would in theory be a sound procedure since, for any particular formula, α, only models with no more than a certain finite number of members of W (depending on the structure of α) need be considered, and for any finite number of members of W only a finite number of distinct S-models can be constructed. Nevertheless, the number of distinct S-models, though always finite for any formula, is apt to be extremely large, and this method would involve us in millions of calculations in order to test even a quite simple formula.

Fortunately there are shorter methods. The one we shall describe[1] is an extension of the Reductio test for PC-validity outlined on pp. 11−12, with which we shall assume that the reader is familiar. Briefly, we attempt to find, for a given wff, α, a falsifying S-model (i.e., an S-model in which, for at least one $w \in W$, $V(\alpha,w) = 0$). The method will enable us to construct such an S-model if this is possible, or else it will demonstrate the impossibility of there being such an S-model. In the former case of course, α is invalid; in the latter case, α is valid.

Semantic diagrams

We shall describe the method of testing for validity by working through a number of examples, and will concentrate initially on the system K. Our first example will be the wff **K** itself. Of course we have already established its validity on p. 20, and again on p. 41, but we will use it here to illustrate the method of testing. For variety we shall consider **K** in a form which is equivalent to it in PC.

[1] $(Lp \wedge L(p \supset q)) \supset Lq$

We begin by supposing that in some K-model there is a world (say w_1) such that $V([1],w_1) = 0$. The rule [V$\supset$] then immediately gives 1 as the value (in w_1) of the antecedent, and 0 as the value of the consequent; i.e. we have $V(Lp \wedge L(p \supset q),w_1) = 1$ and $V(Lq,w_1) = 0$. [V$\wedge$] then gives $V(Lp,w_1) = 1$ and $V(L(p \supset q),w_1) = 1$. This is as far as purely PC methods can take us at this stage and they give us the following values in w_1:

$$
\begin{array}{cc}
* & * \\
(Lp \wedge L(p \supset q)) & \supset Lq \\
1 \quad\;\; 1\;1 & \quad 0\;0 \\
& *
\end{array}
$$

At the places marked by asterisks we have a wff beginning with an L. If it has the value 1 it has an asterisk above it, while if it has the value 0 it has an asterisk below it. Now in K the fact that Lp and $L(p \supset q)$ are both true in w_1 does not require that p and $p \supset q$ are both true in w_1 (though in T this *would* be required). And the fact that Lq is false in w_1 does not require that q be false in w_1. However it *does* require that there be *some* world, call it w_2, that w_1 can see at which q is false. And since w_1 can see w_2 then p and $p \supset q$ must be true at w_2. We can set out the whole calculation diagrammatically as follows:

A contradiction arises at the places underlined, which shows that the wff is K-valid.

Our second example will involve the operator M.

[2] $M(p \wedge Lq) \supset M(p \wedge Mq)$

If we suppose $V([2],w_1) = 0$ then the PC rules give us the following values (in w_1):

The asterisk under the first M indicates that we need a world, w_2, accessible to w_1, in which $p \wedge Lq$ is true. The asterisk *over* the second M indicates that in w_2 $p \wedge Mq$ has to be false. The diagram is as follows:

74

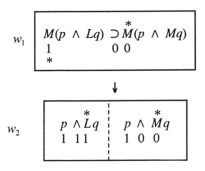

At this point we have two wff with asterisks above their operators. What do we do? Well, if we are in K we need do nothing. For if w_2 is a dead end then Lq will be true at w_2 and Mq will be false. And this shows that [2] is not K-valid.

When a diagram ends without an inconsistency this fact can be used to construct a model in which the wff being tested is false at some world. The present diagram leads to the following K-model. $W = \{w_1, w_2\}$ $w_1 R w_2$. (w_1 cannot see itself, and w_2 is a dead end − it cannot see anything.) The values of p and q in w_1 are arbitrary, since they do not make a difference to the value of the whole wff, and the value of q in w_2 is also arbitrary. We must have $V(p,w_2) = 1$, and for definiteness, let us also put $V(p,w_1) = V(q,w_1) = V(q,w_2) = 1$. Since w_2 is a dead end $V(Lq,w_2) = 1$ and $V(Mq,w_2) = 0$ and so $V(p \wedge Lq,w_2) = 1$ and $V(p \wedge Mq,w_2) = 0$. Since w_2 is the only world that w_1 can see, $V(M(p \wedge Lq),w_1) = 1$ and $V(M(p \wedge Mq),w_1) = 0$, and that is enough to give $V([2],w_1) = 0$. In the diagram each rectangle represents a world and the arrow represents the accessibility relation.

We shall call a diagram of the kind we have just constructed a *semantic diagram*, and the whole method the *method of semantic diagrams*. Before proceeding to further examples we shall now set out explicitly the rules for constructing semantic diagrams.

I *Rule for putting in asterisks*
An asterisk is put above every L which has a 1 beneath it and above every M which has a 0 beneath it. An asterisk is put below every L which has a 0 beneath it and below every M which has a 1 beneath it.

II *Rules for a new world*

A. If in a world w there occurs a formula $L\alpha$ with an asterisk above the L then, in every world accessible to w, α must be assigned 1.

B. If in a world w there occurs a formula $M\alpha$ with an asterisk above the M then, in every world accessible to w, α must be assigned 0.

C. If in a world w there occurs a formula $L\alpha$ with an asterisk below the L then there must be a world accessible to w in which α is assigned 0.

D. If in a world w there occurs a formula $M\alpha$ with an asterisk below the M then there must be a world accessible to w in which α is assigned 1.

It should be clear that when we construct new worlds in accordance with these rules we do so in a way which complies with [VL] and [VM]. In terms of the diagrams a world, w_i, is represented by a rectangle with 'w_i' written beside it; and when a world, w_j, accessible to w_i, is required in order to satisfy C or D, we draw a rectangle labelled 'w_j', with an arrow to it from w_i to represent accessibility. Certain formulae will have to be written in w_j and certain values assigned to them as dictated by the rules in II (A−D). We shall refer to these values as the *initial* values in w_j; values which we then have to assign to various well-formed parts of the formulae in w_j in order to comply with the conditions for a value-assignment we shall call *consequential* values in w_j.

Although [2] is not a theorem of K, it *is* a theorem of D. And the reason is not hard to see. In D-frames R is serial. In other words there can be no dead ends. This means that there must be a world w_3, accessible to w_2 in the semantic diagram for [2], and so the diagram must continue as follows:

$$w_3 \quad \boxed{\begin{array}{c|c} q & q \\ \underline{1} & \underline{0} \end{array}}$$

q must be given 1 in w_3 because of the asterisk over the L in w_2, and must be given 0 in w_3 because of the asterisk over M. And this leads to a contradiction.

Our third example is:

[3] $M(p \supset Lp)$

This is T2 on p. 42 and we shall test it in D.

$$w_1 \quad \boxed{\begin{array}{c} * \\ M(p \supset Lp) \\ 0 \end{array}}$$

Seriality requires a w_2 that w_1 can see, and the asterisk over the M requires $p \supset Lp$ to be false there :

$$w_2 \quad \boxed{\begin{array}{c} p \supset Lp \\ 1 \;\; 0 0 1 \\ * \end{array}}$$

The asterisk under Lp requires a world w_3 that w_2 can see with p false.

$$w_3 \quad \boxed{\begin{array}{c} p \\ 0 \end{array}}$$

At this point all required values have been put in. However, seriality requires a world that w_3 can see. If this had to be a world different from all that have gone before we should be in trouble, since we should have to be constructing new worlds endlessly, but to no purpose. However, there is nothing to stop the world w_3 can see being w_3 itself, and that is what we shall assume. The diagram then leads to the following D-model:

$W = \{w_1, w_2, w_3\}$, $w_1 R w_2$, $w_2 R w_3$, $w_3 R w_3$.
$V(p, w_1) = V(p, w_2) = 1$, $V(p, w_3) = 0$.

The situation with [3] is, however, different in T. T-frames are reflexive, and this means that where an asterisk occurs over an L then the wff that follows L must be given 1 in that world, and where an asterisk occurs over an M the wff that follows the M must be false in that world.

77

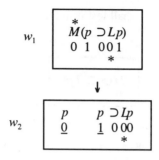

The asterisk over M in w_1 requires, in a T-diagram, that $p \supset Lp$ be 0 in w_1, which requires Lp to be false there. And so the asterisk under Lp requires a world w_2 that w_1 can see at which p is false. However the asterisk over M in w_1 requires $p \supset Lp$ to be false in w_2, which would force p to be true there, resulting in an inconsistency.

The next two examples will be tested in T.

Fourth example

[4] $M(p \wedge Mq) \supset (LMp \supset MLq)$

By steps which should now be obvious we reach the following:

$$
\begin{array}{c}
\overset{*}{} \qquad \overset{*}{} \\
w_1 \quad \boxed{
\begin{array}{l}
M(p \wedge Mq) \supset (\overset{*}{L}Mp \supset \overset{*}{M}Lq) \\
1 \qquad\qquad\quad 0\ 1\ 1 \quad 0\ \ 00 \\
* \qquad\qquad\qquad\quad\ *\qquad\quad *
\end{array}}
\end{array}
$$

We have, as yet, no definite values for p, q, or Mq in w_1. It is clear, however, that the value of $(p \wedge Mq)$ in w_1 does not matter so long as there is some world (accessible to w_1) in which its value is 1. Similarly, all that is required in the case of p and q is that in some world (accessible to w_1) $V(p) = 1$, and that in some world (accessible to w_1) $V(q) = 0$.

In other words the fact that no further values have been assigned in w_1 does not in any way prevent the application of rules A−D. Continuing the procedure we get the following diagram which shows [4] to be invalid in T:

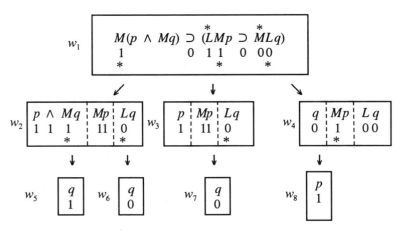

In this diagram the rules have been modified in the following way: In w_2 no * has been put under the M in Mp. This is because p has *already* been given the value 1, and so no further world is required. Similarly no asterisk has been put under Mp in w_3 or Lq in w_4. In a T-diagram, where α has 0 in a rectangle then $L\alpha$ must also have 0 in that rectangle and where α has 1 $M\alpha$ must also have 1, and no new rectangle need be constructed, and no further action need be taken in respect of such Ls and Ms. Since the purpose of the * is to indicate that something needs to be done we leave them out in these cases.

We can often shorten a diagram such as the one above, since instead of constructing a new rectangle whenever we need one we may find that a rectangle we have already constructed contains the values which are required in the new rectangle, or that it can be made to contain them by filling in values which, although not required in the already existing rectangle, are compatible with it. In this way our present diagram can be shortened to the following:

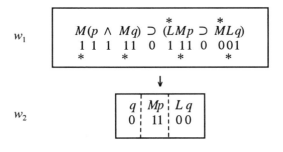

79

What has happened here is that we find that it is possible to let w_1 itself take over the functions for which we previously constructed many new rectangles and that only one other rectangle is required.

Although short cuts such as these can obviously save a lot of time in practice, we shall assume in our theoretical discussion of diagrams that no use has been made of them. In a diagram in which short cuts are not used no values will occur in any rectangle unless they are explicitly required by the rules of the method.

Alternatives in a diagram
Fifth example

[5] $L(Mp \equiv Mq) \supset L(p \equiv Lq)$

The first rectangle in the diagram for [5] will be:

$$w_1 \quad \boxed{\begin{array}{l} * \\ L(Mp \ \equiv \ Mq) \ \supset \ L(p \ \equiv \ Lq) \\ 1 \qquad\quad 1 \qquad\ \ 0 \ \ 0 \\ \dagger \qquad\qquad * \end{array}}$$

At the place marked by a † we have a situation which can also arise in the PC Reductio test (pp. 11−12): a truth-functional operator has a value under it, but we cannot determine unambiguously the values of its arguments. We shall call such an operator, for brevity, a †-operator. In the present case, the first $\equiv$ in [5] is a †-operator in w_1, and by [V$\equiv$], if $Mp \equiv Mq$ is to have the value 1 in w_1, then Mp and Mq must have the same value in w_1, but the assignment so far does not tell us which value this is. So we have two cases to consider, one in which Mp and Mq are both assigned 1, and one in which they are both assigned 0. We can represent these in this way:

$$w_1(\mathrm{i}) \quad \boxed{\begin{array}{l} * \\ L(Mp \ \equiv \ Mq) \ \supset \ L(p \ \equiv \ Lq) \\ 1 \ \ 1 \quad\ 1 \ \ 1 \qquad 0 \ \ 0 \\ * \qquad\ \ * \qquad\quad\ * \end{array}}$$

80

$$w_1(\text{ii}) \quad \boxed{\begin{array}{l} \;\;*\;\;*\qquad\;* \\ L(Mp \;\equiv\; Mq) \;\supset\; L(p \;\equiv\; Lq) \\ \;\;1\;\;0\quad\;1\;\;0\qquad 0\;0 \\ \qquad\qquad\qquad\qquad\quad * \end{array}}$$

As in the parallel cases in the PC Reductio test, it is only if each of these assignments leads to an inconsistency that [5] is valid; i.e., if either of them leads to a falsifying model, [5] is invalid. Now neither $w_1(\text{i})$ nor $w_1(\text{ii})$ contains any †-operators, so we can begin a diagram with each of them by our earlier rules. We take $w_1(\text{ii})$ first, since it is the simpler. This does lead to an inconsistency, as the following diagram shows:

$$w_1(\text{ii}) \quad \boxed{\begin{array}{l} \;\;*\;\;*\qquad\;\;* \\ L(Mp \;\equiv\; Mq) \;\supset\; L(p \;\equiv\; Lq) \\ \;\;1\;\;00\;\;1\;\;00\;\;\;\;0\;0\;0\qquad 00 \\ \qquad\qquad\qquad\qquad * \qquad\qquad\; * \end{array}}$$

$$\downarrow$$

w_2

$p \equiv Lq$	$Mp \equiv Mq$	p	q
$\underline{0\;0\;0\;0}$	1	0	0

$w_1(\text{i})$, however, gives us this:

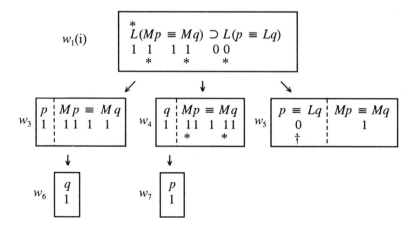

Here, in w_5, we find the same situation arising as in w_1, viz. the occurrence of a †-operator. (In fact in w_5 we have two †-operators, though we have only put a † under one of them, in accordance with a rule which we shall state shortly.) By $[V\equiv]$ if $(p \equiv Lq)$ is to have the value 0 in w_5, p and Lq must have different values in w_5, but the assignments so far do not tell us what these values are to be. So we have two cases to consider for p and Lq in w_5, exactly as we had for Mp and Mq in w_1, and w_5 will count as containing an inconsistency iff each of these leads to an inconsistency. We represent the two cases as follows:

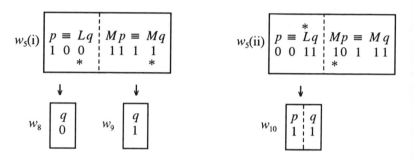

Neither w_5(i) nor w_5(ii) leads to an inconsistency, though of course in order to show that w_5 is not inconsistent it would have been sufficient for one of them not to lead to an inconsistency. So if we replaced w_5 by either w_5(i) or w_5(ii) in the diagram beginning with w_1(i), we could use the diagram so obtained to construct a falsifying model for [5] and thus show it to be invalid. We leave the reader to verify this.

Note that in the present case neither w_5(i) nor w_5(ii) contains any †-operators, since in each case the assignments to p and Lq enable us to give definite values to Mp and Mq, the arguments of the other †-operator in w_5. But if this had not happened — if, e.g., in w_5(i) we had not had definite values for Mp and Mq — we should have put a † under the $\equiv$ in $Mp \equiv Mq$ in that rectangle and constructed alternatives for it, which we should have called $(w_5(i))$(i) and $(w_5(i))$(ii). In general, if †-operators appear for whatever reason in any rectangle, w_i, we put a † under one of them (let us say, for the sake of having a definite rule, the leftmost one) and construct alternatives in the way we have described. Since w_i can contain only a finite number of truth-functional operators, the task of

82

constructing alternatives, alternatives of alternatives, and so on, of w_i is bound to be a finite one.

We shall now state a general rule for dealing with any †-operators that may occur in the construction of a diagram. It may be as well to restate here what a †-operator is. A †-operator in a rectangle, w_i, is a truth-functional operator which has a value beneath it in w_i but whose arguments do not have their values determined unambiguously in w_i. (If a modal operator has a value under it but we cannot determine the value of its argument unambiguously, we handle the case by the rule for asterisks below operators, not by constructing alternative diagrams.) Note that if we follow strictly the practice of putting a † under only one †-operator in any given rectangle, the largest number of alternatives we can have for any rectangle is 3: this will occur when the operator in question is ∨ or ⊃ with 1 beneath it, or ∧ with 0 beneath it, and the values of both arguments are undetermined. In other cases there will be only two alternatives.

III *Rule for alternatives*

If a rectangle, w_i, contains one or more †-operators, we place a † under the leftmost of them. We let $w_i(i)$ and $w_i(ii)$ (or $w_i(i)$, $w_i(ii)$ and $w_i(iii)$) be the two (or three) rectangles, each of which reproduces w_i exactly and in addition contains one of the value-assignments to the arguments of the operator below which the † appears in w_i which are compatible with the value under that operator. We call these rectangles the alternatives of w_i, and beginning with each of them in turn we construct a fresh diagram. Iff each of these diagrams contains an inconsistency we regard w_i itself as inconsistent.

In each alternative of w_i the initial values are all the initial values in w_i together with the values assigned in that alternative to the arguments of the operator under which the † appears in w_i.

N.B. No arrows are drawn from a rectangle containing a †-operator.

In the case of wff involving alternatives it is often a good strategy to postpone dealing with them for as long as possible, since sometimes values elsewhere in the diagram may force values to wff left open by a †-operator. A simple example is

$$(Lp \lor Lq) \supset L(p \lor q)$$

We know this is K-valid since it is theorem K6 on p. 34. Look at what happens when we test it.

$$w_1 \quad \boxed{\begin{array}{c} (Lp \ \lor \ Lq) \ \supset L(p \ \lor \ q) \\ 1 \qquad\quad 0\,0 \\ \dagger \qquad\quad * \end{array}}$$

The point about this wff is that, whatever we decide to do about the $\lor$ with a $\dagger$ under it, the asterisk under the L requires a world w_2 accessible to w_1 as follows:

$$w_1 \quad \boxed{\begin{array}{c} (Lp \ \lor \ Lq) \ \supset L(p \ \lor \ q) \\ 1 \qquad\quad 0\,0 \\ * \end{array}}$$

$$\downarrow$$

$$w_2 \quad \boxed{\begin{array}{c} p \ \lor \ q \\ 0 \ \ 0 \ \ 0 \end{array}}$$

Now w_1 can see w_2, and both p and q are false at w_2. So both Lp and Lq are false at w_1 and we end up with the following:

$$w_1 \quad \boxed{\begin{array}{c} (Lp \ \lor \ Lq) \ \supset L(p \ \lor \ q) \\ \underline{0 \ \ 1 \ \ 0} \ \ \ \ 0 \ 0 \\ * \end{array}}$$

$$\downarrow$$

$$w_2 \quad \boxed{\begin{array}{c} p \ \lor \ q \\ 0 \ \ 0 \ \ 0 \end{array}}$$

In this example what has happened is that the rule for 1 under an L (the overstar rule) has been used contrapositively. That rule says that if you have an L with a 1 under it the wff that follows the L must have 1 in all accessible worlds. So if it already has 0 in an accessible world the L must have 0 in the original world. In the present example this leads to contradiction without the need for alternatives.

S4 diagrams

We now show how to apply the method to S4, and then to S5. The frames for S4 and S5 are all T-frames, though of course not all T-frames are S4-frames, and not all S4-frames are S5-frames. The only difference between our definitions of T-validity and S4-validity is that in an S4-model the relation R must be transitive.

Let us apply this to the diagrams. We shall say that in a semantic diagram a series of rectangles $w_1, \ldots, w_n$ form a chain if an arrow goes from each (except the last) to the next rectangle in the series. Thus in the diagram on p. 79, w_1, w_2, w_5 form a chain, and so do w_1, w_2, w_6 and so on. To take care of the transitivity requirement, an S4-diagram will differ from a T-diagram in the following way: an arrow must go from every rectangle to every other rectangle which occurs later in every chain to which the first belongs. This means that to satisfy rules A and B, whenever in any rectangle we have $L\alpha = 1$ (or $M\beta = 0$) we must now write α with a 1 under it (or β with 0 under it), not only in the next rectangle in the chain but in every subsequent one as well. When a rectangle, w_j, contains a †, then each alternative of w_j is regarded as belonging to the chain to which w_j belongs: thus if an arrow goes from a rectangle, w_i, to w_j, arrows must be drawn from w_1 to each of $w_j(i)$, $w_j(ii)$ and $w_j(iii)$.

Clearly the transitivity requirement will make no difference in the case of a diagram in which no chain is more than two rectangles long. When, however, the T-diagram for a formula contains any longer chain than this, there will be a difference between its T-diagram and its S4-diagram. Consider, e.g., the formula:

(1) $L(p \wedge q) \supset LL(Mp \supset Mq)$

Its T-diagram is

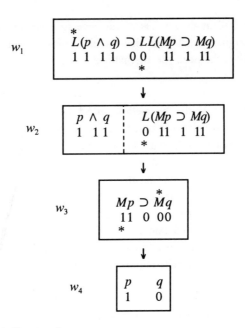

But its S4-diagram is:

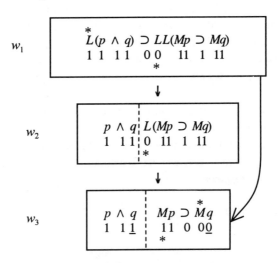

Here the assignment of the value 1 to $L(p \wedge q)$ in w_1 requires the presence of p $\wedge$ q (= 1) not merely in w_2 but in w_3 as well. This kind of addition to the contents of rectangles creates new possibilities of inconsistencies in the diagrams. When we find an inconsistency in the S4-diagram of a formula but not in its T-diagram, that formula is S4-valid but not T-valid. (1), in fact, is a case in point, as the diagrams show.

In order to show that the method of semantic diagrams provides a decision procedure for S4, we have to show that for every wff an S4-diagram of finite length can be constructed; or more exactly, that for every wff, α, we can construct an S4-diagram which will in a finite number of steps either (a) show α to be valid (by containing an inconsistency in some rectangle), or (b) enable us to construct a falsifying S4-model for α.

Now it was easy to show that every T-diagram is finite. For in every chain in a T-diagram the number of modal operators is constantly diminishing. Hence every chain must at worst lead us to a rectangle containing nothing but PC formulae, and such formulae never generate further rectangles. This does not, however, apply to S4-diagrams. In fact in S4 the following tantalizing situation can arise. Consider the formula:

(2) $LMp \supset MLp$

This is not S4-valid but its S4-diagram (by our present rules) goes like this:

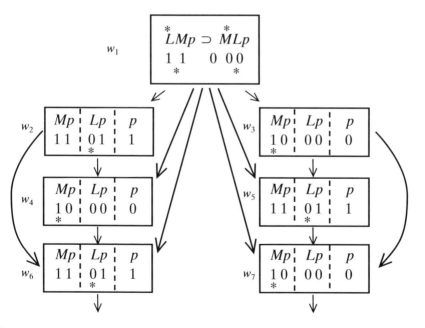

Here rectangle w_6 is needed because of the asterisk in w_4. But an arrow goes from w_1 to w_6 as well as from w_4 to w_6, and as a result the contents of w_6 turn out to be identical with those of w_2; hence we need yet another rectangle below w_6 whose content will turn out to be the same as those of w_4 and so on for ever. And the same situation obtains on the right-hand side of the diagram. Thus a falsifying model for (2) always seems to be within our grasp at the next step, but once we take that step seems to be one step further on still. Yet we never strike inconsistency in the diagram either.[2]

Clearly this diagram is not giving us a decision for (2). A simple modification of it, however, will do so: we delete rectangle w_6 altogether, and run the arrow from w_4 upwards to w_2 instead, and we treat the other side of the diagram in the same way. We then have a five-world falsifying model for (2), as we can easily check by a truth-table. The diagram will be this:

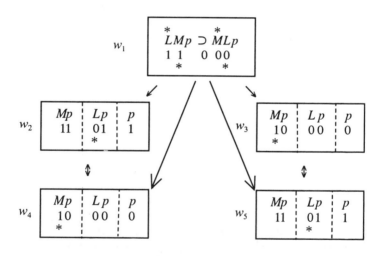

That this diagram fulfils the conditions which previously looked as if they would lead us to an infinite diagram, can be seen as follows:

1. We needed a world w_6 (accessible to w_4) in the first diagram to enable the initial values to be consistently assigned to the formulae in w_4. Since the formulae in w_2 and the values assigned to them there are the same as those in w_6, making w_2 accessible to w_4 is equally satisfactory.

2. The conditions for the assignment of the initial values in w_6 were that it in turn should be succeeded by a further world in which certain

value-assignments should obtain. But since w_6 is identical with w_2 these are precisely the conditions for the initial value-assignments in w_2, and we have already provided for their fulfilment in making w_4 accessible to w_2.

In short, instead of the endless chain, w_1, w_2, w_4, w_6 ... we have w_1 followed by w_2 and w_4 in endless alternation; and for this we only need three worlds. Exactly the same considerations apply to the right-hand side of the diagram. In the case of the present example we can in fact do better than this. Since w_3 and w_4 are identical, and w_2 and w_5 are too, we could abandon w_4 and w_5 altogether, and instead draw arrows from w_2 to w_3, and from w_3 to w_2. We then obtain a three-world falsifying model for (2). Indeed by using 'optional' values in w_1 we can do better still and produce the following diagram which gives a two-world falsifying model:

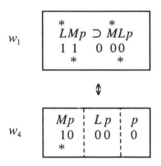

(Note that this, as will appear later, is an S5-diagram as well as an S4-diagram, and shows that (2) is invalid in S5, not only in S4.) But these possibilities depend on special features of (2) and we cannot generalize from them. We now show how to generalize this procedure to avoid infinite diagrams in all cases.

We note first of all that although in the above example the contents of w_2 were exactly the same as those of w_6, it would not have mattered if w_2 had contained some extra formulae as well. So long as all the formulae in w_6 had occurred in w_2 (with the same values assigned to them), it would have been equally satisfactory to lead the arrow back from w_4 to w_2; for all the conditions for the consistent assignment of the required values in w_6 would be included in those for the assignment of the values in w_2, and by hypothesis these are fulfilled by the successors of w_2 in the chain. When all the formulae which occur in a rectangle, w_j, also occur in a rectangle w_i with the same values assigned to them we shall say that

w_j is contained in w_i.

A further point to notice is that the distance between w_2 and w_6 in the chain (the number of intervening rectangles) was irrelevant. Even had w_6 occurred much later in the chain than it did, we could with equal propriety have led the arrow from its predecessor back to w_2, provided of course that at the same time we also directed to w_2 all the arrows which would have gone to w_6. We now state the following additional rule for S4-diagrams.

Rule of repeating chains

Whenever in any chain in an S4-diagram a rectangle, w_j, is contained in a rectangle, w_i, which occurs earlier in that chain, we delete w_j and lead every arrow which would have gone to w_j to w_i instead. We shall call a chain to which we have applied this rule, a *repeating* chain.

Observing the rule of repeating chains will guarantee that every chain in an S4-diagram is of finite length, and hence that every diagram contains only a finite number of rectangles, for the following reason. It is clear from the rules for constructing the diagrams that in the diagram for a wff, α, every formula which occurs in any rectangle must be a well-formed part of α itself. Now α has only a finite number of well-formed parts; and hence there can be only a finite number of sets of formulae selected from these, and of course only a finite number of ways of assigning values to the formulae in any such set. So while the contents of the rectangles in a chain can vary a great deal, they cannot vary *indefinitely*; therefore in an infinite chain we must sooner or later come across a rectangle which is contained in an earlier rectangle, and to which we can therefore apply the rule of repeating chains. Once we have done so, of course, the chain will only contain a finite number of rectangles.

Each chain in an S4-diagram, then, is finite. Now an S4-diagram consists of a set of chains each beginning with w_1. Each rectangle (apart from w_1) is generated, in accordance with rules C and D on p. 76, by a modal operator below which an asterisk appears in the immediately preceding rectangle in the chain; and since each rectangle only contains a finite number of modal operators, there can only be a finite number of chains in any S4-diagram. Hence every S4-diagram contains a finite number of rectangles. The presence of †-operators and the consequent construction of alternatives cannot affect this result, for the same reason as in the case of T.

S5-diagrams

The method of diagrams can be extended to provide a decision procedure for S5. In an S5-model every world stands in the relation R to every other world. The extra rule that has to be observed in constructing an S5-diagram is therefore that an arrow must go from every rectangle to every other one. This means that whenever we add a new rectangle in constructing an S5-diagram we must draw an arrow from it to every rectangle already in the diagram, as well as from all other rectangles to it, and then enter in these rectangles any formulae which the new arrows make necessary. In this way the possibilities of inconsistencies arising in rectangles are increased − as, of course, we should expect, since a formula can be S5-valid without being S4-valid.

As an illustration take the following formula:

$$L(Lp \lor q) \supset (Lp \lor Lq)$$

We shall first show that this wff is not valid in S4, and then that it *is* valid in S5:

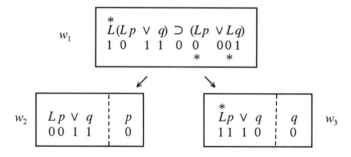

This leads to the construction of a model with three worlds, w_1, w_2 and w_3 where each world can see itself and w_1 can see w_2 and w_3, and in w_2 p is false and q is true, while in w_3 p is true and q is false. (Note that because p is false in w_2 Lp must be false in w_1, and so q must be true in w_1. The value of p in w_1 does not affect the value of the whole formula.) The frame of this model is an S4-frame since R is transitive, but it is not an S5-frame since R is not symmetrical. When we make R symmetrical we must have w_3Rw_1. But then transitivity requires that w_3Rw_2. But Lp is true in w_3 and this would contradict the fact that p is false in w_2. The S5 diagram would look like this:

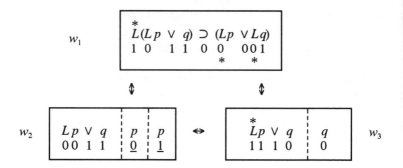

Exercises — 4

4.1 Test each of the following wff for validity in K. If a wff is not K-valid use the diagram to construct a falsifying K-model and then test the wff for validity in D. If it is not D-valid construct a falsifying D-model and then test the wff for validity in T. If it is not T-valid construct a falsifying T-model.

(a) $(M(p \wedge q) \vee M(p \wedge r)) \supset Mp$

(b) $Lq \supset M(p \supset q)$

(c) $(M(p \supset p) \wedge Lq) \supset M(p \supset q)$

(d) $M(p \supset p) \supset \sim L(Lp \wedge L\sim p)$

(e) $L(p \equiv q) \supset (Lp \equiv Lq)$

(f) $L(p \supset L(q \supset r)) \supset M(q \supset (Lp \supset Mr))$

(g) $((LMp \supset MLq) \wedge L(Mq \supset \sim Mr)) \supset M(Lp \supset M\sim r)$

(h) $M(Lp \supset p) \supset M(p \supset Lp)$

(i) $M(Mp \wedge \sim q) \vee L(p \supset Lq)$

4.2 Show that $\vdash \alpha \supset L(\beta \supset \gamma) \rightarrow \vdash \beta \supset L(\alpha \supset \gamma)$ is not a rule of K.

4.3 Test the following wff for validity in T. If a wff is not T-valid use the diagram to construct a falsifying T-model and then test the wff for validity in S4. If it is not S4 valid construct a falsifying S4-model and then test the wff for validity in S5. If it is not S5-valid construct a falsifying S5-model.

(a) $L(p \supset Mq) \supset (Mp \supset Mq)$

(b) $L(Lp \supset q) \vee L(Lq \supset p)$

(c) $L(p \equiv q) \equiv L(Lp \equiv Lq)$

4.4 (a)   Show that $MLp \supset LMp$ is invalid in S4. Give a falsifying model.

(b)   Consider a frame in which R satisfies the condition that if a world (say w_1) can see two worlds (say w_2 and w_3) then there must be a world (say w_4) that both w_2 and w_3 can see. Show that in that case the wff in (a) is valid.

(c)   Consider a frame in which R satisfies the condition that if a world w_1 can see two worlds w_2 and w_3, then either w_2Rw_3 or w_3Rw_2. Show that in that case 4.3(b) is valid, and that if R in addition is transitive then $L(Lp \supset Lq) \lor L(Lq \supset Lp)$ is also valid.

(d)   Consider a frame in which R satisfies the condition that if a world w_1 can see two worlds w_2 and w_2 then these two worlds can see each other. Show that **E**, $(Mp \supset LMp)$, is valid in such a case. Use this fact to show that KE is weaker than S5.

Notes

[1] Our procedure is similar in essentials to the method of semantic tableaux found in Kripke 1963a and elsewhere. For other decision procedures for some of the systems discussed in this chapter, see von Wright 1951 and Anderson 1954 (modified in Hanson 1966).

[2] Adapting a phrase from Kripke 1963a (p. 71), we might call diagrams constructed in accordance with our present rules 'tree' diagrams. Thus $LMp \supset MLp$ cannot be falsified in a finite tree diagram in In T, however, every invalid formula can be falsified in a finite tree diagram. In fact, as we shall show on p. 131 the appropriate definition of validity for S4 + $LMp \supset MLp$ will involve frames in which every world must be able to see a world which can see only itself. Every finite (reflexive) tree frame satisfies this requirement, but not every finite reflexive transitive frame. A study of tree frames (there called 'subordination frames') may be found in Chapter 7 of Hughes and Cresswell 1984.

5

CONJUNCTIVE NORMAL FORM

We have already proved the soundness of K, D, T, S4, B and S5, and given an indication of how to prove the soundness of a number of other systems, each with respect to an appropriate class of frames. In Chapter 6 we shall introduce a technique for proving the completeness of a system, that is, for proving that every valid wff is a theorem — using of course the definition of validity appropriate to that system. This technique will be very general and very powerful. It will not, however, lead to a decision procedure for theoremhood in the system in question; it will not, that is, provide us with a method whereby, given any arbitrary valid wff, we can show how actually to construct a proof of it in that system. Nor will it provide a mechanical method of establishing whether any given wff is valid or not.

The method of validity testing we described in the last chapter can also be adapted to give a completeness proof for each of the systems we have mentioned, and one of a kind which will show how, given any valid wff, we can construct mechanically a proof of it in the relevant system. The details of these completeness proofs are, however, quite complicated, and since we can much more easily establish completeness by another more general method, we shall not pursue them in this book. In the special case of S5, however, there is available a method which yields both a straightforward decision procedure and an easy completeness proof, and the main aim of this chapter is to set out this method.

Equivalence transformations
In our axiomatic presentation of modal systems we have made frequent use of the rule of Substitution of Equivalents (Eq). This rule states that if

α is any theorem of the system in question and we form β from α by replacing some well-formed part of it, γ, by a wff δ, where $\gamma \equiv \delta$ is a theorem, then β is also a theorem. But when we showed on p. 32 that Eq is a rule of K (and of all its normal extensions) we in fact proved something more general than this, viz. that if α is any wff at all, theorem or otherwise, and we form β from it in the way described, then $\alpha \equiv \beta$ is a theorem. And clearly we can make any number of moves of this kind, and the wff with which we begin will be equivalent to the one with which we end; for if we have a sequence of equivalential theorems

$$\alpha_1 \equiv \alpha_2$$
$$\alpha_2 \equiv \alpha_3$$
.
.
.
$$\alpha_{n-1} \equiv \alpha_n$$

we can use the PC-tautology $(p \equiv q) \supset ((q \equiv r) \supset (p \equiv r))$ as often as necessary to obtain $\alpha_1 \equiv \alpha_n$ as a theorem. This process may be described as the performing of an *equivalence transformation* of α into β (or of α_1 into α_n).

The method we are about to describe will enable us to take any modal wff α and convert it by equivalence transformations into a wff β which is of a special kind, for which we shall be able to give a straightforward effective test for whether or not it is a theorem of S5. All the equivalences used in these transformations will be theorems of S5, and hence $\alpha \equiv \beta$ will also be a theorem of S5.

Some of the equivalences we shall need are PC-valid wff. These include some of the formulae listed on p. 13 – in particular PC12−21 – and in addition the following, which we number in sequence with them:

PC22 $(p \wedge (q \vee r)) \equiv ((p \wedge q) \vee (p \wedge r))$
PC23 $(p \vee (q \wedge r)) \equiv ((p \vee q) \wedge (p \vee r))$
[Distributive Laws−Distrib]

We shall also need some modal equivalences, which we shall list later on.

Repeated applications of the Associative Laws enable us to re-group the disjuncts (or conjuncts) in any purely disjunctive (or conjunctive) wff, or in any substitution-instance of such a wff, in any way we please. In view of this, it is convenient to dispense with interior bracketing in such wff, writing, e.g., $p \vee q \vee r \vee s$ to mean that at least one of p, q, r and s is true, and $p \wedge q \wedge r \wedge s$ to mean that p, q, r and s are all true. Our formation rules do not at present permit such expressions, so we license them by the definitions:

$$(\alpha \vee \beta \vee \gamma) =_{Df} ((\alpha \vee \beta) \vee \gamma)$$
$$(\alpha \wedge \beta \wedge \gamma) =_{Df} ((\alpha \wedge \beta) \wedge \gamma)$$

Repeated applications of Comm (together with Assoc if necessary) enable us to rearrange disjuncts or conjuncts in any order.

In virtue of PC20 and PC21, any wff is equivalent to the disjunction (or conjunction) of itself and itself. We shall therefore when convenient speak of any wff at all as a disjunction or conjunction with one argument, or alternatively as a *degenerate* disjunction or conjunction.

Conjunctive normal form

A wff is said to be in *Conjunctive Normal Form* (CNF) if it is a conjunction (possibly degenerate), each conjunct of which is a disjunction (again possibly degenerate) of wff of a kind which we shall call *atoms*. By specifying the wff which are to count as atoms in varying ways we can define a number of different types of CNF. In the simplest type, which is applicable to PC wff and which we shall call PC-CNF, the atoms consist only of propositional variables and their negations. Thus the following wff are in PC-CNF:

(1) p
(2) $p \wedge (q \vee p)$
(3) $p \vee q \vee r$
(4) $(p \vee \sim p \vee q) \wedge (q \vee r \vee \sim r) \wedge (p \vee r \vee \sim r)$.

Wff in PC-CNF have this important property: they are valid iff every conjunct contains among its disjuncts some unnegated variable and also the negation of that variable. Thus of the examples given above, (4) is valid but the others are not.

By using the equivalences referred to in the previous section we can transform any wff of PC, α, into an equivalent wff, α', which is in PC-CNF, and α is then said to be *reduced to (PC-)CNF*. (We shall not give a formal proof of this here, but to see how such a proof might run consider the following: All operators other than $\sim$, $\vee$ and $\wedge$ can be eliminated by their definitions; the De Morgan laws can be used to ensure that $\sim$ occurs only immediately before variables; and conjunctions within disjunctions can be transformed into disjunctions within conjunctions, or *vice versa*, by the Distributive laws.) Since α and α' are equivalent PC wff, each will be valid iff the other is valid. Hence, since we have given a mechanical validity-test for wff in PC-CNF, reduction to CNF can be used as an alternative decision procedure for all wff of PC.

The type of CNF in which we are chiefly interested here, however, is not this, but one which is applicable to modal wff and which we shall call Modal Conjunctive Normal Form (MCNF).[1] We define it by specifying as atoms all PC wff and all wff of the form $L\alpha$ or $M\alpha$, where α is a PC wff. Thus the following wff are in MCNF:

$(p \lor Lp) \land q$
$(M((p \lor q) \supset r) \lor Lp \lor (r \land s)) \land (M(p \lor q) \lor Lr)$

but the following are not:

$(M(p \lor q) \land r) \lor s$
$L(M(p \lor q) \lor r) \land (Lp \lor Mq)$

Now it is not immediately obvious, and for systems weaker than S5 it is mostly not even true, that every wff is equivalent to a wff in MCNF. For instance, in S4 the wff $M(p \land M\sim p)$ is not equivalent to any such wff.[2] But in S5 every wff is equivalent to some wff in MCNF, and our next main task will be to prove this. As a preliminary, however, we need to discuss the notion of the *modal degree* of a wff.

Modal functions and modal degree

Any wff which contains a modal operator is said to be a *modal function* of its variables (just as any wff of PC is a truth-function of its variables). If a wff contains one or more modal operators, but none of these is within the scope of any other modal operator, it is said to be a modal formula of *first degree* (or a first-degree formula, or a first-degree modal function of its variables). In general a formula of degree n is one in which at least one modal operator has an argument of degree $n-1$ but no modal operator has an argument of any higher degree than $n-1$. It is convenient to regard wff which do not contain any modal operators as modal formulae of degree 0, in much the same way as we have counted $-$ and $\sim$ as modalities, and a precise definition of the *modal degree of a formula* can then be given as follows (it is assumed that formulae are written in primitive notation):[3]

1. A propositional variable is of degree 0.
2. If α is of degree *n*, then $\sim\alpha$ is of degree *n*.
3. If α is of degree *n* and β is of degree *m*, then if $n \geq m$, ($\alpha \vee \beta$) is of degree *n*; otherwise it is of degree *m*.
4. If α is of degree *n*, then $L\alpha$ is of degree $n + 1$.

The notion of a modal function of degree *n* is wider than that of a formula containing a modality with *n* modal operators, and should not be confused with it. Certainly *LLp* and *MLp* $\supset$ *Mq* are second-degree formulae, and are made so by the presence in them of the modalities *LL* and *ML*; but *M(p* $\supset$ *Lq)* is also a second-degree formula, though it contains no iterated modalities at all. Any formula containing a modality with *n* modal operators will be of at least degree *n*; but a formula can be of degree *n* (however great *n* may be) without containing any modalities with *n* modal operators, or indeed any iterated modalities at all.

If a formula of degree *n* is equivalent in a given system to some formula of lower degree than *n*, we say that it is *reducible* (in that system) to that formula. We have already seen that in S5 any wff which is of higher than first degree *solely* because of the presence in it of iterated modalities can be reduced to a first-degree formula by the reduction laws R1−R4. It is possible, however, to prove the following much stronger result:

S5 reduction theorem

Every formula of higher than first degree is reducible in S5 to a first-degree formula.

We prove this theorem by describing an effective procedure for reducing any wff of higher than first degree to one of first degree by equivalence transformations. It will be sufficient to show how any second-degree wff can be reduced to first degree, since repetition of the procedure will then enable us to deal with wff of higher degree. The only equivalences required are the PC equivalences referred to earlier in this chapter, the equivalences given by LMI, the laws of *L*- and *M*-distribution (theorems K3 and K6), the reduction laws R1−R4, and theorems S5(4)−S5(7), which we repeat here for convenience:

S5(4) $L(p \vee Lq) \equiv (Lp \vee Lq)$

S5(5) $L(p \lor Mq) \equiv (Lp \lor Mq)$
S5(6) $M(p \land Mq) \equiv (Mp \land Mq)$
S5(7) $M(p \land Lq) \equiv (Mp \land Lq)$

All are of course in S5.

The law of L-distribution $(L(p \land q) \equiv (Lp \land Lq))$ entitles us to distribute L over any conjunction whatsoever. If either conjunct already begins with a modal operator, the appropriate reduction law will enable us to delete the L when it meets that operator. Thus $L(p \land Mq)$ becomes not merely $Lp \land LMq$ by L-distribution but $Lp \land Mq$ by R1. In such a case we shall say that the L has been *absorbed* by the M. S5(4) and S5(5) entitle us to practise the same kind of distribution and absorption when L precedes a disjunction, *provided* that at least one of the original disjuncts begins with a modal operator. (S5(4) and S5(5) are stated for two-membered disjunctions only. If we want to practise L-distribution over an n-membered disjunction we must gather together all but one of the modalized members of the disjunction and treat them as a single disjunct. E.g., if we have $L(p \lor Mq \lor r \lor Ls)$, we form $L((p \lor r \lor Ls) \lor Mq)$ and then distribute to get $L((p \lor r) \lor Ls) \lor Mq$ and then again to get $L(p \lor r) \lor Ls \lor Mq$. We do *not* go to $Lp \lor Mq \lor Lr \lor Ls$.) The law of M-distribution $(M(p \lor q) \equiv (Mp \lor Mq))$ and S5(6) and S5(7) similarly allow us to practise distribution and absorption of M unrestrictedly over a disjunction and, subject to the same proviso as before, over a conjunction. These manœuvres are key steps in the process of reduction to first degree.

As we remarked earlier, it is sufficient to show how to reduce a second-degree formula to a first-degree one. There are four steps in this procedure, though of course not all will be needed in every case. The first three are straightforward and should by now be familiar.

1. We first eliminate all operators except $\sim$, L, M, $\lor$ and $\land$ by using the appropriate definitions.

2. We then eliminate every occurrence of $\sim$ immediately before a bracket or a modal operator by the De Morgan laws and LMI. (As a result $\sim$ will be prefixed only to PC wff.)

3. We next reduce all iterated modalities to single modalities by the reduction laws R1−R4.

4. If the formula we have as a result of steps 1−3 is still of second degree, this can only be because it, or some part of it, is of the form $L\alpha$ or $M\alpha$, where α is of first degree and is either a conjunction or a

disjunction.

We consider the case of $L\alpha$. There are three possibilities: (a) α is a conjunction; in that case, since L distributes unrestrictedly over conjunctions, we distribute L over the conjuncts in α, letting it be absorbed by any modal operator it meets in the process. (b) α is a disjunction at least one of whose disjuncts begins with a modal operator; in that case we again distribute L and let that operator be absorbed. (c) α is a disjunction none of whose disjuncts begins with a modal operator. Since α is of first degree, this can only be because some disjunct in α is a conjunction with a modal operator inside it. To handle this case we transform α into a conjunction by the PC distributive law $(p \lor (q \land r))$ $\equiv ((p \lor q) \land (p \lor r))$, and distribute L over the conjunction so obtained. E.g., if $L\alpha$ is $L(p \lor (q \land Mr))$, we transform this by Distrib into

$$L((p \lor q) \land (p \lor Mr))$$

and then by L-distribution into

$$L(p \lor q) \land L(p \lor Mr)$$

We can then *either* proceed as in case (b), obtaining in the example just cited

$$L(p \lor q) \land (Lp \lor Mr)$$

or else, if this is impossible, apply Distrib and L-distribution once more. Repetition of these moves will always allow the L to meet each modal operator, no matter how deeply it is embedded in α, and be absorbed by it.

The case of $M\alpha$ can be dealt with analogously, except that this time it is when α is a conjunction none of whose conjuncts begins with a modal operator that we cannot proceed directly, and that the PC distributive law we then need is

$$(p \land (q \lor r)) \equiv ((p \land q) \lor (p \land r))$$

(To make all this clearer we shall give one or two examples of reduction to first degree on p. 102.)

Every wff, then, is equivalent in S5 to some first-degree modal function of its variables. (This is true even of a wff containing no modal operators; for any wff α is equivalent to $\alpha \wedge (Lp \vee \sim Lp)$, where p is some variable in α.) Now it is not difficult to see that there can be only a finite number of distinct first-degree modal functions of any finite set of variables. For every first-degree formula (written in primitive notation) is a truth-function of (i) propositional variables and (ii) wff consisting of L followed by a truth-function of propositional variables; and there is only a finite number of non-equivalent truth-functions of any finite number of formulae. Hence the S5 reduction theorem shows that in S5 there are only a finite number of non-equivalent modal functions of any finite number of variables.

It is worth noting that in showing that there are only a finite number of distinct *first-degree* modal functions of a finite number of variables we do not make use of any principles belonging specifically to S5; this result holds equally for any other normal system. Moreover it can easily be generalized to show that there are only a finite number of distinct modal functions (of a finite number of variables) of *any* given finite degree. Hence if we had a system in which, although we could not reduce every wff (as in S5) to first degree, yet we could reduce them all to some specified degree (say, fourth), that would be enough to show that in that system there were only a finite number of distinct modal functions of any finite number of variables.

Our aim, as we mentioned earlier when we defined modal conjunctive form, is to prove the following:

MCNF theorem
Any wff can be reduced in S5 to MCNF.
What this means is that there is an effective procedure whereby for any wff, α, we can find a wff, α', such that α' is in MCNF and $\alpha \equiv \alpha'$ is a theorem of S5.

Proof: (i) If α is a wff of PC, it is in MCNF already.

(ii) If α is a first-degree formula, it is a truth-function of wff each of which is either a PC wff or one of the form $L\beta$ or $M\beta$, where β is a PC wff. Taking each such wff as an atom we reduce the whole formula to CNF by PC methods. We then replace $\sim L$ and $\sim M$ everywhere by $M\sim$ and $L\sim$ respectively. The resulting formula, α', is in MCNF.

(iii) If α is of higher than first degree, we begin by reducing it to first degree by the method explained above, and then obtain α' by proceeding as in (ii). (In fact the only further step required in such a case will be the application of the PC distributive law, together with Comm if necessary.)

Since the only transformations involved are licensed by equivalences which are in S5, $\alpha \equiv \alpha'$ is a theorem of S5 in every case.

We give here some examples of reduction to MCNF. These will also illustrate reduction to first degree.

EXAMPLE 1

$$L(MMp \supset p) \supset L(p \supset Lp)$$

We first reduce to first degree as follows:

Step 1: $\sim L(\sim MMp \lor p) \lor L(\sim p \lor Lp)$
Step 2: $M \sim (\sim MMp \lor p) \lor L(\sim p \lor Lp)$
$\qquad M(MMp \land \sim p) \lor L(\sim p \lor Lp)$
Step 3: $M(Mp \land \sim p) \lor L(\sim p \lor Lp)$
Step 4: $(Mp \land M \sim p) \lor (L \sim p \lor Lp)$

We now have a first-degree formula. To put it into MCNF we apply Comm and Distrib and obtain

$$(Mp \lor L \sim p \lor Lp) \land (M \sim p \lor L \sim p \lor Lp)$$

EXAMPLE 2

$$L(L(p \supset (q \land Mr)) \supset \sim M(p \land \sim q \land \sim Mr))$$

We again begin by reducing to first degree.

Step 1: $L(\sim L(\sim p \lor (q \land Mr)) \lor \sim M(p \land \sim q \land \sim Mr))$
Step 2: $L(M \sim (\sim p \lor (q \land Mr)) \lor L \sim (p \land \sim q \land \sim Mr))$
$\qquad L(M(p \land \sim (q \land Mr)) \lor L(\sim p \lor q \lor Mr))$
$\qquad L(M(p \land (\sim q \lor \sim Mr)) \lor L(\sim p \lor q \lor Mr))$
$\qquad L(M(p \land (\sim q \lor L \sim r)) \lor L(\sim p \lor q \lor Mr))$
Step 4: $M(p \land (\sim q \lor L \sim r)) \lor L(\sim p \lor q \lor Mr)$
$\qquad M((p \land \sim q) \lor (p \land L \sim r)) \lor L((\sim p \lor q) \lor Mr)$
$\qquad M(p \land \sim q) \lor M(p \land L \sim r) \lor L(\sim p \lor q) \lor Mr$
$\qquad M(p \land \sim q) \lor (Mp \land L \sim r) \lor L(\sim p \lor q) \lor Mr$

This is a first-degree formula. Comm and Distrib now give us the

102

following formula in MCNF:

$$(Mp \lor M(p \land {\sim}q) \lor L({\sim}p \lor q) \lor Mr)$$
$$\land\ (L{\sim}r \lor M(p \land {\sim}q) \lor L({\sim}p \lor q) \lor Mr)$$

We are shortly going to formulate a test which can be applied to wff in MCNF. In order to make this test simpler both to formulate and to apply, we make the following two modifications, where necessary, in the way a wff in MCNF is presented:

1. In each conjunct we use Comm to arrange the disjuncts in the following order: first, all unmodalized disjuncts (i.e. PC wff); next, all disjuncts beginning with L; finally all disjuncts beginning with M. Since a disjunction of PC wff is itself a PC wff, each conjunct will then have the form:

$$\beta \lor L\gamma_1 \lor \ldots \lor L\gamma_n \lor M\delta_1 \lor \ldots \lor M\delta_m$$

where $n \geq 0$, $m \geq 0$. β, all the γs and all the δs are PC wff, and of course there may be no unmodalized disjunct β or no $L\gamma$s or no $M\delta$s.

2. We then use the law of M-distribution to replace $M\delta_1 \lor \ldots \lor M\delta_m$ by $M(\delta_1 \lor \ldots \lor \delta_m)$. Since $\delta_1, \ldots, \delta_m$ are all PC wff, their disjunction is also a PC wff, and can be referred to simply as δ. Each conjunct is therefore now of the form:

(1) $\beta \lor L\gamma_1 \lor \ldots \lor L\gamma_n \lor M\delta$

where $\beta, \gamma_1, \ldots, \gamma_n$ and δ are all wff of PC.

When each conjunct in a formula in MCNF is in this form, we shall say that the formula is in *ordered MCNF*. We shall assume in what follows that MCNF formulae are in ordered MCNF.

Testing formulae in MCNF

We shall now state a test which can be applied to any wff in (ordered) MCNF. We shall then show that this test acts as a test for whether or not the wff (and any wff that can be reduced to it) is (a) S5-valid and (b) a theorem of S5. But we shall state the test itself first.

Every wff in MCNF is of the form

$$C_1 \land \ldots \land C_k$$

where each $C_i (1 \leq i \leq k)$ is of the form (1) above. For each C_i form $n+1$ disjunctions, each of which has δ as one conjunct and a distinct one of β, γ_1, ... , γ_n as the other. I.e., form the $n+1$ PC wff $(\beta \lor \delta)$, $(\gamma_1 \lor \delta)$, ... , $(\gamma_n \lor \delta)$. C_i *passes the test* iff at least one of these is PC-valid. (If there is no $M\delta$ then we simply test β and γ_1, ... , γ_n.) The whole MCNF $C_1 \land \ldots \land C_k$ passes the test iff each conjunct in it passes the test.

As illustrations we consider the two formulae we reduced to MCNF earlier. The MCNF formula we arrived at in Example 1 was

$$(Mp \lor L\sim p \lor Lp) \land (M\sim p \lor L\sim p \lor Lp)$$

In ordered MCNF this becomes

$$(L\sim p \lor Lp \lor Mp) \land (L\sim p \lor Lp \lor M\sim p)$$

This will pass the test iff each conjunct does. In the first conjunct there is no β, since all disjuncts are modalized, γ_1 is $\sim p$, γ_2 is p, and δ is also p. Therefore this conjunct passes the test if either $\sim p \lor p$ or $p \lor p$ is PC-valid, and clearly the former is. So this conjunct passes the test. The second conjunct passes the test iff either $\sim p \lor \sim p$ or $p \lor \sim p$ is PC-valid, and the latter is. Thus both conjuncts pass the test, and therefore so does the whole formula.

In Example 2 we reached the formula

$$(Mp \lor M(p \land \sim q) \lor L(\sim p \lor q) \lor Mr)$$
$$\land (L\sim r \lor M(p \land \sim q) \lor L(\sim p \lor q) \lor Mr)$$

In ordered MCNF this is

$$(L(\sim p \lor q) \lor M(p \lor (p \land \sim q) \lor r))$$
$$\land (L\sim r \lor L(p \lor \sim q) \lor M((p \land \sim q) \lor r))$$

The first conjunct passes the test iff $(\sim p \lor q) \lor (p \lor (p \land \sim q) \lor r)$ is PC-valid — which it is. The second passes the test iff either $\sim r \lor ((p \land \sim q) \lor r)$ or $(\sim p \lor q) \lor ((p \land \sim q) \lor r)$ is PC-valid, and in fact both are. So once more the whole formula passes the test.

Neither of these examples contains any unmodalized formulae, so we add a third example which does:

$$(Lq \lor M{\sim}p \lor r \lor L{\sim}(p \land r) \lor ((p \land q) \supset r))$$
$$\land (Mp \lor L{\sim}p)$$

In ordered MCNF the first conjunct becomes

$$(r \lor ((p \land q) \supset r)) \lor Lq \lor L{\sim}(p \land r) \lor M{\sim}p$$

Here β is $(r \lor ((p \land q) \supset r))$, γ_1 is q, γ_2 is ${\sim}(p \land r)$, and δ is ${\sim}p$. This conjunct passes the test iff at least one of (i) $(r \lor ((p \land q) \supset r)) \lor {\sim}p$, (ii) $q \lor {\sim}p$, or (iii) ${\sim}(p \land r) \lor {\sim}p$ is PC-valid, and in fact none of them is. Hence this conjunct does not pass the test, and therefore neither does the whole formula (we do not need to test the other conjunct).

The completeness of S5

We want to show that reduction to MCNF, together with the test we have just described, gives us a completeness proof for S5 — i.e. a proof that every S5-valid wff is a theorem of S5.

We have already shown that for every wff α there is a wff α' in ordered MCNF such that $\alpha \equiv \alpha'$ is a theorem of S5; and from this it follows by the soundness of S5 and [V$\equiv$] that α is S5-valid iff α' is S5-valid. Now α' is a conjunction of wff each of which is of the form

$$(1) \quad \beta \lor L\gamma_1 \lor \dots \lor L\gamma_n \lor M\delta$$

where β, $\gamma_1, \dots, \gamma_n$ and δ are all wff of PC. By [V$\land$], a conjunction is S5-valid iff each of its conjuncts is, and by Adj if each conjunct of α' is a theorem so is α'. So in order to prove the completeness of S5 it will be sufficient to show that every S5-valid wff of the form (1) is a theorem of S5; and to show *this*, it will clearly be sufficient to prove the following two things:

A: Every S5-valid wff of the form (1) passes the test.

B: Every wff of the form (1) which passes the test is a theorem of S5.

We prove A by contraposition; i.e. we prove that if (1) does not pass the test then it is not S5-valid. So let us assume that (1) does not pass the test, i.e. that none of $(\beta \lor \delta)$, $(\gamma_1 \lor \delta)$, $\dots$, $(\gamma_n \lor \delta)$ is PC-valid. We show that in that case (1) is not S5-valid by showing how to construct a falsifying S5 model for it. Since we are dealing solely with S5 we may assume that every world can see every world, and dispense with reference to the accessibility relation R. The model will then be this: W is to consist of exactly $n+1$ worlds, w_0, w_1, ... , w_n. With w_0 we associate $(\beta \lor \delta)$, and with each of w_1, ... , w_n we associate a distinct one of $(\gamma_1 \lor \delta)$, ... , $(\gamma_n \lor \delta)$, as indicated by the subscript to the γ. We define V as follows. In w_0, V makes some value-assignment to the variables which will give $V((\beta \lor \delta),w_0) = 0$; and in each w_i among w_1, ... , w_n, V makes some assignment to the variables which will give $V((\gamma_i \lor \delta), w_i) = 0$. (Since each of $(\beta \lor \delta)$, $(\gamma_1 \lor \delta)$, ... , $(\gamma_n \lor \delta)$ is by hypothesis an invalid PC wff, there will be for each of them a PC-assignment which falsifies it. We simply let the V in our S5 model give in w_0 the values given by one which falsifies $(\beta \lor \delta)$, and in each w_i the values given by one which falsifies $(\gamma_i \lor \delta)$.)

We now show that in such a model, $V((1),w_0) = 0$, and therefore that (1) is not S5-valid. By the way we have defined V, $V((\beta \lor \delta),w_0) = 0$. Hence by $[V\lor]$, $V(\beta,w_0) = 0$ and $V(\delta,w_0) = 0$. Similarly, for each w_i among w_1, ... ,w_n, $V(\gamma_i,w_i) = 0$ and $V(\delta,w_i) = 0$. Thus for every $w \in$ W, $V(\delta,w) = 0$, and hence by $[VM]$, $V(M\delta,w_0) = 0$. Moreover, for each γ_i among γ_1, ... , γ_n, there is some $w \in$ W (viz. w_i) such that $V(\gamma_i,w_i) = 0$; and hence by $[VL]$, $V(L\gamma_i,w_0) = 0$ in each case. Therefore each disjunct in (1) has the value 0 in w_0, and so by $[V\lor]$, $V((1),w_0) = 0$.

(If (1) contains no unmodalized disjunct β, we omit w_0 from the model. We can then prove by the same method that for any $w_i \in$ W whatever, $V((1), w_i) = 0$. If (1) contains no $L\gamma$s we omit w_1, ... ,w_{n+1}. If (1) contains no $M\delta$ the PC-invalidity of β and each γ_i will guarantee that $V((1),w_0) = 0$.)

We can illustrate the construction of a falsifying S5 model in a particular case by the first conjunct in our third example above, which turned out to be invalid. This is:

$$(r \lor ((p \land q) \supset r)) \lor Lq \lor L\sim(p \land r) \lor M\sim p$$

Here β is $(r \lor ((p \land q) \supset r))$, γ_1 is q, γ_2 is $\sim(p \land r)$, and δ is $\sim p$. Now

1. $(r \lor ((p \land q) \supset r)) \lor \sim p$ is not PC-valid and is falsified by the following PC-assignment V_1:

$V_1(p) = 1$, $V_1(q) = 1$, $V_1(r) = 0$

2. $q \lor \sim p$ is not PC-valid and is falsified by the assignment:

$V_2(p) = 1$, $V_2(q) = 0$, $V_2(r) = 1$

3. $\sim(p \land r) \lor \sim p$ is not PC-valid and is falsified by the assignment:

$V_3(p) = 1$, $V_3(q) = 1$, $V_3(r) = 1$

We therefore construct the following S5-model: $W = \{w_0, w_1, w_2\}$.
$V(p, w_0) = V_1(p) = 1$, $V(q, w_0) = V_1(q) = 1$, $V(r, w_0) = V_1(r) = 0$.
$V(p, w_1) = V_2(p) = 1$, $V(q, w_1) = V_2(q) = 0$, $V(r, w_1) = V_2(r) = 1$.
$V(p, w_2) = V_3(p) = 1$, $V(q, w_2) = V_3(q) = 1$, $V(r, w_2) = V_3(r) = 1$.

From this it is easy to show that (a) $V((r \lor ((p \land q) \supset r)), w_0) = 0$;
(b) $V(q, w_1) = 0$, and hence $V(Lq, w_0) = 0$; (c) $V(\sim(p \land r), w_2) = 0$, and
hence $V(L\sim(p \land r), w_0) = 0$; (d) $V(\sim p, w_0) = V(\sim p, w_1) = V(\sim p, w_2)$
$= 0$, and hence $V(M\sim p, w_0) = 0$. As a result, $V((r \lor ((p \land q) \supset r))$
$\lor Lq \lor L(p \land r) \lor Mp), w_0) = 0$, and so this conjunct (and therefore
the whole conjunction) is invalid.

This completes the proof of A. We now turn to prove B. What we
have to prove is that if any of $(\beta \lor \delta)$, $(\gamma_1 \lor \delta)$, ... ,$(\gamma_n \lor \delta)$ is PC-
valid, then

(1) $\beta \lor L\gamma_1 \lor ... \lor L\gamma_n \lor M\delta$

is a theorem of S5.

Suppose that $(\beta \lor \delta)$ is PC-valid. Then by the axiom-schema **PC**, $\vdash_{S5}$
$(\beta \lor \delta)$. By T1, $\vdash_{S5} (\delta \supset M\delta)$. Hence by $(q \supset r) \supset ((p \lor q) \supset (p \lor r))$ and MP, $\vdash_{S5} (\beta \lor M\delta)$; and hence by PC10 and Comm, $\vdash_{S5}$ (1).
The same method will apply to the degenerate case when (1) is just $M\delta$,
and δ is PC-valid.

Suppose now that one of $(\gamma_1 \lor \delta)$, ... , $(\gamma_n \lor \delta)$, say $(\gamma_j \lor \delta)$, is PC-
valid. Then as before, $\vdash_{S5} (\gamma_j \lor \delta)$, and so by N, $\vdash_{S5} L(\gamma_j \lor \delta)$. Hence
by K9, $\vdash_{S5} (L\gamma_j \lor M\delta)$. From this it follows as before that $\vdash_{S5}(1)$. If
there is no $M\delta$ N alone will take us from the PC-validity of γ_i to $\vdash_{S5} L\gamma_i$.

This completes the proof of B, and with it the proof of the
completeness of S5.

The completeness proof that we have given does not merely assure us that if α is any S5-valid wff there is in principle a proof of α in the axiomatic system S5; it gives us an effective procedure for constructing such a proof. For we can proceed as follows. We reduce α to a wff α' in MCNF by using S5 equivalences. We then construct the proof by first deriving each conjunct in α' in the way we have just described, then conjoining these by Adj, and finally using Eq to retrace our steps back through the reduction to MCNF until we reach α itself. Such a proof may not be the most economical or elegant that could be devised, but it will be a correctly constructed one nevertheless.

A decision procedure for S5-validity

We have shown that any wff is S5-valid iff it is a theorem of S5. It follows that any effective procedure for determining whether or not a wff is a theorem of S5 will also be an effective procedure for determining whether or not it is S5-valid. So if we wish to test whether any wff α is S5-valid, all we have to do is to reduce it to a wff α' in MCNF, and then check whether or not α' passes the test described on p. 104. Clearly this is a finite and mechanical procedure in each case.

Triv and Ver again

At the end of Chapter 3 we gave a proof that every normal modal system is contained either in Triv or in Ver, except that we postponed the proof of lemma 3.2, which says that every consistent extension of K which is not contained in Ver contains D. We can now fill in this gap.

Let S be any system which is a consistent extension of K and has some theorem α which is not a theorem of Ver. We have to prove that S contains D; and for this it will be sufficient to show that S has some theorem of the form $M\beta$, since we proved on p. 44 that every normal system with any theorem of that form contains D.

Every wff of propositional modal logic is a truth-function of wff, each of which is either (a) a wff of PC, or (b) a wff of the form $L\alpha$, or (c) a wff of the form $M\alpha$, where in cases (b) and (c) α is a modal wff which may be of any degree of complexity. A little reflection on the procedure for reducing PC wff to PC-CNF should make it clear that by using only PC equivalences we can reduce any such wff to a conjunction of disjunctions, each disjunct in which is either a PC wff or a wff of type (b) or type (c) or the negation of such a wff. Moreover, having done so, we can use LMI to eliminate $\sim$ in front of any negation of a wff of type (b) or (c), and then use Comm and M-distribution to ensure that only one wff beginning with M occurs in any one conjunct. Let us suppose that we have reduced our wff α (which is a theorem of S but not of Ver) to a wff α' of this kind. Then α' will be a conjunction

$$C_1 \wedge \dots \wedge C_n$$

where each C_i is either

(1) a wff of PC, or

(2) a disjunction containing a disjunct of the form $L\alpha$, or

(3) a wff of the form $M\alpha$, or

(4) a wff of the form $\beta \vee M\alpha$, where β is a wff of PC.

Now since all the equivalences we have used in reducing α to α' are in K, $\alpha \equiv \alpha'$ is a theorem of every normal system, and hence of both S and Ver. So α' is a theorem of S, and hence so is each C_i; but α' is not a theorem of Ver, and hence at least one C_i is not a theorem of Ver. So let us ask, what C_i in α' could be a theorem of S but not of Ver (remembering that S is a consistent system)? No wff of type (1) could satisfy this condition; for if it is PC-valid it is a theorem of Ver, and if it is not PC-valid, then, as we proved on p. 47, this would mean that S is inconsistent. Nor can any wff of type (2) satisfy the condition, since every wff of the form $L\alpha$ is a theorem of Ver, and therefore so is every disjunction in which such a wff is a disjunct. So some wff of type (3) or (4) must be a theorem of S. If $M\alpha$ is a theorem then S has a theorem of the form $M\alpha$. So suppose there is some wff $\beta \vee M\alpha$ in which β is a PC wff and $\beta \vee M\alpha$ is a theorem of S. In this wff β must not be PC-valid, since if it were, $\beta \vee M\alpha$ would be a theorem of Ver. Now we showed on p. 47 that every invalid wff of PC has an unsatisfiable substitution-instance. So let us make substitutions in $\beta \vee M\alpha$ to obtain a wff $\beta^* \vee M\alpha^*$ in which β^* is unsatisfiable. By US, $\beta^* \vee M\alpha^*$, and therefore $\sim\beta^* \supset M\alpha^*$, is a theorem of S. But since β^* is unsatisfiable, $\sim\beta^*$ is PC-valid, and therefore a theorem of S. Hence by MP, $\vdash_S M\alpha^*$, and so in this case also S has some theorem of the form $M\alpha$, which is what we had to prove.

This completes the proof that every consistent extension of K is contained either in Triv or in Ver.

Exercises — 5

5.1 Reduce the following wff to MCNF. Where a wff passes the test give a sketch proof using the method described on p. 107. Where it does not pass the test use the method described on pp. 105-107 to construct a falsifying S5-model.

(a) $L(p \lor (q \land (r \lor Ls)))$

(b) $M(p \land q) \supset L(L(Lp \supset Lq) \supset Mq)$

(c) $L(p \supset (q \supset L(p \supset q))) \supset (\sim L(p \supset q) \supset L(p \supset \sim q))$

(d) $L(\sim p \land \sim q) \supset (L(L(p \lor q) \supset r) \land (r \supset L(p \supset p)))$

(e) $L(p \supset q) \supset L(M(p \land \sim Lp) \supset M(q \land L(p \supset Lp)))$

(f) $L(p \supset L(q \supset r)) \supset (q \supset L(p \supset r))$

(g) $L(L(p \equiv q) \supset Mq) \supset L(L(p \equiv q) \supset q)$

(h) $L(L(p \supset Lp) \supset Lp) \supset (MLp \supset Lp)$

(i) $(L(L(p \supset q) \supset q) \supset p) \supset M(Lq \supset p)$

(j) $L(L(Lp \supset Lq) \supset L(p \supset q))$

5.2 Prove that $M(p \land M \sim p)$ is not equivalent in S4 to any first-degree wff.

Notes

[1] The name 'modal conjunctive normal form' is ours, but the idea derives from Carnap 1946. Carnap calls the formula in MCNF to which a wff α can be reduced the *MP-reductum* of α. In Wajsberg 1933 a slightly more complicated normal form is described in which each disjunct consists of L or $\sim L$ followed by a disjunction of variables (negated or unnegated). Schumm 1975 points out that Wajsberg's method has to be adapted to deal with unmodalized disjuncts. One can apply the method of MCNF to some systems in which reduction to first degree is not possible by forming a CNF whose atoms are PC wff or wff of the form $L\alpha$ or $M\alpha$, and then reducing α to a CNF with similar atoms and so on. See Ōhama 1982.

[2] Makinson 1966a uses a generalization of this wff to show that a system containing S4, and therefore S4 itself, has infinitely many non-equivalent modal functions of a single variable, with no upper limit therefore on their modal degree.

[3] This definition is given in Parry 1939, p. 144.

6

COMPLETENESS

In this chapter we shall prove the completeness of K, D, T, S4, B and S5. But the technique we use will generalize to all modal systems of a certain class, and we shall begin by making a few remarks about systems and validity in general.

The first point to note is that we can define a modal system in two ways, in terms of its axiomatic basis, or in terms of its theorems. For instance, in our discussion of the system D we showed that in place of the wff **D**, $(Lp \supset Mp)$, we could have chosen $M(p \supset p)$, and have obtained exactly the same theorems. Although it would be possible to call the two different ways of axiomatizing D two different systems, for most purposes nothing is to be gained by this, and we shall say that S and S' are the same system iff they have the same theorems. In fact it is convenient to *define* a system S as simply a class of wff, and then $\vdash_S \alpha$ and $\alpha \in$ S, are just alternative ways of saying the same thing.

Of course not just *any* collection of wff of modal logic will count as a system. We shall, in most of this book, be interested in extensions of K. This class of systems is the class of what are called *normal* systems. A normal system of modal propositional logic is a class S of wff of modal propositional logic which contains all PC-valid wff and **K**, and has the property that if α and β are in S then so is anything obtainable from them by the use of US, MP and N.

This means that every modal system may be expressed as K + Λ, using the notation introduced on p. 39, since Λ could be simply S itself. But typically we can choose Λ to be much smaller, often a single wff (or, what comes to the same thing, a finite set of wff − since we may always form the single wff which is their conjunction).

111

In defining validity for a system S we have done so in terms of a class $\mathscr{E}$ of frames. Let us use the notation $\mathscr{E}$-valid, to mean, of a wff α, that for every $\langle W,R \rangle \in \mathscr{E}$, and every model $\langle W,R,V \rangle$ based on $\langle W,R \rangle$, $V(\alpha,w) = 1$ for every $w \in W$.

Where $\langle W,R,V \rangle$ is a particular model, then it is convenient to say that α is *valid* in $\langle W,R,V \rangle$ iff $V(\alpha,w) = 1$ for all $w \in W$. We must be careful about this use of 'valid' since, e.g., there will be models in which the single variable p is valid, and if we wish validity to mean truth for every value of the variables then validity in a model will not capture this in all models. Despite this, we shall speak of validity in a model, and in fact many of the models we shall be using will have the property that if α is valid in that model so is every substitution-instance of α.

The key result of the present chapter is that for every (consistent) normal modal system S there is a special kind of model, called the *canonical model* of S, which has the remarkable property that a wff α is valid in the canonical model of S iff $\vdash_S \alpha$.

The connection between this fact and completeness is this. Suppose that we have a class $\mathscr{E}$ of frames, and we wish to show that a wff α of a system S is $\mathscr{E}$-valid iff $\vdash_S \alpha$. We need to show first that S is sound with respect to $\mathscr{E}$, i.e. that every theorem of S is $\mathscr{E}$-valid. This we do by showing that the axioms are $\mathscr{E}$-valid, for theorem 2.1 on p. 39 then assures us that all the theorems will be. Now suppose that we can establish that the frame of the canonical model of S is in $\mathscr{E}$. If α is $\mathscr{E}$-valid then α will be valid on the frame of the canonical model for S, and so *a fortiori* valid in the canonical model itself. But that means that $\vdash_S \alpha$. So if α is $\mathscr{E}$-valid then $\vdash_S \alpha$, which is what the completeness of S with respect to $\mathscr{E}$ means.

In all of this procedure the part that is specific to each system is to establish that the frame of the canonical model is indeed in $\mathscr{E}$. For K this is immediate for $\mathscr{E}$ in the case of K is the class of all frames. For D, $\mathscr{E}$ is the class of serial frames and so we must show that the frame of the canonical model for D is serial; for T we must show that it is reflexive; for S4, B, S5 that it is reflexive and, respectively, transitive, symmetrical, and both transitive and symmetrical.

Although establishing that the frame of the canonical model is in $\mathscr{E}$ is sufficient to give completeness it is not necessary in that $\mathscr{E}$ need not contain the frame of the canonical model. Indeed we shall in Part II look at some systems where although, as guaranteed by the results of the present chapter, every theorem is valid on the canonical model itself, not every theorem is valid on the frame of the canonical model.

Be all that as it may, our task is now to construct, for any system S, the canonical model of S. As we observed on p. 37 the worlds in a model can be anything we please. One very tempting candidate is to make the worlds *sets of wff*. For then we could think of a wff as true in a world iff that wff is in the set of wff which constitutes that world. However, if we do this only certain sets will be able to count as worlds. For instance, since any wff α is either true or false at a world, and since $\sim\alpha$ is true iff α is false, then the set which is that world will have to contain either α or $\sim\alpha$, but not both. And it will have to contain $\alpha \lor \beta$ iff it contains at least one of α and β. Sets like this are described in the next section.

Maximal consistent sets of wff

Where Λ is a set of wff of modal logic we say that Λ is *S-inconsistent* iff there are $\alpha_1, \ldots, \alpha_n \in \Lambda$ such that

$$\vdash_S \sim(\alpha_1 \land \ldots \land \alpha_n)$$

The idea is that in S you can prove that a contradiction arises from the members of Λ. Λ is then *consistent* if there is *no* finite collection $\{\alpha_1, \ldots \alpha_n\} \subseteq \Lambda$, i.e. no $\alpha_1, \ldots, \alpha_n \in \Lambda$, such that

$$\vdash_S \sim(\alpha_1 \land \ldots \land \alpha_n)$$

In the case of a finite set, say $\{\beta_1, \ldots, \beta_k\}$ this definition simply means that

$$\dashv_S \sim(\beta_1 \land \ldots \land \beta_k)$$

(where $\dashv$ means 'not $\vdash$'). In the case of a single wff γ, $\{\gamma\}$ is consistent iff $\dashv_S \sim\gamma$. Thus $\{\sim\gamma\}$ is consistent iff $\dashv_S \sim\sim\gamma$, i.e. iff $\dashv_S \gamma$. (In the above definitions $\subseteq$ is the symbol for *class inclusion*. Where A and B are any classes then A $\subseteq$ B iff every a in A is also in B. I.e., if $a \in$ A then $a \in$ B. $\subseteq$ and $\in$ should not be confused. One important difference is that A $\subseteq$ A for every A, while A $\in$ A is false in most set theories.)

A set Γ of wff is said to be *maximal* iff for every wff α either $\alpha \in \Gamma$ or $\sim\alpha \in \Gamma$. Γ is said to be *maximal consistent* with respect to a system S (or *maximal S-consistent*) iff it is both maximal and S-consistent. We now establish a lemma which shows that in respect of the PC-operators, a maximal consistent set of wff does indeed look like a world, at which the true wff are the wff in the set.

113

LEMMA 6.1   Suppose that Γ is any maximal consistent set of wff with respect to S. Then

6.1a   for any wff α, exactly one member of $\{\alpha, \sim\alpha\}$ is in Γ;
6.1b $\alpha \lor \beta \in \Gamma$ iff either $\alpha \in \Gamma$ or $\beta \in \Gamma$;
6.1c $\alpha \land \beta \in \Gamma$ iff $\alpha \in \Gamma$ and $\beta \in \Gamma$;
6.1d   if $\alpha \in \Gamma$ and $\alpha \supset \beta \in \Gamma$ then $\beta \in \Gamma$.

Proof: One half of 6.1a, viz. that at least one member of $\{\alpha, \sim\alpha\}$ is in Γ, is directly given by Γ's maximality. The other half, that they are not both in Γ, follows directly from its consistency; for if both were in Γ, then $\{\alpha, \sim\alpha\}$ would be a subset of Γ; but $\{\alpha, \sim\alpha\}$ is inconsistent since $\vdash_S \sim(\alpha \land \sim\alpha)$, and therefore Γ itself would be inconsistent. To prove 6.1b, suppose first that $\alpha \lor \beta$ is in Γ but that neither α nor β is. Then by 6.1a, $\sim\alpha$ and $\sim\beta$ would both be in Γ, and hence $\{\alpha \lor \beta, \sim\alpha, \sim\beta\}$ would be a subset of Γ. But this would again make Γ inconsistent, since by PC, $\vdash_S \sim((\alpha \lor \beta) \land \sim\alpha \land \sim\beta)$. Suppose next that one of α and β, say α, is in Γ but that $\alpha \lor \beta$ is not. Then $\{\alpha, \sim(\alpha \lor \beta)\}$ would be a subset of Γ. But this would make Γ inconsistent since $\vdash_S \sim(\alpha \land \sim(\alpha \lor \beta))$. The proof of 6.1c is analogous using the definition of $\alpha \land \beta$ as $\sim(\sim\alpha \lor \sim\beta)$. 6.1d holds because if we had $\alpha \in \Gamma$, $\alpha \supset \beta \in \Gamma$ but not $\beta \in \Gamma$ then $\{\alpha, \alpha \supset \beta, \sim\beta\}$ would be a subset of Γ. But this would make Γ inconsistent since $\vdash_S \sim(\alpha \land (\alpha \supset \beta) \land \sim\beta)$. This proves lemma 6.1.

The next lemma illustrates an important connection between maximal consistent sets and theorems of S.

LEMMA 6.2   Suppose that Γ is any maximal consistent set of wff with respect to S. Then

6.2a   if $\vdash_S \alpha$ then $\alpha \in \Gamma$;
6.2b   if $\alpha \in \Gamma$ and $\vdash_S \alpha \supset \beta$ then $\beta \in \Gamma$.

Proof: For 6.2a, if $\vdash_S \alpha$ then $\{\sim\alpha\}$ is S-inconsistent. So $\sim\alpha$ cannot be in Γ and so α must be. 6.2b follows immediately from 6.2a and 6.1d. This proves lemma 6.2.

Maximal consistent extensions
The idea behind the kind of model we are about to construct is this. The worlds of the model are maximal consistent sets of wff with respect to

some particular system S. Lemma 6.2a guarantees that if $\vdash_S \alpha$ then α is in every maximal consistent set of wff. But we said that the canonical model validates *all and only* theorems of S. This means that if α is *not* a theorem of S then there ought to be a maximal S-consistent set Γ such that $\alpha \notin \Gamma$. Now if α is not a theorem of S then $\{\sim\alpha\}$ is S-consistent, since otherwise $\vdash_S \sim\sim\alpha$ and so $\vdash_S \alpha$. The result we are about to prove guarantees that *every* S-consistent set Λ, whether finite like $\{\sim\alpha\}$ or infinite, can be extended to a maximal S-consistent set Γ. So if $\{\sim\alpha\}$ is consistent then there will be a maximal consistent Γ such that $\sim\alpha \in \Gamma$, and so, by lemma 6.1a, $\alpha \notin \Gamma$.

THEOREM 6.3   Suppose that Λ is an S-consistent set of wff. Then there is a maximal S-consistent set of wff Γ such that $\Lambda \subseteq \Gamma$.

Proof: Let us assume that the wff of modal propositional logic are arranged in some determinate order and labelled α_1, α_2, ... and so on. The idea behind the proof is that we make the set maximal by adding in turn every wff or its negation. We define a sequence Γ_0, Γ_1, ... of sets of wff in the following way.

(1) Γ_0 is Λ itself.
(2)   Given Γ_n we let Γ_{n+1} be $\Gamma_n \cup \{\alpha_{n+1}\}$ if this is S-consistent and let Γ_{n+1} be $\Gamma_n \cup \{\sim\alpha_{n+1}\}$ otherwise.

(The symbol $\cup$ means that where A and B are classes A $\cup$ B is their *union*, the class of things in either A or B. I.e. $a \in$ A $\cup$ B iff $a \in$ A or $a \in$ B. So in the present case $\Gamma \cup \{\alpha_{n+1}\}$ means Γ together with α_{n+1}, and $\Gamma \cup \{\sim\alpha_{n+1}\}$ means Γ together with $\sim\alpha_{n+1}$.)

We next show that, for any n, if Γ_n is S-consistent then so is Γ_{n+1}. The proof is that if Γ_{n+1} is not S-consistent this means that neither $\Gamma_n \cup \{\alpha_{n+1}\}$ nor $\Gamma_n \cup \{\sim\alpha_{n+1}\}$ is S-consistent. This in turn means that there are some wff β_1, ..., β_m in Γ_n such that

$$\vdash_S \sim(\beta_1 \wedge ... \wedge \beta_m \wedge \alpha_{n+1}) \tag{i}$$

and also some wff γ_1, ..., γ_k in Γ_n such that

$$\vdash_S \sim(\gamma_1 \wedge ... \wedge \gamma_k \wedge \sim\alpha_{n+1}) \tag{ii}$$

Now from (i) and (ii) it follows by PC that

$$\vdash_S \sim(\beta_1 \land \ldots \land \beta_m \land \gamma_1 \land \ldots \land \gamma_k)$$

i.e. that $\{\beta_1, \ldots, \beta_m, \gamma_1, \ldots, \gamma_k\}$ is S-inconsistent. But this is a subset of Γ_n, and therefore Γ_n is itself inconsistent.

Now let Γ be the union of all the Γ_ns. Then (a) Γ is consistent. For if it were not then some finite subset of Γ would be inconsistent. But clearly every finite subset of Γ is a subset of some Γ_n, and we have shown that no Γ_n is inconsistent. (b) Γ is maximal. For consider any wff α_i. By the construction of Γ_i, either $\alpha_i \in \Gamma_i$ or $\sim\alpha_i \in \Gamma_i$; and so, since $\Gamma_i \subseteq \Gamma$, either $\alpha_i \in \Gamma_i$ or $\sim\alpha_i \in \Gamma_i$. This completes the proof of theorem 6.3.

Consistent sets of wff in modal systems

All the results we have proved so far depend only on the fact that S contains PC. They therefore hold for any system, whether modal or not, which contains PC. We now go on to consider features of maximal consistent sets which have to do with their modal properties. In particular, in constructing a model in which the worlds are maximal consistent sets of wff we will have to specify when one world is accessible from another. Now if a set Γ is to see a set Δ then one thing that is required is that if a wff β is *necessary* in Γ, i.e., if $L\beta \in \Gamma$, then β must be *true* in Δ, ie. $\beta \in \Delta$. In fact we shall use this as a *definition* of R in the canonical model. We shall say that $\Gamma R\Delta$ iff for every wff β, if $L\beta \in \Gamma$, then $\beta \in \Delta$. In order to express this more succinctly we shall introduce some new notation. Suppose that Λ is any set of wff of modal logic. Then we write $L^-(\Lambda)$ to denote that set consisting precisely of every wff β for which $L\beta$ is in Λ. More formally expressed:

$$L^-(\Lambda) = \{\beta : L\beta \in \Lambda\}$$

where $\{\alpha : L\alpha \in \Lambda\}$ denotes the class whose members are precisely the αs such that $L\alpha \in \Lambda$. Using this notation we can say that $\Gamma R\Delta$ iff $L^-(\Gamma) \subseteq \Delta$. Our next lemma will depend on the modal properties of S. Its purpose is the following. If $\sim L\alpha$ is in a set Λ of wff, and that set is supposed to represent a world in a model, there had better be a set which represents an accessible world, and which contains $\sim\alpha$. We need a guarantee that it will always be consistent to suppose this, and that means that we need to know that $L^-(\Lambda)$ is consistent with $\sim\alpha$. The lemma can be stated as follows:

LEMMA 6.4   Let S be any normal system of propositional modal logic, and let Λ be an S-consistent set of wff containing $\sim L\alpha$. Then $L^-(\Lambda) \cup \{\sim\alpha\}$ is S-consistent.

Proof: We prove the lemma by showing that if $L^-(\Lambda) \cup \{\sim\alpha\}$ is *not* consistent then neither is Λ. So suppose that $L^-(\Lambda) \cup \{\sim\alpha\}$ is not S-consistent. This means that there is some finite subset $\{\beta_1, \dots ,\beta_n\}$ of $L^-(\Lambda)$ such that

$$\vdash_S \sim(\beta_1 \wedge \dots \wedge \beta_n \wedge \sim\alpha)$$

hence by PC

$$\vdash_S (\beta_1 \wedge \dots \wedge \beta_n) \supset \alpha$$

So by DR1 (p. 30)

$$\vdash_S L(\beta_1 \wedge \dots \wedge \beta_n) \supset L\alpha$$

So by L-distribution (K3, p. 28) and Eq (p. 32),

$$\vdash_S (L\beta_1 \wedge \dots \wedge L\beta_n) \supset L\alpha$$

and finally by PC,

$$\vdash_S \sim(L\beta_1 \wedge \dots \wedge L\beta_n \wedge \sim L\alpha)$$

But this means that $\{L\beta_1, \dots ,\beta_n, \sim L\alpha\}$ is not S-consistent; so, since it is a subset of Λ, Λ is not S-consistent, which is what we had to prove. (If Λ should happen to contain no wff of the form $L\beta$ then $L^-(\Lambda)$ would be empty and so if $L^-(\Lambda) \cup \{\sim\alpha\}$ is not consistent then $\vdash_S \alpha$. But then by N $\vdash_S L\alpha$, and so Λ is inconsistent in this case also.) This ends the proof.

In conjunction with theorem 6.3 lemma 6.4 guarantees that there will be a maximal consistent set Γ such that $L^-(\Lambda) \subseteq \Gamma$ and $\sim\alpha \in \Gamma$. This means that for any wff β, if $L\beta \in \Lambda$ then $\beta \in \Gamma$ so if Λ is itself maximal consistent then $\Lambda R\Gamma$.

Canonical models

The canonical model for S is, like any other model for a normal propositional modal system, a triple $\langle W,R,V \rangle$. W is the set of all sets of maximal S-consistent sets of wff. I.e. $w \in W$ iff w is maximal S-consistent.[1] If w and w' are both in W then wRw' iff for every wff β if $L\beta \in w$ then $\beta \in w'$ — using the L^- notation wRw' iff $L^-(w) \subseteq w'$. Finally we define V in the canonical model for S by stipulating that $V(p,w) = 1$ iff $p \in w$. I.e., a variable is true in a world in the canonical model iff it is a member of that world, i.e., a member of that set of formulae.

Given the assignment to the variables, $[V \sim]$, $[V \vee]$ and $[VL]$ then give a value in every world to every wff. Our aim is now to show that every wff — not merely every variable — is true in a world in the canonical model iff it is a member of that world. This will have the consequence that $\vdash_S \alpha$ iff α is valid in the canonical model, since, as we observed on p. 115, α is a theorem of S iff it is a member of every maximal S-consistent set. So α will be a theorem of S iff it is a member of every world in the canonical model of S. Therefore if being a *member* of w is equivalent to being *true* in w then α will be a theorem of S iff it is true in every world in the canonical model of S, i.e. iff it is valid in the canonical model of S.

In the case of the variables the V in the canonical model of S was defined so that a variable is true in a world iff it is a member of that world. In the case of other wff this has to be proved, and our next theorem is sometimes called the fundamental theorem for canonical models.

THEOREM 6.5   Let $\langle W,R,V \rangle$ be the canonical model for a normal propositional model system S. Then for any wff α and any $w \in W$, $V(\alpha,w) = 1$ iff $\alpha \in w$.

Proof: The result is defined to hold for the propositional variables. To show that it holds for all wff it will be sufficient to show the following:

(a) If the theorem holds for α then it holds for $\sim \alpha$;
(b) If the theorem holds for α and β then it holds for $\alpha \vee \beta$;
(c) If the theorem holds for α then it holds for $L\alpha$.

Since every wff (in primitive notation) is made up from the variables in one of the ways mentioned in (a)−(c) this will show that the theorem holds for all wff. This style of proof is often called a proof by *induction on the construction of a wff* (or sometimes on the *length* of a wff).[2] The hypothesis that the theorem holds for α (and β) is called the *hypothesis of the induction* or the *inductive hypothesis*.

As we have observed, if α is a variable the theorem holds by definition. We now prove each of (a)−(c) in turn.

(a)   Consider a wff $\sim\alpha$ and any $w \in$ W. By [V$\sim$] we have $V(\sim\alpha,w) = 1$ iff $V(\alpha,w) = 0$. Since the theorem is assumed to hold for α we have $V(\alpha,w) = 0$ iff $\alpha \notin w$. But by lemma 6.1a, $\alpha \notin w$ iff $\sim\alpha \in w$. Hence finally we have $V(\sim\alpha,w) = 1$ iff $\sim\alpha \in w$ as required.

(b)   Consider next $\alpha \lor \beta$. By [V$\lor$] we have $V(\alpha \lor \beta,w) = 1$ iff either $V(\alpha,w) = 1$ or $V(\beta,w) = 1$. Since the theorem is assumed to hold for α and β we therefore have $V(\alpha \lor \beta,w) = 1$ iff either $\alpha \in w$ or $\beta \in$ W. Hence by lemma 6.1b we have $V(\alpha \lor \beta,w) = 1$ iff $\alpha \lor \beta \in w$, as required.

(c)   Consider finally $L\alpha$. (A) Suppose that $L\alpha \in w$. Then by definition of R we have $\alpha \in w'$ for every w' such that wRw'. Since the theorem is assumed to hold for α we therefore have $V(\alpha,w') = 1$ for every w' such that wRw'. Hence by [VL], $V(L\alpha,w) = 1$. (B) Suppose now that $L\alpha \notin w$. Then by lemma 6.1a, $\sim L\alpha \in w$. Hence by lemma 6.4, $L^-(w) \cup \{\sim\alpha\}$ is S-consistent. So by theorem 6.3 and the definition of W, there is some $w' \in$ W such that $L^-(w) \cup \{\sim\alpha\} \subseteq w'$, and therefore such that (i) $L^-(w) \subseteq w'$ and (ii) $\sim\alpha \in w'$. Now (i) gives us wRw', by the definition of R, and by lemma 6.1a (ii) gives us $\alpha \notin w$; and so, since the theorem is assumed to hold for α, $V(\alpha,w') = 0$. So by [VL] we have $V(L\alpha,w) = 0$.

This completes the proof of theorem 6.5.

COROLLARY 6.6. Any wff α is valid in the canonical model of S iff $\vdash_S$ α.

Proof: Let $\langle W,R,V \rangle$ be the canonical model of S. Then by lemma 6.2a α is in every maximal S-consistent set of wff. Hence α is in every $w \in$ W, and so, by theorem 6.5, $V(\alpha,w) = 1$ for every $w \in$ W; i.e. α is valid in $\langle W,R,V \rangle$. Suppose now that $\dashv_S \alpha$. Then $\{\sim\alpha\}$ is S-consistent and so, by theorem 6.3 there is some maximal S-consistent set − i.e. some $w \in$ W − such that $\sim\alpha \in w$ and hence $\alpha \notin w$. So by theorem 6.5, $V(\alpha,w) = 0$. So in this case α is not valid in $\langle W,R,V \rangle$.

The completeness of K, T, B, S4 and S5

Let us take stock of the position we have now reached. We assume we have a normal system S and a class $\mathscr{E}$ of frames. To say that S is complete with respect to $\mathscr{E}$ is to say that every $\mathscr{E}$-valid wff α is a theorem of S; where a $\mathscr{E}$-valid wff is a wff that is valid on every frame in $\mathscr{E}$, which in turn means that where $\langle W,R,V \rangle$ is any model such that $\langle W,R \rangle$ $\in \mathscr{E}$, and w is any member of W, $V(\alpha,w) = 1$. Now if the frame of the canonical model is in $\mathscr{E}$ then every $\mathscr{E}$-valid wff is valid on that frame, and therefore valid in the canonical model itself. But in that case, by corollary 6.6, that wff will be a theorem of S.

This should make it clear that in order to prove the completeness of S by the canonical model method it will be sufficient to prove that the canonical model of S is based on a frame in $\mathscr{E}$. This means that we have immediately a completeness result for K, since in the case of K, $\mathscr{E}$ is the class of all frames, and the frame of the canonical model in this case is, trivially, in $\mathscr{E}$.

THEOREM 6.7   T is complete with respect to the class of all reflexive frames.

All we have to prove is that in the canonical model for T, R is reflexive, i.e. for every $w \in W$, wRw. By the definition of R in the canonical model this means that we must prove that for any wff α, if $L\alpha \in w$ then $\alpha \in w$. But from **T** and US we have $\vdash_s L\alpha \supset \alpha$, and so the result follows by lemma 6.2b.

THEOREM 6.8   D is complete with respect to the class of all serial frames.

To prove that D is complete it is sufficient to prove that R in its canonical model is serial. By D1 $M(p \supset p)$ is a theorem of D and so, for any w in the canonical model of D, $M(p \supset p) \in w$. So, by theorem 6.5 $V(M(p \supset p),w) = 1$. So there must be some w' such that wRw', and so R is serial as required.

THEOREM 6.9   S4 is complete with respect to the class of all reflexive and transitive frames.

We prove that the canonical model of S4 is based on a frame which is reflexive and transitive. Since S4 contains **T** the proof of theorem 6.7 establishes that it is reflexive. For transitivity suppose that wRw' and $w'Rw''$. To show that wRw'' we must show that for any wff α, if $L\alpha \in$ w then $\alpha \in w''$. Now $\vdash_{S4} L\alpha \supset LL\alpha$, and so, by lemma 6.2b, if $L\alpha \in$

w then $LL\alpha \in w$, and then since wRw', by the definition of R, $L\alpha \in w'$ and so, since $w'Rw''$, again by the definition of R, $\alpha \in w''$ as required. (Note that this proof also gives us the result that the system K4, mentioned on p. 64, is complete with respect to the class of transitive frames, whether or not R in those frames is reflexive.)

THEOREM 6.10   B is complete with respect to the class of all reflexive and symmetrical frames.

Reflexiveness is as for T. For symmetry suppose that wRw'. To show that $w'Rw$ we must show that if any wff α, if $L\alpha \in w'$ then $\alpha \in w$. So suppose $\alpha \notin w$. Then $\sim\alpha \in w$, and, since $\vdash_B \sim\alpha \supset L\sim L\alpha$, by lemma 6.2b, $L\sim L\alpha \in w$, and since wRw', by the definition of R, $\sim L\alpha \in w'$ and so $L\alpha \notin w'$. (The proof also establishes that KB is complete with respect to the class of all symmetrical frames, whether or not they are reflexive.)

THEOREM 6.11   S5 is complete with respect to the class of all equivalence frames.

The presence in S5 of **T**, **4** and **B** means that the completeness of S5 follows from the proofs of theorems 6.7, 6.9 and 6.10.

Triv and Ver again

At the end of Chapter 3 we mentioned the Trivial system and the Verum system. What we said there has the consequence that the Trivial system is sound with respect to reflexive one-world frames, and the Verum system is sound with respect to irreflexive one-world frames (or what comes to the same thing, one-world frames in which the world is a dead end). Now in fact the frame of the canonical model for neither of these systems is a one-world frame. However we can show, and quite easily too, that every world in the frame of the canonical model of Triv can see itself, and itself alone, and that every world in the canonical model of Ver is a dead end. Clearly if α is valid on every model based on a one-world reflexive frame then it will be valid on a frame all of whose worlds are like this, and so will be valid on the frame of the canonical model of Triv, and so $\vdash \alpha$ similarly if α is valid on every model based on a dead end it will be valid in the canonical model of Ver.

It is easy to show that the canonical model of Triv contains only reflexive end points (i.e. worlds which can see themselves and themselves alone). From $\vdash Lp \equiv p$ we have $\vdash Lp \supset p$ and so the frame is reflexive, so suppose that in the canonical model for Triv there is a world w such that wRw' but $w \neq w'$. Then there will be a wff α such that $\alpha \in w$ but $\alpha \notin w'$. Now $\alpha \in w$ and $\vdash \alpha \supset L\alpha$, so $L\alpha \in w$. But wRw' and so $\alpha \in w'$ which is a contradiction. For Ver we note that $\vdash_{\text{Ver}} L(p \wedge \sim p)$. But that can only happen at a dead end, and so every world in the canonical model of Ver is a dead end. Each world in the canonical model of Triv can be thought of as based on the one-world reflexive frame, and each world in the canonical model of Ver as based on the one-world dead end frame and so these frames respectively characterize Triv and Ver.

When we look at Triv and Ver in this way we see why it is that they collapse into PC. For in one-world frames there is no way of making a distinction between wff which are true in one world but false in another. Further, since there are only two one-world frames, one in which the single world can see itself, and one in which it cannot, we can see why it is that there are only two ways in which a normal modal system can collapse into PC.

Exercises — 6

6.1 Call Γ *maximal consistent** iff Γ is consistent and for every wff α, if $\Gamma \cup \{\alpha\}$ is consistent then $\alpha \in \Gamma$. Prove that Γ is maximal consistent* iff Γ is maximal consistent as defined in this chapter.

6.2 Prove that if Γ is maximal consistent then $\alpha \supset \beta \in \Gamma$ iff $\alpha \notin \Gamma$ or $\beta \in \Gamma$.

6.3 Let Γ and Λ both be maximal consistent. Show that if $\Lambda \subseteq \Gamma$ then $\Lambda = \Gamma$.

6.4 Show that if Γ and Λ are both maximal consistent then $\{\alpha : L\alpha \in \Gamma\} \subseteq \Lambda$ iff $\{M\alpha : \alpha \in \Lambda\} \subseteq \Gamma$.

6.5 Show that if Λ is consistent and $M\alpha \in \Lambda$ then $L^-(\Lambda) \cup \{\alpha\}$ is consistent.

6.6 Let wR^nw' mean that w can see w' in n R-steps. Where S is any normal modal system show that in the canonical model of S wR^nw' iff $\{\alpha : L^n\alpha \in w\} \subseteq w'$.

6.7 Where S contains S4 show that if $\{L\gamma_1, \ldots , L\gamma_n, \sim L\beta\}$ is S-consistent, so is $\{L\gamma_1, \ldots ,L\gamma_n, \sim\beta\}$.

6.8 Show that K + $Mp \supset Lp$ is complete with respect to the class of frames in which each world can see at most one world, itself or another.

6.9 Let W2 be T with the additional axiom

W2 $(p \wedge q \wedge M(p \wedge \sim q)) \supset Lp$

Show that any wff α is a theorem of W2 iff it is valid in all models in which every world can see at most one other world besides itself.

6.10 Show that K + $L(Lp \supset q) \vee L(Lq \supset p)$ is complete with respect to the class of frames in which if w_1Rw_2 and w_1Rw_3 then either w_2Rw_3 or w_3Rw_2.

6.11 Show that K + $p \supset Lp$ is complete with respect to the class of frames in which every world is either a dead end or can see only itself.

6.12 Show that K + **E** is complete with respect to frames which satisfy the condition stated in exercise 3.11.

6.13 Consider the class of frames in which R is replaced by a subset N of W and $V(L\alpha,w) = 1$ iff $V(\alpha,w') = 1$ for every $w' \in$ N. Prove that K + **E** is characterized by frames of this kind.

Notes
[1] The use of maximal consistent sets in proving the completeness of systems of modal logic goes back at least as far as Bayart 1959. Other early works are Kaplan 1966, Makinson 1966b and Lemmon and Scott 1977. Completeness proofs of a different kind are found in Kripke 1959 and 1963a. The method was originally used for non-modal predicate logic in Henkin 1949.
[2] Although we have not used the word 'induction' before we have used this method of proof in earlier chapters, for instance in our proof of Eq on p. 32 and in the proof of lemma 3.1 on p. 66. A proof by induction, more precisely *mathematical induction*, applies when we have a class of objects made up from simple parts by a finite number of steps. So, for instance, the natural numbers are all obtained from 0 by the successor operation, the operation of adding 1, or as here any wff is obtained from the primitive symbols by successive operations of the formation rules. If we wish to show that every member of such a class has a certain property it is sufficient to show that the simple members of the class have

it, and that anything made up from members which have the property also has the property. Other examples of inductive proofs are in soundness proofs such as that for K on pp. 39-41.

Part II

NORMAL MODAL SYSTEMS

7

CANONICAL MODELS

In the last chapter we introduced canonical models for normal modal systems and used them to prove the completeness of the systems we had been studying in Part I. As we remarked there there are many more normal modal systems, and in this part of the book we shall have a look at some of them with a view to illustrating some general techniques and properties of them. This chapter will be concerned to look at some features of canonical models. We first introduce three other systems: S4.3, S4M and S4.2, and include completeness proofs for them using canonical models. We shall then look at the structure of the frames of canonical models for a selection of systems, and finally we will discuss some limitations of the canonical model technique for proving completeness by looking at a system where the frame of its canonical model does not validate all its theorems.

Temporal interpretations of modal logic

In order to motivate the next two systems we shall look at what can be called *temporal interpretations of modal logic*. These systems have a special interest in connection with an issue raised by A. N. Prior in *Time and Modality*.[1] Prior was thinking of propositions as things which could change their truth-values (could become true or become false) with the passage of time, and he wanted to be able to interpret Lp to mean 'It is and always will be the case that p'. He therefore suggested that we think of time as a series of moments, at each of which a given proposition could have the value 1 (true) or the value 0 (false), without prejudice to its value at any other moment; and he defined the value of Lp at any given moment as 1 if p has the value 1 at that moment and at every subsequent moment, and otherwise as 0. A formula can then be said to be valid iff it has the value 1 at every moment, irrespective of the values assigned to its variables at any moment.

The problem is to find an axiomatic system whose theorems shall coincide with the formulae which are valid by this criterion. In *Time and Modality* Prior made the conjecture that S4 was the required system,[2] but this was discovered to be incorrect and he abandoned it shortly afterwards.[3] One reason why S4 is too weak is because Prior's interpretation requires that the moments are all *connected* in the following sense. Suppose we have a point (world) w. A relation R is connected iff it holds, in one direction or the other, between every pair of worlds that w can see. Using the language of the lower predicate calculus (see Part III) we can say that a frame $\langle W, R \rangle$ is *connected* iff

Conn $\forall w \forall w' \forall w''((wRw' \land wRw'') \supset (w'Rw'' \lor w''Rw'))$

Conn means that if w can see both w' and w'' then either w' can see w'' or w'' can see w'; in other words no world can see two incomparable worlds. One kind of frame in which it would be natural to think of R as connected over W would be one in which the members of W are moments of time and R is the relation 'either contemporaneous with or earlier than'; for we normally think of the moments of time as all lying, so to speak, on a single straight line. And in fact if we require that R be reflexive, transitive and connected over W we obtain an account of validity for the 'temporal' system S4.3.[4] S4.3 is S4 with the addition of the axiom

D1 $L(Lp \supset q) \lor L(Lq \supset p)$

The method of semantic diagrams can easily be adapted to the system S4.3. As an illustration, we show how to prove the validity of $L(Lp \supset q)$ $\lor L(Lq \supset p)$ when R is connected (as well as reflexive and transitive). The T-diagram for this formula (which shows it to be invalid in T) is:

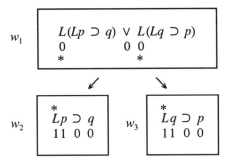

Clearly this is the only kind of T-diagram which could falsify the formula. If, however, we require that R be connected, then one thing that will follow is that we must have either w_2Rw_3, or w_3Rw_2. If we have the former then p must be assigned 1 in w_3, thus making it inconsistent. If we have the latter, then for a similar reason q must be assigned 1 in w_2, making it inconsistent.

This establishes the soundness of S4.3 with respect to (reflexive and transitive) connected frames. We now proceed to establish completeness. Since S4.3 contains S4, we know from the proof of theorem 6.9 on p. 120 that R is reflexive and transitive in its canonical model. So all that remains to prove completeness is to prove that R is also connected. In other words we have to show that it is impossible to have the following situation for any w_1, w_2, w_3 in the canonical model for S4.3:

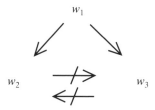

(where $w \to w'$ means that wRw', and $w \not\to$ means that not wRw').

The proof is this. Suppose that such a situation were to obtain somewhere in the canonical model of S4.3. Then, since w_2 cannot see w_3, there must be some wff α such that

(1) $L\alpha \in w_2$ but $\alpha \notin w_3$.

129

Similarly, since w_3 cannot see w_2 there must be some wff β such that

(2) $L\beta \in w_3$ but $\beta \notin w_2$.

Putting (1) and (2) together we have

(3) $L\alpha \supset \beta \notin w_2$ and

(4) $L\beta \supset \alpha \notin w_3$.

But since w_1Rw_2 and w_1Rw_3, (3) and (4) give us

(5) $L(L\alpha \supset \beta) \notin w_1$ and

(6) $L(L\beta \supset \alpha) \notin w_1$.

So

(7) $L(L\alpha \supset \beta) \vee L(L\beta \supset \alpha) \notin w_1$.

This however is impossible since this wff is a substitution instance of **D1** and therefore must be in every world in the canonical model of S4.3. So the situation envisaged cannot arise. This establishes the completeness of S4.3.

Although this proof does yield completeness with respect to the class of connected frames as defined above it does not on its own give completeness for frames which reflect linear time. This is because connected models allow what Krister Segerberg calls *clusters*.[5] In a cluster every world can see every other world in the same cluster, and in the case of time this would mean that you could have a cluster of distinct but contemporaneous moments; and this would contradict the fact that time is usually imagined to be *antisymmetrical*, in that if wRw' and $w'Rw$ then $w = w'$. To obtain a linear frame from a connected frame Segerberg uses an operation he calls *bulldozing*.[6] This consists of ordering each cluster in some arbitrary way and replacing the cluster by an infinite chain of copies of that cluster. Where a world used to see another world which is now above it in the same cluster it no longer does so, but instead sees a copy of that other world in a copy of the cluster lower (i.e. further on) in the chain that replaces the cluster.

Ending time

In a temporal interpretation, whether or not we conceive of time as linear, another question which might be raised is whether time has an end. With L meaning 'It is and always will be that', then a final point will be one in which, because there is no future, everything that is the case both is and always will be. In terms of frames a final point will be one which can only see itself, and the claim that time has an end will be the claim that every point can see a final point. Without linearity there need be no unique final point, but the claim that time ends could still perhaps be that every world (i.e. every moment of time) can see a final world. The appropriate system for this is S4 + **F**, where **F** is the wff

F $(LMp \land LMq) \supset M(p \land q)$

Although **F** on its own captures the idea that time has an end, in the presence of S4 we can in fact use a weaker axiom. S4M is S4 with the addition of the wff

M $LMp \supset MLp^7$

It is interesting to note that if **M** were added to S5 rather than merely to S4 then the resulting system would collapse into PC; i.e. it would be Triv, since in S5 LMp is equivalent to Mp and MLp is equivalent to Lp. However, when added to S4 we obtain a system which is characterized by the condition on frames that in addition to reflexiveness and transitivity every world can see at least one world that can see only itself. This condition was called $(m\infty)$ by E.J.Lemmon.[8] As far as we can tell it has no recognized name so we shall call it finality. (In modal systems with a temporal interpretation it can express the idea that time has an end – a final point.) The condition can be expressed formally as

Fin $\forall w \exists w'(wRw' \land \forall w''(w'Rw'' \supset w' = w''))$

It is not hard to check that **M** is valid on all final frames and we now use the canonical model method to prove its completeness. In fact the completeness proof goes more straightforwardly in S4 + **F**, since **F** corresponds exactly to Fin. But in the presence of S4, **F** can be derived from **M**. We first prove a theorem of K:

K14 $(Lp \land Mq) \supset M(q \land p)$

PROOF

K[~q/q]	(1)	$L(p \supset \sim q) \supset (Lp \supset L\sim q)$	
(1) × PC × Eq	(2)	$L\sim(q \wedge p) \supset (Lp \supset L\sim q)$	
(2) × LMI	(3)	$\sim M(q \wedge p) \supset (Lp \supset \sim Mq)$	
(3) × PC	(4)	$(Lp \wedge Mq) \supset M(q \wedge p)$	**Q.E.D.**

The PC-principle used in getting from (3) to (4) is $(\sim p \supset (q \supset \sim r)) \supset ((q \wedge r) \supset p)$ with $M(q \wedge p)/p$, Lp/q and Mq/r.

Proof of **F** in S4M:

M × PC	(1)	$(LMp \wedge LMq) \supset (LMp \wedge MLq)$	
K14[Mp/p,Lq/q]	(2)	$(LMp \wedge MLq) \supset M(Lq \wedge Mp)$	
K14[q/p,p/q]	(3)	$(Lq \wedge Mp) \supset M(p \wedge q)$	
(3) × DR3	(4)	$M(Lq \wedge Mp) \supset MM(p \wedge q)$	
R3a[p ∧ q/p]	(5)	$MM(p \wedge q) \supset M(p \wedge q)$	
(1)(2)(4)(5) × PC	(6)	$(LMp \wedge LMq) \supset M(p \wedge q)$	**Q.E.D.**

The following rule is an immediate consequence of **F**:

DR5 $\vdash M\alpha, \vdash M\beta \rightarrow \vdash M(\alpha \wedge \beta)$

DR5 obviously generalizes to more than two wff, so that we have

DR5′ $\vdash M\alpha_1, \dots , \vdash M\alpha_k \rightarrow \vdash M(\alpha_1 \wedge \dots \wedge \alpha_k)$

From T2 (p. 42), since S4M contains T, we have, for $1 \leq i \leq k$,

$\vdash \quad M(\alpha_i \supset L\alpha_i)$

and so, by DR5′,

S4M1 $M((\alpha_1 \supset L\alpha_1) \wedge \dots \wedge (\alpha_k \supset L\alpha_k))$

To prove the completeness of S4M with respect to final transitive and reflexive frames it is sufficient to show that its canonical model satisfies Fin. We first prove a lemma. Say that w is a *final* world in a frame iff $\forall w'(wRw' \supset w = w')$. Then the following holds for every world w in the canonical model of any normal modal system:

LEMMA 7.1 w is final iff $\alpha \supset L\alpha \in w$ for every wff α.

Proof: First suppose that $\alpha \supset L\alpha$ *is* in w for every wff α, and suppose that wRw' but $w \neq w'$. If $w \neq w'$ then there is a wff β with $\beta \in w$ but $\beta \notin w'$. But since $\beta \supset L\beta \in w$ then $L\beta \in w$ and so $\beta \in w'$, which would make w' inconsistent. And if there is some $\alpha \supset L\alpha$ not in w, then $\alpha \in w$ but $L\alpha \notin w$. So there is some w' such that wRw' and $\sim\alpha \in w'$. So there is some w' such that wRw' and $w \neq w'$. This proves lemma 7.1.

We now show that the canonical model of S4M satisfies Fin. It will be sufficient to prove the following:

THEOREM 7.2   If w is any world in the canonical model of S4M, then $L^-(w) \cup \{\alpha \supset L\alpha : \alpha$ any wff$\}$ is consistent in S4M.

We shall first explain why theorem 7.2 gives us the result we want. If $L^-(w) \cup \{\alpha \supset L\alpha : \alpha$ any wff$\}$ is consistent then it will have an extension w' in the canonical model of S4M. Since $L^-(w) \subseteq w'$ we have wRw', and since $\alpha \supset L\alpha \in w'$ for every wff α, w' is final. So, as a result of the theorem, every world in the canonical model of S4M can see a final world.

Proof of theorem 7.2:   Suppose $L^-(w) \cup \{\alpha \supset L\alpha : \alpha$ any wff$\}$ were *not* consistent. Then there would be $\alpha_1, \ldots, \alpha_n, \beta_1, \ldots, \beta_k$ such that $L\alpha_1, \ldots,$ $L\alpha_n \in w$ and

$$\vdash_{S4M} \sim(\alpha_1 \wedge \ldots \wedge \alpha_n \wedge (\beta_1 \supset L\beta_1) \wedge \ldots \wedge (\beta_k \supset L\beta_k))$$

so

$$\vdash_{S4M} (\alpha_1 \wedge \ldots \wedge \alpha_n) \supset \sim((\beta_1 \supset L\beta_1) \wedge \ldots \wedge (\beta_k \supset L\beta_k))$$

so, by principles of K,

$$\vdash_{S4M} (L\alpha_1 \wedge \ldots \wedge L\alpha_n) \supset \sim M((\beta_1 \supset L\beta_1) \wedge \ldots \wedge (\beta_k \supset L\beta_k))$$

But $(L\alpha_1 \wedge \ldots \wedge L\alpha_n) \in w$, and so $\sim M((\beta_1 \supset L\beta_1) \wedge \ldots \wedge (\beta_k \supset L\beta_k)) \in w$. But by S4M1

$$\vdash M((\beta_1 \supset L\beta_1) \wedge \ldots \wedge (\beta_k \supset L\beta_k))$$

which would make w inconsistent.

Convergence

Our third example is the system S4.2 which is S4 with the additional axiom

G1 $MLp \supset LMp$[9]

G1 is in fact the converse of **M** and the relevant class of frames is the class of frames which are reflexive transitive and *convergent* where a frame $\langle W,R \rangle$ is convergent iff R satisfies the condition that for any w_1, w_2 and w_3 in W, if w_1Rw_2 and w_1Rw_3, there is some w_4 such that w_2Rw_4 and w_3Rw_4. (Connected reflexive frames are convergent frames in which w_4 is either w_2 or w_3.) Soundness is straightforward. To prove completeness we show that the canonical model of S4.2 is convergent. This means that we have to show that wherever the following pattern occurs in the canonical model for S4.2

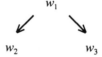

there is always a world w_4 in the model which continues the pattern in this way:

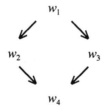

To prove this it is sufficient to show that the set of wff

(Λ) $L^-(w_2) \cup L^-(w_3)$

is S4.2-consistent. For then theorem 6.3 guarantees the existence of a world w in the canonical model such that $\Lambda \subseteq w$. It might be worth remarking on this way of using the canonical model. For it may easily happen, as here, that we need to show that there *is* in the canonical model a world w which has a certain property, and we may be able to express that property by saying that w has to contain a certain set of wff, say the set Λ. It is here that theorem 6.3 comes to our aid, for it says that provided Λ is consistent then it is included in a set which is maximal consistent, with respect to the system in question, and therefore included in a world in the canonical model of that system.

Suppose then that Λ is not S4.2-consistent. Then there are wff $L\alpha_1$, ... , $L\alpha_n$ in w_2 and wff $L\beta_1$, ... , $L\beta_m$ in w_3 such that

$$\vdash_S \sim (\alpha_1 \wedge \ldots \wedge \alpha_n \wedge \beta_1 \wedge \ldots \wedge \beta_m)$$

If we let α denote $\alpha_1 \wedge \ldots \wedge \alpha_n$ and β denote $\beta_1 \wedge \ldots \wedge \beta_m$, then lemma 6.1c (on p. 114) and L-distribution (p. 28) tell us that $L\alpha \in w_2$, and $L\beta \in w_3$, and

$$\vdash_S \sim (\alpha \wedge \beta)$$

By PC this gives us

$$\vdash_S \alpha \supset \sim\beta$$

And hence by DR3 (p. 35) and LMI (p. 33)

(1) $M\alpha \supset \sim L\beta$

We now note that since w_1Rw_2 and $L\alpha \in w_2$, $ML\alpha \in w_1$. (It is not hard to see quite generally that if wRw' and $\gamma \in w'$ then $M\gamma \in w$. For if not, by lemma 6.1a and LMI, $L\sim\gamma \in w$ and then $\sim\gamma \in w'$ making w' inconsistent.) So by **G1** and lemma 6.2b, $LM\alpha \in w_1$, and since w_1Rw_3, $M\alpha \in w_3$. So by (1) $\sim L\beta \in w_3$, making w_3 inconsistent.

This means that Λ is S4.2-consistent and so is contained in some w in its canonical model. Clearly this w will serve as the required w_4. This establishes the completeness of S4.2.[10]

It should be noted that in our proof that R is convergent in the canonical model of S4.2 (as also in our proof that it is connected in the canonical model of S4.3) we appealed only to **G1 (D1)** in addition to principles common to all normal systems, and made no use of any theorems that depend on **T** or **4**. This shows that K + **G1** is complete for frames in which R is convergent, and K + **D1** is complete for frames in which R is connected, irrespective of whether it is also reflexive or transitive.

The frames of canonical models

The canonical model for a given modal system, like any other model, is based on a certain frame. So far we have said a good deal about canonical models, but very little about the frames on which they are based, except to note that, although every normal system is characterized by its canonical model, it does not follow that every such system is characterized by the frame of its canonical model, because that frame may not be a frame for the system at all. (Obviously, if the frame of the canonical model for S is a frame for S, then that frame characterizes S.) We shall now say something more about the frames of canonical models.

Although it is obvious that the frame of the canonical model is a frame it can be easy to forget just what that implies. In the canonical model the worlds are sets of wff and a wff α is *true* in a world w iff $\alpha \in w$. Now where a world is a set of wff it is so natural to think that a wff is *true* in a set of wff, just in case it is a member of that set, that we might forget that you could, for instance, elect to set a variable p as true in a world iff p was *not* a member of that world. Or even, if the variables were arranged in a determinate order you could put $V(p_i, w) = 1$ if i is odd and $p_i \in w$, or if i is even and $p_i \notin w$, and there is no limit to the assignments that could be made. An examination of the members of a world would of course not then give you any clue about whether a wff is true or not at that world.

In order to look more closely at frames it will be useful to introduce the ideas of an *R-step* in an *R-chain*. We say that every world w is 0 R-steps from itself, i.e. wR^0w' iff $w = w'$. We then say that there is an n + 1-step R-chain from w to w' (written $wR^{n+1}w'$) iff there is some w'' such that wR^nw'' and $w''Rw'$. The idea is simple. If w_1Rw_2 then w_2 is one R-step from w_1, and if w_2Rw_3 then w_3 is two R-steps from w_1. Notice that w_3 might also be only one R-step from w_1, as it will be if R is transitive. If R is reflexive then every world will be n R-steps from itself for arbitrarily large (finite) n. Sometimes we don't even care about the direction of a relation. Thus in the frame you can't get from w_1 to w_2 by a sequence of R-steps, though you can if you are allowed to go backwards as well as forwards. Now some frames are composed of a number of parts, each completely isolated from any of the others. For example the frame

is like this. We shall call such frames *non-cohesive* frames. By contrast a *cohesive* frame is one in which each world can see each other world in a number of forward or backward R-steps. For many purposes a non-cohesive frame is most conveniently thought of as a collection of the cohesive frames of which it is composed. Nevertheless it is certainly a frame and in some contexts it is important to think of it as a single frame.[11]

When we look at the frames of canonical models we see that the frames of *some* of them are not cohesive. An extreme example is provided by the Verum system. We showed on p. 121 that in the canonical model for this system each world is a dead end. The frame of this model therefore consists of a collection of worlds none of which is related to itself or to any of the others, and is thus as radically non-cohesive as any frame could be. We may, indeed, feel that it is more natural to regard it as a collection of distinct frames than as a single frame; and in fact the Verum system is characterized not only by the frame of its canonical model but also by the frame which consists of a single dead end. There is, however, this important difference between these two frames, that whereas there is a model based on the former (viz. the canonical model) which characterizes Ver, there can be no model based on the latter which characterizes it. The reason is that in any model based on a one-world frame, either p is true in every world or else $\sim p$ is true in every world; yet neither p nor $\sim p$ is a theorem of Ver. The case of the Trivial system is analogous. The frame of the canonical model for Triv consists of a collection of worlds each of which can see itself but none of the others. Triv is characterized both by this frame and by a one-world reflexive frame; but, for the same reason as in the case of Ver, it is characterized by a model based on the former, but not by any model based on the latter.

Another canonical model whose frame is not cohesive is the canonical model for S5. This is not as obvious as for Ver or Triv, but in fact the frame of this model is split up into a number of disjoint sets of worlds, each isolated from all the others. The relation R is universal within each such set (i.e. each world is related to every world in its own set), but it is not universal over the whole frame. How do we know that the frame of the canonical model for S5 is like this? One simple proof is this: p is an S5-consistent wff, and therefore is true in some world in the canonical model for S5. Now if R were universal in that model, then Mp would be true in *every* world in it; and therefore, by corollary 2.5, it would be a theorem of S5. But we know that it is not.

At this point one might perhaps begin to suspect that the frame of the canonical model for a normal modal system is never a cohesive frame. But in fact, for a quite wide range of systems we can prove that the frames of their canonical models actually contain a world that can see every world. For this to happen it will be sufficient to show, for a given system S, that $\{\sim L\alpha :\dashv_S \alpha\}$ is consistent. If this set is consistent then the canonical model of S will contain a world w^* such that $L\alpha \in w^*$ only when α is a theorem of S. But when α is a theorem it is a member of every world, and so if $L\alpha \in w^*$ then $\alpha \in w$ for every $w \in W$, and so w^*Rw.

How can we prove that this does happen for a given system S? One way is as follows.[12] We take the canonical model of S, and we extend it in the following way. We form a new model for S (call it $\langle W^+, R^+, V^+ \rangle$) containing a world w^* such that if $V(L\alpha, w^*) = 1$ then $\vdash_S \alpha$. Let $\langle W, R, V \rangle$ be the canonical model of S and let $\langle W^+, R^+, V^+ \rangle$ be defined as follows: Choose some $w^* \notin W$ and let $W^+ = W \cup \{w^*\}$, $R^+ = R \cup \{\langle w^*, w \rangle : w \in W\}$. For $w \in W$, $V^+(p, w) = V(p, w)$. $V^+(p, w^*)$ is arbitrary. Since every $w \in W$ can see by R^+ all and only the worlds it can see by R an easy induction establishes that for all α and all $w \in W$, $V(\alpha, w) = V^+(\alpha, w)$,

(A) If $V(L\alpha, w^*) = 1$ then $\vdash_S \alpha$;

(B) $\langle W^+, R^+, V^+ \rangle$ is a model for S.

Proof of A: If $V^+(L\alpha,w^*) = 1$ then $V^+(\alpha,w) = 1$ for all $w \in W$. So $V(\alpha,w) = 1$ for all $w \in W$ and so, since $\langle W,R,V \rangle$ is the canonical model for S, $\vdash_S \alpha$.

The proof of (B) is specific to S. In some cases it is easy. If S is K then the extended frame $\langle W^+,R^+ \rangle$ automatically validates all K theorems, and therefore so does $\langle W^+,R^+,V^+ \rangle$. If S is T then by making $w^*R^+w^*$, $\langle W^+,R^+ \rangle$ is reflexive and so $\langle W^+,R^+,V^+ \rangle$ validates all T theorems, and so on. But of course if no $w \in W$ can see w^* then R cannot be symmetrical. And if we made it so we might well change the truth-values of wff in worlds in W since such worlds can now see worlds they could not see before. That is not surprising in view of such results as that the canonical model of S5 is not cohesive.

Since there is a model for S satisfying (A) then $\{\sim L\alpha:\dashv_S \alpha\}$ is S-consistent and so there is in its canonical model a world w such that for any wff α if $L\alpha \in w$ then $\vdash_S \alpha$. In that case $\alpha \in w$ and so $L^-(w) \subseteq w$, i.e. wRw. Note that even if R^+ is defined so that not $w^*R^+w^*$, if $V^+(L\alpha,w^*) = 1$, $V(\alpha,w^*) = 1$, since $\vdash_S \alpha$ and $\langle W^+,R^+,V^+ \rangle$ is a model for S. So if it were allowed that w^*Rw^* the values of all wff in $\langle W^+,R^+,V^+ \rangle$ would remain the same. Notice also that although in $\langle W^+,R^+,V^+ \rangle$ w^* is not in the canonical model of S yet a result of the construction is that $\{\sim L\alpha: \dashv_S \alpha\}$ is S-consistent and so there must be a world w *already in* the canonical model whose only necessities are theorems, and which therefore can see every world, including itself, whether or not we set w^* to see itself.

A non-canonical system

In this section we introduce a system, KW, which will appear from time to time in this part of the book. This system is K +

W $L(Lp \supset p) \supset Lp$

We give it Segerberg's name,[13] though it is frequently called G after Gödel since it has been widely studied as the modal logic of 'provability'. If L means 'it is provable that' then one way of interpreting one of Gödel's incompleteness theorems is that if you could prove the consistency of arithmetic, which might be described by saying that you could prove that whatever is provable is true, i.e. $L(Lp \supset p)$, then you could prove anything, i.e. Lp. At any rate it is possible to give a precise interpretation to L which has the consequence of validating exactly the wff which are theorems of KW. (We trust that the use of **W** as the name of a wff will cause no confusion with the use of W for the set of worlds in a frame.) In this book we will not discuss the provability interpretation of KW, but it turns out that KW is a very interesting modal system in that it lacks many features that we have come to expect in modal systems.

The first of these features is that it is not what is called *canonical*.[14] Recall what happened in proving the completeness of T. We showed that the frame of the canonical model of T is reflexive. That means that not only is every theorem of T valid in the canonical model itself − *that* fact holds of every modal system − but it remains valid however bizarre a value-assignment we give to the variables on that frame. That includes assignments like the one mentioned above, where p_i is true in a world if i is odd and p_i is a member of that world, or i is even and p_i is not a member of that world. We call a system S *canonical* iff the frame of S's canonical model is a frame for S. In the case of KW, although every theorem is (obviously) valid on the canonical model itself this does not remain true when we vary the assignments on that same frame.

We show this as follows. We first use the technique described above to show that where $\langle W,R,V \rangle$ is the canonical model of KW then (B) holds. This establishes that the frame of the canonical model of KW contains a world that can see itself. We then show that **W** is not valid on any frame that contains such a world. First, then, to prove (B) for KW. Since $\langle W,R,V \rangle$ is a model for KW then for any wff β, $V(L(L\beta \supset \beta) \supset L\beta,w) = 1$ and so $V^+(L(L\beta \supset \beta) \supset L\beta,w) = 1$. So it is sufficient to show that $V^+(L(L\beta \supset \beta) \supset L\beta,w^*) = 1$. Suppose $V^+(L(L\beta \supset \beta),w^*) = 1$. Then, by A, $\vdash_{KW} L\beta \supset \beta$. So by N, $\vdash_{KW} L(L\beta \supset \beta)$, so by **W** $\vdash_{KW} L\beta$ and so $\vdash_{KW} \beta$ and so $V(\beta,w) = 1$ for all $w \in W$, and so $V^+(\beta,w) = 1$ for all w such that w^*R^+w. So $V^+(L\beta,w^*) = 1$.

Now to show that **W** fails on every frame containing a world that can see itself. Let $\mathscr{F}$ be such a frame and w^* such a world, and consider a model $\langle \mathscr{F},V \rangle$ in which $V(p,w^*) = 0$ and $V(p,w) = 1$ for every $w \in W$ other than w^*. Then clearly

(1) $V(Lp,w^*) = 0$

and so

(2) $V(Lp \supset p,w^*) = 1$.

140

But since p is true at all worlds other than w^* we also have

(3) $V(Lp \supset p,w) = 1$

for every $w \in W$ other than w^*. Hence by (2) and (3) we have $V(Lp \supset p,w) = 1$ for every $w \in W$, and therefore

(4) $V(L(Lp \supset p),w^*) = 1$.

But (4) and (1) mean that **W** is false at w^*, and thus that it fails on $\mathcal{F}$.

Since the only assumption we have made about $\mathcal{F}$ is that it contains a world that can see itself, and since the canonical model for KW contains such a world, we have shown that **W** is not valid on the frame of its canonical model. That is we have proved that KW is not canonical.

Exercises — 7

7.1 Use canonical models to prove the completeness of the systems which result by adding to K the axiom listed, with respect to the conditions indicated:

(a)   **MV** $MLp \lor Lp$ (Every world is or can see a dead end)

(b)   **R1** $MLp \supset (p \supset Lp)$

                        (If wRw' and $w \neq w'$ then if wRw'', $w''Rw'$)

(c) $p \supset LMMp$ (If wRw' then $w'R^2w$)

(d) $MLp \supset Mp$

      (If wRw' then there is some w'' such that wRw'' and $w'Rw''$.)

(e) $ML(p \land \sim p) \lor (q \supset LMq)$

              (Either w can see a dead end or if wRw' then $w'Rw$.)

7.2 Prove that T +

  Mk $L(LLp \supset Lq) \supset (Lp \supset q)$

is characterized by reflexive frames which satisfy the condition

  C $\forall w_1 \exists w_2(w_1Rw_2 \land w_2Rw_1 \land \forall w_3(w_2R^2w_3 \supset w_1Rw_3))$

7.3 Use canonical models to prove the completeness of the systems which result by adding to K4 the axiom listed, with respect to transitive frames which satisfy the conditions indicated:

Lem₀ $L((p \land Lp) \supset q) \lor L((q \land Lq) \supset p)$

        (If wRw' and wRw'' and $w' \neq w''$ then $w'Rw''$ or $w''Rw'$)

H1 $\quad p \supset L(Mp \supset p)$

$\qquad$ (If wRw' and $w'Rw''$ then either $w = w'$ or $w' = w''$)

G$_0$ $\quad M(p \wedge Lq) \supset L(p \vee Mq)$

$\qquad$ (If w_1Rw_2 and w_1Rw_3 and $w_2 \neq w_3$ then there is some w_4 such that w_2Rw_4 and w_3Rw_4)

7.4 $\quad$ KAlt$_n$ is K +

Alt$_n$ $\quad Lp_1 \vee L(p_1 \supset p_2) \vee \ldots \vee L((p_1 \wedge \ldots \wedge p_n) \supset p_{n+1})$

Prove that KAlt$_n$ is characterized by the class of frames in which every world can see at most n worlds.

7.5 $\quad$ Prove that S5 is characterized by a single cohesive frame.

7.6 $\quad$ Prove that no consistent system containing **B** has a canonical model based on a cohesive frame.

7.7 $\quad$ Prove that KB + $(Lp \wedge p) \supset LLp$ is characterized by frames in which

$\qquad$ (i) $\quad$ if wRw' and $w \neq w''$ and $w'Rw''$ then wRw''

$\qquad$ (ii) $\quad wRw'$ iff $w \neq w'$

7.8 $\quad$ RD (the 'rule of disjunction') is the rule that if $\vdash L\alpha_1 \vee \ldots \vee L\alpha_n$ then either $\vdash \alpha_i$ for some $1 \leq i \leq n$. Prove that if RD is a rule of S then the canonical model of S contains a world that can see every world.

7.9 $\quad$ Prove that K, T, S4, and KW provide the rule of disjunction.

7.10 $\quad$ Prove that B, S4.2 and S5 do not provide the rule of disjunction

7.11 $\quad$ Prove that K1.1 (S4 + **J1**, $L(L(p \supset Lp) \supset p) \supset p$) is not canonical. (Hughes and Cresswell 1982.)

Notes

[1] Prior 1957, Chapter 2. For a later and fuller introduction to the whole topic of the temporal interpretation of modal logics see Prior 1967.

[2] Prior 1957, p. 23. See also Prior 1955b.

[3] Prior 1958.

[4] The name S4.3 comes from Dummett and Lemmon 1959, p. 252. See also Kripke 1963a, p. 95. The completeness of S4.3 is proved (algebraically) in Bull

1965a. See also Prior 1962.

[5] Segerberg 1971, p. 75

[6] Segerberg 1971, p. 78. Hughes and Cresswell 1984, pp. 84–86. The completeness of S4.3 when time has the structure of the rational numbers of the real numbers with R as $\leq$ is proved in Segerberg 1970. When time has the structure of the natural numbers the system required is stronger than S4.3. (It is S4.3.1, see p. 180.) Where L means 'it always will be the case that' (so that R is irreflexive) the required system is K4.3, i.e. K4 + $\mathbf{Lem_0}$ $L((p \land Lp) \supset q) \lor L((q \land Lq) \supset p)$.

[7] The name $\mathbf{M}$ is given in Lemmon and Scott 1977, p. 74 after a system discussed in McKinsey 1945 and called by him S4.1. This name is misleading since S4M is not a subsystem of S4.2. Further, Sobociński 1964a, 1964c has used the name S4.1 for a system between S4 and S4.2. (See Hughes and Cresswell 1968, pp. 265–67.) Sobociński's name for S4M is K1. The derivation of $\mathbf{F}$ in S4M is on p. 75.

[8] Lemmon and Scott 1977, p. 74.

[9] $\mathbf{G1}$ was so named (see Dummett and Lemmon 1959, p. 252) after P.T. Geach, who had suggested it as an addition to S4 to reduce the number of distinct modalities and order them linearly. S4.2 is S4, i.e. K + $\mathbf{T}$ ($= Lp \supset p$) + $\mathbf{4}$ ($= Lp \supset LLp$), + $\mathbf{G1}$.

[10] Examples of further extensions of K4 (i.e K + $Lp \supset LLp$) with a fairly extensive discussion may be found in volume 2 of Segerberg 1971. He also contains a discussion of the Alt systems mentioned in exercise 7.14. For a discussion of modalities in the Alt logics added to B see Ullrich and Byrd 1977 and Byrd 1978.

[11] Cohesive frames allow chains to go forwards or backwards. For some purposes we might want to consider what are called *generated frames*. A frame $\langle W,R \rangle$ is *generated* iff there is some $w^* \in W$ such that every $w \in W$ is on an R-chain from w^* – i.e., if $w \in W$ then w^*R^nw for some n $\geq$ 0. Where $\langle W,R \rangle$ is any frame, generated or not, and $w^* \in W$ then $\langle W^*,R^* \rangle$ is called the *subframe of* $\langle W,R \rangle$ *generated by* w^* iff (i) $w \in W^*$ provided $w \in W$ and w^*R^nw for some n $\geq$ 0, and (ii) for w, $w' \in W^*$, wR^*w' iff wRw'. Where $\langle W,R,V \rangle$ is any model and $\langle W^*,R^* \rangle$ is the subframe of $\langle W,R \rangle$ generated by w^* then $\langle W^*,R^*,V^* \rangle$ is called the *sub-model of* $\langle W,R,V \rangle$ generated by w^* iff for $w \in W^*$, $V^*(p,w) = V(p,w)$. A straightforward induction establishes that for $w \in W^*$ and any wff α, $V^*(\alpha,w) = V(\alpha,w)$. From this it follows that a wff is valid on a frame iff it is valid on all its generated subframes, and so any class of frames can be replaced by a class of generated frames. See Hughes and Cresswell 1984, pp. 77–81. Generated frames are used in Segerberg 1980 to formalize the logic of 'elsewhere' (where R is $\neq$) mentioned in von Wright 1979. See exercise 7.7 and Jansana 1994.

[12] This proof is a variation of that given on p. 96 of Hughes and Cresswell 1984 that the canonical model of any system which provides the rule of disjunction (see

p. 71) has a world which can see every world. This result was obtained by a different method in van Benthem 1979a.

[13] Segerberg 1971, p. 84. It is called G in Boolos 1979. For a more recent survey of the history of provability logic see Boolos and Sambin 1990. The system dates at least from Löb 1966.

[14] The use of 'canonical' in this sense is due to Fine 1975a.

8

FINITE MODELS

The finite model property

So far all our completeness proofs have been based on canonical models, and the technique has been to show that for any system S which is to be proved complete with respect to a class $\mathscr{E}$ of frames, the frame of S's canonical model is in $\mathscr{E}$. This gives an immediate completeness result since only the theorems of S are valid in S's canonical model. But we saw at the end of the last chapter that you can have systems where the frame of the canonical model cannot be in *any* class of frames which characterizes S, since not all theorems are valid on that frame. In this chapter we shall look at the question of when a system can be characterized by a class of *finite* frames. It will turn out that the standard systems, including KW, are so characterized, but that not every system is. Systems for which we can prove soundness and completeness with respect to a class of finite frames are said to have the *finite model property*.

Establishing the finite model property

Now the canonical model of a system S proved very useful because in a single model you have as valid all and only the theorems of S. But that is a stronger result than we need for completeness. Look at it this way. We need to show that for any wff α, if α is $\mathscr{E}$-valid then $\vdash_S \alpha$. Put in an equivalent way we need to show that if $\dashv_S \alpha$, then there is a model based on a frame in $\mathscr{E}$ in which α is not valid. And this in turn can be shown if we can show that for any S-consistent set of the form $\{\alpha\}$ there is a model $\langle W,R,V \rangle$ where $\langle W,R \rangle \in \mathscr{E}$ and for some $w \in W$, $V(\alpha,w) = 1$. It is clear that the frame of the canonical model is not finite, but in producing a model to falsify α we do not need to consider *all* the wff of modal logic, since the truth-value of α depends only on the truth-values, in the worlds of the model, of its well-formed parts, i.e. its sub-formulae.

The idea of a wf part of a wff α should be clear. If α is $L(p \lor \sim L(\sim p \lor q)) \lor \sim q$, its wf parts are α itself and $L(p \lor \sim L(\sim p \lor q))$, $\sim q$, $(p \lor \sim L(\sim p \lor q))$, $\sim L(\sim p \lor q)$, $L(\sim p \lor q)$, $(\sim p \lor q)$, $\sim p$, p and q. Note that α is always a wf part of itself. If we wish to exclude this we speak of a *proper* part of α.

For a given wff α then the idea is that we make a kind of 'mini canonical model' using only the wf parts of α. For each α this model will be finite, but otherwise it will behave just like the real canonical model, and we can use it to establish the finite model property for many systems.[1] In the case of KW we shall be able to use it to establish a completeness result where the canonical model method does not work.

We define the mini canonical model based on a wff α as follows. Let Φ_α be the set $\{\beta : \beta$ is a sub-formula of $\alpha\}$ and let Φ_α^+ be $\Phi_\alpha \cup \{\sim\beta : \beta \in \Phi_\alpha\}$. Clearly both Φ_α and Φ_α^+ are finite. Say that a set Γ of wff is α-maximal S-consistent (for short mc) iff $\Gamma \subseteq \Phi_\alpha^+$ and

(i) For all $\beta \in \Phi_\alpha$ either $\beta \in \Gamma$ or $\sim\beta \in \Gamma$ (α-maximality)

(ii) Where $\Gamma = \{\gamma_1, \ldots, \gamma_n\}$ then not $\vdash_S \sim(\gamma_1 \land \ldots \land \gamma_n)$ (S-consistency)

[Note that (ii) is equivalent to the 'regular' definition – *viz* there is no *subset* $\Lambda \subseteq \Gamma$, where $\Lambda = \{\gamma_1, \ldots, \gamma_n\}$ and $\vdash_S \sim(\gamma_1 \land \ldots \land \gamma_n)$.] The results which follow parallel those obtained in chapter 6 except that the sets here are mc only in Φ_α^+.

LEMMA 8.1 If $\beta \in \Phi_\alpha$ then exactly one of β and $\sim\beta \in \Gamma$.

Proof: By maximality at least one is and by consistency both cannot be, since $\vdash_S \sim(\beta \land \sim\beta)$.

LEMMA 8.2 If $\beta \lor \gamma \in \Phi_\alpha$ then $\beta \lor \gamma \in \Gamma$ iff either $\beta \in \Gamma$ or $\gamma \in \Gamma$.

Proof: If $\beta \lor \gamma \in \Gamma$ but $\beta \notin \Gamma$ and $\gamma \notin \Gamma$ then if $\beta \lor \gamma \in \Phi_\alpha$ so are β and γ and so $\sim\beta \in \Gamma$ and $\sim\gamma \in \Gamma$. But then $\{\sim\beta, \sim\gamma, \beta \lor \gamma\} \subseteq \Gamma$ and $\vdash_S \sim(\sim\beta \land \sim\gamma \land (\beta \lor \gamma))$ so Γ would not be consistent. If

$\beta \lor \gamma \notin \Gamma$ then since $\beta \lor \gamma \in \Phi_\alpha$, $\sim(\beta \lor \gamma) \in \Gamma$, but if $\beta \in \Gamma$, $\{\sim(\beta \lor \gamma), \beta\} \subseteq \Gamma$, but $\vdash_S \sim(\sim(\beta \lor \gamma) \land \beta)$ so $\beta \notin \Gamma$ and if $\gamma \in \Gamma$ then $\{\sim(\beta \lor \gamma), \gamma\} \subseteq \Gamma$, but $\vdash_S \sim(\sim(\beta \lor \gamma) \land \gamma)$ so $\gamma \notin \Gamma$.

LEMMA 8.3   If $\Lambda \subseteq \Phi_\alpha^+$ and Λ is S-consistent then there is an mc Γ such that $\Lambda \subseteq \Gamma$.

Proof: Construct Γ as follows. Order the wff of Φ_α^+, $\beta_1, \ldots, \beta_n$. Let $\Gamma_0 = \Lambda$ and for $0 \leq k < n$ let $\Gamma_{k+1} = \Gamma_k \cup \{\beta_{k+1}\}$ if this is consistent and $\Gamma_k \cup \{\sim\beta_{k+1}\}$ otherwise. If neither is consistent then where β_0 is the conjunction of wff in Λ, we have $\vdash_S (\beta_0 \land \ldots \land \beta_k) \supset \beta_{k+1}$ and $\vdash_S (\beta_0 \land \ldots \land \beta_k) \supset \sim\beta_{k+1}$, and so $\vdash_S \sim(\beta_0 \land \ldots \land \beta_k)$, i.e. Γ_k is inconsistent. So given that Γ_0 is consistent so is Γ_n. But Γ_n is mc.

Given that α is not a theorem of S the aim is to construct a model based on a frame in $\mathcal{E}$ in which α is false. Call this model $\langle W_\alpha, R_\alpha, V_\alpha \rangle$, though unless it matters we may speak simply of $\langle W, R, V \rangle$. W is the set of all α-maximal S-consistent sets of wff. Where S is K, T or D, we let R be defined as in the canonical model. To be specific, for $w, w' \in W$, wRw' iff for all $L\gamma \in w$, $\gamma \in w'$, i.e. iff $L^-(w) \subseteq w'$. For $p \in \Phi_\alpha$, let $V(p,w) = 1$ iff $p \in w$. For $p \notin \Phi_\alpha$ the definition is arbitrary.

THEOREM 8.4   For $\beta \in \Phi_\alpha$ and $w \in W$, $V(\beta,w) = 1$ iff $\beta \in w$.

Proof: The result is defined to hold for the variables. Consider $\sim\beta \in \Phi_\alpha$. Since $\sim\beta \in \Phi_\alpha$ then so is β, and we may assume the result for β. So $V(\sim\beta,w) = 1$ iff $V(\beta,w) = 0$, iff $\beta \notin W$ iff $\sim\beta \in w$. Consider $\beta \lor \gamma$. If $\beta \lor \gamma \in \Phi_\alpha$ then so are β and γ and we may assume the result for both β and γ. So $V(\beta \lor \gamma,w) = 1$ iff $V(\beta,w) = 1$ or $V(\gamma,w) = 1$, iff $\beta \in w$ or $\gamma \in w$. But $\beta \lor \gamma \in \Phi_\alpha$. So by lemma 8.2 this last holds iff $(\beta \lor \gamma) \in w$.

Suppose $L\beta \in w$ and wRw', then $\beta \in w'$, and so $\beta \in \Phi_\alpha$, so $V(\beta,w') = 1$. So $V(L\beta,w) = 1$.

Suppose $L\beta \notin w$ but $L\beta \in \Phi_\alpha$. Then $\sim L\beta \in w$. Lemma 6.4 on p. 117 guarantees that $\{\gamma: L\gamma \in w\} \cup \{\sim\beta\}$ is S-consistent. Now note that every member of $\{\gamma: L\gamma \in w\} \cup \{\sim\beta\}$ is in Φ_α except possibly $\sim\beta$. But $\sim\beta \in \Phi_\alpha^+$. So if $\{\gamma: L\gamma \in w\} \cup \{\sim\beta\}$ is consistent then by lemma 8.3 there will be an mc w' with wRw', and $\sim\beta \in w'$. So $\beta \notin w'$. But $\beta \in \Phi_\alpha$ since $L\beta \in \Phi_\alpha$ and so $V(\beta,w') = 0$ and so $V(L\beta,w) = 0$. This proves theorem 8.4.

This immediately gives us the fact that K has the finite model property since $\langle W_\alpha, R_\alpha \rangle$ is certainly a frame, and in the case of K, $\mathscr{E}$ is the class of all frames.

For T we must show that $\langle W_\alpha, R_\alpha \rangle$ is reflexive, and for D that it is serial. In the case of T we have to show that for any $w \in W$ and any $L\beta \in w$, if $L\beta \in w$ then $\beta \in w$. (Obviously if $L\beta \in \Phi_\alpha$ then $\beta \in \Phi_\alpha$.) Note that there may not be any wff at all of the form $L\beta$ in w, as for instance if α contains no modal operators. In that case $L^-(w)$ would be empty, and trivially $L^-(w) \subseteq w$. If $L^-(w) \not\subseteq w$ then there would have to be some $\beta \in \Phi_\alpha$ such that $L\beta \in w$ but $\beta \notin w$. Since $\beta \in \Phi_\alpha$ but $\beta \notin w$, $\sim\beta \in w$. But then $\{L\beta, \sim\beta\} \subseteq w$, and since $\vdash_T \sim(L\beta \land \sim\beta)$, w would be inconsistent. In the case of D, if R were not serial there would have to be a $w \in W$ such that there is no w' such that $L^-(w) \subseteq w'$. But this means that $L^-(w)$ is inconsistent. So there are $L\beta_1, \dots, L\beta_n \in w$ such that

$$\vdash_D \sim(\beta_1 \land \dots \land \beta_n)$$

So by N,

$$\vdash_D L\sim(\beta_1 \land \dots \land \beta_n)$$

so by **D**

$$\vdash_D \sim L(\beta_1 \land \dots \land \beta_n)$$
so
$$\vdash_D \sim(L\beta_1 \land \dots \land L\beta_n).$$

But $\{L\beta_1, \dots, L\beta_n\} \subseteq w$, and this would make w inconsistent.

Even in these cases it can be seen that the proofs need to be a little more complicated than in the case of the proofs by canonical models, for the worlds in these frames are made up using only sub-formulae of α or their negations. When we move to S4 this becomes even more of a problem. For recall how we proved that R in the canonical model of S4 is transitive. We reasoned that since $L\beta \in w$ then (by $Lp \supset LLp$) $LL\beta \in w$. However we now have no guarantee that $LL\beta$ will be in Φ_α just because $L\beta$ is, and so we cannot use this method. There are a number of ways around this problem. The simplest is to *change the definition* of R.[2] Instead of saying that wRw' if wherever $L\beta \in w$ then $\beta \in w'$ we say that wherever $L\beta \in w$ then $L\beta \in w'$. (If we use $L(w)$ for $\{L\beta : L\beta \in w\}$

then we could say that wRw' iff $L(w) \subseteq w'$.) Now it is clear that R as so defined is transitive. It is also clear that theorem 8.4 holds in respect of the variables and the truth-functional operators. But because we have changed the definition of R we now have to establish the induction for L:

Suppose $L\beta \in w$ and wRw', then $L\beta \in w'$. Since $L\beta \in \Phi_\alpha$, $\beta \in \Phi_\alpha$ and so by the T-axiom $\beta \in w'$ (since otherwise $\sim\beta$ would be, making w' inconsistent). So $V(\beta,w') = 1$. So $V(L\beta,w) = 1$. Suppose $L\beta \notin w$ but $L\beta \in \Phi_\alpha$. Then $\sim L\beta \in w$. We show that the following set is S-consistent:

$$\Lambda = \{L\gamma : L\gamma \in w\} \cup \{\sim\beta\}$$

Note that every member of Λ is in Φ_α except possibly $\sim\beta$. But $\beta \in \Phi_\alpha$. So if Λ is consistent then by lemma 8.3 there will be an mc w' with $\Lambda \subseteq w'$. For such a w' we have wRw'. Let $L\gamma_1, \ldots , L\gamma_n$ be all the wff beginning with L in w. Then if Λ were inconsistent

$$\vdash_{S4} \sim(L\gamma_1 \wedge \ldots \wedge L\gamma_n \wedge \sim\beta)$$

so $\quad \vdash_{S4} (L\gamma_1 \wedge \ldots \wedge L\gamma_n) \supset \beta$

so $\quad \vdash_{S4} L(L\gamma_1 \wedge \ldots \wedge L\gamma_n) \supset L\beta$

so $\quad \vdash_{S4} (LL\gamma_1 \wedge \ldots \wedge LL\gamma_n) \supset L\beta$

so, since $\vdash_{S4} Lp \equiv LLp$,

$$\vdash_{S4} (L\gamma_1 \wedge \ldots \wedge L\gamma_n) \supset L\beta$$

so $\vdash_{S4} \sim(L\gamma_1 \wedge \ldots \wedge L\gamma_n \wedge \sim L\beta)$.

But $\{L\gamma_1, \ldots , L\gamma_n, \sim L\beta\} \subseteq w$, and so w would be inconsistent. Since wRw' and $\sim\beta \in w'$ then $\beta \notin w'$. But $\beta \in \Phi_\alpha$ since $L\beta \in \Phi_\alpha$ and so $V(\beta,w') = 0$ and so $V(L\beta,w) = 0$. This proves that theorem 8.4 also holds in the case of S4. Since $\dashv_S \alpha$ then $\{\sim\alpha\}$ is consistent and so, since $\alpha \in \Phi_\alpha$, $\sim\alpha \in w$ for some $w \in W$. So $V(\alpha,w) = 0$. Thus S4 has the finite model property.

We can adapt the result to K4 by defining wRw' iff $L(w) \cup L^-(w) \subseteq w'$. For B we have wRw' iff $L^-(w) \subseteq w'$ and $L^-(w') \subseteq w$; for S5 wRw'

iff $L(w) = L(w')$, and so on. What is of course specific to each system is the definition of R. Given any system S, to prove by this method that S has the finite model property, we must find a definition of R which (a) makes the resulting frame a frame for S, and (b) enables us to prove the analogue for S of theorem 8.4 – i.e. the theorem that establishes that truth at a world is equivalent to membership of that world. And this is a non-trivial task, which must be attempted system by system.[3]

The completeness of KW

We showed in the last chapter that KW is not canonical. Nevertheless it is complete, and its completeness can be proved by the methods of the present chapter.[4] For KW the relevant class $\mathscr{E}$ of frames is frames which are finite, irreflexive and transitive. It is not hard to see that **W** is valid on all such frames, and therefore that KW is sound with respect to $\mathscr{E}$-validity. We now prove completeness. We note first that **4** – $Lp \supset LLp$ – is a theorem of KW. The proof is as follows:

PC	(1)	$p \supset ((Lp \wedge LLp) \supset (p \wedge Lp))$
$(1) \times$ DR1	(2)	$Lp \supset L((Lp \wedge LLp) \supset (p \wedge Lp))$
$(2) \times$ K3	(3)	$Lp \supset L(L(p \wedge Lp) \supset (p \wedge Lp))$
$(2) \times$ **W**	(3)	$Lp \supset L(p \wedge Lp)$
$(3) \times$ K1 $\times$ PC	(4)	$Lp \supset LLp$ Q.E.D.

We assume the methods of the previous section, but will prove the appropriate version of theorem 8.4 explicitly for KW. We proceed as follows. Given that α is not a KW-theorem the aim is to construct a finite irreflexive and transitive model in which α is false. W is the set of all α-maximal KW consistent sets of wff. For w, $w' \in W$, wRw' iff

(i) For all $L\gamma \in w$, $L\gamma$, $\gamma \in w'$
(ii) There is some $L\beta \in w'$ such that $L\beta \notin w$.

Note that if $L\gamma \in w$ and $L\beta \in w'$ then $L\gamma \in \Phi_\alpha$ and $L\beta \in \Phi_\alpha$. For $p \in \Phi_\alpha$, let $V(p,w) = 1$ iff $p \in w$. For $p \notin \Phi_\alpha$ the definition is arbitrary.

THEOREM 8.4′   For $\beta \in \Phi_\alpha$ and $w \in W$, $V(\beta,w) = 1$ iff $\beta \in w$.

Proof: As before the result is defined to hold for the variables and is preserved by $\sim$ and $\vee$.
Suppose $L\beta \in w$ and wRw'. Then $\beta \in w'$, and so $\beta \in \Phi_\alpha$, so

150

$V(\beta,w') = 1$. So $V(L\beta,w) = 1$. Suppose $L\beta \notin w$ but $L\beta \in \Phi_\alpha$. Then $\sim L\beta \in w$. We show that the following set is KW consistent:

$$\Lambda = \{L\gamma: L\gamma \in w\} \cup \{\gamma: L\gamma \in w\} \cup \{L\beta, \sim\beta\}$$

Note that every member of Λ is in Φ_α except possibly $\sim\beta$. But $\beta \in \Phi_\alpha$. So if Λ is consistent then by lemma 8.3 there will be an mc w' with $\Lambda \subseteq w'$. For such a w' we have

(i) If $L\gamma \in w$ then $L\gamma \in w'$
(ii) If $L\gamma \in w$ then $\gamma \in w'$
(iii) $L\beta \in w'$ but $L\beta \notin w$.

These three conditions ensure that wRw'. Let $L\gamma_1, \ldots, L\gamma_n$ be all the wff beginning with L in w. Then if Λ were inconsistent

$$\vdash_{KW} \sim(L\gamma_1 \wedge \ldots \wedge L\gamma_n \wedge \gamma_1 \wedge \ldots \wedge \gamma_n \wedge L\beta \wedge \sim\beta)$$

so $\quad \vdash_{KW} (L\gamma_1 \wedge \ldots \wedge L\gamma_n \wedge \gamma_1 \wedge \ldots \wedge \gamma_n) \supset (L\beta \supset \beta)$

so $\quad \vdash_{KW} L(L\gamma_1 \wedge \ldots \wedge L\gamma_n \wedge \gamma_1 \wedge \ldots \wedge \gamma_n) \supset L(L\beta \supset \beta)$

so $\quad \vdash_{KW} (LL\gamma_1 \wedge \ldots \wedge LL\gamma_n \wedge L\gamma_1 \wedge \ldots \wedge L\gamma_n) \supset L(L\beta \supset \beta)$

so, since $\vdash_{KW} Lp \supset LLp$,

$$\vdash_{KW} (L\gamma_1 \wedge \ldots \wedge L\gamma_n) \supset L(L\beta \supset \beta)$$

so, by **W**,

$$\vdash_{KW} (L\gamma_1 \wedge \ldots \wedge L\gamma_n) \supset L\beta$$

so $\quad \vdash_{KW} \sim(L\gamma_1 \wedge \ldots \wedge L\gamma_n \wedge \sim L\beta)$.

But $\{L\gamma_1, \ldots, L\gamma_n, \sim L\beta\} \subseteq w$ and so w would be inconsistent. Since wRw' and $\sim\beta \in w'$ then $\beta \notin w'$. But $\beta \in \Phi_\alpha$ since $L\beta \in \Phi_\alpha$ and so $V(\beta,w') = 0$ and so $V(L\beta,w) = 0$. This proves theorem 8.4'.

Since $\alpha \in \Phi_\alpha$ and $\dashv_{KW} \alpha$ then $\{\sim\alpha\}$ is consistent and so $\sim\alpha \in w$ for some $w \in W$. So $V(\alpha,w) = 0$. It is clear that $\langle W_\alpha, R_\alpha, V_\alpha \rangle$ is finite, irreflexive and transitive, so α fails in such a model.

The word 'finite' here is crucial. The system characterized by *all* transitive irreflexive frames is K4. That does not mean that K4 lacks the finite model property – in fact we proved on p. 149 that K4 has that property. But although K4 is characterized by the class of all finite transitive frames and by the class of all transitive and irreflexive frames it is not characterized by any class of finite transitive and irreflexive frames.

Decidability

A system S (not necessarily a modal system) is said to be decidable iff there is an effective procedure whereby, for any given wff α, it can be determined in a finite number of steps whether or not α is a theorem of S. Some systems of logic are known to be decidable, others are known not to be decidable, and of yet others it is not known whether they are decidable or not. This is so for modal as well as for non-modal systems. There is no effective procedure for determining, for an arbitrary system of logic, even for an arbitrary normal modal system, whether or not it is decidable.

There is, however, a certain connection between possession of the finite model property and decidability. We shall now prove that this connection holds.[5]

THEOREM 8.5   If S is a finitely axiomatizable normal modal system which has the finite model property, then S is decidable.

Proof: Let S be a system of the kind described. To say that S is finitely axiomatizable (see p. 50) is to say that there is a finite collection Λ of wff such that the theorems of S are precisely those wff which can be derived from the formulae in Λ, together with PC-tautologies and K, by the rules US, MP and N. This means that any frame $\mathscr{F}$ is a frame for S iff every wff in Λ is valid on $\mathscr{F}$. Moreover, if $\mathscr{F}$ is finite, there will be a finite (and obviously effective) procedure for checking whether or not all the (finitely many) wff in Λ are valid on $\mathscr{F}$, and thus whether or not $\mathscr{F}$ is a frame for S. Now it is not difficult to see that, if we disregard isomorphic duplicates, there is an effective procedure for generating all finite frames in some definite order, and therefore for generating all the finite frames for S in some definite order (since each finite frame can be effectively checked for whether or not it is a frame for S). Since S has the finite model property, if α is not a theorem of S then it is invalid on some finite frame for S; and therefore, in our effectively generated sequence of finite frames for S there will (eventually!) appear one on which α is invalid. If α is a theorem of S, then of course a frame on which it is invalid will never appear in the sequence we have described. There is, however, also an effective procedure for generating all the proofs of theorems of S in some definite order. (A proof of a theorem α of S is a finite sequence of wff in which each wff is either a PC-tautology, or K, or a member of Λ, or a wff derived from some earlier wff in the sequence by US, MP or N, and in which α is the last member. α is a theorem of S iff there is such a proof of α.) Hence if α is a theorem of S, a proof of α will (again, eventually!) appear in this generated sequence of proofs. Since any wff α either is or is not a theorem of S, therefore, either a frame on which α is invalid will appear in a finite number of steps in the first sequence, or a proof of α will appear in a finite number of steps in the second sequence (but not, of course, both). In the former case, α is not a theorem of S; in the latter case it is.

This gives an effective procedure for determining of any wff whether or not it is a theorem of S, and so proves the theorem. (We are not, of course, suggesting that the procedure we have described would be of much use in actual practice for discovering whether some particular formula is a theorem of S or not. For some of the best-known systems more practical procedures are described in Chapter 4, and the methods explained there can easily be adapted for many other systems as well.)

It is important to notice what theorem 8.5 does not say as well as what it does. First, it is only for finitely axiomatizable systems that possession of the finite model property guarantees decidability. There are, in fact, systems which have the finite model property but are undecidable, though of course they are not finitely axiomatizable.[6] Second, even if we confine our attention to finitely axiomatizable systems, possession of the finite model property, although a sufficient condition of decidability, is not a necessary one. There are, in fact, finitely axiomatizable systems which are decidable but which lack the finite model property. Third, theorem 8.5 does not say that every decidable system with the finite model property is finitely axiomatizable. There are in fact systems of this kind which are not.[7]

Systems without the finite model property

That a system has the finite model property is by no means a trivial fact, for there are systems which lack this property. The first published proof that a normal propositional modal system lacks the finite model property was given by David Makinson and we shall adapt his proof.[8] The system we shall discuss may be called Mk and is T with the addition of the single extra axiom.

Mk $L(LLp \supset Lq) \supset (Lp \supset q)$

Mk is characterized by the class of reflexive frames which satisfy the condition

C $\forall w_1 w_2(w_1 R w_2 \land w_2 R w_1 \land \forall w_3(w_2 R^2 w_3 \supset w_1 R w_3))$

where $w_2 R^2 w_3$ means that there is some w such that $w_2 R w$ and $w R w_3$. C says that every world can see some world which (a) can see it in return, and (b) is such that whatever it can see in two steps, the original world can see in one. It is easy to check that Mk is sound with respect to models satisfying C, and it is also straightforward to establish that the canonical model of Mk satisfies C, thus yielding completeness.

Our present task however is to establish that Mk does indeed lack the finite model property. We shall do this by showing that every *finite* reflexive frame on which **Mk** is valid is transitive. So if $\mathcal{E}$ is any class of finite frames for Mk, $Lp \supset LLp$ would be $\mathcal{E}$-valid; and so if such a class were to characterize Mk, $Lp \supset LLp$ would have to be a theorem. But we shall show that $Lp \supset LLp$ is not a theorem of Mk, and so Mk does not have the finite model property.

First then to show that every finite reflexive frame on which **Mk** is valid is transitive. If $\langle W,R \rangle$ is any frame then we say that $w_1, \dots, w_n$ form a *non-transitive chain of length n* (for $n \geq 3$) iff for $1 \leq i < n$, $w_i R w_{i+1}$, where $w_i \neq w_j$ for $1 \leq i \neq j \leq n$, and not $w_1 R w_i$ for any $i > 2$. A non-transitive chain looks like this

$w_1 \to w_2 \dots \to w_n$

where each w_i is distinct and w_1 cannot see any other world in the chain besides itself and w_2. If $\langle W,R \rangle$ is non-transitive then it has at least one non-transitive chain, and if it is finite it will have a maximal non-transitive chain, where a maximal chain is a chain of length n and there is no non-transitive chain of greater length in the frame, though there may be other chains of equal length.

Given that $\langle W,R \rangle$ is a finite non-transitive reflexive frame and that $w_1, \dots, w_n$ is a maximal non-transitive chain, we show that **Mk** is not valid on $\langle W,R \rangle$ by showing that it can be falsified at w_1. Let $\langle W,R,V \rangle$ be a model based on $\langle W,R \rangle$ in which p is true everywhere *except* at w_3, ... , w_n, and q is true everywhere *except* at w_1. Then $Lp \supset q$ is false at w_1. Now consider $L(LLp \supset Lq)$ and consider any w such that w_1Rw. (a) If not wRw_1, then $V(Lq,w) = 1$ since q is only false at w_1, and so in this case $V(LLp \supset Lq,w) = 1$. (b) If wRw_i for any $1 < i \le n$, $V(LLp,w) = 0$ and so again $V(LLp \supset Lq,w) = 1$. From (a) and (b), if w_1Rw then wRw_1 but not wRw_i for $1 < i < n$. But then, if w_1Rw and not wRw_i for $1 < i \le n$, then $w, w_1, \ldots, w_n$ will be a non-transitive chain of length greater than n, contradicting the fact that $w_1, \ldots, w_n$ is a maximal chain. (Reflexiveness is needed for the case i = n.) So $V(LLp \supset Lq,w) = 1$ for every w such that w_1Rw and so $V(L(LLp \supset Lq),w_1) = 1$ so **Mk** is false at w_1.

It only remains to show that $Lp \supset LLp$ is not a theorem of Mk. For that purpose we produce a reflexive and non-transitive infinite frame on which **Mk** is valid. Since $Lp \supset LLp$ fails on any non-transitive frame this will show that $Lp \supset LLp$ is not a theorem of Mk. The frame we shall use is called the recession frame.[9] Its worlds are just the natural numbers 0, 1, ... etc. Each number can see (a) itself, (b) its immediate predecessor and (c) each greater number. Formally we say that wRw' iff $w \le w' + 1$. So let $\langle W,R \rangle$ be the recession frame and suppose that **Mk** is false at some n. Then

(i) $V(L(LLp \supset Lq),n) = 1$
(ii) $V(Lp,n) = 1$
(iii) $V(q,n) = 0$

From (ii) we have that $V(p,k) = 1$ for every $k \ge n-1$, and thus $V(Lp,k) = 1$ for every $k \ge n$, and thus

(iv) $V(LLp,n+1) = 1$

so from (i)

(v) $V(Lq,n+1) = 1$

But this contradicts (iii), and so establishes, by reductio ad absurdum, the validity of **Mk** on the recession frame. Since 2R1 and 1R0 but not 1R0, then the recession frame is non-transitive. In fact $Lp \supset LLp$ fails at 2 when p is false at 0 but true everywhere else.

This establishes that Mk lacks the finite model property.[10]

Exercises — 8

8.1 A modality is an unbroken sequence, possibly empty, of monadic operators ($\sim$, L, M). For any wff α, let Φ_α^M be the set of all wff $A\beta$ where β is any sub-formula of α and A is any modality. Let $\langle W,R,V \rangle$ be the mini canonical model for S4 based on Φ_α^M with R defined so that wRw' iff for every $L\gamma \in w$, $\gamma \in w'$. Show that R is reflexive and transitive, and explain why this shows that S4 has the finite model property.

8.2 Prove that the systems S4.2, S4.3, S4M all have the finite model property.

8.3 Prove that KW + **Lem$_0$** $(L((p \wedge Lp) \supset q) \vee L((q \wedge Lq) \supset p))$ is characterized by frames in which W is a finite initial segment of the natural numbers and R is $>$.

8.4 Prove that K1.1 (i.e. K + **J1**: $L(L(p \supset Lp) \supset p) \supset p)$) is characterized by finite frames in which W is reflexive, transitive and antisymmetrical. (You may assume that **4** is a theorem of K1.1.)

8.5 Let $\langle W,R \rangle$ be the following frame:
  (i) W is the set of all pairs $\langle n,m \rangle$ of natural numbers;
  (ii) $\langle n,m \rangle R \langle j,k \rangle$ iff $n \leq j$.
Prove that $\langle W,R \rangle$ characterizes S4.3.

8.6 Prove that every proper extension of S5 is S5Alt$_n$ for some n. (This is a difficult exercise. See Segerberg 1971, pp. 122–128.)

8.7 Mk* is T + $L(LLp \supset LLLp) \supset (Lp \supset LLp)$. Prove that Mk* lacks the finite model property.

8.8 Prove that K3.1 (i.e. K1.1 + **Lem$_0$**) is characterized by frames in which W is a finite initial segment of the natural numbers and R is $\geq$.

Notes

[1] The method described in the text shows how to give a direct construction of a finite model. A more widely used method is found in Lemmon and Scott 1977.

This method has become known as the method of 'filtrations' and consists in taking a model together with a wff α and making a finite model which is equivalent to it in respect of sub-formulae of α, or in respect of some nominated set of wff. An exposition of this method is found on pp. 136–145 of Hughes and Cresswell 1984. (Note that the completeness proof given for KW on pp. 145–148 of that work is defective. A correct proof appears in Hughes and Cresswell 1986.) The term 'filtration' appears to be due to Segerberg 1968a. The method of filtrations is also described and used to prove that a system has the finite model property in Segerberg 1971, Gabbay 1976 and Chellas 1980. A method of proving that a system has the finite model property without using filtrations may be found in Fine 1975b. Fine's method uses normal forms, and may be applied to all the systems discussed in this section. He is also able to use his method to prove that the system KM (i.e. K + the wff M discussed on p. 131 above) has the finite model property. Fine's method can be modified to yield a completeness proof for KM which has affinities with the mini canonical model type of completeness proof used in the present chapter (see Cresswell 1983a). The earliest proofs of the finite model property were obtained algebraically. See McKinsey 1941 (for S2 and S4), Bergmann 1949 (for S5), Bull 1964, 1965b (for various extensions of S4). Every extension of S5 not only has the finite model property but is characterized by a single finite frame. In fact it is Alt_n for some n. See Segerberg 1971, pp. 122–128 and Scroggs 1951. S5 itself is not so characterized; see Dugundji 1940.

[2] For some systems we may also need to extend Φ_α^+. (See Cresswell 1983b.)

[3] An even stronger result is known about S4.3. It was proved long ago, in Bull 1966, that not only S4.3 itself, but every normal extension of it, has the finite model property. Bull's proof was algebraic, but the same result has more recently been proved semantically in Fine 1971, Segerberg 1973a and Gabbay 1976. (See also Goldblatt 1987, pp. 60–63.) Fine, op. cit., has also proved that every normal extension of S4.3 is finitely axiomatizable. Another result which has been proved about S4.3 (in Segerberg 1975) is that in any system which contains all the theorems of S4.3 and has the rules US and MP, we can obtain N as a derived rule. In that sense, N would be a redundant item in an axiomatic basis for such a system. Bellissima and Mirolli 1983 show how to provide an axiomatization of the modal logic characterized by any particular finite frame.

[4] A completeness proof for KW is given on pp. 86–88 of Segerberg 1971 and in Chapter 7 of Boolos 1979. Boolos also provides a decision procedure for KW in the style of Chapter 4 above and extracts a completeness proof from it. (Indeed the techniques of that chapter yield alternative proofs of the finite model property for the systems treated there.) The proof of **4** given here is adapted from Boolos 1979, p. 30.

[5] This theorem is proved in Segerberg 1971, pp. 34–36. Note, however, that Segerberg uses the term 'axiomatizable' to mean what we mean by 'finitely axiomatizable', and uses 'finitely axiomatizable' to mean finitely axiomatizable *without* using N. In our terminology a (normal) logic S would be said to be

axiomatizable iff there is some effectively specifiable set Λ of wff such that S is $K + \Lambda$. The system presented in Urquhart 1981 can be adapted so that its axioms correspond to an arbitrary non-recursively enumerable set of numbers, and the resulting system will not be axiomatizable in the sense we are using.

[6] Urquhart 1981 has produced an example of such a system. Although it is not finitely axiomatizable, its axioms are effectively specifiable. Kracht 1991 provides a similar example which is an extension of S4. Conversely, there are finitely axiomatizable undecidable systems (which of course lack the finite model property). See Isard 1977.

[7] See the proof of this for the system BSeg in Cresswell 1979. (BSeg is $(MMp_1 \wedge \ldots \wedge MMp_n) \supset M(Mp_1 \wedge \ldots \wedge Mp_n)$, for $n > 1$. See Hughes and Cresswell 1975.)

[8] Makinson 1969. Makinson's system is in fact slightly weaker than Mk. It is T $+ L(LLp \supset LLLp) \supset (Lp \supset LLp)$. Interestingly no completeness proof appears to have been provided for this system. An extension of S4 without the finite model property is provided in Fine 1972.

[9] This name appears to be due to van Benthem 1978, p. 30. Blok 1979 axiomatizes the logic characterized by the recession frame in which the 'truth sets' of wff are finite or cofinite. (See p. 162.)

[10] As Gabbay 1976, pp. 258–265 shows, the fact that a system lacks the finite model property does not stop it from being decidable. See also Cresswell 1984.

9

INCOMPLETENESS

In previous chapters we have proved the completeness of a number of systems of modal logic, but always relative to some given class $\mathscr{E}$ of frames. In this chapter we show that there exist systems which are *incomplete* in the sense that there is *no* class $\mathscr{E}$ of frames such that their theorems are precisely the $\mathscr{E}$-valid wff. But we must first make some remarks about the difference between frames and models.

Frames and models

If we were to pose the question of completeness in terms of models, that is to say if we were to ask whether, for a given system S, there is always a class $\mathscr{E}$ of *models* such that α is $\mathscr{E}$-valid iff $\vdash_S \alpha$, the answer would have to be (trivially) yes. For the class consisting of the canonical model on its own would do the trick. But as we remarked on p. 112 validity in models may not be quite the appropriate notion. In fact validity in models lacks an important property: it is not preserved by all the transformation rules. In other words just because all members of a set Λ of wff of modal logic are valid in a model $\langle W,R,V \rangle$, it does not mean that all theorems of K + Λ are. It is, indeed, easy to show that MP and N are validity-preserving in a single model. For if both α and $\alpha \supset \beta$ are true in every world in W, then by [V$\supset$] so is β. And if α is true in every world in W, then *a fortiori* it is true in every world that any world in W can see; so $L\alpha$ will also be true in every world in W. The same, however, does not hold for US. For to say that US is validity-preserving in a single model would be to say that if a wff α is true in every world in a model, then so is every substitution-instance of α; and it is easy to see that this does not hold generally. To take the simplest case, it is a straightforward matter to define a model in which p is true in every world but q is not; yet q is certainly a substitution-instance of p. Of course, p is not an axiom of any normal modal system (at least not of any consistent one), but the same situation obtains even for a wff that is such an axiom. There is no difficulty, for instance, in defining a model in which $Lp \supset p$ is true in every world but $Lq \supset q$ is not. An example would be a model consisting of only two worlds, w_1 and w_2, where we have $w_1 R w_2$ but neither world is related to itself, and in which p is true in both worlds and q is false in w_1 and true in w_2.

So we cannot be sure that if a collection of wff are all valid in a given model, all the wff derived from them by US, MP and N are also valid in that model. What we *can* be sure of, however, is that these derived wff will be valid in the model if not only they themselves but all their substitution-instances are valid in it. This result can be stated as follows:

THEOREM 9.1   If every substitution-instance of every member of a set Λ of wff is valid in a model $\langle W, R, V \rangle$ then every theorem of K + Λ is valid in $\langle W, R, V \rangle$.

We outline how this theorem can be proved, but leave the details to the reader. Suppose we have a model $\langle W, R, V \rangle$. Let us say that a wff is *generalizable* iff all its substitution-instances are valid in $\langle W, R, V \rangle$. Then the hypothesis of the theorem is that all the axioms of S, i.e. all wff in Λ, are generalizable. The proof then takes the form of showing that any wff that is obtained from generalizable wff by any of the transformation rules (including US) is itself generalizable.

An incomplete modal system

KH is K with the addition of the single wff

H $L(Lp \equiv p) \supset Lp$

We show that KH is incomplete, i.e. that it is not characterized by any class of frames.[1] In order to show the incompleteness of KH it will be sufficient to show two things:

A   If **H** is valid on $\mathscr{F}$ then so is $Lp \supset LLp$.
B $Lp \supset LLp$ is not a theorem of KH.

First we must show why this establishes the incompleteness of KH. To say that KH is complete is to say that there is a class $\mathscr{E}$ of frames such that

C (i) If $\vdash_{KH} \alpha$ then α is valid on every $\mathscr{F} \in \mathscr{E}$.
   (ii) If α is valid on every $\mathscr{F} \in \mathscr{E}$, then $\vdash_{KH} \alpha$.

We show that C together with A and B leads to a contradiction. For consider any $\mathscr{F} \in \mathscr{E}$. Since $\vdash_{KH}$ **H**, then by C(i) **H** is valid on $\mathscr{F}$. But then, by A, $Lp \supset LLp$ is valid on $\mathscr{F}$. So by C(ii) $\vdash_{KH} Lp \supset LLp$. This contradicts B.

Proof of A: We prove A by contraposition. I.e. we show that if $Lp \supset LLp$ is not valid on $\mathscr{F}$ neither is **H**. Since $Lp \supset LLp$ is valid on every transitive frame, if $Lp \supset LLp$ is not valid on $\mathscr{F}$, there must be w_1, w_2, w_3, such that $w_1 R w_2$, $w_2 R w_3$ but not $w_1 R w_3$.

Divide the worlds into two classes as follows. If there is an R-chain (see p. 136) leading from w to w_3, let $V(p,w) = 0$. (In accordance with the definition of an R-chain given on p. 136 assume that there is a 0-step R-chain leading from w_3 to itself, and so put $V(p,w_3) = 0$.) If there is no such chain let $V(p,w) = 1$. First consider a w from which there is an R-chain leading to w_3. Now, unless w is w_3 itself, if w is on an R-chain to w_3, it can see at least one world w' also on an R-chain to w_3. So $V(p,w) = 0$ and $V(p,w') = 0$, and so $V(Lp,w) = 0$. Thus $V(Lp \equiv p,w) = 1$. Now consider a w from which there is *no* R-chain to w_3. If there is no such chain from w then there is also no such chain from any w' that w can see. So $V(p,w) = 1$ and $V(p,w') = 1$. So $V(Lp, w) = 1$ and so $V(Lp \equiv p, w) = 1$.

This means that $V(Lp \equiv p, w) = 1$, for every w except possibly w_3. But w_1 cannot see w_3, and so $V(Lp \equiv p, w) = 1$ for every w such that $w_1 Rw$. So $V(L(Lp \equiv p),w_1) = 1$. But w_2 is on a chain to w_3 and so $V(p, w_2) = 0$. So $V(Lp, w_1) = 0$ since $w_1 R w_2$. So **H** fails at w_1 in this frame, and thus every frame for **H** must be transitive, and must in consequence validate $Lp \supset LLp$. This establishes A.

Now theorem 9.1 guarantees that if α is any wff (here **H**) then any model which validates every substitution-instance of α, validates every theorem of $K + \alpha$. So, to establish B we must produce a model $\langle W,R,V \rangle$ on which *every instance* of **H** is valid, but $Lp \supset LLp$ is not.

Proof of B: Let $\mathscr{F}$ be the following frame: W consists of two parts. One part consists of the 'ordinary' natural numbers 0, 1, 2, ... etc. The other part is in fact the recession frame introduced in the last chapter and consists of a copy of the natural numbers, 0*, 1*, 2*, ... etc. Call the 'ordinary' part N, and the 'starred' part N*. Then W = N ∪ N*.
R is defined as follows:

(i)   For n, m ∈ N, mRm iff n > m.
(ii) For n*, m* ∈ N*, n* Rm* iff n ≤ m+1.
(iii) For m ∈ N, n* ∈ N*, n*Rm.

It might be easiest to imagine $\mathscr{F}$ (= $\langle$W,R$\rangle$) as follows:

$$\rightarrow$$
$$0^*\ 1^*\ 2^*\ ....\ n^*\ ...\ ...\ m\ ...\ 2\ \ 1\ \ 0$$

$$N^* \qquad\qquad\qquad N$$

The members of N, the 'ordinary' numbers can see only numbers less than themselves, and each member of N*, each starred number, can see itself, its immediate predecessor, all greater starred numbers (that is what (ii) says) and all 'ordinary' numbers.

We now define a model $\langle\mathscr{F},$V$\rangle$ based on $\mathscr{F}$. For every variable p, let V(p,0*) = 0 and for every w ≠ 0*, let V(p,w) = 1.

LEMMA 9.2   V($Lp \supset LLp$, 2*) = 0

Proof: Since 1*R0* and V(p,0*) = 0, then V(Lp,1*) = 0. Since 2*R1*, V(LLp,2*) = 0. But since not 2*R0*, then V(p,w) = 1 for every w such that 2*Rw. So V(Lp,2*) = 1. Thus V($Lp \supset LLp$,2*) = 0.
    The hard part is now to prove that every instance of **H** is valid in $\langle\mathscr{F},$V$\rangle$ in the sense of being true at every world in W. To do this we first show that all wff have a certain property. We use $|\alpha|$ to denote the 'truth set' of α:

$$|\alpha| = \{w \in W: V(\alpha,w) = 1\}$$

The truth set of a wff α is simply the set of worlds, in this model, at which α is true. Let us say that a subset A ⊆ W is *cofinite* iff its complement W−A (i.e. $\{w \in W: w \notin A\}$) is *finite*.

LEMMA 9.3   For any wff α, $|\alpha|$ is finite or cofinite.

Proof: The proof is by induction on the construction of α. If α is a variable, then by definition $|\alpha| = W - \{0^*\}$, since every variable is true everywhere except at 0^*. So $|\alpha|$ is cofinite. Obviously if $|\alpha|$ is finite then $|\sim\alpha|$ is cofinite, and *vice versa*. $|\alpha \vee \beta|$ is $|\alpha| \cup |\beta|$. If both $|\alpha|$ and $|\beta|$ are finite then so is $|\alpha| \cup |\beta|$. If either one is cofinite then so is $|\alpha| \cup |\beta|$.

For $L\alpha$, suppose first that $V(\alpha,n) = 0$ for some $n \in N$. Where $w \in N$ and $w > n$, or where $w \in N^*$, $V(L\alpha,w) = 0$, and so $|L\alpha|$ is finite. If $V(\alpha,n) = 1$ for all $n \in N$, then $|\alpha|$ is certainly not finite. So it must be cofinite, and since it is true throughout N, there must be a highest n^* for which $V(\alpha,n^*) = 0$. But then $V(L\alpha,w) = 1$ for $w = m^*$ with $m > n+1$, and for all $w \in N$. So $|L\alpha|$ is cofinite. (Obviously if $|\alpha| = W$ then also $|L\alpha| = W$.)

This proves lemma 9.3. To prove B all that remains is to prove the following theorem:

THEOREM 9.4   For every wff α, $L(L\alpha \equiv \alpha) \supset L\alpha$ is valid in $\langle \mathscr{F}, V \rangle$

Proof: First note that if $V(\alpha,w) = 1$ for all $w \in W$, then $V(L\alpha, w) = 1$ for all $w \in W$, and so (every instance of) H holds in this case. So suppose that $V(\alpha,w) = 0$ for some $w \in W$.

First suppose that $V(\alpha,n) = 0$ for some $n \in N$. (Possibly $n = 0$.) Without loss of generality we may suppose n to be the least number such that $V(\alpha,n) = 0$. Then for all $m < n$, $V(\alpha,m) = 1$ and so $V(L\alpha,m) = 1$ for all $m \leq n$, and so H is true at all such worlds. Since $V(\alpha,n) = 0$, and $V(L\alpha,n) = 1$ then $V(L\alpha \equiv \alpha,n) = 0$. So, where $w \in N$ and $w > n$, or where $w \in N^*$, $V(L(L\alpha \equiv \alpha), w) = 0$. So H is true at all these worlds also. So H is true at every world if $V(\alpha,n) = 0$ for some $n \in N$.

Finally consider the possibility that $V(\alpha,n) = 1$ for all $n \in N$. Then $|\alpha|$ is not finite, and so by lemma 9.3, $|\alpha|$ is cofinite. But also it is true throughout N, and so there must be a highest $n^* \in N$ for which $V(\alpha,n^*) = 0$. But then for all $m > n+1$, $V(L\alpha,m^*) = 1$ and for all $m \in N$, $V(L\alpha,m) = 1$. Thus H is true at all such worlds. But $V(L\alpha,(n+1)^*) = 0$, while $V(\alpha,(n+1)^*) = 1$. So $V(L\alpha \equiv \alpha,(n+1)^*) = 0$, and so for all $m \leq n+1$, $V(L(L\alpha \equiv \alpha),m^*) = 0$, and so H is true at all these worlds also. This proves the theorem and establishes the incompleteness of KH.

Notice how when α fails at $n \in N$, it is $L(L\alpha \supset \alpha)$ which fails, while when α fails at $n^* \in N^*$ it is $L(\alpha \supset L\alpha)$ which fails. The equivalential antecedent is thus crucial.

It might be instructive to see what happens to the result in A when we look at $\mathscr{F}$. In proving that $Lp \supset LLp$ fails on $\mathscr{F}$ the w_1, w_2, w_3 of A are 2*, 1*, and 0*. The worlds on an R-chain leading to 0* are precisely the worlds in N*, while the worlds not on such a chain are the worlds in N. But then, to get **H** to fail we would have to make p true throughout N and false throughout N*, and so $|p|$ would be neither finite nor cofinite, and would not be the truth set of any wff in the particular model we have put upon $\mathscr{F}$. And of course we have shown that **H** *is* valid in this model.

KH and KW

There is an interesting connection between KH and KW, for it turns out that the system characterized by the class of all frames for KH is precisely KW. We establish this by showing that KH + **4** = KW. We first prove $\vdash_{KH + 4}$ **W**. (**4** is the wff $Lp \supset LLp$.)

PC	(1)	$(q \supset r) \supset ((q \supset p) \supset ((r \wedge q) \equiv (q \wedge p)))$
(1)[$Lp/q,LLp/r$]	(2)	$(Lp \supset LLp) \supset ((Lp \supset p) \supset$ $((LLp \wedge Lp) \equiv (Lp \wedge p)))$
4 (2) MP	(3)	$(Lp \supset p) \supset ((LLp \wedge Lp) \equiv (Lp \wedge p))$
(3) L-dist,Eq	(4)	$(Lp \supset p) \supset (L(Lp \wedge p) \equiv (Lp \wedge p))$
(4) DR1	(5)	$L(Lp \supset p) \supset L(L(Lp \wedge p) \equiv (Lp \wedge p))$
H	(6)	$L(Lp \equiv p) \supset Lp$
(6) [$Lp \wedge p/p$]	(7)	$L(L(Lp \wedge p) \equiv (Lp \wedge p)) \supset L(Lp \wedge p)$
(5)(7) Syll	(8)	$L(Lp \supset p) \supset L(Lp \wedge p)$
PC	(9)	$(q \wedge p) \supset p$
(9) [Lp/q]	(10)	$(Lp \wedge p) \supset p$
(10) DR1	(11)	$L(Lp \wedge p) \supset Lp$
(8)(11) Syll	(12)	$L(Lp \supset p) \supset Lp$	Q.E.D.

The proof that KW contains **4** is on p. 150. Here is a proof that $\vdash_{KW}$ **H**:

PC	(1)	$(q \equiv p) \supset (q \supset p)$
(1) [Lp/q]	(2)	$(Lp \equiv p) \supset (Lp \supset p)$
(2) DR1	(3)	$L(Lp \equiv p) \supset L(Lp \supset p)$
W	(4)	$L(Lp \supset p) \supset Lp$
(3)(4) Syll	(5)	$L(Lp \equiv p) \supset Lp$	Q.E.D.

These two results establish that where $\mathscr{E}$ is the class of frames for KH then α is $\mathscr{E}$-valid iff $\vdash_{KW} \alpha$. For suppose $\vdash_{KW} \alpha$. Then $\vdash_{KH+4} \alpha$, and since every frame in $\mathscr{E}$ is a frame for KH + **4**, (by (B) above) α is $\mathscr{E}$-valid. If $\dashv_{KW} \alpha$ then, from the completeness of KW established in the last chapter, α fails on a frame for KW. But since KW contains KH a frame for KW is also a frame for KH and so α is not $\mathscr{E}$-valid.

H is a formula of modal degree 2 (see p. 97). It is known[2] that any system whose axioms are of degree 1 is complete, so in a sense this is a 'best possible' incompleteness result.

Completeness and the finite model property

There is one class of systems for which completeness follows automatically, that is systems with the finite model property. As we defined the finite model property on p. 145 this is trivial, for we said that S has the finite model property iff for every wff α which is not a theorem of S there is a finite frame for S on which α is not valid, and this has the consequence that where $\mathscr{E}$ is the class of all finite frames for S then $\mathscr{E}$ characterizes S.

But there is a less trivial result. To see why look at the difference between frames and models in the matter of completeness. Every system S has a canonical model, in which all and only S's theorems are valid. Thus S is characterized by the class consisting of just that model, or indeed by any class of models for S, i.e. models in which every S-theorem is valid, which contains the canonical model. This holds even if S is not complete – even if S is not characterized by any class of frames. So one might expect that a system S could be characterized by a class of finite *models* without being characterized by a class of finite frames, or indeed without being characterized by any class of frames at all.

This, however, is not so. Any system S which is characterized by a class of finite models is also characterized by a class of finite frames. The proof of this, due to Krister Segerberg,[3] proceeds by showing that if α fails on a finite model which is a model for S, then that model can easily be converted into a model based on a finite frame for S.

So suppose that $V(\alpha,w) = 0$ for some $w \in W$ in some model $\langle W,R,V \rangle$ on which all theorems of S are valid. Our first step is to make sure that W contains no worlds w and w' which are 'duplicates' in the sense that for every wff α, $V(\alpha,w) = V(\alpha,w')$.[4] If w and w' are duplicates we simply leave one of them out, and if w has many duplicates we get rid of all but one. Let $\langle W^*,R^*,V^* \rangle$ be the model obtained from $\langle W,R,V \rangle$ as follows. W^* is obtained from W by dropping all but one member of any class of duplicates. For R^*, given any w and $w' \in W^*$, we let wR^*w' iff there is a duplicate w'' of w' such that wRw''. For V^*,

$V^*(p,w) = V(p,w)$ for every $w \in W^*$. An induction on the construction of α then establishes that $V^*(\alpha,w) = V(\alpha,w)$ for every $w \in W^*$. This means that if $\langle W,R,V \rangle$ is a model for S then so is $\langle W^*,R^*,V^* \rangle$, and that if a wff α fails on $\langle W,R,V \rangle$ then it also fails on $\langle W^*,R^*,V^* \rangle$ and so if α fails on a finite model of S it also fails on a (finite) model with no duplicates.[5]

Consider a finite model for S with no duplicates. It is not hard to show that in such a model for every world w there is a wff β_w such that $V^*(\beta_w,w') = 1$ iff $w = w'$ — i.e. β_w is true at w and w alone. The reason is this. If W^* contains no duplicates then for each w and each w' there is a wff $\gamma_{w'}$ such that $V^*(\gamma_{w'},w) = 1$ and $V^*(\gamma_{w'},w') = 0$. So if β_w is the conjunction of all these γs then β_w is true at w and w alone. This of course depends on the fact that W^* is finite, since otherwise there could be infinitely many γs, and we could not form their conjunction.

We now show that not only is $\langle W^*,R^*,V^* \rangle$ a *model* for S, but $\langle W^*,R^* \rangle$ is a *frame* for S. Suppose it is not. Then there is a model $\langle W^*,R^*,V' \rangle$ based on $\langle W^*,R^* \rangle$ in which, for some $w^* \in W^*$ and some theorem α of S, $V'(\alpha,w^*) = 0$. Where p is any variable then there will be a finite collection of worlds, $w_1, \ldots, w_n$ such that $V'(p,w) = 1$ if w is one of w_1, $\ldots$, w_n, and 0 otherwise. Then, where β_p is $\beta_{w_1} \vee \ldots \vee \beta_{w_n}$, $V'(p,w) = V^*(\beta_p,w)$ for every $w \in W^*$. What this means is that p has the same values in $\langle W^*,R^*,V' \rangle$ as β_p does in the original $\langle W^*,R^*,V^* \rangle$. Now let δ be any sub-formula of α and let δ' be the result of uniformly replacing each variable p in δ by β_p. A straightforward induction on the construction of wff establishes that $V'(\delta,w) = V^*(\delta',w)$ for every $w \in W^*$. In particular when δ is α itself we have, given that $V'(\alpha,w^*) = 0$, $V^*(\alpha',w^*) = 0$. But α' is a substitution-instance of α, and so, since $\vdash_S \alpha$ then $\vdash_S \alpha'$. So $\langle W^*,R^*,V^* \rangle$ would not after all be a model for S.

A consequence of this is that any incomplete system, such as KH, lacks the finite model property, even if this is defined in terms of models rather than frames. But of course a complete system can lack it too, since Mk discussed on p. 154 is complete, and indeed characterized by frames satisfying a reasonably simple relational condition.

General frames

In proving that $Lp \supset LLp$ is not a theorem of KH we made essential use of a model in which $|\alpha|$ is either finite or cofinite. There is, however, another way in which we could look at what is going on. Instead of thinking of ourselves as starting from a frame as a structure consisting only of a set W and a relation R, we could think of ourselves as starting from a structure consisting of these together with a set P of 'allowable' sets of members of W; and we could then think of a model as being derived from such a structure by adding to it any value-assignment to the variables which satisfies the condition that, for every variable p, $|p|$ is one of the sets in P. Such a structure $\langle W,R,P \rangle$, though not a frame in the sense in which we have been using the term 'frame', would be better described as a frame than as a model, since it would contain no value-assignment and therefore would not determine the values of wff in various worlds. In order to ensure that $\langle W,R,P \rangle$ could yield the sort of proof we gave in lemma 9.3 however, we should have to require that P should be so selected that once we were given that $|p| \in P$ for every variable p, we could be sure that $|\alpha| \in P$ for every wff α. To achieve this, we have to require that P should be so chosen that whenever any set of worlds, A, is in P, then so is A's complement (for the sake of the induction on $\sim$), that whenever A and B are both in P, then so is their union (for the sake of the induction on $\vee$), and that whenever A is in P, so is the set of all worlds that can see only members of A (for the sake of the induction on L). A structure $\langle W,R,P \rangle$ in which P satisfies these conditions is called a *general frame* by van Benthem.[6]

The formal definition is this: $\langle W,R,P \rangle$ is a general frame iff

(a)   W is a non-empty set;
(b)   R is a dyadic relation defined over W;
(c)   P is a set of sets of members of W (i.e. $P \in \mathcal{P}W$) satisfying the following conditions:

  (i)   If $A \in P$, then $W - A \in P$,
  (ii)   If $A \in P$ and $B \in P$, then $A \cup B \in P$, and
  (iii)   If $A \in P$, then $\{w \in W : \forall w' \in W(wRw' \supset w' \in A)\} \in P$.

A model based on a general frame $\langle W,R,P \rangle$ will then be any structure $\langle W,R,P,V \rangle$, where V is a value-assignment to the variables which makes $|p| \in P$ for every variable p. The standard rules $[V\sim]$, $[V\vee]$ and $[VL]$ are assumed to hold. (In lemma 9.3, P would of course be the set of all finite or cofinite subsets of W.) We shall then say, by a natural extension of our earlier definitions, that a wff is valid on a given general frame iff it is valid in (true in every world in) every model based on that general frame; that a general frame is a general frame for a system S iff every theorem of S is valid on that general frame; and that S is characterized by a class $\mathscr{E}$ of general frames iff, for every wff α, α is a theorem of S iff α is valid on every (general) frame in $\mathscr{E}$.

Now suppose we consider the frame $\langle W,R \rangle$ of the canonical model for any normal modal system S, and suppose we define the set P of allowable sets of worlds by saying that A is an allowable set iff there is some wff α which is true in that canonical model in every world in A but in no other world. (I.e. $P = \{A \subseteq W : \exists \alpha (A = |\alpha|)\}$.) Then it is not hard to show that $\langle W,R,P \rangle$, as so defined, is a general frame which characterizes S. And this has the consequence that every normal modal system is characterized by the class of all the general frames for that system. Thus if we were to suggest, as a third possible account of the completeness of a system in some absolute sense, that a system should be said to be complete iff it is characterized by some class of general frames, then this would have the consequence that every normal modal system is complete.

General frames are like models in that each normal modal system is characterized by some class of them, and indeed each is characterized by a single frame. But general frames are unlike models in that if any wff is valid on a general frame, so are all its substitution-instances. Ordinary frames (which are sometimes called Kripke frames in contexts in which it is important to distinguish them from general frames) of course also have this property; but many models do not, as we observed on p. 112. It is this last-mentioned fact which suggests that an intuitively satisfactory account of validity for a modal system should be in terms of frames, of one kind or another, rather than in terms of models. Of the two kinds of frames we have discussed, Kripke frames, unlike general frames, lead to an account of completeness which yields a real distinction between systems which are complete and ones which are not; but general frames sometimes enable us to construct independence proofs where neither Kripke frames nor models would be of service.

What might we understand by incompleteness?

The incomplete system KH which we have discussed in this chapter is certainly one which has a very simple axiomatic basis, but it is difficult to get an intuitive grasp of just how it is incomplete − that is, of how it can be that the system cannot precisely match any condition on a frame and yet can match such a condition if it is combined with a restriction on the permitted value-assignments. (This, indeed, seems also to be true of the other incomplete systems that have been described in the literature.) We may, however, be helped in this matter by comparing KH with an incomplete system of tense logic which has been produced by S.K.

Thomason.[7] Tense logic will be discussed briefly on p. 218, though it lies outside the scope of this book since it contains two 'necessity' operators, one for the past and one for the future; nevertheless it seems worthwhile to mention Thomason's system here, since it seems possible to get an intuitive 'feel' for the source of its incompleteness. One of the consequences of Thomason's axioms, given the interpretation he intends them to have, is that time never comes to an end. Another of their consequences is that every proposition eventually takes on an unvarying truth-value (though, since time is never-ending, there need be no specific moment after which all propositions have unvarying truth-values).

Thomason is able to prove that there are no Kripke frames at all for his system and hence, of course, it is not characterized by any class of frames; and we may well feel, intuitively, that this is not a surprising result, for this reason: if we give the elements in a frame a temporal interpretation (e.g. by taking the 'worlds' as moments of time and R as the relation is earlier than), then a frame, or a class of frames, can be thought of as expressing a possible structure for time; but it is very hard to see how the mere structure of (non-ending) time could by itself be sufficient to ensure that every proposition will eventually have a constant truth-value. It is, however, not difficult in principle to conceive that the structure of time together with some restriction on permitted value-assignments might have just such an effect. The analogy with the semantics for KH is this: our definition of the class of allowable sets of worlds has the effect of ensuring that, for any wff α, either α itself or $\sim\alpha$ will be true at only a finite number of worlds; and this means that for every wff α, except for a finite, possibly empty, portion at each end of the frame, α has an unvarying truth-value. It again seems intuitively reasonable (as it did with Thomason's system) to expect that a system characterized by such a class of models would not be determined solely by a condition on a Kripke frame, but only by this in conjunction with a restriction on value-assignments.

Exercises — 9
9.1 Prove theorem 9.1.

9.2 Let VB be K + **VB**, $MLp \lor L(L(Lq \supset q) \supset q)$. Show (A) that every frame for VB is also a frame for **MV**, $MLp \lor Lp$, but (B) that **MV** is not a theorem of VB. Explain why this shows the incompleteness of VB.

9.3 Prove that K together with the following axioms is not complete:
  (i) $LMq \supset L(Lp \supset p)$
  (ii) $L(L(Lp \supset p) \supset Lp)$

9.4 Let MV be K + **MV**:
(a) Prove that **VB** is a theorem of the system MV.
(b) Prove that MV is precisely the system characterized by the class of all frames for VB.

9.5 Prove that if there is a p-morphism (see note 5) from $\langle W,R \rangle$ to $\langle W^*,R^* \rangle$ then if α is valid on $\langle W,R \rangle$, α is valid on $\langle W^*,R^* \rangle$.

9.6 Set out fully the proof that every normal modal system is characterized by a class of general frames.

Notes

[1] The incompleteness of this system is proved in Boolos and Sambin 1985. The proof given in the text is essentially the simplification of the proof they give which appears in Cresswell 1987. The earliest incomplete logics appeared in Fine 1974b and S.K. Thomason 1974a. Other examples occur in van Benthem 1978, 1979b and Boolos 1980. Ming Xu, 1991, has shown that, for each n, the system KH_n, which is K + $L^n(L(Lp \equiv p) \supset Lp)$ is a distinct system, with KH_n included in KH_m for n > m, but that, for each of them, the class of frames is just the class of frames for KW. Analogous results are obtained for other systems. Blok 1980 shows by algebraic means that either there are none or non-denumerably many incomplete systems whose frames are just those of any given complete system. Fine (op. cit., p. 28) notes that a method which he uses in Fine 1974c will produce non-denumerably many incomplete extensions of S4. The incompleteness of one of the systems discussed in van Benthem 1979b is proved in Chapter 4 of Hughes and Cresswell 1984.

[2] Lewis 1974.

[3] Segerberg 1971, p. 33.

[4] Segerberg 1971 p. 29 calls models with no duplicates 'distinguishable' models.

[5] This way of making a new model from an old one in such a way that it may be guaranteed to satisfy exactly the same formulae is an example of what Segerberg 1968a, p. 13f., calls a *pseudo-epimorphism*, or for short a *p-morphism*. Briefly a p-morphism from a frame $\langle W,R \rangle$ to a frame $\langle W^*,R^* \rangle$ is a function f from W onto W^* such that for w, $w' \in W$, if wRw' then $f(w)R^*f(w')$, and for u, $v \in W^*$, if uR^*v, then for every $w \in W$ such that $f(w) = u$ there is some $w' \in W$ such that wRw' and $f(w') = v$. Provided that for every variable p and every $w \in W$, $V(p,w) = V^*(p,f(w))$ then for every wff α, $V(\alpha,w) = V^*(f(w))$. In the present example of course $f(w)$ is simply the representative of all the duplicates of w.

[6] Van Benthem 1978. (The term 'general', as used here, is derived from its much earlier use in Henkin 1950 in connection with an analogous situation in higher-order predicate logic.) Makinson 1970 calls such structures relational frames, and S.K. Thomason 1972a, p. 151, calls them first-order structures. Thomason (op. cit., p. 154) then imposes two extra conditions on such structures to obtain what he calls refined structures. These conditions are (a) that if $w \neq w'$, then there is an allowable set A such that $w \in A$ but $w' \notin A$; and (b) that if not wRw', then there is an allowable set A such that $w \in A$ but $w' \notin A$. Goldblatt 1976, Part 1, p. 64, imposes still further conditions to obtain what he calls descriptive frames. (Descriptive frames link with canonical models.)

[7] S.K. Thomason 1972a, pp. 153f.

10

FRAMES AND SYSTEMS

Frames for T, S4, B and S5

By *a frame for* a normal modal system S we mean a   ne on which
every theorem of S is valid (i.e. true in every world in every model based
on it). We showed, on pp. 39–41, that validity on a frame is preserved
by the rules US, MP and N. This means that a frame is a frame for S iff
each *axiom* of S is valid on that frame; and in fact we need only consider
the modal axioms other than **K**, since **K** is valid on every frame
whatsoever.

In our soundness and completeness proofs in Chapters 2 and 6 we were
able to show that the system T and the class of reflexive frames match
each other in the sense that any wff is a theorem of T iff it is valid in
every reflexive frame. That is certainly one connection between T and the
class of all reflexive frames. The question we now want to ask, however,
is whether the class *of all frames for T* is the same as the class of all
reflexive frames. The answer is that in fact it is. We have, indeed, proved
one half of this already. For in proving the soundness of T we showed
that every theorem of T is valid on every reflexive frame; and that is just
another way of saying that every reflexive frame is a frame for T. But we
have not yet proved the other half, namely that every frame for T is
reflexive. It is, however, quite easy to do so.

THEOREM 10.1 Every frame for T is reflexive.

Proof: The proof is by contraposition; i.e. we shall show that if any
frame $\mathscr{F}$ is not reflexive, then some theorem of T – in fact $Lp \supset p$ – is
not valid on $\mathscr{F}$. Suppose then that $\mathscr{F}$ is not reflexive. This means that

some $w \in$ W is not related to itself. Let w^* be such a world. Then let $\langle \mathscr{F}, \text{V} \rangle$ be a model based on $\mathscr{F}$ in which $V(p,w^*) = 0$ but $V(p,w) = 1$ for every $w \in$ W *except* w^*. Since w is not related to itself, this will make p true in every world to which w^* *is* related. Thus $V(Lp,w^*) = 1$. But $V(p,w^*) = 0$. Hence $V(Lp \supset p,w^*) = 0$. So $Lp \supset p$ is not valid in this model, and therefore is not valid on $\mathscr{F}$.

This completes the proof of theorem 10.1. It and the soundness of T then give us

COROLLARY 10.2 $\mathscr{F}$ is a frame for T iff $\mathscr{F}$ is reflexive.

It is important to note that theorem 10.1 holds only for frames, not for models. That is, it is not the case that every *model* for T is reflexive, even though every reflexive model is a model for T. To see this, consider a frame $\langle W,R \rangle$ in which W $= \{w_1,w_2\}$ and R $= \{\langle w_1\ w_2 \rangle, \langle w_2,w_1 \rangle\}$ – i.e. a two-world frame in which neither world can see itself but each can see the other. We could picture the frame in this way:

$$\text{o} \quad \Leftrightarrow \quad \text{o}$$
$$w_1 \qquad\qquad w_2$$

Now consider any model based on this frame in which each variable has the same value in both worlds, i.e. any model in which $V(p,w_1) = V(p,w_2)$ for each variable p. It is not hard to prove, by induction on the construction of a wff, that for every wff α, $V(\alpha,w_1) = V(\alpha,w_2)$. We now show that for any wff α, $V(L\alpha \supset \alpha,w_1) = 1$. For suppose that $V(L\alpha,w_1) = 1$. Then since w_1Rw_2 we have $V(\alpha,w_2) = 1$; and hence, since α has the same value at both worlds, $V(\alpha,w_1) = 1$. Clearly an exactly similar argument will show that $V(L\alpha \supset \alpha,w_2) = 1$. This means that every substitution-instance of **T** is valid in the model in question, and therefore, by theorem 9.1 on p. 160, that it is a model for T. But clearly it is not a reflexive model.

Theorem 10.1 and corollary 10.2 should be compared with theorem 6.7 on p. 120. That theorem, in conjunction with the soundness of T, establishes that T is characterized by the class of all reflexive frames. But this by itself does not give us corollary 10.2. For, as we saw in Chapter 8, T is characterized by the class $\mathscr{E}$ of all finite reflexive frames, and also by another class $\mathscr{E}^*$ which contains just the frame of T's canonical model. Not only are $\mathscr{E}$ and $\mathscr{E}^*$ different; they have no members at all in common. The fact that T is characterized by the class of all reflexive

173

frames still leaves open the possibility that it might also be characterized by some class of frames which contains, or even consists solely of, non-reflexive ones. And it is this which corollary 10.2 assures us cannot be so. For the proof of theorem 10.1 shows that $Lp \supset p$ fails on *every* non-reflexive frame, and therefore that no such frame can be a member of *any* class which characterizes T. In other words, every class of frames which characterizes T must consist solely of reflexive frames.

Theorem 10.1, therefore, establishes something that theorem 6.7 does not. Does this mean that it is *stronger* than theorem 6.7, that it proves all that that theorem proves and more besides? If it did, that would indeed be gratifying, since the proof of theorem 10.1 is a great deal simpler than a completeness proof by canonical models. Unfortunately, however, there is no short cut to a completeness proof by this method. Certainly, *if T is characterized by any class of frames at all*, then it will be characterized by the class of all frames for T, and then corollary 10.2 assures us that in that case it is characterized by the class of all reflexive frames. But the hypothesis here is that T is characterized by some class of frames; and that is something that corollary 10.2 does not tell us, and which we need a separate proof to establish.

To make the position clearer, consider again the incomplete system KH. What we proved in Chapter 9 is that the system characterized by the class of all frames for KH is stronger than KH itself, because it contains the wff **4**, which is not a theorem of KH. We also proved that a frame is a frame for KH (a frame on which every theorem of KH is valid) iff it is a frame for KW – which gives us an analogue of corollary 10.2 for KH. But it is *not* true that KH is characterized by the class of all such frames, since this class validates the non-theorem **4**.

What all this means is that the fact that the frames for a certain system are precisely the frames which have a certain property, is neither a necessary nor a sufficient condition of that system's being characterized by the class of all frames which have that property. The case of KH shows that it is not a sufficient condition; and the fact that T is characterized by the class of all finite reflexive frames but that not all frames for T are finite shows that it is not a necessary condition either. The most that we can say is that *if* a system S is complete, in the sense of being characterized by some class of frames, and if the frames for S are precisely those that possess a certain property, then the class of all frames with that property is one of the classes of frames (and in fact the largest of them) which characterize S.

We have gone through the situation in some detail for T. For S4, B and S5 we shall merely survey the analogous results. These are that the frames for S4 are precisely those that are reflexive and transitive, that the frames for B are precisely those that are reflexive and symmetrical, and that the frames for S5 are precisely those that are reflexive, transitive and symmetrical. S4, of course, is T + **4** ($Lp \supset LLp$); B is T + **B** ($\sim p \supset L\sim Lp$); and S5, although in Chapter 2 we axiomatized it as T + **E**, can equally well be axiomatized as T + **4** + **B**. So, since we have already proved the soundness of these systems, all that we still have to do is to prove that every frame on which **4** is valid is transitive, and that every frame on which **B** is valid is symmetrical.

THEOREM 10.3 Every frame on which $Lp \supset LLp$ is valid is transitive.

Proof: Let $\mathscr{F}$ be any non-transitive frame. This means that there are worlds w_1, w_2 and w_3 in W such that w_1Rw_2 and w_2Rw_3 but not w_1Rw_3. Let $\langle \mathscr{F}, V \rangle$ be a model based on $\mathscr{F}$ in which $V(p,w_3) = 0$ but $V(p,w) = 1$ for every $w \in W$ other than w_3. Then clearly $V(Lp,w_1) = 1$. However, $V(Lp,w_2) = 0$ and hence $V(LLp,w_1) = 0$. So $V(Lp \supset LLp,w_1) = 0$, which means that $Lp \supset LLp$ is not valid on $\mathscr{F}$.

THEOREM 10.4 Every frame on which $\sim p \supset L\sim Lp$ is valid is symmetrical.

Proof: Let $\mathscr{F}$ be any non-symmetrical frame. This means that there are worlds w_1 and w_2 in W such that w_1Rw_2 but not w_2Rw_1. Let $\langle \mathscr{F}, V \rangle$ be a model based on $\mathscr{F}$ in which $V(p,w_1) = 0$ but $V(p,w) = 1$ for every $w \in$ W other than w_1. Then (a) $V(\sim p,w_1) = 1$. But since w_2 is not related to w_1, p is true in every world to which w_2 is related. So we have $V(Lp,w_2) = 1$, and therefore $V(\sim Lp,w_2) = 0$. Hence, since w_1Rw_2 we have (b) $V(L\sim Lp,w_1) = 0$. (a) and (b) then give us the result that $V(\sim p \supset L\sim Lp,w_1) = 0$, and so $\sim p \supset L\sim Lp$ is not valid on $\mathscr{F}$.

We can prove analogous results for many other formulae and systems than the ones we have just dealt with. For example, we can prove that every frame on which **D1** (see p. 128) is valid is connected. The proof is that if any frame contains worlds w_1, w_2 and w_3 such that w_1Rw_2 and w_1Rw_3 but neither w_2Rw_3 nor w_3Rw_2, then a model based on that frame which makes p false at w_3 but true everywhere else, and q false at w_2 but true everywhere else, will make **D1** false at w_1. Likewise with the finality condition for S4M. For suppose that in a transitive and reflexive frame there is a world w which cannot see an endpoint. Then, firstly, w must be able to see a world distinct from itself, and, secondly, no world that w can see can see an endpoint either. Thus there must be a chain (possibly a finite but repeating chain) of at least two distinct worlds where each can see all later members. By having p alternately true and false (though not necessarily consecutively) on this chain we may falsify **M**. So every frame for S4M is final.

Irreflexiveness

We have seen that not only is T characterized by reflexive frames, but that all frames for T are reflexive. But we also saw, on p. 173, that there are irreflexive *models* for T. The procedure we used for constructing the irreflexive model on p. 173 can in fact be generalized.[1] For if we take any reflexive world in any model, i.e., any world which can see itself, and replace it by a pair of worlds each able to see the other but neither able to see itself, *and* we give each variable the same value in each world in the new pair as it had in the original world, then the new (irreflexive) model will validate exactly the same wff as the original. If we apply this procedure to the canonical model of K we can therefore falsify any non-theorem of K in a model based on an irreflexive frame, and thereby show that the system characterized by irreflexive frames is simply K itself.

There is another way of looking at the connection between a system and the class of all its frames. In the case of T what we have in fact proved is that any frame $\mathscr{F}$ validates the wff **T** iff $\mathscr{F}$ is reflexive. Put this way the connection is not so much a connection with the *system* T as with the wff **T**. This connection can be described by saying that the modal wff **T** *corresponds* with reflexiveness. The result described above concerning irreflexiveness shows that irreflexiveness does not correspond with any modal wff. For suppose there were a modal wff α such that a frame $\mathscr{F}$ validates α iff $\mathscr{F}$ is irreflexive. Then α must be a theorem of K, for otherwise the class of all irreflexive frames would characterize K + α where this would be different from K, and we showed above that the class of irreflexive frames characterizes K. But if α is a theorem of K then *every* frame validates α, not just irreflexive frames.

Although irreflexiveness does not correspond to a modal *formula* Gabbay[2] has shown that it does, in a sense, correspond to a *rule*. We note first that any irreflexive frame preserves the rule

Gabb $\quad \vdash \alpha_1 \supset L(\alpha_2 \supset \ldots L(\alpha_n \supset (Lp \supset p))\ldots) \to$
$\qquad \vdash \alpha_1 \supset L(\alpha_2 \supset \ldots L\sim\alpha_n)$

where p does not occur in any of $\alpha_1, \ldots, \alpha_n$. This may be proved as follows. Suppose that $\mathscr{F}$ is an irreflexive frame and that $\alpha_1 \supset L(\alpha_2 \supset \ldots L \sim \alpha_n)$ fails on $\mathscr{F}$. Then there is a model $\langle \mathscr{F}, V \rangle$ based on $\mathscr{F}$ such that $V(\alpha_1 \supset L(\alpha_2 \supset \ldots L \sim \alpha_n), w_1) = 0$ for some $w_1 \in W$. If so there is a chain $w_1, \ldots, w_n$ in which $V(\alpha_k, w_k) = 1$ for $1 \leq k \leq n$. Let $\langle \mathscr{F}, V^* \rangle$ be a model based on the same $\mathscr{F}$, in which V^* is just like V except that $V^*(p, w_n) = 0$, and $V^*(p, w) = 1$ unless $w = w_n$. Since p does not occur in $\alpha_1, \ldots, \alpha_n$ we have $V^*(\alpha_k, w_k) = V(\alpha_k, w_k) = 1$. But since $\mathscr{F}$ is irreflexive then not $w_n R w_n$ and so $V^*(Lp \supset p, w_n) = 0$. So $V^*(\alpha_1 \supset L(\alpha_2 \supset \ldots L(\alpha_n \supset (Lp \supset p)) \ldots), w_1) = 0$, and so $\alpha_1 \supset L(\alpha_2 \supset \ldots L(\alpha_n \supset (Lp \supset p)) \ldots)$ fails on $\mathscr{F}$.

Gabbay proves a lemma[3] from which it follows that if a normal modal system S contains the rule Gabb then for any α such that $\dashv_S \alpha$, there is a sub-model of the canonical model of S in which R is irreflexive and α is false, and in that sense the rule Gabb may be said to correspond with irreflexiveness. There are however some differences between the way in which Gabb corresponds to a condition on frames and the way in which a modal formula does. If a condition corresponds to a wff α then that condition defines the class of all frames for K + α. But although irreflexiveness corresponds with the rule Gabb there is no system that Gabb determines. For Gabb is a rule of K (though not of any extensions of T) because K is characterized by irreflexive frames; yet K certainly has frames which are not irreflexive, since all frames are K frames, even reflexive ones. Further, Gabb is preserved by at least some frames which are not irreflexive. For consider the irreflexive frame obtained from the canonical model of K by 'duplicating' every reflexive world in K's canonical model and giving every variable the same value in each duplicate. Since this model is irreflexive it certainly validates Gabb, but also validates only theorems of K. Now add to this model a reflexive world that can see at least one world in the irreflexive model. The new model, and therefore the new frame, also validates only K theorems and so, since Gabb is a rule of K, validity on the new frame is preserved by Gabb. But the new frame contains a reflexive world.

Compactness

In this section we shall look at our old friend KW again as a propositional modal logic which turns out to have a number of interesting features.

The first is that, in a certain sense of that word, KW is not *compact*.[4] To see what is meant here look at what the canonical model does. Suppose that $\dashv_S \alpha$. What this means is that $\{\sim \alpha\}$ is S-consistent. Let $\mathscr{F}^*$

$= \langle W,R \rangle$, where $\langle W,R,V \rangle$ is the canonical model of S. Then for some $w \in W$, $V(\sim\alpha,w) = 1$. But the canonical model theorem can be used to produce a stronger result. For it shows not just that any single S-consistent formula is S-satisfiable (in the sense of being true at some world in a model for S) but more generally that if Λ is any S-consistent set of wff then Λ is simultaneously S-satisfiable, in the sense that there is some $w \in W$ such that for every $\alpha \in \Lambda$, $V(\alpha,w) = 1$. So if $\mathscr{F}^*$ is a frame for S we have the result that any S-consistent set of wff is simultaneously satisfiable in a frame for S.[5] We call S *compact* iff every S-consistent set of wff is satisfiable in a frame for S.

Using a set Λ suggested to the authors by Kit Fine it can be shown that KW is not compact. We will first establish certain facts about frames for KW.

LEMMA 10.5   If $\mathscr{F}$ is a frame for KW then $\mathscr{F}$ is (a) irreflexive and (b) transitive.

Proof: (a) was proved on p. 140. (b) If $\mathscr{F}$ is not transitive there are some w_1, w_2, $w_3 \in W$ with w_1Rw_2, w_2Rw_3, but not w_1Rw_3. Let $V(p,w) = 0$ iff $w = w_2$ or $w = w_3$. Then, since w_1Rw_2, $V(Lp,w_1) = 0$. Now consider every w such that w_1Rw. w cannot be w_3 since not w_1Rw_3. If $w = w_2$ then since w_2Rw_3 and $V(p,w_3) = 0$, $V(Lp,w_2) = 0$, and so $V(Lp \supset p,w_2) = 1$. If w is any other world w_1 can see we have $V(p,w) = 1$ and so $V(Lp \supset p,w) = 1$. So $V(L(Lp \supset p),w_1) = 1$. So W fails in a non-transitive frame.

For the next theorem we define a *chain*, in a frame $\langle W,R \rangle$ to be a sequence $w_1, \ldots ,w_i, \ldots$ such that w_iRw_{i+1}. By an infinite chain we mean a chain in which every term has a successor.

THEOREM 10.6   No frame for KW contains an infinite chain.

Proof: Suppose there is an infinite chain C in $\mathscr{F}$. Call its terms w_1, w_2, ... etc. Define V so that $V(p,w) = 1$ iff $w \notin C$. Now consider any $w_i \in C$. Since C is infinite there is some $w_{i+1} \in C$ and, by definition $V(p,w_{i+1}) = 0$. So $V(Lp,w_i) = 0$. Now consider any w that w_i can see. If $w \in C$ we have $V(Lp,w_i) = 0$ and so $V(Lp \supset p,w_i) = 1$. If $w \notin C$ we have $V(p,w) = 1$ and so here too $V(Lp \supset p,w) = 1$. So $V(L(Lp \supset p),w_i) = 1$. Thus W fails at w_i.

Notice that it is crucial that C be infinite. For if C has a last term then it must be some w_n for which there is no w such that $w_n R w$. In other words w_n must be a *dead end*. Dead ends are characterized by the fact that $L\alpha$ is true for every α, even $L\perp$ is true. So by making p false at w_n we have $Lp \supset p$ false there, and so $L(Lp \supset p)$ is false further up the chain.

Now consider the following set Λ of wff, where the propositional variables are p_0, p_1, ... etc.

$$\Lambda = \{Mp_0\} \cup \{L(p_i \supset Mp_{i+1})\} \ (1 \geq 0)$$

To show that Λ is KW-consistent it will be sufficient to show that any finite subset of it is consistent and to do *that* it will suffice to show that every finite subset of Λ is satisfiable on a frame for KW. (Note that this can be used to give a purely model-theoretic version of non-compactness that there is a set of wff each finite subset of which is simultaneously satisfiable on a frame for the logic, but which is not itself so satisfiable.)

Every finite subset of Λ will also be a subset of some

$$\Lambda_n = \{Mp_0, L(p_0 \supset Mp_1), \dots , L(p_n \supset Mp_{n+1})\}$$

Let $\mathscr{F}_n = \langle\{0, \dots , n+2\}, <\rangle$. It is easy to check that **W** is valid on $\mathscr{F}_n$. Now consider the following model $\langle\mathscr{F}_n, V\rangle$. For $i < n+2$ let $V(p_i, i+1) = 1$, and for all $w \neq i+1$, $V(p_i, w) = 0$. (For $i \geq n+2$, $V(p_i, w)$ can be defined arbitrarily.) So $V(Mp_0, 0) = 1$. Further $V(p_i \supset Mp_{i+1}, i+1) = 1$, and so, since $V(p_i, w) = 0$ for all $w \neq i+1$, $V(p_i \supset Mp_{i+1}, w) = 1$ for all $w \leq n+2$. So $V(L(p_i \supset Mp_{i+1}), 0) = 1$ and so Λ_n is simultaneously satisfiable on $\mathscr{F}_n$.

But for Λ as a whole to be satisfiable on an irreflexive and transitive frame the frame would need to have an infinite chain. For suppose all members of Λ are true at some w_0. Then p_0 must be true at some w_1 and supposing some p_i is true at w_{i+1} then Mp_{i+1} must be too, which means that p_{i+1} must be true at some w_{i+2}. Since R is transitive and irreflexive, and since there is no limit on i, this can only be so if the frame has an infinite chain. But in that case theorem 10.6 assures us that it is not a frame for KW.

S4.3.1

In Chapter 7 we spoke of temporal interpretations of modal logic, and in particular of Prior's desire to think of L as meaning 'it is and always will be the case that'. We noted that when R is interpreted so that wRw' iff w is no later than w', the class of frames required is those which are transitive and connected. But the problem is further complicated by the fact that the criterion of validity can be taken in two ways, depending on whether time is regarded as discrete or continuous. To regard time as discrete is to think of it in such a way that given one moment we can speak of the next moment, the next again, and so forth. To regard time as continuous is to suppose that between any two moments there is a third, and then it will make no sense to speak of the *next* moment after a given one. This distinction is important since it turns out that there are formulae which are not valid when time is taken to be continuous but which are valid when time is taken to be discrete. The stronger system is one Prior called D,[6] but that name has already been used for a quite different system, and the less confusing name of the system we require is S4.3.1. S4.3.1 is obtained by adding to S4.3 the following extra axiom:

N1 $L(L(p \supset Lp) \supset p) \supset (MLp \supset p)$

A frame $\langle W,R \rangle$ for discrete time can be considered to be a frame in which W is the natural numbers, or some finite subset of them, with R as $\leq$. This gives us a definition of validity for the system S4.3.1. We shall not give a completeness proof for S4.3.1. It is quite complicated.[7] The reason is that the canonical model method cannot be used because S4.3.1 is not compact, and it is this latter fact that we shall now prove.

The proof is similar to that given for KW except that in place of Λ we use another set Ψ.[8] To define Ψ we let α_i be $p_i \supset M(\sim p_0 \wedge \ldots \wedge \sim p_i \wedge p_{i+1})$. Then Ψ is

$$(\Psi) \ \{MLp_0, \ \sim p_0, \ M(\sim p_0 \wedge p_1)\} \ \cup \ \{L\alpha_i : i \geq 1\}$$

Our proof will have the same structure as that for KW; i.e. we shall show that (1) any finite subset of Ψ is simultaneously satisfiable on a frame for S4.3.1 but that (2) Ψ as a whole is not.

For (1) we merely observe that where $L\alpha_n$ is the highest of the $L\alpha_i$s in a particular finite subset of Ψ then the S4.3.1 frame $\langle W,R \rangle$, where $W = \{1, \ldots, n+2\}$ and $R = \leq$, will satisfy Ψ when p_0 is true at $n+2$ only and each p_i $(1 \leq i \leq n+1)$ is true just at i.

Since S4.3.1 contains both **T** and **4** we know that any frame for S4.3.1 will be both reflexive and transitive. So to prove (2) suppose that Ψ is true at some world w_0 in a model $\langle W,R,V \rangle$ based on a reflexive and transitive frame. Since MLp_0 is true at w_0, w_0 must see some world w^* at which Lp_0 is true, and since $\sim p_0$ is true at w_0, w^* cannot see w_0. Since $M(\sim p_0 \wedge p_1)$ is true at w_0, w_0 must be able to see some world w_1 at which p_0 is false but p_1 is true. But given a chain of worlds $w_1, \ldots, w_n$ such that w_iRw_j for $0 \le i \le j \le n$, and that each p_i ($1 \le i \le n$) is true at w_i, the truth of $L\alpha_n$ at w_0 requires that α_n is true at w_n, and therefore that w_n can see a world w_{n+1} at which p_{n+1} is true and each of $p_1, \ldots, p_n$ is false. Since each $w_1, \ldots, w_n$ has at least one of these true w_{n+1} must be distinct from each of $w_1, \ldots, w_n$; and so there must be an infinite chain of worlds beginning with w_0 throughout which p_0 is false. Since Lp_0 is true at w^* this means that w^* cannot see any world in this infinite chain. (Think of w^* as coming after all the worlds in the infinite chain.)

Now consider a (possibly different) model based on this same frame at which p is false at w_0, alternately true and false through the chain and true everywhere else in the frame. Then

    (i) p is false at w_0.

    (ii) Since w^* cannot see any world in the chain (including w_0) then Lp is true at w^* and so MLp is true at w_0.

    (iii) If w is any world in the model and p is true at w then so is $L(p \supset Lp) \supset p$. If p is false at w then w must be in the chain and there must be a world w' that w can see at which p is true, but which can in turn see a world at which p is false. This means that $p \supset Lp$ is false at w' and so $L(p \supset Lp)$ is false at w and so $L(p \supset Lp) \supset p$ is true at w. So $L(L(p \supset Lp) \supset p)$ is true at w_0 and so **N1** is false at w_0, and so fails on this frame.

So no reflexive and transitive frame which satisfies Ψ is a frame for S4.3.1. So no frame for S4.3.1 satisfies Ψ. This establishes the non-compactness of S4.3.1.

First-order definability

Consider again the class of frames for the system T. That class is the class of all reflexive frames, by which is meant the class of frames $\langle W, R \rangle$ which validate the condition that for every $w \in W$, wRw. Using the notation of the lower predicate calculus (LPC) to be introduced in Part III we can express reflexiveness in terms of a wff of LPC, the wff $\forall x xRx$. In this wff the italicized R is a two-place predicate whose interpretation is the relation R of $\langle W, R \rangle$. In Chapter 7 we spoke of the possibility of describing classes of frames by wff of the lower predicate calculus (first-order logic) and our next task is to pursue this theme a little further. This section is designed for those who already know a little about first-order logic. Others may like to consult what we say about the lower predicate calculus in Chapter 13. The class of frames for T may be said to be *first-order definable* in the sense that it is the class of those and only those structures which satisfy $\forall x x R x$. Frames for T are definable by a single closed wff of LPC, but we can allow an infinite set of such wff, and allow identity as a logical predicate.[9]

We shall first mention some general characterization theorems. These are theorems which show how to take any modal wff of a certain general kind and 'translate' it into a wff of LPC in such a way that the system formed by adding any number of such modal wff to K will be characterized by precisely those frames which satisfy all the conditions expressed by the corresponding wff of LPC. The first characterization theorem is due to Lemmon and Scott.[10] It covers all wff of the form

G′ $M^m L^n p \supset L^j M^k p$

where m, n, j and k are natural numbers including 0. Thus for instance **T** is the case where n = 1 and m = j = k = 0. **4** where m = 0, n = 1, j = 2 and k = 0, **D** where n = k = 1 and m = j = 0, and so on. The condition corresponding to **G′** is

C: $\forall x \forall y \forall z ((x R^m y \land x R^j z) \supset \exists v (y R^n v \land z R^k v))$

What C means is that if we have four worlds w_1, w_2, w_3 and w_4 (not necessarily distinct) and w_2 is m steps from w_1, and w_3 is j steps, then there is a w_4 which is n steps from w_2 and k steps from w_3. The proof of this result is a generalization of the completeness proof for S4.2 on pp. 134–135.

The other theorem to which we shall refer generalizes a conjecture made by Lemmon and Scott, and has been proved by Sahlqvist.[11] The formulae covered by it are all those of the form

Sahl $L^n(\alpha \supset \beta)$

where n ≥ 0 and α and β are any wff which satisfy the following conditions: α is a wff in which (i) no operators occur except L, M, ∨, ∧ and ∼, (ii) ∼ occurs only immediately before a variable, and (iii) no occurrence of M, ∨ or ∧ lies within the scope of any L. β is a wff in which no operators occur except L, M, ∨ and ∧ (∼ is not permitted).

Although **Sahl** covers all systems covered by **G′** there are instances of

Sahl which cannot be expressed by any instances of *G'*. Thus Ver can be axiomatized as K + *q* ⊃ *Lp*, and S4.3 as S4 + *M(Lp* ∧ *q)* ⊃ *L(Mq* ∨ *p)*. The condition R which corresponds to **Sahl** is quite complicated, and we shall not state it here, but simply refer the interested reader to Sahlqvist's paper. Our reason for referring to these results is simply to make the point that the problem of characterizing systems by means of a condition on R which is expressible in LPC has been definitively solved for an extremely wide range of systems. Nevertheless, there are systems which cannot be so characterized. The simplest is the system obtained by adding the wff **M** discussed on p. 131 not to S4 but directly to K. K + **M** gives a system for which no condition on R describes a class of frames which characterizes it. We shall not here prove that K + **M** cannot be characterized by a first-order condition,[12] but we shall prove that any system which can be so characterized is compact. From this will follow immediately that non-compact systems like KW and S4.3.1 cannot be characterized by any collection of wff of LPC.

To prove this theorem we first note that, given a frame ⟨W,R⟩, the intended interpretation of *R* is the relation R of ⟨W,R⟩. A first-order description of frames involves a language 𝓛 whose only predicates are *R* and =. We shall say that a model ⟨D*,V*⟩ for 𝓛 (see p. 238) *corresponds* with a frame ⟨W,R⟩ iff D* = W and V*(R) = R. ⟨D*,V*⟩ is completely determined by ⟨W,R⟩ and so nothing is lost if we speak as though it is ⟨W,R⟩ which is the LPC interpretation. To describe a *model* we add, as one-place predicates, the symbols which also constitute the propositional variables of modal logic. We call the augmented first-order language 𝓛+, and use it to show that any modal system which can be characterized by a class of frames defined by a collection of sentences of 𝓛 must be compact. From this and the non-compactness of KW, it follows that KW cannot be characterized by any first-order definable class of frames.

In order to prove that first-order characterization implies compactness we first show how to translate any wff *α* of modal logic into a wff *τ*(*α*) of 𝓛+ containing one free variable *x*.

$$\tau(p) = px$$
$$\tau(\sim\alpha) = \sim\tau(\alpha)$$
$$\tau(\alpha \vee \beta) = (\tau(\alpha) \vee \tau(\beta))$$
$$\tau(L\alpha) = \forall y(xRy \supset \tau(\alpha[y/x]))$$

(where *y* is the first variable after *x* for which *x* is free in *τ*(*α*), and

$\tau(\alpha)[y/x]$ is $\tau(\alpha)$ with y replacing free x. See p. 241).

Any model $\langle W,R,V \rangle$ for modal logic assigns a subset of W to each propositional variable. This means that we may define a corresponding LPC model $\langle D^*,V^* \rangle$ by requiring that $D^* = W$, $V^*(R) = R$, and that $V^*(p) = \{w \in W : V(p,w) = 1\}$. Since $\langle W,R,V \rangle$ completely determines $\langle D^*,V^* \rangle$ then $\langle W,R,V \rangle$ may be regarded as providing an interpretation for $\tau(\alpha)$ as well as for α. Let α be a wff of LPC containing only one free variable, say x. For $w \in W$ let V_w^* denote V_μ^*, where μ is an assignment to the variables of $\mathcal{L}$ (see p. 238) such that $\mu(x) = w$. Thus $V_w^*(\tau(\alpha)) = 1$ means, in effect, that $\tau(\alpha)$ is true in $\langle W,R,V \rangle$ for an assignment which gives x the value w. Then an easy inductive argument establishes that $V_w^* \tau(\alpha) = V(\alpha,w)$.

THEOREM 10.7 If S is characterized by a class of frames defined by a collection of closed wff of $\mathcal{L}$ then S is compact.

Proof: Let $\mathcal{E}$ be a class of frames which characterizes S, and suppose that Δ is a (possibly infinite) collection of closed wff of $\mathcal{L}$ such that $\mathcal{F} \in \mathcal{E}$ iff, for every $\delta \in \Delta$, δ is valid in $\mathcal{F}$ (in the ordinary first-order sense). Now let Λ be any S-consistent collection of modal wff and let $\tau(\Lambda) = \{\tau(\alpha) : \alpha \in \Lambda\}$. Consider any finite subset Θ of Λ. Let θ be the conjunction of all the members of Θ. Since Θ is S-consistent $\sim\theta$ is not a theorem of S, and so θ is true for some $w \in W$ in some $\langle \mathcal{F},V \rangle$ based on some $\mathcal{F} \in \mathcal{E}$. So, for every $\delta \in \Delta$, where $\langle D^*,V^* \rangle$ corresponds with $\langle \mathcal{F},V \rangle$, $V_w^*(\delta) = 1$ and $V_w^*(\tau(\theta)) = 1$. But this means that every finite subset of $\Delta \cup \tau(\Lambda)$ is satisfiable, and so, by the compactness of first-order logic (see p. 262), $\Delta \cup \tau(\Lambda)$ is satisfiable. So there is some $\langle W,R,V \rangle$ based on a frame $\mathcal{F}'$ ($= \langle W,R \rangle$) for which there is a $w \in W$, and a corresponding $\langle D^*,V^* \rangle$ such that $V_w^*(\delta) = 1$ for $\delta \in \Delta$ and $V_w^*(\tau(\alpha)) = 1$ for $\alpha \in \Lambda$. So $V(\alpha,w) = 1$ for $\alpha \in \Lambda$ and since δ is a closed wff of $\mathcal{L}$, δ is valid on $\mathcal{F}'$ and so $\mathcal{F}' \in \mathcal{E}$. So Λ is simultaneously satisfiable on a frame for S; so S is compact.

If S is any complete system then S is characterized by the class of all its frames, and so if S is not compact the class of all its frames is not first-order definable. Where S is not complete then S is not characterized by any class of frames and so, *a fortiori*, not by any first-order definable class of frames. Nevertheless it is possible that the class of all frames for an incomplete logic is first-order definable. An example is the system VB.[13] This system is K +

VB $LM\top \supset L(L(Lp \supset p) \supset p)$

VB is not characterized by any class of frames, but the class of all its frames is defined by the condition $\forall x(\sim\exists yxRy \lor \exists y(xRy \land \sim\exists z\, yRz))$. This condition says that every world either is or can see a dead end, and characterizes the system K +

MV $LM\top \supset L\bot$

The incompleteness of VB is established by showing that MV is valid on every frame for VB, but is not a theorem of VB.

So a system's frames can be first-order definable without the system's being first-order characterizable. And the converse can happen too. A simple example of this is the following,[14] though it is not quite as general as it could be as it speaks only of definability by a single LPC sentence. The system in question is characterized by the single condition that every world can see a reflexive world:

(*) $\forall x\exists y(xRy \land yRy)$

Curiously enough this system, called KMT, is not finitely axiomatizable. It is K together with, for every $n \geq 1$

MT$_n$ $M((Lp_1 \supset p_1) \land \ldots \land (Lp_n \supset p_n))$

THEOREM 10.8   KMT is characterized by frames satisfying (*).

Proof: If any world w can see a reflexive world w' then $Lp_i \supset p_i$ is true at w' for all i and so every MT$_n$ is true at w. Thus KMT is sound with respect to the class in question; and it is not difficult to see that every world in its canonical model can see a reflexive world, for if not

$L^-(w) \cup \{L\alpha \supset \alpha\colon \alpha \text{ any wff}\}$

would be inconsistent. And if this were the case then for some $L\beta_1, \ldots,$ $L\beta_k \in w$ and some $\alpha_1, \ldots, \alpha_n$ we would have

$\vdash (\beta_1 \land \ldots \land \beta_k) \supset \sim((L\alpha_1 \supset \alpha_1) \land \ldots \land (L\alpha_n \supset \alpha_n))$

and so by DR1, K3 and LMI

185

$$\vdash (L\beta_1 \wedge \ldots \wedge L\beta_k) \supset \sim M((L\alpha_1 \supset \alpha_1) \wedge \ldots \wedge (L\alpha_n \supset \alpha_n))$$

which would make w inconsistent in KMT.

Although frames satisfying (*) are sufficient to characterize KMT, they are not all the frames for KMT. One other frame is $\langle \text{Nat}, < \rangle$, but more important for our purposes are what can be called *non-identity* frames. $\langle W,R \rangle$ is a non-identity frame (NI-frame for short) iff it satisfies the condition

$$\forall x \forall y (xRy \equiv x \neq y)$$

In other words every world can see every *other* world but cannot see itself. Since non-identity frames are irreflexive they do not satisfy (*). Non-identity frames have the property that an NI-frame is a frame for KMT iff it is infinite. To prove this we proceed as follows:

THEOREM 10.9   If $\mathscr{F} = \langle W,R \rangle$ is an NI-frame where W has $n+1$ members, then KMT_n fails on $\mathscr{F}$.

Proof: Let the members of W be $w_1, \ldots, w_{n+1}$. For $1 \leq i \leq n$, put $V(p_i, w_i) = 1$ but for $w \neq w_i$ put $V(p_i, w) = 0$. Then $Lp_i \supset p_i$ fails at w_i and so

$$(Lp_1 \supset p_1) \wedge \ldots \wedge (Lp_n \supset p_n)$$

fails at every w_i $(1 \leq i \leq n)$. But these are the only worlds w_{n+1} can see, and so KMT_n fails at w_{n+1}.

It is easy to see that if MT_n is valid on a frame so is MT_m for $m \leq n$, since MT_m can be obtained from MT_n by identification of variables. So theorem 10.9 shows that if KMT_n fails on $\mathscr{F}$, so does KMT_m for $m \geq n$. In other words KMT_n fails on $\mathscr{F}$ provided $\mathscr{F}$ has no more than $n+1$ members.

LEMMA 10.10 $L\alpha \supset \alpha$ is false in at most one world in an NI-frame.

Proof: For $L\alpha \supset \alpha$ to be false at w, $L\alpha$ must be true and α false. So α is true at every $w' \neq w$ and so $L\alpha \supset \alpha$ is true at every $w' \neq w$.

THEOREM 10.11   If $\mathscr{F} = \langle W,R \rangle$ is an NI-frame where W has more than $n+1$ members, then KMT_n is valid on $\mathscr{F}$.

186

Proof: From lemma 10.10 we have that $L\alpha \supset \alpha$ is false in at most one world in an NI-frame. So

(†) $(Lp_1 \supset p_1) \wedge \ldots \wedge (Lp_n \supset p_n)$

can be false in at most n worlds. But since $\mathscr{F}$ has more than $n+1$ worlds there must be at least two worlds at which (†) is true. But in an NI-frame any two worlds can between them be seen by the whole frame and so MT_n is valid on $\mathscr{F}$.

Theorems 10.9 and 10.10 have the consequence that the MT_ns produce a strictly ascending chain of systems whose union is KMT. By a standard argument[15] this shows that KMT is not finitely axiomatizable with US, N and MP as sole rules of inference.

THEOREM 10.12   An NI-frame is a frame for KMT iff it is infinite.

This follows immediately from theorems 10.9 and 10.11.

THEOREM 10.13   There is no sentence of LPC which characterizes the class of all KMT frames.

Proof: Suppose that δ were such a sentence. For $n \geq m$, let β_n be defined as

$x_n \neq x_0 \wedge \ldots \wedge x_n \neq x_{n-1}$

and let Λ be the set

$\{\beta_n: n \geq 1\} \cup \{\sim\delta, \forall x \forall y xRy \equiv x \neq y\}$

Now any finite subset of Λ is satisfiable in a finite NI-frame which (by theorem 10.12) will not be a frame for KMT and will therefore satisfy $\sim\delta$. So Λ will be simultaneously satisfied in some frame $\mathscr{F}$. But any frame satisfying the whole of Λ will have to be an infinite NI-frame. By theorem 10.12 it will be a KMT frame and so will validate δ, thus contradicting the fact that $\sim\delta \in \Lambda$.

Although theorem 10.13 does not show that no infinite class of first-order sentences characterizes the frames for KMT, it does nevertheless provide a simple example of a system which can be characterized by a single first-order sentence, but whose class of frames cannot be so characterized.

Second-order logic

In first-order predicate logic the quantifiers only use individual variables. Second-order logic is obtained by allowing predicate variables to be put in quantifiers. This section is intended for those who know a little about second-order logic, and is intended to show that in a certain sense classical modal propositional logic, from a semantical point of view, belongs with second-order logic and not with first-order logic.[16]

We first recall the translation function τ which takes every wff of modal propositional logic to a wff of a language $\mathcal{L}^+$ of predicate logic. Now this translation did not make any use of quantifiers over predicate variables and it may appear that it is a translation into first-order logic. If we stick to truth at a world in a *model* this is indeed so, since a model for modal propositional logic does give particular values to the propositional variables, and so can equally be regarded as giving values to their translations in $\mathcal{L}^+$. But when we are interested in validity on a *frame* – and that remember was always the basic sense of validity – although the frame supplies a domain W and an interpretation for R, the modal wff is valid on the frame iff it is true for *every* assignment to the propositional variables. In other words, where $\tau(\alpha)$ is the translation of a modal wff α containing propositional variables $p_1, \ldots, p_n$ we are considering the truth in $\langle W,R \rangle$ of $\forall p_1 \ldots \forall p_n \tau(\alpha)$. We can illustrate this using the wff **T**, $Lp \supset p$. $\tau(\mathbf{T})$ is

$$\forall x(\forall y(xRy \supset py) \supset px)$$

but of course given a frame $\langle W,R \rangle$ the validity of **T** on $\langle W,R \rangle$ corresponds to the truth in $\langle W,R \rangle$, considered as a structure to interpret second-order logic, of

$$\forall p \forall x(\forall y(xRy \supset py) \supset px)$$

In the case of T, corollary 10.2 on p. 173 tells us that any frame $\langle W,R \rangle$ is a frame for T iff R is reflexive. In terms of the second-order translation this means that we need to show the following:

$$\forall x xRx \equiv \forall p \forall x(\forall y(xRy \supset py) \supset px)$$

We prove the implication in both directions. The first direction does not involve an essential use of second-order logic:

$$\forall y(xRy \supset py) \supset (xRx \supset px)$$

$$xRx \supset (\forall y(xRy \supset py) \supset px)$$

$$\forall x xRx \supset \forall x(\forall y(xRy \supset py) \supset px)$$

$$\forall x xRx \supset \forall p \forall x(\forall y(xRy \supset py) \supset px)$$

The other direction involves the second-order equivalent of the principle we shall call ∀1 in our discussion of LPC in Part III. In the present case we shall use the fact that if *every* property p is true of an individual then the property of being able to be seen by some particular individual x is also true of that individual. To be specific we have, as an instance of that principle

$$\forall p \forall x(\forall y(xRy \supset py) \supset px) \supset \forall x(\forall y(xRy \supset xRy) \supset xRx)$$

We then proceed as follows:

$$\forall x(\forall y(xRy \supset xRy) \supset xRx) \supset \forall x xRx$$

$$\forall p \forall x(\forall y(xRy \supset py) \supset px) \supset \forall x xRx$$

Contrast T with KW. The translation of **W** is

$$\forall p(\forall y(xRy \supset (\forall z(yRz \supset pz) \supset py)) \supset \forall y(xRy \supset py))$$

From the fact that KW is not first-order definable it follows that the second-order formula just mentioned is not equivalent to any wff of first-order logic.

Exercises — 10
10.1   (a) Prove that every frame for D is serial.
        (b)   Prove that every frame for S4.2 is convergent.

10.2 Prove that every frame for K1.1 (K + $L(L(p \supset Lp) \supset p) \supset p$) is transitive.

10.3 Prove that K is characterized by the class of
(a) all irreflexive frames;
(b) all asymmetrical frames;
(c) all intransitive frames.

10.4 Prove that KB is characterized by the class of all irreflexive symmetrical frames.

10.5 Prove that K4 is characterized by the class of all irreflexive transitive frames.

10.6 Prove that KG' is characterized by condition C (p. 182).

10.7 Prove that if $\langle W,R \rangle$ is a frame for KG' then R satisfies C.

10.8 Prove that the second-order translations of the axioms for S4, B, S4.2, S4.3 and S4M correspond to the first-order conditions which characterize those systems.

Notes
[1] See Hughes and Cresswell 1984, pp. 47–51. Other results of this kind are found in Sahlqvist 1975.
[2] Gabbay, 1981. The name 'Gabb' is ours.
[3] Gabbay's result has the consequence that if S is canonical then any non-theorem is rejected by an irreflexive frame, and so S is characterized by a class of irreflexive frames. (There are of course non-canonical systems which are characterized by a class of irreflexive frames, for instance KW.) The lemma that Gabbay actually proves is more general since it covers systems with more than one modal operator. In particular he is interested in applying it to tense logic, where there are two operators, *G* and *H*, meaning, respectively, 'it always will be that', and 'it always has been that'.
[4] Fine 1974a, p. 40.
[5] Conversely, if S is a system for which there exists a Λ which is S-consistent but is *not* satisfiable in any frame for S then, *inter alia*, $\mathcal{F}^*$ cannot be a frame for S. We call S *canonical* iff $\mathcal{F}^*$ is a frame for S. From what we have said canonicity implies compactness. (Rob Goldblatt has informed us that some results obtained by Dov Gabbay for tense logic can be adapted to show that compactness does not always imply canonicity.)
[6] Prior 1967, p. 29. Although **N1** appears on p. 293 of Dummett and Lemmon 1959 the names **N1** and S4.3.1 appear to be due to Sobosiński 1964b. (See Hughes and Cresswell 1968, p. 263.) Another proof that S4.3.1 is not canonical may be found in van Benthem 1980 (where **N1** is referred to as **Dum**). That **4**

follows from **N1** is proved in van Benthem and Blok 1978.

[7] The first completeness proof (by algebraic methods) is in Bull 1965a. Model-theoretic proofs of this and related results are given in Segerberg 1970.

[8] In fact, the result, as shown in Hughes and Cresswell 1986, can be generalized to show the non-compactness of any system between S4.1 (which is S4 + N1) and K3.1, which is S4.3 + **J1** $L(L(Lp \supset Lp) \supset p) \supset p$. (See Hughes and Cresswell 1968, p. 266.) The reason is that the finite model described in the text to establish (1) is based on a frame for K3.1. K3.1 is the logic of finite linear frames, i.e. finite (reflexive and transitive) frames in which each world has a unique immediate successor. The system characterized by frames in which W is the natural numbers and R is $<$ is K4.3 (i.e. K4 + **Lem$_0$**, see p. 141) + **Z**, $L(lp \supset p) \supset (MLp \supset Lp)$. More non-compact logics are presented in Fine 1974a and Schumm 1987. A different sense of compactness is used in S.K. Thomason 1972b.

[9] These issues form an area of modal logic called *correspondence theory*. A fuller discussion may be found in van Benthem 1983 and 1984.

[10] Lemmon and Scott 1977, pp. 151ff. See also Chellas 1980, pp. 85–90.

[11] Sahlqvist 1975, pp. 121ff. Lemmon and Scott's conjecture was less general in that they considered only the cases in which n = 0 and α has the form

$$M^{m_1} L^{j_1} p_1 \wedge \ ... \ \wedge \ M^{m_k} L^{j_k} p_k$$

See also Goldblatt 1975b.

[12] Goldblatt 1976, Part II, pp. 40–42. That the class of *all* frames for KM is not first-order definable is proved in Goldblatt 1975a and in van Benthem 1975. A proof that S4M and K4M are first-order definable is in Lemmon and Scott 1977, p. 75. Goldblatt 1991 proves that KM is not canonical, and Wang 1992 that it is not compact.

[13] See Chapter 4 of Hughes and Cresswell 1984.

[14] Hughes 1990. Fine 1975a establishes that every system which is first-order definable is canonical. Note, however, that Fine's own sense of the term 'first-order definable', and therefore the way in which he himself expresses his result, is not the same as ours. In our sense, every first-order definable system is automatically complete. In Fine's sense, a system S is first-order definable if the class of all the frames for S is first-order definable, and in that sense the first-order definability of a system does not guarantee its completeness. Fine therefore states his result by saying that every complete system which is first-order definable is canonical. In Fine's sense, though not in ours, the system VB is therefore first-order definable.

[15] See Lemmon 1965a. The argument is as follows: To say that K + Λ is not finitely axiomatizable is to say that there is no finite set Θ such that K + Λ = K + Θ. (See p. 50.) To prove this it is sufficient to show that Λ is a set whose members form a sequence $\alpha_1, \alpha_2 \ldots$ etc. such that where $\Lambda_n = \{\alpha_1, \ldots, \alpha_n\}$ then α_{n+1} is not a theorem of K + Λ_n. (In the example in the text α_n is **MT$_n$**.) Suppose there were a finite Θ such that K + Θ = K + Λ. Let β be the conjunction of the

members of Θ. Then β is a theorem of $L + \Lambda$. So there is a proof of β in $K + \Lambda$. But a proof uses only finitely many wff and so there will be a proof of β in some $K + \Lambda_n$. So $K + \Lambda$ will be included in $K + \Lambda_n$. But this is impossible since α_{n+1} is a theorem of $K + \Lambda$ but not a theorem of $K + \Lambda_n$.

[16] The connection between second-order logic and modal logic is quite strong. S.K.Thomason 1974a, 1975a, 1975b, shows that the consequence relation of second-order logic can be expressed in propositional modal logic.

11

STRICT IMPLICATION

Historical preamble

Modal logic was discussed by several ancient authors, notably Aristotle,[1] and also by mediaeval logicians; their work, however, lies outside the scope of this book. The subject then appears to have been almost completely neglected until fairly recent times. In fact the first steps towards modern modal logic seem to have been taken by Hugh MacColl towards the end of the 19th century. MacColl introduces the operations of disjunction $(a + b)$, negation (a') and implication $(a : b)$.[2] He then asserts as a valid principle

$$(a : b) : a' + b$$

but denies the validity of

$$(a : b) = a' + b$$

on the ground that if a means 'He will persist in his extravagancy' and b means 'He will be ruined', then the negation of $a : b$ is 'He may persist in his extravagancy without necessarily being ruined', while the negation of $a' + b$ is 'He will persist in his extravagancy and he will not be ruined'. MacColl objects to the identification of these precisely because the first asserts only possibility while the second asserts something more. What this amounts to is that he regards $a : b$ as expressing necessary implication, and $a' + b$ as expressing material implication. In later papers, and in his book entitled *Symbolic Logic and its Applications*, this becomes even clearer: for he explicitly denies that his implicational connective can be given a truth-functional interpretation, and he defines $(A : B)$ as $(A' + B)^\in$ (or alternatively as $(AB')^\eta$), where $\in$ and η represent necessity and impossibility respectively.[3]

But MacColl does not give any axioms[4] and his system can hardly be called a modal logic of the distinctively modern kind with which this book is concerned. For that we have to wait until shortly after the publication in 1910 of *Principia Mathematica*,[5] a work which did more than any other to establish the axiomatic method in logic. Beginning in 1912 C.I. Lewis published a series of articles and books[6] in which he expressed dissatisfaction with the notion of material implication found in *Principia*. The grounds of his dissatisfaction were very much the same as those of MacColl, but he had the great advantage of being able to use an axiomatic method based on that of *Principia* itself, and he used it to construct a system (or rather a series of systems) in which material implication no longer played the dominant role. It is the work of Lewis which marks the beginning of modern modal logic properly so called.

The 'paradoxes of implication'

In the system of *Principia Mathematica* — indeed in any standard system of PC — there are found the theorems:

(1) $p \supset (q \supset p)$
(2) $\sim p \supset (p \supset q)$

The sense of (1) is often expressed by saying that if a proposition is true, any proposition whatsoever implies it: that of (2) by saying that if a proposition is false, it implies any proposition whatsoever. Together they are often called the 'paradoxes of (material) implication'. Moreover, since for any proposition p, either the antecedent of (1) or the antecedent of (2) must be true, it is easy to derive from (1) and (2) the further theorem:

(3) $(p \supset q) \vee (q \supset p)$

i.e. in any pair of propositions, either the first implies the second or the second implies the first.

Lewis did not wish to reject these theorems. On the contrary, he argued (and surely correctly) that (1) and (2), when properly understood, are 'neither mysterious sayings, nor great discoveries, nor gross absurdities', but merely reflect the truth-functional sense in which Whitehead and Russell were using the word 'imply'. But he also maintained that there is another, stronger, sense of 'imply', a sense in which when we say that p implies q we mean that q follows from p; and that in this sense of 'imply' it is not the case that every true proposition is implied by any proposition whatsoever, nor that every false proposition implies any proposition whatsoever. Moreover in this stronger sense of 'imply' there are pairs of propositions neither of which implies the other. Lewis was thus led to draw the distinction between an implication which holds materially and one which holds necessarily or *strictly*,[7] and to make analogous distinctions for disjunction and equivalence. Before examining Lewis's modal logic we shall have something to say about the relation between propositions that he was attempting to capture.

The symbol Lewis used for strict implication was $\dashv$, and he interpreted $p \dashv q$ to mean that it is impossible that p should be true without q's being true too. An alternative way of expressing the fact that it is impossible for p to be true without q also being true is to say that it is necessary that if p is true so is q, i.e. that $L(p \supset q)$ is true. In view of this equivalence we shall not have to take $\dashv$ as primitive but can define it as follows:

[Def $\dashv$] $(\alpha \dashv \beta) =_{Df} L(\alpha \supset \beta)$

If instead of L we had taken M as primitive we could have defined $\alpha \dashv \beta$ as $\sim M(\alpha \wedge \sim \beta)$.

When two propositions strictly imply each other we say that each is *strictly equivalent* to the other. We use $=$ as the strict equivalence sign and introduce it by the definition:

[Def $=$] $(\alpha = \beta) =_{Df} ((\alpha \dashv \beta) \wedge (\beta \dashv \alpha))$[8]

Material and strict implication

It is not hard to see how replacing $\supset$ with $\dashv$ affects formulae like (1)−(3) on p. 194. Important differences between strict and material implication can be brought out, even in the system K, by comparing certain pairs of formulae. Sometimes a formula containing occurrences of $\supset$ is a theorem, but when $\supset$ is replaced by $\dashv$ the formula ceases to be a theorem. (Of course in any normal system this will never be the case when the only occurrence of $\supset$ so replaced is the main operator, for then either both formulae are theorems or neither is.) For example, in each of the following pairs the first formula is a theorem but the second is not:

(1a) $(p \supset q) \lor (q \supset p)$
(1b) $(p \dashv 3\ q) \lor (q \dashv 3\ p)$
(2a) $(p \land q) \supset (p \supset q)$
(2b) $(p \land q) \supset (p \dashv 3\ q)$

Moreover, sometimes we have an equivalence which is a theorem, but when $\supset$ is replaced by $\dashv 3$ the resulting formula is provable as an implication only. For example,

(3a) $((p \supset r) \lor (q \supset r)) \equiv ((p \land q) \supset r)$

is a theorem, but while

(3b) $((p \dashv 3\ r) \lor (q \dashv 3\ r)) \supset ((p \land q) \dashv 3\ r)$

is also a theorem, its converse is not. Here are some further theorems involving strict implication. They are numbered in sequence with the K theorems in Chapter 2.

K8 $(\sim p \dashv 3\ p) \equiv Lp$

PROOF
PC   (1) $(\sim p \supset p) \equiv p$
(1) × DR2   (2) $L(\sim p \supset p) \equiv Lp$
(2)Def $\dashv 3$ (3) $(\sim p \dashv 3\ p) \equiv Lp$ Q.E.D.

Just as whenever we have $\vdash \alpha \supset \beta$ we also have $\vdash \alpha \dashv 3\ \beta$, so whenever we have $\vdash \alpha \equiv \beta$ we also have $\vdash \alpha = \beta$). I.e., K8 and all other equivalential theorems are also provable as strict equivalences.

K9 $(p \dashv 3 \sim p) \equiv L\sim p$

The proof is similar to that for K8.

K10 $((q \dashv 3\ p) \land (\sim q \dashv 3\ p)) \equiv Lp$

PROOF
PC   (1) $((q \supset p) \land (q \supset \sim p)) \equiv p$
(1) × DR2   (2) $L((q \supset p) \land (\sim q \supset \sim p)) \supset Lp$
(2)K3$[q \supset p/p, \sim q \supset p/q]$ × Eq:

196

$$(3) \quad (L(q \supset p) \wedge L(\sim q \supset p)) \equiv Lp$$
(3)Def -3   (4) $((q \dashv p) \wedge (\sim q \dashv p)) \equiv Lp$ **Q.E.D.**

K11 $((p \dashv q) \wedge (p \dashv \sim q)) \equiv L\sim p$

Proof as for K10.

K8-K11 express important facts about non-contingent propositions (i.e. propositions which are either necessary or impossible). K8 says that a necessary proposition is one which is strictly implied by its own negation. K9 says that an impossible proposition is one which strictly implies its own negation. K10 says that a necessary proposition is one which is strictly implied both by another proposition and by the negation of that other proposition. K11 says that an impossible proposition is one which strictly implies both another proposition and the negation of that other proposition.

K12 $Lp \supset (q \dashv p)$

PROOF
PC   (1) $p \supset (q \supset p)$
(1) × DR1   (2) $Lp \supset L(q \supset p)$
(2)Def -3   (3) $Lp \supset (q \dashv p)$ **Q.E.D**

K13 $L\sim p \supset (p \dashv q)$

Proof as for K12.

K12 and K13 should be compared with (1) and (2) on p. 194. We will come back to them on pp. 202-204, since they have been the occasion of a large amount of controversy, but our immediate task is to return to Lewis's development of modal logic.

The 'Lewis' systems

In his early articles Lewis sometimes took strict disjunction as primitive, sometimes strict implication, sometimes logical impossibility; and in his book *A Survey of Symbolic Logic*,[9] he set out an axiomatic system (the *Survey* system) in which he again took logical impossibility as the primitive modal operator (along with conjunction and negation as primitive truth-functional operators). In 1930 Oskar Becker[10] proposed some additional axioms for the Survey system and showed that they enable all modalities to be reduced (see p. 52) to a small number of non-equivalent ones. But the first comprehensive treatment of systems of strict implication (or indeed of systems of modal logic at all) appeared in 1932 in Lewis and Langford's book *Symbolic Logic*. Here possibility is taken as the primitive modal operator, and two axiomatic systems of strict implication (called S1 and S2 respectively) are developed in considerable detail. In an appendix several other systems are outlined as well: one of these is the system of the Survey (S3); two others, which contain certain of Becker's reduction postulates, are called S4 and S5.

Since Lewis assumed that what is necessary is true it is not to be expected that K would be one of his systems, but in fact T is not either. Nevertheless for purely first-degree wff, of the kind we have just been discussing, there is no difference between T and any of the Lewis systems. We shall set out these systems in the form in which they occur in *Symbolic Logic*, except that we shall use the notation and terminology employed in Chapter 1 of this book.[11]

The system S1
Primitive symbols[12]

$p, q, r, \ldots$	[Propositional variables]
$\sim, M$	[Monadic operators]
$\wedge$	[Dyadic operator]
$(,)$	[Brackets]

Formation rules
1. A propositional variable is a wff.
2. If α is a wff, so are $\sim\alpha$ and $M\alpha$.
3. If α and β are wff, so is $(\alpha \wedge \beta)$.

Definitions[13]

[Def $\vee$] $(\alpha \vee \beta) =_{df} \sim(\sim\alpha \wedge \sim\beta)$
[Def $\dashv$] $(\alpha \dashv \beta) =_{df} \sim M(\alpha \wedge \sim\beta)$
[Def $=$] $(\alpha = \beta) =_{df} ((\alpha \dashv \beta) \wedge (\beta \dashv \alpha))$
[Def L] $L\alpha =_{df} \sim M\sim\alpha$

Axioms[14]

AS1.1 $(p \wedge q) \dashv (q \wedge p)$
AS1.2 $(p \wedge q) \dashv p$
AS1.3 $p \dashv (p \wedge p)$
AS1.4 $((p \wedge q) \wedge r) \dashv (p \wedge (q \wedge r))$
AS1.5 $((p \dashv q) \wedge (q \dashv r)) \dashv (p \dashv r)$

AS1.6 $(p \wedge (p \dashv 3 q)) \dashv 3 q$

Transformation rules
1. *Uniform Substitution*, as in the systems in Part I.
2. *Substitution of strict equivalents*: If $\vdash \alpha$, and β differs from α only in having some wff, δ, at one or more places where α has a wff γ, then if $\vdash \gamma = \delta$, $\vdash \beta$.
3. *Adjunction*: $\vdash \alpha$, $\vdash \beta$, $\rightarrow$ $\vdash \alpha \wedge \beta$.
4. *Modus Ponens (Detachment)*: $\vdash \alpha$, $\vdash \alpha \dashv 3 \beta$, $\rightarrow$ $\vdash \beta$.

There is one striking difference between the above basis for S1 and any of the bases discussed in earlier chapters, and that is that it is not constructed as an extension of PC.[15] In fact none of the axioms of S1 is a wff of PC at all. Moreover, while the rule of Uniform Substitution belongs to PC, the S1 Modus Ponens rule is stated for strict implication, not for material implication as for PC. (We shall often call it the rule of Strict Detachment, and the corresponding PC rule, the rule of Material Detachment.) As a result proofs of theorems in S1 are apt to have a somewhat different 'style' from those in, say, T, since we are not free to help ourselves to any theorem of PC which seems likely to be useful. Nevertheless, S1 contains PC; i.e., every theorem of PC is a theorem of S1. It is easy to introduce the operators $\supset$ and $\equiv$ (as Lewis himself does[16]) by the definitions:

[Def $\supset$] $\quad (\alpha \supset \beta) =_{Df} \sim(\alpha \wedge \sim\beta)$
[Def $\equiv$] $\quad (\alpha \equiv \beta) =_{Df} ((\alpha \supset \beta) \wedge (\beta \supset \alpha))$

The axiom AS1.6 is interdeducible with $Lp \dashv 3 p$. If it is omitted we have a system called S1⁰, which stands to S1 rather as K stands to T.[17] In comparing S1 with T we first notice that the basis of S1 is certainly contained in T. Further, S1 contains the whole of the basis of T *except* for the rule of necessitation. In fact S1 has no theorems of the form $LL\alpha$ at all, and if so much as one is added the other rules enable the derivation of N, and increase S1 to T.[18]

Lemmon's basis for S1
It is in fact possible to axiomatize S1 by making additions to non-modal PC as we did in earlier chapters. The following basis is due to E.J. Lemmon.[19] Lemmon's basis for S1 consists of the following axioms:

(1)   every PC-tautology;
(2) $Lp \supset p$;
(3) $(L(p \supset q) \land L(q \supset r)) \supset L(p \supset r)$.

The transformation rules are Uniform Substitution, Modus Ponens (for $\supset$), and two extra rules. The first is a restricted form of Necessitation:

N′   If α is a PC-tautology or an axiom then $\vdash L\alpha$.

The second is a rule for the substitution of proved strict equivalents:

Eq′   If α differs from β only in having a wff γ in some of the places where β has δ, and $\vdash \gamma = \delta$, then $\vdash \alpha = \beta$.

The system S2
S1 was not in fact Lewis's preferred system. The system he designated as the correct system is one called S2, obtained from S1 by adding

AS2.1 $M(p \land q) \dashv 3 (Mp \land Mq)$

Lewis calls this the *Consistency Postulate*. Its sense is that only a possible (or *consistent*) proposition can be a term in a consistent conjunction. S2 can also be axiomatized in the style of Lemmon. We replace (3) with the wff **K** from p. 25

K $L(p \supset q) \supset (Lp \supset Lq)$.

We keep N′ (now of course applied to **K** rather than (3)) and we replace Eq′ with a rule called *Becker's Rule*.[20]

BR $\vdash L(\alpha \supset \beta) \rightarrow \vdash L(L\alpha \supset L\beta)$

(Using $\dashv3$ BR can be written as $\vdash \alpha \dashv3 \beta \rightarrow \vdash L\alpha \dashv3 L\beta$.)

The system S3
Although Becker's rule belongs to S2 the formula

(4) $(p \dashv3 q) \dashv3 (Lp \dashv3 Lq)$

which might be confused with it, is not a theorem of S2. Nevertheless it could be added to S2, and if it is we obtain a system deductively equivalent to the system Lewis presented in his 1918 book. This system is called S3.[21]

Lewis also discussed S4 and S5. Although axiomatized differently, these systems are deductively equivalent to the S4 and S5 studied in Part I of this book.

Validity in S2 and S3

One reason why we shall have to make a substantial change in our earlier definitions of validity if we are to deal with S2 and S3 is that these definitions — i.e. those for T, S4, S5 and the like — all satisfy the rule of Necessitation. That is to say, if any wff, α, is valid in terms of any of these definitions, $L\alpha$ is also valid. But as we have observed, the rule of Necessitation does not hold, at least unrestrictedly, in S2 and S3.

Another, related, feature of S2 and S3 is that they are compatible with (though they do not contain) the axiom MMp.[22] This means that they are compatible with (though they do not commit us to) the view that every proposition is 'possibly possible'. And this suggests an idea which is in fact the key to S2- and S3-models, that there might be some 'worlds' in which every proposition without exception — even one of the form $p \wedge \sim p$ — is possible. Kripke[23] calls such worlds *non-normal* worlds, and we shall follow him in this terminology. Worlds of the kind that occur in the frames of normal modal systems are by contrast called *normal* worlds. The rules for evaluating non-modal formulae in non-normal worlds are the same as in normal worlds — thus even in a non-normal world we never have $p \wedge \sim p$ false, for example — but for modal formulae in non-normal worlds $M\alpha$ is always true and $L\alpha$ is always false. In this respect non-normal worlds are the reverse of dead ends in normal modal logics.

In an S2 frame there must be at least one normal world, and there may (but need not) be one or more non-normal worlds.[24] Every normal world can see itself, and every non-normal world can be seen by at least one normal world. Otherwise the accessibility relations can be as we please. In an S3 frame there is the additional requirement that the accessibility relation be transitive. A formula will be said to be S2-(S3-)valid iff it is true in every *normal* world in every model based on an S2- (S3-) frame.[25]

More exactly expressed, an S2 frame[26] is a triple $\langle W,R,N \rangle$ where W is a set of objects (worlds), N is a proper subset of W, i.e. $N \subseteq W$ but $N \neq W$, and R is a relation such that (a) R is reflexive over N, i.e. if $w \in N$ then wRw, and (b) for every $w' \in W$ there is some $w' \in N$ such that wRw'. $\langle W,R,N,V \rangle$ is an S2-model iff $\langle W,R,N \rangle$ is an S2 frame and V is a value-assignment as on p. 38, except that [VL] should be changed to read that for any wff, α, and for any $w' \in W$, $V(L\alpha,w) = 1$ if $w \in N$ and for every w' such that wRw', $V(\alpha,w') = 1$. Otherwise $V(L\alpha,w) = 0$. (The effect of this is that if w is normal, $V(L\alpha,w)$ is computed as in a T-model; but if w is non-normal, $V(L\alpha,w) = 0$ in every case — and hence, incidentally, $V(M\alpha,w) = 1$ in every case.)

A wff α is *valid* on an S2 frame $\langle W,R,N \rangle$ iff in every S2-model $\langle W,R,N,V \rangle$ based on $\langle W,R,N \rangle$, $V(\alpha,w) = 1$ for every $w \in N$. A wff is S2-valid iff it is valid on every S2 frame. An S3 frame is defined in the same way as an S2 frame, except that we add the condition that R is transitive. A wff α is S3-valid iff it is valid on every S3 frame.

For those who prefer the approach via the parlour games of Chapter 1, the S2-game is the modal game with the following modifications. Some of the sheets of paper are, say, white, others pink. In every S2-setting at least one player must have a white sheet; but some of the players may have pink sheets instead. No player with a pink sheet may see any other player, but every such player must be seen by at least one player with a white sheet. The rules for responding to calls are, for players with white sheets, exactly as in the modal game. For players with pink sheets, rules 1−3 are as in the modal game, but rules 4 and 5 (those covering calls with L and M) are replaced by the following:

4′. If a call is of the form $L\alpha$, do not raise your hand.
5′. If a call is of the form $M\alpha$, raise your hand.

A call is an S2-successful call iff in every S2-setting it would lead every player with a white sheet to raise his or her hand. A formula is S2-valid iff it would form an S2-successful call. The S3-game will be the S2-game with the added rule that in every setting the seeing-relation must be transitive. S3-successful calls and S3-validity are then defined as above, with 'S3' replacing 'S2' throughout.

S2 and S3 may be shown to be sound and complete with respect to this semantics.[27] The soundness result also enables us to establish that they are distinct systems, and that neither contains S4. T contains S2 but neither contains nor is contained in S3. S1 is not susceptible of this kind of treatment and the only known semantics for it is unintuitive.[28]

Entailment

An important modal notion is that of entailment. By this we understand the converse of the relation of *following logically from* (when this is understood as a relation between *propositions*, not wff) i.e. to say that a proposition, *p*, entails a proposition, *q*, is simply an alternative way of saying that *q* follows logically from *p*, or that the inference from *p* to *q* is logically valid.[29] It is clear from the writings we have already referred to that Lewis wished to interpret ⤙ as 'entails'. Now there has been a good deal of philosophical controversy about the correct analysis of entailment and in particular K12 and K13 on p. 197 are sometimes known as the 'paradoxes of strict implication',[30] and are often considered problematic when ⤙ is interpreted as 'entails'. We shall look at them and some associated formulae in the following forms:

(1) $(p \wedge \sim p) \dashv 3\ q$
(2) $q \dashv 3\ (p \vee \sim p)$
(3) $\sim Mp \supset (p \dashv 3\ q)$
(4) $Lq \supset (p \dashv 3\ q)$[31]

When ⤙ is interpreted as 'entails', (1) means that from any proposition of the form $(p \wedge \sim p)$ any proposition whatever can be deduced, and (2) means that from any proposition whatever there can be deduced any proposition of the form $(p \vee \sim p)$. (3) and (4) are more general: (3) means that from any logically impossible proposition (whether of the form $(p \wedge \sim p)$ or not) any proposition whatever can be deduced, and (4) means that every necessary proposition (whether of the form $(p \vee \sim p)$ or not) can be deduced from any proposition whatever.

If these are not sound principles of deducibility, that would of course tell against the claim of the standard modal systems to be correct logics of entailment. But in order to decide whether they are sound principles of deducibility or not we have to look into what we take ourselves to be asserting when we assert that one proposition is deducible from another.

Now one plausible account is that to say that *q* is deducible from *p* is to say that it is logically impossible for *p* to be true but *q* false. Deducibility is after all the relation which obtains between the conclusion and the premiss(es) of a valid deductive inference, and what we require in a valid inference is the logical guarantee that we shall not have the premiss(es) true but the conclusion false. Now by this account the 'paradoxes' are sound principles of deducibility; and hence it is not their presence in but their absence from a system which would tell against its claim to be a correct logic of entailment. To take the case of (1): to say that $(p \wedge \sim p)$ entails *q* is on this account to say that it is logically impossible for $(p \wedge \sim p)$ to be true but q false, i.e. it will amount to saying that $(p \wedge \sim p \wedge \sim q)$ is logically impossible; but since $(p \wedge \sim p)$ is itself impossible, so is $(p \wedge \sim p \wedge \sim q)$. Similar comments will apply to the other 'paradoxes'. Moreover, this account will guarantee that ⊰3 can be interpreted as 'entails'; for in all the standard systems α ⊰3 β is defined as $\sim M(\alpha \wedge \sim \beta)$ (or, what comes to the same thing, as $L(\alpha \supset \beta)$), where M is interpreted as 'it is logically possible that'.

No one is likely to deny that the logical impossibility of $(p \supset q)$ is a necessary condition of q's deducibility from p, but it has been suggested that it is not a sufficient condition on the ground that a further condition of q's deducibility from p is that there should be some connection of 'content' or 'meaning' between p and q. But even those who are inclined to accept this further requirement for deducibility, however, have to face the following argument. On any account we shall have to regard q as deducible from p when it can be derived from p by some valid principle or principles of deductive inference. Now the following principles seem intuitively to be valid:[32]

A. Any conjunction entails each of its conjuncts.
B. Any proposition, p, entails $(p \vee q)$, no matter what q may be.
C. The premisses $(p \vee q)$ and $\sim p$ together entail the conclusion q (the principle of the disjunctive syllogism).
D. Whenever p entails q and q entails r, then p entails r (the principle of the transitivity of entailment).

C.I. Lewis has shown that by using these principles we can always derive any arbitrary proposition, q, from any proposition of the form $(p \wedge \sim p)$, in the following way:

	(i)	$p \wedge \sim p$
From (i), by A:	(ii)	p
From (ii), by B:	(iii)	$p \vee q$
From (i), by A:	(iv)	$\sim p$
From (iii) and (iv), by C:	(v)	q[33]

By D we then have the result that $(p \wedge \sim p)$ entails q. This derivation shows that the price which has to be paid for denying that $(p \wedge \sim p)$ entails q is the abandonment of at least one of A–D.

The most fully developed formal response to these 'paradoxes' consists of abandoning C, the principle of disjunctive syllogism. Logics which do this are called *relevance logics* and there is now an enormous body of literature on them.[34] These systems are well beyond the scope of the present book, and in fact relevance logics differ from all the logics we have so far considered in that they require a non-standard interpretation of the PC symbols, in particular of negation.

Exercises — 11

11.1   Prove that adding $LL(p \supset p)$ to S1 gives T.

11.2   Prove that Lemmon's basis for S1(S2) on pp. 199−200 is equivalent to Lewis's.

11.3   Where S7 is S3 + MMp, prove that $\vdash_{S3} \alpha$ iff $\vdash_{S4} \alpha$ and $\vdash_{S7} \alpha$.

11.4   Let E2 be $\{\alpha : L\alpha \in S2\}$.
   (a)   Prove that N is not a rule of E2.
   (b)   Prove that E2 is sound with respect to the class of S2 frames but with the definition of validity changed so that a wff is E2-valid iff it is true in *all* worlds, not just normal worlds, in every frame.
   (c)   Give completeness proofs for E2 and S2 by defining a canonical model in which W is the set of all maximal E2-consistent sets of wff and $w \in N$ iff $L(p \supset p) \in w$.

11.5   Show that E2 can be axiomatized by PC, **T**, **K**, and the rules US, MP and R*: $\vdash \alpha \supset \beta \to \vdash L\alpha \supset L\beta$.

11.6   Where E3 is E2 with $L(p \supset q) \supset L(Lp \supset Lq)$ show that E3 is characterized by S3 frames when validity is truth in all worlds in every S3 frame.

11.7   S3.5 is S3 + $Mp \supset LMp$ (see note 27). Where an S3.5 frame is an S3 frame in which R is symmetrical over N (i.e. if w, $w' \in N$ and wRw' then $w'Rw$) show that S3.5 frames characterize S3.5.

11.8   S0.5 is just like T except that N is replaced by the rule:
   N'   If α is a PC-valid wff then $\vdash \alpha$.
A model for S0.5 consists of a set of worlds, of which one, w^*, is a 'distinguished' world. For w^*, $V(L\alpha, w^*) = 1$ iff $V(\alpha, w) = 1$ for every $w \in W$. For every other world $L\alpha$ has an arbitrary value. A wff α is

S0.5-valid iff $V(\alpha,w^*) = 1$ in every S0.5 model.

   (a)   Prove that S0.5 is sound with respect to this definition of validity.

   (b)   Prove that N is not a rule of S0.5.

   (c)   Prove that Eq is not a rule of S0.5.

11.9   Construct a canonical model for S0.5 in which w^* is a set of maximal S0.5-consistent sets of wff and every other world is a maximal PC-consistent set of wff (i.e. w is maximal and there is no set $\{\alpha_1, \ldots ,\alpha_n\}$ such that each of $\alpha_1, \ldots ,\alpha_n$ is in w and $\sim(\alpha_1 \wedge \ldots \wedge \alpha_n)$ is a substitution-instance of a PC-tautology). Use this to prove the completeness of S0.5.

Notes

[1] Aristotle, 350 BC, 29b29–40b16. An attempt to formalize Aristotle's modal logic will be found in McCall 1963. For a general history of ancient and mediaeval modal logic see Kneale and Kneale 1962, pp. 81–96, 117–138, 212, 232, 236, 243, or Bocheński 1961, pp. 81–88, 101–103, 114–115, 224–230.

[2] MacColl 1880, pp. 50–55.

[3] MacColl 1903, 1906a, 1906b, (see especially 1903, pp. 356–7.

[4] He does give (1906a, p. 8) a list of 'self-evident formulae' and it would be interesting to know which of the more recent modal systems is the weakest in which all these are true.

[5] Whitehead and Russell 1910.

[6] Lewis 1912, 1913, 1914a, 1914b, 1918. Lewis and Langford 1932.

[7] As far as we have been able to discover, the term 'strict implication' first occurs in Lewis 1912, p. 526 n. 1. The symbol 3 appears in Lewis 1918.

[8] = as defined here and $=_{Df}$ should not be confused. The former is an operator which occurs in wff of a modal system; the latter is a metalogical symbol which never occurs in wff but is used only in discoursing about a system.

[9] Lewis 1918, ch. 5 (emended in Lewis 1920).

[10] Becker 1930.

[11] These names ('S1' etc.), by which the systems have since become generally known, are given on pp. 500–501 of Appendix II (written by Lewis) in Lewis and Langford 1932. They do not occur in Chapter 6, where S1 and S2 are developed (unless we count a brief reference to 'System 1' and 'System 2' on pp. 177–178). Lewis's S4 and S5 are deductively equivalent to the S4 and S5 of Part I of this book, though they have different bases. S4 and S5 appear in Lewis and Langford 1932 only in the appendix on p. 500f., and are rejected by Lewis as acceptable systems of strict implication. S3 is the system of Lewis 1918, and S1 and S2 are the systems developed in Chapter 6 of Lewis and Langford 1932. For a more detailed survey of the axioms, theorems and rules of the various Lewis systems see Feys 1965, Chapters 12 and 13 of Hughes and Cresswell 1968, and Zeman

1973.

[12] Lewis uses $\sim$ for negation, juxtaposition for conjunction, and $\Diamond$ for M.

[13] We write these definitions in the style adopted in Part I. Lewis writes them as strict equivalences, using propositional variables. Lewis does not have a single symbol for necessity, but writes $\sim \Diamond \sim$ throughout. (His $\Diamond$ = our M). However, the abbreviation provided by this definition is an obvious convenience.

[14] Our numbering of these axioms is not the same as that of Lewis and Langford. Moreover we omit the axiom $p \, 3 \, \sim \sim p$ since this was shown to be non-independent in McKinsey 1934. Instead of AS1.6 we may have $\sim Mp \, 3 \, \sim p$, or $p \, 3 \, Mp$.

[15] The first axiomatization of modal logic starting from a PC basis and adding extra axioms and rules to it (as in Part I) appears to be that in Gödel 1933.

[16] Lewis and Langford 1932, p. 13ff.

[17] Feys 1965, p. 43.

[18] Yonemitzu 1955.

[19] Lemmon 1957. Lemmon also considers a weaker system, which he calls S0.5, in which (3) is replaced by **K**, and N′ by the rule N″ that if α is a PC-tautology then $\vdash L\alpha$. Interestingly S0.5 does not satisfy the rule Eq, even for proved strict equivalents. (See Hughes and Cresswell 1968, pp. 286–288.) By omitting $Lp \supset p$ we obtain S0.5^0. In Lemmon 1959, p. 31, there is the suggestion that in S0.5 the necessity operator might mean 'it is tautologous by truth tables that … '.

[20] Becker 1930. The name 'Becker's Rule' was given in Churchman 1938.

[21] S3 was subsequently discovered to be stronger than S2, but Lewis in 1932 (p. 496) had no proof of this and declared that if S2 should turn out to contain S3 he would fall back on S1, which he knew to be weaker than S2. Parry 1939 proves that S3 has only 42 distinct affirmative modalities. The systems which result from S3 by adding all possible modality reduction laws are classified in Pledger 1972 and given a possible-worlds semantics in Goldblatt 1973.

[22] This wff is called C13 on p. 497 of Lewis and Langford 1932.

[23] Kripke 1965b, p. 208 uses a slightly different axiomatization based on an infinite (though effectively specifiable) set of axioms with material detachment as the only primitive rule of inference. His axiomatic basis may be easily shown equivalent to Lemmon's and for our purposes there is nothing to choose between them though, unlike the bases we are using, Kripke's basis allows the addition of $LL(p \supset p)$ to S2 without obtaining the unrestricted rule of Necessitation and permits an infinity of systems to be generated by the axioms $L^n(p \supset p)$ (for each n). For some suggestions for interpreting S2 see Cresswell 1967b. A canonical model completeness theorem for S2 appears in Cresswell 1982.

[24] If we insist that there must be at least one non-normal world then MMp becomes valid. S2 + MMp has been called S6 (Alban 1943) and S3 + MMp S7. (Halldén 1949a, Hughes and Cresswell 1968, pp. 281–284.) S3 is the intersection of S4 and S7. S3 + $LMMp$ is called S8. In S8 frames every normal world can see a non-normal world.

[25] If we define validity as truth in *all* worlds we get a semantics for the 'E-systems' of Lemmon 1957 (see Hughes and Cresswell 1968, pp. 302f). In these systems N is replaced by the rule R* $\vdash \alpha \supset \beta \rightarrow \vdash L\alpha \supset L\beta$. Unlike normal systems, which contain N, these systems have no theorems of the form $L\alpha$, and their canonical models contain maximal consistent sets with no wff of that form. Segerberg 1971, Chapter 4, calls such systems 'regular' and calls systems like S2 and S3 'quasi-regular'. That Chapter shows how to apply techniques from normal modal logic to regular and quasi-regular logics. One can also study logics in which all worlds are normal but in which validity is defined as truth in a designated subset of worlds. Chapter 3 of Segerberg 1971 calls these 'quasi-normal' systems. They all contain (all the theorems of) K, and the rules US and MP, but not the rule of necessitation. An example of a quasi-normal system is studied in Langholm 1987. It is K $+ p \supset L^nMp$ and is intended to formalize a system of logic advocated in Smith 1936.

[26] Kripke 1965b does not take N as primitive but defines it via R. He calls R 'quasi-reflexive' provided that for any w, $w' \in$ W, if wRw' then wRw (i.e. a world which can see anything can see itself) and then defines a world as normal iff wRw. We have used N to make the semantics easier to follow. (Also using N generalizes more easily to systems where R is not reflexive over normal worlds.)

[27] Where a normal system S is characterized by a class of frames there is of course the non-normal system characterized by the class of all frames obtained from frames for S by the addition of non-normal worlds with the condition that every non-normal world can be seen by a normal world. All such systems will be extensions of the system Feys 1950, 1965, p.68, calls S2^0, i.e., in Lemmon's axiomatization, S2 without $Lp \supset p$. This system is characterized by frames in which no restrictions are placed on R, except that every non-normal world can be seen by a normal world. S2^0 corresponds to K as S2 corresponds to T and S3 to S4. Corresponding to S5 is a system called S3.5, which is obtained by adding E to S3 (Åqvist 1964). Note that the strict form of E, $L(Mp \supset LMp)$ strengthens S3 to S5. A completeness theorem for S3.5 is found in Cresswell 1967a. For S3.5 we may also prove a conjunctive normal form theorem (Cresswell 1969a). The system corresponding to B is S2 $+$ **B**. (S3 $+$ **B** is S3.5.) S3.5 $+$ MMp has been called S9. (See Hughes and Cresswell 1968, pp.172 and 285f.)

[28] Cresswell 1995a.

[29] This use of 'entails' has for some time been standard in philosophy. It derives from Moore 1919 (reprinted in his *Philosophical Studies*; see esp. p. 291). It is important at this point to stress that we are here thinking of a relation between propositions rather than wff. For there is a quite different, though equally legitimate, use of the term 'logically follows from', whereby a wff β 'logically follows from' a wff α in a logical system S iff $\vdash_S \alpha \supset \beta$. The distinction between these two senses of 'logically follows from' parallels the distinction between validity and necessary truth. We shall have more to say on this on p. 225.

[30] Tendentiously; for those on the other side in the controversy regard the formulae as expressing perfectly sound principles of deducibility, and on anyone's account they express sound and quite unparadoxical truths about strict implication. The 'paradoxes' seem to have been first stated (and incidentally accepted as unparadoxical) in modern logic by MacColl 1906b, p. 613. For some information about mediaeval anticipations of them see Kneale and Kneale 1962, pp. 281ff.

[31] In S2 and stronger systems we can also prove $\sim Mp \; 3 \; (p \; 3 \; q)$ and $Lq \; 3 \; (p \; 3 \; q)$. Two early attempts to formalize a relation which does not lead to the 'paradoxes' (Emch 1936 and Vredenduin 1939) avoided them in the S2 forms but contained our (1) and (2) as theorems.

[32] To say that q may be derived from p by some valid principle(s) of inference is (as noted in Lewis and Langford 1932, pp. 252–255) not the same as saying that it may be derived by the principles of a given system, or by principles we have already established up to a given point in the development of a system. Rather it is to say that the principles which enable us to pass from p to q are sound ones, whether they occur in any particular system or not. See Pollock 1966, pp. 184–185, for a discussion of this confusion in writers later than Lewis.

[33] Cf. Lewis and Langford 1932, pp. 250–251, where there is also found an analogous derivation, relevant in a similar way to our (2), of $\sim q \lor q$ from p. For a mediaeval anticipation of Lewis's derivation of q from $p \land \sim p$ see Kneale and Kneale 1962 and Kneale 1956, pp. 239–240. It is also possible to derive the result that $(p \land \sim p)$ entails $\sim q$ (a simple and equally general variant of the 'paradox' in question) by starting from the principle that $(p \land \sim q)$ entails p and applying to it the principle of antilogism, viz. that if $(p \land q)$ entails r then $(p \land \sim r)$ entails $\sim q$ (see Lewis 1914a, p. 246n, and Moh Shaw-Kwei 1950, p. 70).

[34] A survey of relevance logic is found in Dunn 1986.

12

GLIMPSES BEYOND

Our aim in earlier chapters has been to set out as much modal propositional logic as we can in the space at our disposal. But of course there is much more to modal logic than we have been able to cover, and there are many directions in which the ideas involved in modal logic can be extended. In this chapter we shall try to give a few hints of some of these. Nothing we say here is at all complete or definitive, and much of it reflects our own ideas of what topics may be of interest and importance. In most cases all we can do is suggest topics that can be further pursued elsewhere and we shall try to indicate some other works where this can be done.[1]

Axiomatic PC

In the axiomatic presentation of modal systems in this book our axioms have included all valid PC wff. It would have been possible, had our aim been to study the propositional calculus, to have presented even PC axiomatically. For instance instead of the schema **PC** we could have used a variant of the axiomatic system of *Principia Mathematica*[2] and replaced **PC** by

PCA1 $(p \lor p) \supset p$
PCA2 $q \supset (p \lor q)$
PCA3 $(p \lor q) \supset (q \lor p)$
PCA4 $(q \supset r) \supset ((p \lor q) \supset (p \lor r))$

With the rules US and MP the whole of PC may be obtained, and so any modal system K + Λ may be axiomatized by PCA1−PCA4, **K**, every member of Λ, and the rules US, MP and N.

Natural deduction

We have defined a modal system as a set of formulae called its theorems. There is however another way of looking at a system of logic, and that is to think of it as a system of *rules* whereby a conclusion may be deduced from a number of premisses. Where Λ is a set of premisses and α the conclusion, the fact that α may be derived from Λ in a system S can be written as $\Lambda \vdash_S \alpha$. For a system containing the classical propositional calculus − and all the modal systems discussed in this book do − there is no extra power to be gained by this notation since we may define $\Lambda \vdash_S \alpha$ to hold iff either Λ is empty and $\vdash_S \alpha$, or there are β_1, ... , $\beta_n \in \Lambda$ such that

$$\vdash_S (\beta_1 \wedge ... \wedge \beta_n) \supset \alpha$$

Given this definition we have that $\Lambda \vdash \alpha \supset \beta$ iff $\Lambda \cup \{\alpha\} \vdash \beta$. For clearly there will be γ_1, ... ,$\gamma_n \in \Lambda$ such that

(i) $\vdash_S (\gamma_1 \wedge ... \wedge \gamma_n) \supset (\alpha \supset \beta)$

iff there are γ_1, ... , γ_n, $\alpha \in \Lambda \cup \{\alpha\}$ such that

(ii) $\vdash_S (\gamma_1 \wedge ... \wedge \gamma_n \wedge \alpha) \supset \beta$

This fact is often called the *deduction theorem* and it is tempting to read the expression $\Lambda \vdash_S \alpha$ as meaning that there is a proof of α in which the members of Λ are treated as axioms. However, if this is done we need to be very careful since a proof in a modal system may appeal to three transformation rules, US, MP and N. Of these, only MP applies to $\Lambda \vdash_S \alpha$. If S is consistent then we cannot have $\{p\} \vdash_S q$, so US cannot be allowed; and if S is not Triv or Ver or their intersection we cannot have $\{p\} \vdash_S \{Lp\}$, and so N cannot be allowed.

Since $\Lambda \vdash_S \alpha$ can be defined in terms of theoremhood in S, the notation $\Lambda \vdash_S \alpha$ has not appeared in earlier chapters. There is however an approach to logic in which $\Lambda \vdash \alpha$ is taken as basic. This approach can be implemented in a variety of ways, and we shall refer to them all as systems of natural deduction. We shall show how natural deduction methods may be incorporated into modal logic, but we shall not be specific, except by way of illustration, about the particular form a system

211

of natural deduction might take.

A system of natural deduction is an axiomatic system in which the axioms and theorems are no longer single wff, but pairs of the form $\langle \Lambda, \alpha \rangle$ in which Λ is a set of wff and α is a wff. Such a pair is called a *sequent*. Where a sequent $\langle \Lambda, \alpha \rangle$ is a theorem of such an axiom system we write $\Lambda \vdash \alpha$.[3] Just which axioms and rules are taken as basic is a matter for the system in question. Since we are not interested in axiomatizing the propositional calculus, either directly or via natural deduction, we shall content ourselves with indicating how the method works in the case of PC, and how it may be extended to deal with modal systems. The following rules are based on those given by E.J. Lemmon.[4] We will illustrate the ones he gives for wff involving only $\supset$. There is one axiom schema:

A (Assumption) $\{\alpha\} \vdash \alpha$ for any wff α

There are three rules.

Add (addition of assumptions) If $\Lambda \vdash \alpha$ and $\Lambda \subseteq \Gamma$ then $\Gamma \vdash \alpha$.
MPP (Modus Ponens for natural deduction) If $\Lambda \vdash \alpha$ and $\Lambda \vdash \alpha \supset \beta$ then $\Lambda \vdash \beta$.
CP (conditional proof) If $\Lambda \cup \{\alpha\} \vdash \beta$ then $\Lambda \vdash \alpha \supset \beta$.

The PC-tautologies on this account will turn out to be just those wff α such that $\varnothing \vdash \alpha$, where $\varnothing$ is the symbol for the empty set. As an example we show how to establish

Syll' $\qquad \varnothing \vdash (q \supset r) \supset ((p \supset q) \supset (p \supset r))$

A	(1)	$\{p\} \vdash p$
A × **Add**	(2)	$\{p \supset q, p\} \vdash p \supset q$
(1) × **Add** (2) × MPP	(3)	$\{p \supset q, p\} \vdash q$
A × **Add**	(4)	$\{q \supset r, p \supset q, p\} \vdash q \supset r$
(3) × **Add** (4) × MPP	(5)	$\{q \supset r, p \supset q, p\} \vdash r$
(5) × CP	(6)	$\{q \supset r, p \supset q\} \vdash p \supset r$
(6) × CP	(7)	$\{q \supset r\} \vdash ((p \supset q) \supset (p \supset r))$
(7) × CP	(8)	$\varnothing \vdash (q \supset r)$
		$\supset ((p \supset q) \supset (q \supset r))$ Q.E.D.

Lemmon in fact sets out proofs a little differently. He would set out this proof of syll as

Syll″

1	(1)	p	A
1 2	(2)	$p \supset q$	A
1 2	(3)	q	1 2 MPP
1 2 4	(4)	$q \supset r$	A
1 2 4	(5)	r	3 4 MPP
2 4	(6)	$p \supset r$	5 CP
4	(7)	$(p \supset q) \supset (p \supset r)$	6 CP
	(8)	$(q \supset r) \supset ((p \supset q) \supset (p \supset r))$	7 CP

In this way of setting out the proof of syll' the numbers to the left of the parentheses serve to identify the wff which make up the set of assumptions on which the wff on that line depends. Thus 2 4 refers to the set {(2),(4)}, i.e. to {$p \supset q$, $q \supset r$} and so on. So line (6), say, abbreviates the sequent {$p \supset q$, $q \supset r$} ⊢ $p \supset r$ which of course is exactly the same as line (6) in syll'. A system adequate for deriving all and only tautologies (in $\sim$, $\supset$, $\vee$, $\wedge$ and $\equiv$) is given by Lemmon as **A, Add, MPP** and **CP**, together with the following additional rules:

MTT If $\Lambda \vdash \alpha \supset \beta$ and $\Lambda \vdash \sim\beta$ then $\Lambda \vdash \sim\alpha$.

∧I If $\Lambda \vdash \alpha$ and $\Lambda \vdash \beta$ then $\Lambda \vdash \alpha \wedge \beta$.

∧E If $\Lambda \vdash \alpha \wedge \beta$ then $\Lambda \vdash \alpha$ and $\Lambda \vdash \beta$.

∨I If $\Lambda \vdash \alpha$ then $\Lambda \vdash \alpha \vee \beta$, and if $\Lambda \vdash \beta$ then $\Lambda \vdash \alpha \vee \beta$.

∨E If $\Lambda \vdash \alpha \vee \beta$ and $\Lambda \cup \{\alpha\} \vdash \gamma$ and $\Lambda \cup \{\beta\} \vdash \gamma$ then $\Lambda \vdash \gamma$.

RAA If $\Lambda \cup \{\alpha\} \vdash \beta \wedge \sim\beta$, then $\Lambda \vdash \sim\alpha$.

DN If $\Lambda \vdash \alpha$ then $\Lambda \vdash \sim\sim\alpha$.

To extend this, or some other adequate system of natural deduction for PC, to the language $\mathcal{L}$ of modal logic we add a version of US:

US′ If $\Lambda \vdash \alpha$ and Λ' and α' result from the simultaneous and uniform substitution of wff for the variables of Λ and α, then $\Lambda' \vdash \alpha'$.

From here on we shall assume our PC basis includes US′. Lemmon's rules are given by way of example only since it is not our intention to be committed to any particular natural deduction basis for PC. A complete set of rules for PC will have the consequence that where Λ is a set of PC wff and α is a PC wff then $\Lambda \vdash \alpha$ iff every assignment of truth-values which makes all members of Λ true also makes α true. Given such a natural deduction basis for PC it may be extended to a system for normal modal logic by the addition of one new rule. To formulate this let $L^+(\Lambda)$ be $\{L\alpha : \alpha \in \Lambda\}$. Then the rule is

LR If $\Lambda \vdash \alpha$ then $L^+(\Lambda) \vdash L\alpha$.

Now consider any modal system S and let AS be a set of wff which provides an axiomatic basis for S. (I.e. $S = K + AS$.) We add as extra axioms

NDS If $\alpha \in AS$ then $\varnothing \vdash \alpha$.

What NDS means in natural deduction terms is that any axiom of S may be introduced at any stage on the basis of no assumptions. This is in contrast to the axiom **A** which means that any wff whatsoever may be introduced, but only on the basis of itself as an assumption. Different notations for natural deduction signal the dependence of a wff on a set of assumptions in different ways, so the precise terminology according to which **NDS** is presented will depend on which method of signalling dependence is used. Where S is a system of normal modal logic let NDS denote the natural deduction system formed from it in the way described above. To avoid confusion in what follows we shall write $\vdash_{NDS}$ to indicate the $\vdash$ defined by the basis of NDS. We shall write $\vdash_S$ as usual to indicate theoremhood in S, and $\Lambda \vdash_S \alpha$ to mean that either $\vdash_S \alpha$ or there exist $\beta_1, \ldots, \beta_n \in \Lambda$ such that

(i) $\vdash_S (\beta_1 \wedge \ldots \wedge \beta_n) \supset \alpha$.

Our aim is to show $\Lambda \vdash_{NDS} \alpha$ iff $\Lambda \vdash_S \alpha$. We shall prove this in each direction.

THEOREM 12.1 If $\Lambda \vdash_{NDS} \alpha$ then $\Lambda \vdash_S \alpha$.

We shall prove this by induction on the proof of sequents in NDS. Say that a sequent $\Lambda \vdash_{NDS} \alpha$ *satisfies* $\vdash_S$ iff $\Lambda \vdash_S \alpha$. We show that any axiomatic sequent, i.e. instance of **A** or AS, satisfies $\vdash_S$, and that if a set of sequents satisfies $\vdash_S$ then so does any sequent obtainable from them by an application of the transformation rules of NDS. For **A** we need to show that $\{\alpha\}$ $\vdash_S \alpha$. Since $\alpha \supset \alpha$ is a PC-tautology we have, by **PC** and US, $\vdash_S \alpha \supset \alpha$ and so $\{\alpha\}$ $\vdash_S \alpha$. For **AS** we note that if α is an axiom of S then $\vdash_S \alpha$ and so $\varnothing$ $\vdash_S \alpha$. We now turn to the transformation rules of NDS. For **Add** if $\Lambda \subseteq \Gamma$ and there are $\beta_1, \ldots, \beta_n \in \Lambda$ such that (i) obtains then there are $\beta_1, \ldots, \beta_n \in \Gamma$ such that (i) obtains and so $\Gamma \vdash \alpha$. We noted on p. 211 that if Λ $\vdash_S \alpha$ and Λ $\vdash_S \alpha \supset \beta$ then Λ $\vdash_S \beta$, and that if $\Lambda \cup \{\alpha\}$ $\vdash_S \beta$ then Λ $\vdash_S \alpha \supset \beta$. In a similar way we may show that any new sequents obtained by application of the other PC rules from sequents which satisfy $\vdash_S$ must themselves satisfy $\vdash_S$.

For **LR** suppose that Λ $\vdash_S \alpha$. Then (i) holds. So as in the proof of lemma 6.4 on p. 117 we have

(ii) $\quad \vdash_S (L\beta_1 \wedge \ldots \wedge L\beta_n) \supset L\alpha$

and so $L^+(\Lambda)$ $\vdash_S L\alpha$. This proves theorem 12.1.

THEOREM 12.2   If Λ $\vdash_S \alpha$ then Λ $\vdash_{NDS} \alpha$.

It will be sufficient to prove the following lemma:

LEMMA 12.3   If $\vdash_S \alpha$ then $\varnothing$ $\vdash_{NDS} \alpha$.

We first show that theorem 12.2 follows from lemma 12.3 and then we shall prove lemma 12.3. Assume lemma 12.3 and suppose that Λ $\vdash_S \alpha$. Then there are $\beta_1, \ldots, \beta_n \in \Lambda$ such that (i) holds. So

(iii) $\quad \vdash_S \beta_1 \supset (\ldots(\beta_n \supset \alpha)\ldots)$

so by lemma 12.3

(iv) $\quad \varnothing$ $\vdash_{NDS} \beta_1 \supset (\ldots(\beta_n \supset \alpha)\ldots)$

so by repeated applications of CP

(v) $\quad \{\beta_1, \ldots, \beta_n\}$ $\vdash_{NDS} \alpha$.

But $\{\beta_1, \ldots, \beta_n\} \subseteq \Lambda$ and so by **Add**, Λ $\vdash_{NDS} \alpha$.

Proof of lemma 12.3:
The proof is by induction on the proof of α in S. If α is a PC-tautology

then, since we are assuming that the natural deduction rules are complete for PC we have $\varnothing \vdash_{NDS} \alpha$. If $\alpha \in$ AS then $\varnothing \vdash_{NDS} \alpha$ by **NDS**. For **K** proceed as follows:

A × **Add**	(1)	$\{p, p \supset q\} \vdash p$
A × **Add**	(2)	$\{p, p \supset q\} \vdash p \supset q$
(1) (2) × MPP	(3)	$\{p, p \supset q\} \vdash q$
(3) × LR	(4)	$\{Lp, L(p \supset q)\} \vdash Lq$
(4) × CP	(5)	$\{L(p \supset q)\} \vdash Lp \supset Lq$
(5) × CP	(6)	$\varnothing \vdash L(p \supset q) \supset (Lp \supset Lq)$ **Q.E.D.**

US obviously follows from US'. For N if $\varnothing \vdash_{NDS} \alpha$ then, by LR, $L^+(\varnothing) \vdash_{NDS} L\alpha$; but $L^+(\varnothing) = \varnothing$. For MP if $\varnothing \vdash_{NDS} \alpha$ and $\varnothing \vdash_{NDS} \alpha \supset \beta$ then, by MPP $\varnothing \vdash_{NDS} \beta$. This proves lemma 12.3, and therefore theorem 12.2.

In this natural deduction formulation of modal logic we have achieved generality at a cost. For in every case the natural deduction rule corresponding to a proper axiom α of S, is simply $\varnothing \vdash \alpha$. In some cases this rule may be replaced with one which looks more like a regular kind of natural deduction rule. If a special axiom of S has the form $\alpha \supset \beta$ then we may add either the axiomatic sequent

$$\{\alpha\} \vdash \{\beta\}$$

or the rule

If $\Lambda \vdash \alpha$ then $\Lambda \vdash \beta$.

So, for instance, T could be axiomatized by adding $\{L\alpha\} \vdash \{\alpha\}$ or

If $\Lambda \vdash \{L\alpha\}$ then $\Lambda \vdash \{\alpha\}$.

Other possible natural deduction bases are not so predictable from the axioms. For instance S4 can be axiomatized by adding to T the following rule and omitting LR.

NDS4   If $L^+(\Lambda) \vdash \alpha$ then $L^+(\Lambda) \vdash L\alpha$.

(K4 can be axiomatized by adding NDS4 to K, keeping LR.)
If we define $M^+(\Lambda)$ to be $\{M\alpha: \alpha \in \Lambda\}$, then B may be obtained by

adding to T:

NDB   If $M^+(\Lambda) \vdash \alpha$ then $\Lambda \vdash L\alpha$.

S5 may be obtained by adding to T the following rule and omitting LR:

NDS5   If $\Lambda \vdash \alpha$ then $\Lambda \vdash L\alpha$ provided every variable in every member of Λ is inside the scope of a modal operator.

Multiply modal logics

All the systems so far considered in this book have involved only one (primitive) necessity operator. It is possible to have logics which involve more than one. A language $\mathcal{L}_k$ of *multi-modal* (propositional) logic contains a family of operators $L_1, \dots , L_k$, with the formation rules being extended so that if α is a wff then so is $L_n\alpha$ for each L_n ($n \leq k$). A frame for a multi-modal logic consists of a pair $\langle W, R \rangle$ where W is a set (of worlds) and R is a function from a natural number $n \leq k$ to a relation R_n between members of W. A model based on $\langle W, R \rangle$ is a triple $\langle W, R, V \rangle$ in which everything is as for ordinary modal logic except that for L_n we have

[VL$_n$] $V(L_n\alpha, w) = 1$ if $V(\alpha, w) = 1$ for every w' such that wR_nw', and 0 otherwise.

Obviously $M_n\alpha$ may be defined as $\sim L_n \sim \alpha$.

In any system of multi-modal logic we have the result that where α is a theorem of K in ordinary modal logic and α'_n results from α by the replacement of every L by L_n, then α'_n is valid in every frame. We let K_k denote the system defined as any collection of wff of $\mathcal{L}_k$ which contains every PC-tautology, every instance for $n \leq k$ of,

K_n $L_n(p \supset q) \supset (L_np \supset L_nq)$

and is closed under US, MP and N_n ($\vdash \alpha \rightarrow \vdash L_n\alpha$) for every $n \leq k$.

For every such system we may define, in the usual way, a canonical model by letting wR_nw' iff for every wff α, if $L_n\alpha \in w$ then $\alpha \in w'$. The canonical model will characterize the system in question for the same reasons as in the ordinary case. So much is relatively unexciting. The interest in multi-modal logics comes when we have relations between different necessity operators. For instance we might have a necessity operator L_1, say, which is stronger than L_2 in the sense that $L_1 p \supset L_2 p$. The canonical model for such a system would obey the restriction that for all w, $w' \in W$, if wR_1w' then wR_2w'.

One particularly important class of multi-modal systems is the class of *tense logics*.[5] A tense logic has two operators, L_1 and L_2, where L_1 means 'it always will be the case that' and L_2 means 'it always has been the case that'. In frames for a tense logic R_1 and R_2 are so related that one is the converse of the other, i.e. wR_1w' iff $w'R_2w$. Alternatively we may think of a frame for tense logic as the same as for ordinary modal logic, a pair $\langle W,R \rangle$ where R is just a relation, and in a model $\langle W,R,V \rangle$ based on $\langle W,R \rangle$ we have

[VL_1TL] $V(L_1\alpha,w) = 1$ if $V(\alpha,w') = 1$ for all w' such that wRw' and 0 otherwise.

[VL_2TL] $V(L_2\alpha,w) = 1$ iff $V(\alpha,w') = 1$ for every w' such that $w'Rw$ and 0 otherwise.

(In a tense logic L_1 and L_2 are often written G and H with their possibility versions as P, for $\sim H\sim$, and F, for $\sim G\sim$.)

To guarantee that R_2 is the converse of R_1 we need the axioms

TL1 $\sim p \supset L_1 \sim L_2 p$
TL2 $\sim p \supset L_2 \sim L_1 p$

It is not hard to see that TL1 and TL2 are valid in every model satisfying [VL_1TL] and [VL_2TL]. Further, in the canonical model for any system containing TL1, one may prove that if wR_1w' then $w'R_2w$, and for any system containing TL2 if wR_2w' then $w'R_1w$. We shall prove the former. Suppose that in the canonical model (i) wR_1w' but (ii) not $w'R_2w$. From (ii) there is a wff α such that $L_2\alpha \in w'$ but $\alpha \notin w$. So $\sim\alpha \in w$ and so, by TL1, $L_1 \sim L_2\alpha \in w$. So by (i) $\sim L_2\alpha \in w'$ making w' inconsistent. The proof of the case for TL2 is exactly analogous.

An interesting class of temporal logics are those called omnitemporal logics. These are ordinary modal logics in which the rule for L is

[VLO] $V(L\alpha,w) = 1$ iff $V(\alpha,w') = 1$ for every w' such that either wRw' or $w'Rw$ or $w = w'$.

L interpreted by [VLO] means 'it was, is now, and always will be the case that'. One can equally describe it as governed by its own accessibility relation R^+ where wR^+w' iff wRw' or $w = w'$ or $w'Rw$. If time is linear in both directions then the appropriate omnitemporal logic is S5. If no conditions are imposed on R the correct logic is B. If R is transitive it is still B. An interesting case is where R is linear in the past but allowed to branch in the future. Then the correct logic[6] is B +

$$Lp \supset (Mq \supset L(Lp \lor Mq))$$

Tense logic is a whole topic in itself and is beyond the scope of this book.

The expressive power of multi-modal logics

From the point of view of modal logic one of the interesting features of multi-modal systems is their expressive power. In one recent study Lloyd Humberstone[7] discusses logics where R_2 is the complement of R_1 in the sense that wR_2w' iff not wR_1w'. The minimal logic of such frames, i.e. the system determined by the class of all frames $\langle W,R \rangle$ in which R_2 is the complement of R_1, may be axiomatized as follows. Define an operator $\square$ as

$$\square\alpha =_{df} (L_1\alpha \land L_2\alpha)$$

Now add to K_2 all instances of the S5 axioms for $\square$. I.e.

$$\square p \supset p$$
$$\sim\square p \supset \square \sim \square p$$

This system is called K~. As an example of the extra expressive power of bi-modal logic we recall from p. 176 that there is no wff of ordinary modal logic which, when added to K, imposes irreflexiveness on a frame. When we move to K~, however, the situation is different. We may think of a frame for K~ either as a frame with two relations or alternatively as a frame in which L_2 has a non-standard evaluation,

[VL~] $V(L_2\alpha,w) = 1$ iff $V(\alpha,w') = 1$ for every $w' \in W$ such that *not* wRw'.

Now if we add to K~ the axiom

$\mathbf{T}^{\sim}$ $L_2p \supset p$

We can see that, just as $\mathbf{T}$ imposed reflexiveness on R, $\mathbf{T}^{\sim}$ imposes it on R_2. But wR_2w' iff not wR_1w'. So if R_2 is reflexive, R_1 is irreflexive. Using [VL$^{\sim}$] this means that R is irreflexive. Similarly asymmetry can be expressed by $p \supset L_1M_2p$ and intransitivity by $L_2p \supset L_1L_1p$.

Propositional symbols

Another way of increasing the expressive power of propositional modal logic is to add new propositional symbols. An example of this is connected with the fact noted on p. 187 that there is no modal wff which can define the class of frames in which every world can see a reflexive world. Valentin Goranko suggests adding a symbol **loop** such that $V(\mathbf{loop},w) = 1$ iff wRw.[8] Obviously $M\mathbf{loop}$ will be valid in a frame iff every world can see a reflexive world.

A second example of a propositional symbol is a special kind of variable. Patrick Blackburn investigates a class of propositional symbols he calls *nominals*.[9] Where n is a symbol of this kind the rule is that in every model there is some w such that

$$V(n,w') = 1 \text{ iff } w = w'$$

This means that a nominal is true in exactly one world. It is easy to see that $n \supset L\sim n$, where n is a nominal, is valid on a frame iff that frame is irreflexive.

Dynamic logic

In the presentation of multiply modal logics we have assumed that the necessity operators L_1, L_2, ... etc. are indexed by the natural numbers. Another way of indexing them is suggested by a possible interpretation of modal logic in computer science. In this interpretation the 'worlds' are states in the running of a program. If π is a computer program then $[\pi]\alpha$ means that after program π has been run α will be true. If w is any 'world' then $wR_\pi w'$ means that state w' results from the running of program π. This interpretation of modal logic is called *dynamic logic*.[10]

What gives dynamic logic its interest is the possibility of combining simple programs to get more complex ones. Thus if π_1 and π_2 are two programs then the expression $\pi_1;\pi_2$ refers to the program 'first do π_1 and then do π_2', and $[\pi_1;\pi_2]\alpha$ means that α will be true if this is done. The relation corresponding to $[\pi_1;\pi_2]$ may be defined to hold between w and

w' iff $\exists u(wR_{\pi_1}u \wedge uR_{\pi_2}w')$.

Other complex programs include:

$\pi_1 \cup \pi_2$: 'do either π_1 or π_2' (its relation is $R_{\pi_1} \cup R_{\pi_2}$)
π^*: 'do π finitely many times' ($\exists n\ wR_\pi^n v'$)
$[\alpha?]\beta$: 'β is true provided α is' ($wR_{[\alpha?]}w'$ iff $w = w'$ and $V(\alpha,w)$
$= 1$)

Other constructs may be introduced by definition.

Goldblatt shows that a system he calls PDL (propositional dynamic logic) is complete with respect to this interpretation.[11] Using π_1, π_2, ... etc., as schematic letters for simple or complex programs PDL may be specified as the smallest normal multi-modal logic containing

Comp $[\pi_1;\pi_2]p \equiv [\pi_1][\pi_2]p$
Union $[\pi_1 \cup \pi_2]p \equiv ([\pi_1]p \wedge [\pi_2]p)$
Test $[\alpha?]p \equiv (\alpha \supset p)$
Mix $[\pi^*]p \supset (p \wedge [\pi][\pi^*]p)$
Ind $[\pi^*](p \supset [\pi]p) \supset (p \supset [\pi^*]p)$

Neighbourhood semantics

In this section we look at the most general kind of possible-worlds semantics compatible with keeping the classical truth-table semantics for the truth-functional operators.

The idea is based on that of the 'truth set' of a formula. In any model we can define $|\alpha|$ as $\{w \in W: V(\alpha,w) = 1\}$. Now in evaluating $L\alpha$ in a world w all the input that we require is to know which set of worlds forms the truth set of α. Whatever L means, what it has to do is to declare $L\alpha$ true at w for some truth sets and false for others. So the meaning of L must specify which sets of worlds form acceptable truth sets in world w. These sets of worlds are called the *neighbourhoods*[12] of w, and a *neighbourhood frame* for a language $\mathcal{L}$ of (mono-) modal propositional logic is a pair $\langle W,R \rangle$ in which W is a set (of worlds) and R is a 'neighbourhood relation'. A neighbourhood relation is a relation between a world w and a subset A of W and A is a neighbourhood of w iff wRA. The rule for L in such a frame is

$[VL\dagger]$ $V(L\alpha,w) = 1$ iff $wR|\alpha|$

A frame of the kind assumed in the rest of this book in which R is a relation between worlds is often called a *relational* frame, and it is not difficult to see that every relational frame is a special case of a neighbourhood frame. To be precise, a relational frame is a neighbourhood frame in which for every $w \in W$ there is a set B of those and only those worlds which are accessible to w (i.e. B is the set of worlds w can 'see') and wRA iff $B \subseteq A$. What this means is that α's truth set is a neighbourhood of w iff it contains all the worlds accessible from W, which is of course precisely what the truth of $L\alpha$ in a relational frame amounts to.

As an example of a neighbourhood frame which is not a relational frame let W consist of the natural numbers and let the neighbourhoods of all worlds be the set of odd numbers or the set of even numbers. Then we can easily falsify such K-theorems as $Lp \supset L(p \supset p)$ − by making, say, p true just at the odd numbers.

The logic characterized by the class of all neighbourhood frames is very simple. Its axioms are the valid PC-wff and its rules are US, MP and the single rule

RE $\vdash \alpha \equiv \beta \rightarrow \vdash L\alpha \equiv L\beta$

This rule will also be a rule of all logics determined by any class of neighbourhood frames provided validity is defined as truth in every world in every model based on that frame.[13]

Neighbourhood frames give the appropriate generality for operators whose semantics are provided by a non-standard evaluation rule. For instance Humberstone[14] discusses the logic of an operator whose semantics is

$V(L\alpha,w) = 1$ iff, for every $w' \in W$, $V(\alpha,w') = 1$ iff wRw'

(where R is now an ordinary accessibility relation). He interprets L to mean 'α is true in all and only accessible worlds'. Here A is a neighbourhood of w iff $A = \{w' : w$R$w'\}$.

Another interesting class of logics which can be studied by neighbourhood frames are logics which have been called 'non-aggregative' logics.[15] In these logics the accessibility relation R is replaced by an n-place relation for some n > 1. For 3 the evaluation rule is:

$V(L\alpha,w) = 1$ iff for every w', w'' such that $wRw'w''$, $V(\alpha,w') = 1$ or $V(\alpha,w'') = 1$.

In such logics **K**, and therefore K2 $((Lp \wedge Lq) \supset L(p \wedge q))$ does not hold, although

K2$'$ $(Lp \wedge Lq \wedge Lr) \supset L((p \wedge q) \vee (p \wedge r) \vee (q \wedge r))$

Along with PC, US, MP and the rule R* ($\vdash \alpha \supset \beta$, $\vdash L\alpha \supset L\beta$), **K2$'$** provides an axiomatization for this logic. The frames for this logic can be thought of as neighbourhood frames in which A is a neighbourhood of w iff for every w' and $w'' \in W$ such that $wRw'w''$, either $w' \in A$ or $w'' \in A$. The case involving a three-place relation can be generalized to any n.

Neighbourhood semantics can of course be devised for systems with more than one necessity operator, and even for systems with operators taking more than one argument. A philosophically important example here is the logic of counterfactuals as developed in the late 60s and early 70s. We shall present a version of David Lewis's semantics.[16] Counterfactual logic is based on a dyadic operator $\square\!\!\rightarrow$ where $\alpha \square\!\!\rightarrow \beta$ is to mean that if α were to be the case then β would be the case. Lewis's idea is that, given a possible world w, some worlds are closer to w than others. If we write $w' <_w w''$ to mean that w' is closer to w than w'' is then the semantics for $\square\!\!\rightarrow$ will be that $\alpha \square\!\!\rightarrow \beta$ is to be true in w iff either α is not true at any world or there is a world w' at which α and β are both true which is closer to w than any world w'' at which α is true but β is not. A counterfactual frame can be described as a neighbourhood frame in the following way. Since $\square\!\!\rightarrow$ is dyadic its neighbourhood relation R will relate worlds to pairs $\langle A,B\rangle$ where $A \subseteq W$ and $B \subseteq W$. The standard rule for dyadic operators will of course be

$V(\alpha \square\!\!\rightarrow \beta,w) = 1$ iff $wR\langle|\alpha|,|\beta|\rangle$

A frame $\langle W,R\rangle$ will be a counterfactual frame iff it is based on a nearness relation $<$ in such a way that $wR\langle A,B\rangle$ iff either

(a) $A = \varnothing$ or

(b) There is some w' such that $w' \in A \cap B$ and for every w'', if $w'' \in A \cap -B$ then $w' <_w w''$.

Which counterfactual logic you get will depend on what kind of conditions you put on $<$. For instance, under the plausible assumption that the closest world to w is w itself you get a frame which validates the wff

$$p \supset ((p \;\Box\!\!\rightarrow q) \equiv q)$$

By contrast, on any plausible account of nearness, many wff which are valid for $\supset$ or for $\dashv$ fail for $\Box\!\!\rightarrow$. For instance in standard systems of counterfactual logic neither

$$((p \;\Box\!\!\rightarrow q) \wedge (q \;\Box\!\!\rightarrow r)) \supset (p \;\Box\!\!\rightarrow r) \text{ nor}$$

$$(p \;\Box\!\!\rightarrow q) \supset (\sim q \;\Box\!\!\rightarrow \sim p)$$

are valid.

A logic may be said to be neighbourhood complete if it is characterized by a class of neighbourhood frames. It is known that there are normal incomplete modal logics which are neighbourhood complete and others which are not neighbourhood complete.[17]

Intermediate logics

In Chapter 11 we introduced the symbol $\dashv$ in such a way that $\alpha \dashv \beta$ can be defined as $L(\alpha \supset \beta)$. Many valid PC-wff become invalid if $\supset$ is replaced by $\dashv$, and so one could regard a propositional logic in which $\supset$ is replaced by $\dashv$ as a weaker version of PC. Indeed one might even argue that Lewis thought of it in just this way. Other versions of propositional logic can be studied like this, and they are often called *intermediate logics*, the principal example being intuitionistic logic. The intuitionistic propositional calculus IC treats $\vee$ and $\wedge$ as in classical PC, but interprets negation and implication differently. We shall use $\neg$ for intuitionistic negation and $\rightarrow$ for intuitionistic implication. A set of axioms for IC is the following:[18]

H1 $\quad p \rightarrow (p \wedge p)$
H2 $\quad (p \wedge q) \rightarrow (q \wedge p)$
H3 $\quad (p \rightarrow q) \rightarrow ((p \wedge r) \rightarrow (q \wedge r))$
H4 $\quad ((p \rightarrow q) \wedge (q \rightarrow r)) \rightarrow (p \rightarrow r)$
H5 $\quad p \rightarrow (q \rightarrow p)$
H6 $\quad (p \wedge (p \rightarrow q)) \rightarrow q$
H7 $\quad p \rightarrow (p \vee q)$

H8 $(p \lor q) \to (q \lor p)$
H9 $((p \to r) \land (q \to r)) \to ((p \lor q) \to r)$
H10 $\neg p \to (p \to q)$
H11 $((p \to q) \land (p \to \neg q)) \to \neg p$

The most notable omissions from IC are $p \lor \neg p$ and $\neg\neg p \to p$. (However, $p \to \neg\neg p$ is a theorem.)

To understand IC we bear in mind that it is intended to formalize intuitionistic mathematics in which truth means established truth and $\neg \alpha$ means that α has been established to be false. Thus, since α may neither be established to be true, nor established to be false it is not surprising that $\alpha \lor \neg \alpha$ should fail to be valid. IC can be interpreted in modal logic by the definitions:

Def $\neg$: $\neg \alpha =_{df} L{\sim}\alpha$
Def $\to$: $\alpha \to \beta =_{df} L(\alpha \supset \beta)$

With these definitions IC becomes a subsystem of S4 in the sense that, provided every variable p is replaced by Lp, then any wff will be a theorem of IC iff the result of such replacements (using Def $\neg$ and Def $\to$) is a theorem of S4.

The standard semantics for S4 can then be used to provide a direct interpretation for IC, in which, if $V(p,w) = 1$ then $V(p,w') = 1$ for every w' such that wRw', $V(\neg\alpha,w) = 1$ iff $V(\alpha,w') = 0$ for every w' such that wRw', and $V(\alpha \to \beta,w) = 1$ iff for every w' such that wRw', either $V(\alpha,w') = 0$ or $V(\beta,w') = 1$.

If we interpret the language of IC in S5 rather than S4 it turns out that we get classical PC. If we interpret it in systems between S5 and S4 we can get extensions of IC. Thus, in S4.3 $(p \to q) \lor (q \to p)$ becomes valid.[19] Such intermediate logics form an interesting application of modal logic.

'Syntactical' approaches to modality

This book has been concerned to present the semantics of modal logic by means of possible worlds. That technique has proved by far the most valuable in terms of the generality of its applicability. It is however not the only way of studying modal logic semantically. Many philosophers are suspicious of the idea of a possible world when thought of as an alternative to our actual world. While such suspicions give rise to important debates in metaphysics we have been at pains to insist that from the point of view of modal *logic* it does not in the least matter what the worlds are. For instance in the canonical model of a normal modal system the worlds are maximal consistent sets of wff. Seen in this way possible-worlds semantics is the most neutral of semantic frameworks since many 'alternatives' to it are better seen as implementations of it, provided by giving an account of what possible worlds might be held really to be. However, even a semantics which might in the end turn out to be of this form can be worth looking at to see just how the implementation works.

One very powerful idea behind modal logic is the connection between necessity and validity. The rule of necessitation makes it clear that if α is *valid* then this is necessarily so, since $L\alpha$ is then also valid. The version of this approach that we shall discuss is a generalization of one presented by Brian Skyrms,[20] though the idea of treating modality 'syntactically' by thinking of necessity as a property of wff has a longer history. However, we have to be careful since validity is a property of *wff* while necessity is a property of propositions. The importance of this distinction may be easily seen. The variable p is certainly not valid. So if we identified validity with necessity it would seem that Lp should always be false, or that $\sim Lp$ should always be true. But obviously if $\sim Lp$ were a theorem of any normal modal system we would have, by US, $\sim L(p \supset p)$ and since $L(p \supset p)$ is a theorem of every normal system the resulting system would be inconsistent. The idea underlying Skyrms's account is this. Although the variable p is not valid in the sense that it is not true in *every* PC model, yet it might well be true in a more restricted class of models. In the present section we shall use the notion of an *extensional model*. An extensional model is simply an assignment of truth-values to the wff of propositional modal logic which respects the standard truth-tables; specifically it is an assignment m such that

   (i) $m(\sim \alpha) = 1$ if $m(\alpha) = 0$ and 0 otherwise;
   (ii) $m(\alpha \lor \beta) = 1$ if $m(\alpha) = 1$ or $m(\beta) = 1$ and 0 otherwise.

We say that a family M of extensional models is a *modal family* iff there is a relation R* between members of M such that for $m \in M$, for every wff α of $\mathcal{L}$,

   (iii) $m(L\alpha) = 1$ iff $m'(\alpha) = 1$ for every $m' \in M$ such that mR*m'.

It should not be difficult to see that every 'ordinary' model $\langle W,R,V \rangle$

which contains no duplicates (in the sense described on p. 165) may be represented by a modal family M in which each member m of M can be indexed by a world w in such a way that $m_w(\alpha) = V(\alpha,w)$. And of course every modal family may be considered to be a model $\langle W,R,V \rangle$ in such a way that W is simply M, R is R*, and $V(\alpha,m) = m(\alpha)$.

In the case of S5 (which is the system that Skyrms considered) we can in fact do better. Recall that an S5-model may be considered to be simply a pair $\langle W,V \rangle$ in which W is a set of worlds and [VL] is amended to

[VLS5] $V(L\alpha,w) = 1$ iff $V(\alpha,w') = 1$ for every $w' \in$ W.

[VLS5] has the consequence that any wff of the form $L\alpha$ is either true throughout the model or false throughout the model. And *this* means that any two worlds which coincide on the values to the variables, coincide on the values to all wff. So the extensional models in the corresponding modal family in this case need give values only to the variables. This procedure will not work in general. Consider for instance a model in which there are two worlds, w_1 and w_2, where w_1 is a dead end while w_2 is not. In such a case a model in which every variable has the same value in w_1 as in w_2, will still not give every wff the same value in both these worlds since $L(p \wedge \sim p)$ will be true in w_1 but false in w_2.

Another 'syntactic' interpretation is to think of L as meaning 'is a theorem'. Skyrms shows how to give an interpretation for S4 in which L has this meaning.[21] Care must be taken here too since we have already observed (p. 140) that if 'provable' means 'provable in the language of arithmetic' the correct logic is KW, and if we add the wff $Lp \supset p$ as an extra axiom to KW, by N we have $L(Lp \supset p)$ and so by W, Lp and thus by $Lp \supset p$ we have p and the inconsistent system.[22]

Probabilistic semantics

Another alternative to possible-worlds semantics involves probability theory. Instead of assigning truth-values in possible worlds a probability function Pr assigns values from the interval of real numbers from 0 to 1 (including 0 and 1 themselves as limiting cases). Where $Pr(\alpha,\beta) = r$ is read as 'the probability of α given β is r', a probability function, for PC, may be defined as satisfying the following:[23]

PR1 $0 \leq Pr(\alpha,\beta) \leq 1$
PR2 $Pr(\alpha,\alpha) = 1$

PR3 If $\Pr(\beta,\delta) = \Pr(\gamma,\delta)$ for every wff δ then $\Pr(\alpha,\beta) = \Pr(\alpha,\gamma)$ for every wff α.

PR4 If there is at least one wff γ such that $\Pr(\gamma,\beta) \neq 1$, then for every wff α, $\Pr(\sim\alpha,\beta) = 1 - \Pr(\alpha,\beta)$.

PR5 $\Pr(\alpha \wedge \beta,\gamma) = \Pr(\alpha,\beta \wedge \gamma) \times \Pr(\beta,\gamma)$

PR6 $\Pr(\alpha \wedge \beta,\gamma) = \Pr(\beta \wedge \alpha,\gamma)$

A wff α is called probabilistically valid iff $\Pr(\alpha,\beta) = 1$ for every wff β. The probabilistically valid PC-wff are precisely the PC-valid wff. Charles Morgan[24] extends this account to modal logic by adding the following conditions:

PR7 If $\Pr(\alpha,\gamma) \leq \Pr(\beta,\gamma)$ for every wff γ then $\Pr(L\alpha,\gamma) \leq \Pr(L\beta,\gamma)$ for every wff γ.

PR8 $\Pr(L(\alpha \wedge \beta),\gamma) = \Pr(L\alpha \wedge L\beta,\gamma)$

PR9 There is at least one wff α such that $\Pr(L\alpha,\beta) = 1$ for every wff β.

It is not difficult to see that these conditions mimic the axiomatic basis of K, and Morgan is able to provide a soundness and completeness result. Other systems may be obtained by adding conditions which correspond analogously with their axioms. Thus a probabilistic semantics for T is obtained by adding

PR10 $\Pr(L\alpha,\beta) \leq \Pr(\alpha,\beta)$

and for S4

PR11 $\Pr(L\alpha,\beta) \leq \Pr(LL\alpha,\beta)$

and so on.

Morgan's is not the only way to present a probabilistic semantics for modal logic. For those who prefer a semantics which does more than simply mimic the axioms. Charles Cross[25] has a semantics for modal logic in which the role played by possible worlds in standard treatments is played by probability functions. Using an accessibility relation between probability functions, and requiring that the value of $L\alpha$ conditional on β for a given probability function be less than the value of α conditional on β for all accessible probability functions, Cross is able to prove soundness for T, B, S4 and S5. The use of degenerate functions whose values are 0 or 1 enables standard completeness results to apply to his semantics.

Algebraic semantics

An algebra is a set of 'elements' together with operations on them. An especially important kind of algebra is called a Boolean Algebra. The most intuitive way to link Boolean Algebra with modal logic is to think of the elements as sets of worlds and the operations as intersection, union and complementation. The accessibility relation R then defines a further operation O on sets of worlds such that where A is a set of worlds, O(A) is the set $\{w: \forall w'(wRw' \supset w' \in A)\}$, i.e. O(A) is the set of worlds in which A is 'necessary' − and w is such a world iff every world accessible to it is in A. In speaking this way we are thinking of A as the truth set of a wff.[26]

The study of frames and models as algebraic structures provides an insightful way of looking at modal logic for those who want to link it with mathematics. Such a study is beyond the scope of the present book.[27]

Exercises — 12

12.1   Prove that $\Lambda \vdash \alpha$ in NDS4, NDB and NDS5 iff $\Lambda \vdash_{S4} \alpha$, $\vdash_B \alpha$ and $\vdash_{S5} \alpha$ respectively.

12.2   Provide an axiomatization for tense logic in which time is
  (a)   connected in both directions,
  (b)   connected in the past but branching in the future.

12.3   Prove that B is omnitemporally characterized by frames in which time is transitive but permitted to branch in both directions.

12.4   Prove that the system axiomatized by PC, US, MP and RE is characterized by the class of all neighbourhood frames.

12.5   (open problem) Is KH complete for neighbourhood frames?

12.6   Show that in standard systems of counterfactual logic neither
  $((p \,\Box\!\!\rightarrow q) \land (q \,\Box\!\!\rightarrow r)) \supset (p \,\Box\!\!\rightarrow r)$
nor
  $(p \,\Box\!\!\rightarrow q) \supset (\sim q \,\Box\!\!\rightarrow \sim p)$
is valid.

12.7   Show that the following are valid in the intermediate logics based on the following extensions of S4:
  $\neg p \lor \neg \neg p$ [S4.2]

$(p \rightarrow q) \vee (q \rightarrow p)$ [S4.3]
All PC-tautologies   [S5]

Notes

[1] A standard reference work for most topics mentioned in this chapter may be found in Gabbay and Guenthner 1984.

[2] Whitehead and Russell 1910 have a basis consisting of the four axioms listed in the text together with one subsequently found to be derivable from the others. The basis given here was assumed for modal logic in Hughes and Cresswell 1968.

[3] Strictly speaking it might be more correct to write $\vdash \langle \Lambda, \alpha \rangle$, since the sequent itself is the pair $\langle \Lambda, \alpha \rangle$. However we shall frequently use the notation $\Lambda \vdash \alpha$ to refer to the sequent itself rather than to the fact that the sequent is a theorem. Our development is based on Lemmon 1965b but natural deduction methods go back to Gentzen 1934 and are found in many logic texts. One of the earliest natural deduction systems for modal logic is in Fitch 1952, though Fitch did not aim for or achieve the generality we assume here. For a survey of natural deduction methods in modal logic see Fitting 1983. Other discussion occurs in Hawthorn 1990. We do not make a distinction between a system of natural deduction and a sequent calculus, since we regard the latter as a way of making the former precise and explicit. Different systems of natural deduction are in effect different notations for keeping track of the premisses (i.e. the members of Λ) on which the wff α depends. Some systems use vertical lines starting under a wff to be assumed as part of Λ. Others box subproofs, and so on, but what they all have in common is that they are establishing a relation between a wff and a set of wff.

[4] Lemmon 1965b, pp. 9–15. Lemmon does not explicitly state the rule **Add** but it is in fact required. (Or else **A** and **Add** can be combined into a single axiom $\mathbf{A^+}$: If $\alpha \in \Lambda$ then $\Lambda \vdash \alpha$.)

[5] An introduction to tense logic is found in Burgess 1984.

[6] See Hughes 1975 and 1982. Logics of this kind are there called 'omnitemporal logic'.

[7] Humberstone 1983. Such logics are also discussed in Goranko 1990, and the axiom system we provide in the text is his.

[8] **loop** is found on p. 102f. of Goranko 1990.

[9] Blackburn 1993. Bull 1970 had already introduced the same idea for tense logic. See also Gargov and Goranko 1993.

[10] This section summarizes material presented at greater length in Chapter 10 of Goldblatt 1987. Further references to the literature may be found in that volume.

[11] It is also possible to develop dynamic predicate logic. For an introductory survey see Part III of Goldblatt 1987.

[12] For some remarks on the history of neighbourhood semantics see Segerberg 1971, pp. 72f.

[13] If, as in S2 and S3 as described on p. 201 we define validity as truth only in every 'normal' world (however this may be defined) then RE may no longer hold.

(We observed on p. 46 that a rule may hold in a system but may fail in an extension of that system.) The semantics for S1 given in Cresswell 1995a uses an accessibility relation for normal worlds, but for non-normal worlds uses an arbitrary neighbourhood relation R^* satisfying the restriction that if wR^*A and wR^*B then (i) $w \in A$ and $w \in B$ and (ii) $A \cup B \neq W$.

[14] Humberstone 1987. The operator in this paper is a sort of fusion of the operators that appeared in Humberstone 1983.

[15] Schotch and Jennings 1980.

[16] Lewis 1973. The same idea is also found in Stalnaker 1968 and Åqvist 1973.

[17] See Bull and Segerberg 1984, p. 72 and the references listed there. (Also Gerson 1975 and Gabbay 1975.)

[18] These axioms are given in Heyting 1930. The connection between IC and S4 seems to have first been noticed in Gödel 1933 and is stated explicitly in McKinsey and Tarski 1948. A connection of a different kind between modal logic and IC is noted in Becker 1930 (see p. 70). The intuitionist predicate calculus is studied in Kripke 1965a. See also Fitting 1983. A survey of intuitionistic logic is found in van Dalen 1986.

[19] See Dummett and Lemmon 1959.

[20] Skyrms 1978. Skyrms's ideas are generalized to propositional languages with propositional operators having neighbourhood semantics in Cresswell 1985. The idea that a necessary proposition is one which has the form of a valid wff is found in McKinsey 1945. Kripke 1959 for S5 predicate logic treats worlds as value assignments. Further development of Skyrms's approach, including a discussion of how it works in modal predicate logic, may be found in Schweizer 1992, 1993 and elsewhere.

[21] Skyrms 1978, pp. 375–382.

[22] Montague 1963 shows that when L is a predicate applicable to sentences of formal arithmetic then $Lp \supset p$ cannot be consistently added to any normal modal logic. (In fact even S1 is inconsistent.) Skyrms 1978, pp. 382–387, points out that Montague's argument need not apply to weaker languages.

[23] We have used the definition presented in Morgan 1982, p. 445. Morgan takes $\sim$ and $\wedge$ as the basic PC-operators and we have followed him in this.

[24] Morgan 1982, p. 445f.

[25] Cross 1993.

[26] An early algebraic study of modal logic is found in McKinsey 1941. See also McKinsey and Tarski 1944 and Jónsson and Tarski 1951, and Lemmon 1960a. A fuller survey is found in Lemmon 1966a and 1966b, and a more introductory survey in Chapter 17 of Hughes and Cresswell 1968.

[27] A modal algebra turns out to look more like the general frames described on p. 167 since not every set of worlds need be an element.

Part III

MODAL PREDICATE LOGIC

13

THE LOWER PREDICATE CALCULUS

In this part of the book we shall examine what happens when modal logic is combined with the Lower Predicate Calculus. We shall assume that readers are familiar with the ordinary non-modal LPC (as we shall refer to it) but we shall make our development self-contained, and explain all our terminology as we proceed.[1] In essence the predicate calculus extends the propositional calculus by the addition of symbols which enable us to speak about 'all' or 'some' things which satisfy a certain condition. These symbols are called *quantifiers*. The symbol ∀ is used to say that everything satisfies a certain condition and is called the *universal quantifier*, while the symbol ∃ is used to say that there exists something which satisfies a certain condition and is called the *existential quantifier*. Each can be defined in terms of the other, and we shall set out a version of LPC which takes ∀ as primitive.

Primitive symbols and formation rules of non-modal LPC
In what follows we shall have occasion to extend the language of LPC by adding extra symbols. We shall therefore define what is to count as a language $\mathcal{L}$ of LPC. Where we have a fixed language in mind we shall usually omit explicit reference to $\mathcal{L}$. A language $\mathcal{L}$ of (non-modal) LPC takes as primitive the following symbols.

(1) For each natural number n (≥ 1) a set (possibly finite but at most denumerably infinite) of n-place *predicates*. We refer to these as ϕ, ψ, χ, ... etc.

(2) A denumerably infinite set of *individual variables*, which we refer to as x, y, z, ... etc.

(3) The five symbols $\sim$, $\vee$, $\forall$, (, and).

The formation rules are these:

FR1 Any sequence of symbols consisting of an n-place predicate followed by n (not necessarily distinct) individual variables is a wff. (Such a wff is called an *atomic wff*.)

FR2 If α is a wff so is $\sim\alpha$.

FR3 If α and β are wff so is $(\alpha \vee \beta)$.

FR4 If α is a wff and x is an individual variable then $\forall x\alpha$ is a wff.

We adopt the definitions of $\wedge$, $\supset$ and $\equiv$ used in propositional logic, and add the definition

[Def $\exists$] $\exists x\alpha =_{df} \sim\forall x\sim\alpha$

As we said above $\forall$ and $\exists$ are called quantifiers. More strictly we should say that $\forall$ or $\exists$ followed by a variable is the quantifier since $\forall x$ and $\forall y$ have different meanings. In a wff of the form $\forall x\alpha$, α is said to be the *scope* of the quantifier $\forall x$. An occurrence of a variable x in a wff α (not as part of a quantifier) is said to be *free* or *bound* in α. If it does not lie within the scope of any quantifier which contains x it is said to be *free* in α. Otherwise it is said to be bound in α; and if x is free in α it is said to be *bound by* $\forall x$ in $\forall x\alpha$. Thus in the wff

(1) $\forall x(\phi x \vee \psi y)$

the x occurring immediately after ϕ is bound (by the quantifier $\forall x$ at the beginning) but y is free. Note however that even when we are speaking of (1) we say that x is free in $(\phi x \vee \psi y)$ since no quantifier containing x occurs in *that* expression, though of course x is not free in (1) itself. Note also that it is *occurrences* of variables that are bound or free, and that the same variable may occur both bound and free in the same formula, as, e.g., x does in $\forall x\phi x \supset \phi x$. Note thirdly that in a wff like $\forall x(\phi x \vee \forall x\psi x)$ the first occurrence of x is bound by the outermost (initial) quantifier, and the second by the innermost quantifier.

In Chapter 17 we shall consider languages of LPC which have individual constants and function symbols. For the present we do not have these.

Interpretation

In order to see how to interpret wff of LPC we shall look at the kind of things such a language can be used to say which go beyond the resources of PC. Suppose we wanted to express the fact that all cats are animals. If we interpret the one-place predicates ϕ and ψ as, respectively, 'is a cat' and 'is an animal' then we can express this fact by the wff

(1) $\forall x(\phi x \supset \psi x)$.

(1) says that for every x, if x is a cat then x is an animal. At least it does this on the assumption that $\forall x$ means 'for every x' or perhaps 'no matter what x may be'.

If we were to keep the predicate ϕ to mean 'is a cat', but re-interpret ψ to mean 'is black' then we could express the fact that some cats are black by the wff

(2) $\exists x(\phi x \wedge \psi x)$

where $\exists x$ may be read as 'there exists an x such that'. If ϕ is a two-place predicate and is interpreted as 'admires' then we can express

(3) everyone admires someone

as

(4) $\forall x \exists y \phi xy$.

(4) allows each person to admire someone different. If (3) is understood to imply that there is someone whom everyone admires we would have to use

(5) $\exists y \forall x \phi xy$.

In (4) and (5) we have used $\forall$ and $\exists$ to mean 'everyone' and 'someone'. That is to say we have understood ourselves to be restricting the things we are speaking about to people. In general, whenever we use quantifiers we have in mind what is often called a 'universe of discourse' or in technical terms a *domain*. The quantifiers are then said to *range over* the domain. This means that they refer to everything or to something from the domain in question. So to interpret a wff of LPC we must first specify a domain D.

Given a domain D we must now interpret the predicates. Consider (1). If D is a domain which includes animals then some subset of D will be those which are cats. If A is the set of those members of the domain which are cats, then A will be the interpretation of the predicate ϕ when ϕ means 'is a cat'. And if B is the set of animals in D then B will be the interpretation of the predicate ψ when ψ means 'is an animal'. For a two-place predicate it is a little more complicated. If ϕ means 'admires' then we need to consider pairs from the domain. If C is the set of pairs $\langle u,v \rangle$ where u and v are both in D and u admires v, then C will be the interpretation of ϕ when it means 'admires'. To get a model for a language $\mathscr{L}$ of LPC we form the pair $\langle D,V \rangle$ where D is any class of objects we please, and V is a function such that where ϕ is an n-place predicate in $\mathscr{L}$ then $V(\phi)$ is a class of n-tuples from D. The idea is that $\langle u_1, \dots ,u_n \rangle \in V(\phi)$ iff $u_1, \dots ,u_n$ (in that order) stand in the n-place relation which is the meaning of ϕ.

We must now give rules for evaluating wff of $\mathscr{L}$. In defining $\langle D,V \rangle$ we have made no mention of the individual variables. The reason is this. The kind of LPC wff that we are ultimately interested in are those like (1), (2), (4) and (5) in which there are no free variables. Such wff are called *closed* wff, or sometimes *sentences*. The simplest kind of closed wff is a wff like

(6) $\forall x \phi x$.

In any interpretation $\langle D,V \rangle$ (6) will be true if $V(\phi) = D$, and false otherwise and this fact does not depend on the value of x. By contrast consider a wff with a free variable, say

(7) ϕx.

Is (7) true or false? Well, it depends on what x is. We could of course require V to give values, from D, to the individual variables as well as to the predicates. But in obtaining the value of (6) from (7) we need to refer to all the possible values x might have. For this reason it is convenient to separate the value-assignment to the individual variables from the model itself. So where $\langle D,V \rangle$ is an LPC model we say that μ is a *value-assignment* based on $\langle D,V \rangle$ provided that, for every variable x in

$\mathscr{L}$, $\mu(x)$ is a member of D. We shall then write

$$V_\mu(\alpha) = 1$$

to mean that α is true in the model $\langle D, V \rangle$ when the individual variables are given the values assigned them by μ. Thus for atomic wff we have

[Vϕ] $V_\mu(\phi x_1...x_n) = 1$ if $\langle \mu(x_1), ... , \mu(x_n) \rangle \in V(\phi)$ and 0 otherwise.

What [Vϕ] means is that $\phi x_1...x_n$ is true, with respect to μ, iff the n-tuple made up from the individuals μ assigns to $x_1, ... , x_n$, is in the set of n-tuples that V assigns to ϕ. For $\sim$ and $\vee$ the procedure is obvious.

[V$\sim$] $V_\mu(\sim \alpha) = 1$ if $V_\mu(\alpha) = 0$ and 0 otherwise.

[V$\vee$] $V_\mu(\alpha \vee \beta) = 1$ if either $V_\mu(\alpha) = 1$ or $V_\mu(\beta) = 1$ and 0 otherwise.

The complexity comes with the quantifiers. For we want $V_\mu(\forall x \alpha)$ to be true not only when $V_\mu(\alpha) = 1$, but when $V_\rho(\alpha) = 1$ for whatever value from D ρ may assign to x. But we must be careful. For consider the wff $\forall x \phi xy$. In evaluating this wff with respect to μ we permit ρ to give any value whatsoever to x, but we need to keep the same value for y as μ gives, since y remains free in $\forall x \phi xy$. So we say that ρ is an *x-alternative* of μ iff for every variable y except (possibly) x, $\rho(y) = \mu(y)$. We then say

[V$\forall$] $V_\mu(\forall x \alpha) = 1$ if $V_\rho(\alpha) = 1$ for every *x*-alternative ρ of μ, and 0 otherwise.

By Def $\exists$ this means that we have

[V$\exists$] $V_\mu(\exists x \alpha) = 1$ if there is an *x*-alternative ρ of μ such that $V_\rho(\alpha) = 1$, and 0 otherwise.

A wff α is said to be *valid* in a model $\langle D, V \rangle$ iff $V_\mu(\alpha) = 1$ for every assignment μ in $\langle D, V \rangle$ to the individual variables of $\mathscr{L}$. A wff which is valid in every model is said to be *universally valid* or sometimes *LPC-valid* or just plain *valid*.

The principle of replacement

In order to motivate this important principle of LPC we shall look at some examples of LPC-valid wff which depend on the meaning of the quantifiers. Consider the wff

(1) $\forall x\phi x \supset \phi y.$

(1) expresses the principle that if ϕ is true of everything in D then it will be true of whatever member of D is assigned to y. Now (1) should be expected to hold not only of atomic wff, but also of complex wff. Consider

(2) $\forall x(\phi xx \wedge \exists x\phi xy) \supset (\phi yy \wedge \exists x\phi xy).$

In (2) we notice first that every x free in $\phi xx \wedge \exists x\phi xy$ has been replaced by y. The x bound by $\exists x$ however has been left alone. (Recall that although x cannot be free in $\forall x(\phi xx \wedge \exists x\phi xy)$ it can be, and is, free in $\phi xx \wedge \exists x\phi xy$). Second we notice that the fact that y already occurs in $\phi xx \wedge \exists x\phi xy$, does not affect the validity of (2). Readers should convince themselves that (2) is indeed valid. The general form of (2) is

∀1 $\forall x\alpha \supset \alpha[y/x]$

where $\alpha[y/x]$ is α with y replacing every free x in α.

This is almost right, but in order to rule out an unwanted instance we must impose another restriction. For, suppose ϕ means 'is less than'. Then the following would appear to be an instance of **∀1**

(3) $\forall x\exists y\phi xy \supset \exists y\phi yy.$

This says that if everything is less than something then something is less than itself, and this is false in the domain of natural numbers.

The problem with (3) is that although x is free in $\exists y\phi xy$, the y that replaces it becomes bound. So we must require that $\alpha[y/x]$ has *free y* where α has free x. Now in $\exists y\phi xy$, the fact that we have a y quantifier is accidental in the following sense. $\exists y\phi xy$ simply says that x is related by ϕ to *something*, and in place of $\exists y\phi xy$ we could equally have $\exists z\phi xz$. And now there is no problem. For we certainly have as valid

(4) $\forall x\exists y\phi xy \supset \exists z\phi yz$.

∃yφxy and ∃zφxz are called *bound alphabetic variants*. More strictly α and β (in primitive notation) are bound alphabetic variants iff they differ only in that α has a wf part ∀xγ where β has ∀yδ and γ and δ differ only in that γ has free x where and only where δ has free y. We then let α[y/x] be the result of taking a bound alphabetic variant of α in which there is no y quantifier, and then replacing every x free in the resulting variant by y. The validity of ∀1 then follows from the *principle of replacement*:

PR Let α be any wff, x and y any variables, ⟨D,V⟩ any model for $\mathcal{L}$, and μ any assignment to the variables. Then, where ρ is just like μ except that $ρ(x) = μ(y)$, $V_ρ(α) = V_μ(α[y/x])$.

PR is a standard result in non-modal predicate logic.

The other principle we require is that where μ and ρ agree on all the variables free in a wff α then $V_μ(α) = V_ρ(α)$. We can call this the *principle of agreement*, **PA**. PA has the consequence that where α contains no free variables then $V_μ(α) = V_ρ(α)$ for every μ and ρ.

Axiomatization
Our style of axiomatization will differ from that used in Part I in that we will not have any rule of uniform substitution. This means that all our axioms will be stated as axiom schemata, i.e. general principles to the effect that any wff of a certain form is an axiom. Parallel to axiom schemata we shall frequently prove theorem schemata. Even in Part I we stated PC as a schema which provided infinitely many axioms. For LPC we define an *LPC substitution-instance* of a PC-wff α as any expression which results from uniformly replacing every propositional variable in α by a wff of $\mathcal{L}$. The axioms of LPC, for a given language $\mathcal{L}$ are

PC Any LPC substitution-instance of a valid wff of PC is an axiom of LPC.

∀1 If α is any wff and x and y any individual variables then ∀xα ⊃ α[y/x] is an axiom of LPC.

The transformation rules of LPC are first, Modus Ponens.

MP ⊢ α, ⊢ α ⊃ β → ⊢ β

and second

241

∀2 ⊢ $\alpha \supset \beta$ → ⊢ $\alpha \supset \forall x\beta$, provided x is not free in α.

It is routine to prove that every instance of PC and ∀1 is valid in every model, and that MP and ∀2 preserve validity in a model. (We shall in fact go through this proof for the modal extensions of LPC.) From this it follows that every LPC theorem is universally valid.

Some theorems of LPC

We list here some theorems of LPC (in the form of schemata) and rules which will be useful in later developments. We omit proofs, which are in any case quite standard. Where a rule is proved here that rule will hold in all the modal extensions of LPC which are based on the present axiomatization of LPC. α and β are any wff and x, y and z any individual variables.

UG ⊢ α → ⊢ $\forall x\alpha$
UG$^\supset$ ⊢ $\alpha \supset \beta$ → ⊢ $\forall x\alpha \supset \forall x\beta$
UG$^=$ ⊢ $\alpha \equiv \beta$ → ⊢ $\forall x\alpha \equiv \forall x\beta$

UG$^=$, in conjunction with the PC principles listed on p. 32, enables the proof of a rule of substitution of equivalents:

Eq If ⊢ $\alpha \equiv \beta$ and $\gamma[\alpha]$ differs from $\gamma[\beta]$ only in having α at 0 or more places where $\gamma[\beta]$ has β, then ⊢ $\gamma[\alpha] \equiv \gamma[\beta]$.

RBV $\forall x\alpha \equiv \forall y\beta$ where α and β differ only in that α has free x where and only where β has free y.

$\forall x\alpha$ and $\forall y\beta$ are bound alphabetic variants (see p. 241). RBV shows that bound alphabetic variants are equivalent, and so by Eq we may replace them in any wff, and the result of the replacement will give a wff probably equivalent to the original. Such replacement is often called *relettering* of bound variables.

LPC1 $\forall x(\alpha \supset \beta) \supset (\forall x\alpha \supset \forall x\beta)$
LPC2 $\forall x(\alpha \supset \beta) \supset (\alpha \supset \forall x\beta)$ provided x is not free in α
LPC3 $\exists y(\alpha[y/x] \supset \forall x\alpha)$ provided y is not free in $\forall x\alpha$.
QI $\sim\exists x\sim\alpha \equiv \forall x\alpha$

QI is a principle of *quantifier interchange* and generalizes to strings of quantifiers in exactly the same way that K5 on p. 33 generalizes to LMI. We shall refer to such generalizations also as QI.

Modal LPC

A language $\mathscr{L}$ of modal LPC is simply the language formed out of LPC by the addition of the modal operator L and by changing FR2 to

FR2′ If α is a wff of $\mathscr{L}$ then so are $\sim\alpha$ and $L\alpha$.

The interpretation of modal LPC is the obvious generalization of that for LPC.[2] A model for modal LPC now consists of a quadruple $\langle W,R,D,V \rangle$ in which $\langle W,R \rangle$ is a frame and D is a domain of 'individuals'. In interpreting the predicates each n-place predicate must now be given a set of n-tuples from D in each world;[3] or, what comes to the same thing, must be assigned a set of $n+1$-tuples, in each of which the first n terms are from D and the final term is from W. To say that $\langle u_1, \ldots ,u_n,w \rangle \in V(\phi)$ is to say that in world w, ϕ is true of $u_1, \ldots ,u_n$ (in that order.) We can sum this up by defining explicitly a model for a language $\mathscr{L}$ of modal LPC.

Semantics for modal LPC

A model for a language $\mathscr{L}$ of modal LPC is a quadruple $\langle W,R,D,V \rangle$ in which W is a set (of 'worlds'), R a relation on W, D another set and V a function such that, where ϕ is an n-place predicate, $V(\phi)$ is a set of $n+1$-tuples each of the form $\langle u_1, \ldots ,u_n,w \rangle$ for $u_1, \ldots ,u_n \in D$ and $w \in W$. In such a model an assignment μ to the variables is a function such that, for each variable x, $\mu(x) \in D$. Where ρ is also an assignment to the variables μ and ρ are x-*alternatives* iff for every y except possibly x, $\rho(y) = \mu(y)$. Every wff has a truth-value at a world relative to an assignment μ as follows:

[$V\phi$] $V_\mu(\phi x_1...x_n,w) = 1$ if $\langle \mu(x_1), \ldots ,\mu(x_n),w \rangle \in V(\phi)$ and 0 otherwise.

[$V\sim$] $V_\mu(\sim\alpha,w) = 1$ if $V_\mu(\alpha,w) = 0$, and 0 otherwise.

[$V\vee$] $V_\mu(\alpha \vee \beta,w) = 1$ if $V_\mu(\alpha,w) = 1$ or $V_\mu(\beta,w) = 1$, and 0 otherwise.

[VL] $V_\mu(L\alpha,w) = 1$ if $V_\mu(\alpha,w') = 1$ for every w' such that wRw', and 0 otherwise.

[$V\forall$] $V_\mu(\forall x\alpha) = 1$ if $V_\rho(\alpha,w) = 1$ for every x-alternative ρ of μ, and 0 otherwise.

A wff is valid in $\langle W,R,D,V \rangle$ iff $V_\mu(\alpha,w) = 1$ for every $w \in W$ and every assignment μ. A wff is valid on a frame $\langle W,R \rangle$ iff it is valid in every model based on $\langle W,R \rangle$. Among valid principles of modal LPC are the obvious generalizations of PR and PA.

Systems of modal predicate logic

Where S is a system of normal modal propositional logic then LPC + S is defined as follows, where the wff are now wff of a language $\mathcal{L}$ of modal LPC:

S′ If α is an LPC substitution-instance of a theorem of S then α is an axiom of LPC + S.

∀1 If α is any wff and x and y any variables and $\alpha[y/x]$ is α with free y replacing every free x, then $\forall x\alpha \supset \alpha[y/x]$ is an axiom of LPC + S.

N If α is a theorem of LPC + S then so is $L\alpha$.

MP If α and $\alpha \supset \beta$ are theorems of LPC + S then so is β.

∀2 If $\alpha \supset \beta$ is a theorem of LPC + S and x is not free in α then $\alpha \supset \forall x\beta$ is a theorem of LPC + S.

An additional principle is known as the *Barcan Formula*, which may be stated by the schema

BF $\forall xL\alpha \supset L\forall x\alpha$

S + BF is LPC + S with the addition of BF. BF has the rather curious property that for some choices of a propositional system S, e.g. B or S5, BF is a theorem schema of LPC + S, while for other choices, e.g. K, T or S4, it is not. For uniformity, we shall in this chapter consider only systems which contain the Barcan Formula.

Theorems of modal LPC

Many theorems of modal LPC are of course obvious instances of theorems of propositional modal logic, e.g. $L(\forall x\phi x \supset \exists x\psi x) \supset (L\forall x\phi x \supset L\exists x\psi x)$, while others are instances of theorems of non-modal LPC, e.g. $\forall xL\phi x \supset L\phi y$. However the interest of modal predicate logic lies mainly in 'mixed' principles which exhibit interrelations among modal operators and quantifiers which cannot be stated in propositional modal logic or non-modal LPC alone. One of these we have already mentioned, the Barcan Formula.[4] In order to see BF at work we shall look at how to

244

generalize LPC1.

LPC1 $\forall x(\alpha \supset \beta) \supset (\forall x\alpha \supset \forall x\beta)$.

As we saw in Chapter 11, in the early days of modal logic an important concern was to study principles involving strict implication. If we use the symbol $\dashv$ as in Chapter 11 in such a way that $\alpha \dashv \beta$ is defined as $L(\alpha \supset \beta)$ then the appropriate generalization of LPC1 would seem to be

(1) $\forall x(\alpha \dashv \beta) \supset (\forall x\alpha \dashv \forall x\beta)$.

Although (1) seems intuitively valid its proof requires BF. If we write (1) out without using $\dashv$ we notice that it is

(2) $\forall xL(\alpha \supset \beta) \supset L(\forall x\alpha \supset \forall x\beta)$.

This looks like a combination of LPC1 and **K**, but in the antecedent the modal operator is within the scope of the quantifier, while in the consequent the quantifiers are within the scope of the modal operator, and it is this feature which prevents it being derivable without BF. What we can prove quite easily in LPC + K is

(3) $L\forall x(\alpha \supset \beta) \supset L(\forall x\alpha \supset \forall x\beta)$

but to get from (3) to (2) we require

(4) $\forall xL(\alpha \supset \beta) \supset L\forall x(\alpha \supset \beta)$.

(4) is of course the special case of BF in which α is $\alpha \supset \beta$. So (2) may be derived using BF. We leave it as an exercise to show that BF may be derived from (2). In Chapters 15 and 16 we shall say a little about the controversy which surrounds BF.

The converse of the Barcan formula is provable in LPC + K as it stands.

BFC $L\forall x\alpha \supset \forall xL\alpha$

PROOF

$\forall 1$	(1)	$\forall x\alpha \supset \alpha$
(1) × DR1	(2)	$L\forall x\alpha \supset L\alpha$

(2) × ∀2   (3) $L\forall x\alpha \supset \forall xL\alpha$ **Q.E.D.**

(Clearly x cannot be free in $L\forall x\alpha$ and so the application of ∀2 in obtaining (3) from (2) is legitimate.)

Hence if we had the Barcan Formula we could easily derive

$L\forall x\alpha \equiv \forall xL\alpha$

and from this by LMI and QI

$M\exists x\alpha \equiv \exists xM\alpha.$

Two related theorems which may be easily proved without the Barcan formula are

(5) $\exists xL\alpha \supset L\exists x\alpha$

and

(6) $M\forall x\alpha \supset \forall xM\alpha$

Their converses however are not provable, and in fact are not valid. Consider the converse of (5).

(7) $L\exists x\phi x \supset \exists xL\phi x.$

To see that (7) is not valid under the intended interpretation let ϕx be 'x is the number of the planets'. Then the antecedent is true, for there must be some number which is the number of the planets (even if there were no planets at all there would still be such a number, viz. 0); but the consequent is false, for since it is a contingent matter how many planets there are, there is no number which must be the number of the planets. It is equally easy to see that the converse of (6) is not valid. (See, however, pp. 332-333)

As we shall see on p. 276 there are many modal systems S, among them S4, and so *a fortiori* K, T, and D, such that the Barcan Formula is not a theorem of LPC + S. It is however a theorem of LPC + S where S contains the Brouwerian system B. Such systems contain $MLp \supset p$ (p. 62) and the rule DR4 (p. 62). The proof of BF is as follows:[5]

∀1	(1)	$\forall x L\alpha \supset L\alpha$
(1) × DR3	(2)	$M\forall x L\alpha \supset ML\alpha$
$MLp \supset p$	(3)	$ML\alpha \supset \alpha$
(2) (3) × PC	(4)	$M\forall x L\alpha \supset \alpha$
(4) × ∀2	(5)	$M\forall x L\alpha \supset \forall x\alpha$
(5) × DR4	(6)	$\forall x L\alpha \supset L\forall x\alpha$

Q.E.D.

Validity and soundness

Our definition of validity for modal LPC will be exactly analogous to our definition for propositional modal systems. Since the modal LPC models defined on p. 243 all validate the Barcan Formula we shall often speak of them as BF models. If $\langle \mathcal{F}, D, V \rangle$ is a BF model and $\mathcal{F}$ is the frame $\langle W, R \rangle$, we say that a wff α of modal LPC is valid in $\langle \mathcal{F}, D, V \rangle$ iff $V(\alpha, w) = 1$ for every $w \in W$. We say that a model $\langle \mathcal{F}, D, V \rangle$ is based on the frame $\mathcal{F}$, and that α is valid on $\mathcal{F}$ iff it is valid in every BF model based on $\mathcal{F}$. We say that $\mathcal{F}$ is a frame for a system S + BF iff every theorem of S + BF is valid on $\mathcal{F}$, and that a class $\mathcal{E}$ of frames characterizes S + BF iff, for every wff α of modal LPC, α is valid on every frame in $\mathcal{E}$ iff it is a theorem of S + BF. A frame in a BF model, of course, is just the same kind of thing as a frame in a propositional model; so we can speak of one and the same frame as being a frame for a modal propositional system or a frame for a modal predicate system. Our first two theorems state important connections between propositional and predicate systems.

THEOREM 13.1 Suppose that $\mathcal{F}$ is a frame for a normal propositional modal system S. Then $\mathcal{F}$ is a frame for S + BF.

Proof: Let $\mathcal{E}$ be the class of all BF models based on $\mathcal{F}$. We prove the theorem by showing that each instance of the axiom schemata of S + BF, viz. S, ∀1 and BF, is valid in every model in $\mathcal{E}$, and then that the transformation rules MP, N and ∀2 preserve the property of being valid in every such model.

(1) For the axiom schema S, we have to verify that if β is a wff of modal LPC obtained by substituting modal LPC wff $\gamma_1, \ldots, \gamma_n$ for propositional variables $p_1, \ldots, p_n$ in some theorem α of S, then β is valid in every model in $\mathcal{E}$. Suppose that β is not valid in every such model, i.e. that for some $\langle \mathcal{F}, D, V \rangle \in \mathcal{E}$ and some $w \in W$, $V(\beta, w) = 0$. Let $\langle \mathcal{F}, V' \rangle$ be a model for propositional modal logic in which $\mathcal{F}$ is precisely the same frame as in $\langle \mathcal{F}, D, V \rangle$ and in which, for every $w \in W$ and every p_i ($1 \leq i \leq n$), $V'(p_i, w) = V(\gamma_i, w)$. Then a straightforward inductive proof will

show that $V'(\alpha,w) = 0$, i.e. that α is invalid in $\langle \mathscr{F},V' \rangle$. Since by hypothesis $\mathscr{F}$ is a frame for S, this means that α is not a theorem of S. Thus if α is a theorem of S, β is valid in every model in $\mathscr{E}$.

(2) For $\forall 1$, suppose that for some $w \in W$ in some BF model, $V_\mu(\forall x\alpha,w) = 1$. Let ρ be the x-alternative of μ in which $\rho(x) = \mu(y)$. By $[V\forall]$ $V_\rho(\alpha,w) = 1$, and so by PR $V_\mu(\alpha[y/x],w) = 1$. This shows that every instance of $\forall 1$ is valid in every BF model, and hence in every model in $\mathscr{E}$.

(3) For BF, suppose that for some $w \in W$ and some assignment μ, $V_\mu(\forall xL\alpha,w) = 1$. Let ρ be any x-alternative of μ, and let wRw'. By $[V\forall]$ $V_\rho(L\alpha,w) = 1$, and hence by $[VL]$, $V_\rho(\alpha,w') = 1$. Since this holds for every x-alternative ρ of μ we have $V_\mu(\forall x\alpha,w') = 1$; and since this holds for every w' such that wRw' we finally have $V(L\forall x\alpha,w) = 1$. This shows that every instance of BF is also valid in every BF model, and so in every model in $\mathscr{E}$.

(4) MP and N are validity-preserving in a model for the same reasons as in propositional modal logic.

(5) Finally, for $\forall 2$ we assume that $\alpha \supset \beta$ is valid in every model in $\mathscr{E}$, and show that in that case so is $\alpha \supset \forall x\beta$ (where x is not free in α). We prove (5) by contraposition. Suppose $\alpha \supset \forall x\beta$ is not valid in some model $\langle W,R,D,V \rangle$. Then there is some assignment μ in $\langle W,R,D,V \rangle$ such that $V_\mu(\alpha,w) = 1$ and $V_\mu(\forall x\beta,w) = 0$. So there is some x-alternative ρ of μ such that $V_\rho(\alpha,w) = 0$. Now x is not free in α and so by PA on p. 241, $V_\rho(\alpha,w) = V_\mu(\alpha,w) = 1$. But then $V_\rho(\alpha \supset \beta,w) = 0$, contradicting the assumption that $\alpha \supset \beta$ is valid in $\langle W,R,D,V \rangle$.

This completes the proof of theorem 13.1. The next theorem is the converse of the previous one.

THEOREM 13.2 If $\mathscr{F}$ is a frame for S + BF, then $\mathscr{F}$ is a frame for S.

Proof: Suppose that $\mathscr{F}$ is not a frame for S. Then there is some model $\langle \mathscr{F},V \rangle$, based on $\mathscr{F}$, such that for some wff α which is a theorem of S, and some $w^* \in W$, $V(\alpha,w^*) = 0$. Let $p_1, \ldots, p_n$ be the propositional variables in α; let $\phi_1, \ldots, \phi_n$ be n distinct one-place predicate letters and x some individual variable; and let β be the wff of modal LPC which is obtained from α by uniformly replacing $p_1, \ldots, p_n$ by $\phi_1 x, \ldots, \phi_n x$ respectively. Clearly β is a substitution-instance of α, and is therefore a theorem of S + BF. To show that $\mathscr{F}$ is not a frame for S + BF it is clearly sufficient to exhibit a BF model $\langle \mathscr{F},D,V' \rangle$, based on $\mathscr{F}$, in which, for some μ, $V'_\mu(\beta,w^*) = 0$. This can be accomplished by letting D be any domain whatsoever and, for any $u \in D$, let $\langle u,w \rangle$ be in $V'(\phi_i)$ iff $V(p_i,w) = 1$, for each $w \in W$ and each i $(1 \leq i \leq n)$. By $[V\phi]$ this will ensure that $\phi_i x$ is true in w in $\langle \mathscr{F},D,V \rangle$, for any assignment μ, at precisely those worlds at which p_i is true in $\langle \mathscr{F},V \rangle$. Since β contains no quantifiers, it is built up from $\phi_1 x, \dots , \phi_n x$ by $\sim$, $\vee$ and L in precisely the same way as α is from $p_1, \dots , p_n$. Hence at any $w \in W$, β will have the same truth-value in $\langle \mathscr{F},D,V' \rangle$ as α has in $\langle \mathscr{F},V \rangle$; and in particular, $V'_\mu(\beta,w^*) = 0$. Thus $\mathscr{F}$ is not a frame for S + BF.

This proves the theorem. Theorems 13.1 and 13.2 give us

COROLLARY 13.3 $\mathscr{F}$ is a frame for S iff $\mathscr{F}$ is a frame for S + BF.

We have defined a frame for modal LPC in the same way as for modal propositional logic, as a pair $\langle W,D \rangle$. It could however be argued that D is really part of the frame rather than the model, since it does not depend on the assignment V to the predicates of $\mathscr{L}$. In ordinary LPC the choice of D can affect validity. Thus if D has only one member $\phi x \supset \phi y$ is valid, but not if D has more. If D has two members $((\phi x \wedge \phi y) \wedge (\psi x \wedge \sim \psi y)) \supset \phi z$ is valid, but not if D has more, and so on. However, this fact does not affect theorems 13.1 and 13.2. Obviously, by theorem 13.1, if $\mathscr{F}$ is a frame for S then $\langle \mathscr{F},D \rangle$ is a frame for S + BF for every D. If $\mathscr{F}$ is not a frame for S then the proof of theorem 13.2 shows that $\langle \mathscr{F},D \rangle$ is not a frame for S + BF, *whatever D may be*. Thus, for any D, $\mathscr{F}$ is a frame for S iff $\langle \mathscr{F},D \rangle$ is a frame for S + BF.

It follows immediately from theorem 13.1 that every theorem of K + BF is valid on every frame. Moreover, the soundness results we proved in Chapter 1, together with this theorem, show that each of the following systems is sound with respect to the class of frames listed beside it:

T + BF: reflexive frames
K4 + BF: transitive frames
KB + BF: symmetrical frames
S4 + BF: reflexive transitive frames
B + BF: reflexive symmetrical frames
S5 + BF: equivalence frames

Theorem 13.1, in fact, provides us with a general soundness result to the effect that whenever a normal propositional modal system S is sound with respect to a certain class of frames, so is the corresponding predicate system S + BF.

Theorem 13.2, however, although it is the converse of theorem 13.1, does not give us a corresponding general completeness result, nor does corollary 13.3 give us a general characterization result. What theorems 13.1 and 13.2 together tell us about T + BF, for example, is that the class of all frames for T + BF is precisely the class of all reflexive frames − given, that is, the result that we established in Chapter 10, that the frames for T itself are precisely the frames that are reflexive. But as we explained on p. 174, that result does not prove that T is complete with respect to the class of all such frames; and for just the same reasons, our present result does not give us a completeness result for T + BF either. In fact we shall see in the next chapter that there are complete propositional systems S such that S + BF is not characterized by the class of frames that characterize S, and so not characterized by any class of frames. I.e. S is complete but S + BF is not.

De re and *de dicto*

When we look at the 'mixed' principles which are proper to modal predicate logic, and not merely generalizations of modal propositional logic or of non-modal predicate logic we notice a significant fact. We can illustrate this with the formula

(1) $L\exists x\phi x \supset \exists x L\phi x$

discussed above as (7) on p. 246. We noted that although the converse of this is a theorem of LPC + S for any normal system S yet (1) is not. The feature of modal LPC that makes (1) interesting may be seen by contrasting its antecedent and consequent. In the antecedent there is a variable x free inside the scope of the modal operator L, while in the consequent there are no free variables inside L. To see the importance of this difference look at the meanings of these two wff. $\exists x L\phi x$ says that there is a thing (in Latin a *res*) and concerning this thing (*de re*) *it*, the very same thing, is ϕ in every accessible world. $L\exists x\phi x$ does not carry this implication. It says that in every accessible world the proposition (*dictum*) that *something* (not necessarily the same thing in each world) is ϕ is true. Whether or not the Latin descriptions are accurate the fact remains that wff of modal predicate logic divide into those called *de dicto*, in which no variable occurs free within the scope of a modal operator, and those called *de re*, in which some do.

Now some *de re* wff are equivalent to *de dicto* wff in every S + LPC.

For instance $\forall x(L\phi x \supset L\phi x) \wedge L\exists x\phi x$ is always equivalent to $L\exists x\phi x$. Other wff are sometimes so. For instance $\forall x L\phi x$ is equivalent to $L\forall x\phi x$ in systems with BF, but not otherwise. So the question arises as to whether there are modal systems in which *all de re* wff are equivalent to *de dicto* wff. The answer is no, unless the system is Triv or Ver. We shall first prove the result for S5 + BF by looking at the simplest kind of S5 model in which there is more than one world and show that the wff $\exists x L\phi x$ is not equivalent to any *de dicto* wff.[6]

The technique we shall use is this. We shall show that *de dicto* formulae do not depend on just how we match up an individual in one world with an individual in another. Consider the following two models, which coincide in W, R and D, but differ in the interpretation to the predicates. In each case $W = \{w_1, w_2\}$, $R = W^2$ (i.e. every world can see every world) and $D = \{u_1, u_2\}$. In the first model, $\langle W,R,D,V \rangle$, V is as follows: For any predicate ψ except for ϕ, $V(\psi) = \varnothing$, i.e., these predicates hold of nothing in any world. $V(\phi) = \{\langle u_1,w_1 \rangle, \langle u_1,w_2 \rangle\}$. In the second model $\langle W,R,D,V^* \rangle$, $V^*(\psi) = V(\psi) = \varnothing$, but $V^*(\phi) = \{\langle u_1,w_1 \rangle, \langle u_2,w_2 \rangle\}$. In other words, in w_1 u_1 is ϕ in both models, but in w_2 it is u_1 which is ϕ in the first model, and u_2 which is ϕ in the second model. The idea behind the proof which follows is that for *de dicto* wff a model which 'switches' u_1 and u_2 in w_2 is equivalent, from the point of view of w_1, to one which does not. This means that the difference between the models cannot be shown up by a *de dicto* wff, but can be shown up by a *de re* wff.

We note that since these two models have the same D then the class of assignments to the variables is the same in each. Given an assignment μ we let μ^* denote the 'anti-assignment' such that for every variable x, $\mu(x) \neq \mu^*(x)$. (In other words if $\mu(x) = u_1$ then $\mu^*(x) = u_2$, and vice versa.)

THEOREM 13.4 If α is *de dicto* then $V_\mu(\alpha,w_1) = V^*_\mu(\alpha,w_1)$ and $V_\mu(\alpha,w_2) = V^*_{\mu^*}(\alpha,w_2)$.

Proof: The proof is by induction on the construction of formulae. For atomic wff the theorem clearly holds for every wff $\psi x_1...x_n$, for every predicate except ϕ. So consider ϕx.

$V_\mu(\phi x,w_1) = 1$ iff $\langle \mu(x),w_1 \rangle \in V(\phi)$, iff $\mu(x) = u_1$, iff $\langle \mu(x),w_1 \rangle \in V^*(\phi)$ iff $V^*_\mu(\phi x,w_1) = 1$.

$V_\mu(\phi x,w_2) = 1$ iff $\langle \mu(x),w_2 \rangle \in V(\phi)$ iff $\mu(x) = u_1$, iff $\mu^*(x) = u_2$, iff $\langle \mu^*(x),w_2 \rangle \in V^*(\phi)$ iff $V^*_{\mu^*}(\phi x,w_2) = 1$.

251

The induction is clearly preserved for $\sim$ and $\vee$. Consider $\forall x\alpha$. Note that if $\forall x\alpha$ is *de dicto* then so is α. So $V_\mu(\forall x\alpha, w_1) = 1$ iff for every x-alternative ρ of μ, $V_\rho(\alpha, w_1) = 1$, iff (by the induction hypothesis) $V_\rho^*(\alpha, w_1) = 1$ for every x-alternative ρ of μ, i.e., iff $V_\mu^*(\forall x\alpha, w_1) = 1$.

$V_\mu(\forall x\alpha, w_2) = 1$ iff for every x-alternative ρ of μ, $V_\mu(\alpha, w_2) = 1$, iff (by the induction hypothesis) $V_{\rho^*}^*(\alpha, w_2) = 1$. Now every x-alternative ν of μ^* will be ρ^* for some x-alternative ρ of μ, and so $V_\rho(\alpha, w_2) = 1$ for every x-alternative ρ of μ iff $V_\nu^*(\alpha, w_2) = 1$ for every x-alternative ν of μ^*, i.e. iff $V_{\mu^*}^*(\forall x\alpha, w_2) = 1$.

For L we note that if $L\alpha$ is *de dicto* then α must contain no free variables and so, by PA, $V_\mu(\alpha, w) = V_\rho(\alpha, w)$ and $V_\mu^*(\alpha, w) = V_\rho^*(\alpha, w)$ for every μ, ρ and w. Now for any $w \in W$,

(1) $\quad V_\mu(L\alpha, w) = 1$ iff

(2) $\quad V_\mu(\alpha, w_1) = 1$ and

(3) $\quad V_\mu(\alpha, w_2) = 1$.

By the induction hypothesis (2) holds iff

(4) $\quad V_\mu^*(\alpha, w_1) = 1$

and (3) holds iff

(5) $\quad V_{\mu^*}^*(\alpha, w_2) = 1$.

But α is closed and so (5) holds iff

(6) $\quad V_\mu^*(\alpha, w_2) = 1$.

So (6) holds iff (3) does. Thus (2) and (3) hold iff (4) and (5) hold. But (4) and (5) hold iff

(7) $\quad V_\mu^*(L\alpha, w) = 1$.

So (1) holds iff (7) holds. This gives the result immediately for $w = w_1$. For $w = w_2$, since $L\alpha$ is closed (7) holds iff

(8) $V_{\mu^*}^*(L\alpha,w_2) = 1$.

This proves theorem 13.4.

We now show that $\exists x L\phi x$ is not equivalent in S5 + BF to any *de dicto* wff. We note first that both $\langle W,R,D,V \rangle$ and $\langle W,R,D,V^* \rangle$ are models which satisfy all theorems of S5 + BF. So suppose there were some *de dicto* wff α such that $\vdash_{S5+BF} \exists x L\phi x \equiv \alpha$. Then for every μ and every w,

$V_\mu(\exists x L\phi x,w) = V_\mu(\alpha,w)$ and

$V_\mu^*(\exists x L\phi x,w) = V_\mu^*(\alpha,w)$.

But α is *de dicto* and so, by theorem 13.4,

$V_\mu(\alpha,w_1) = V_\mu^*(\alpha,w_1)$

and so

$V_\mu(\exists x L\phi x,w_1) = V_\mu^*(\exists x L\phi x,w_1)$.

But it is easy to see that

$V_\mu(\exists x L\phi x,w_1) = 1$ and

$V_\mu^*(\exists x L\phi x,w_1) = 0$.

So $\exists x L\phi x$ is not equivalent to any *de dicto* formula in S5 + BF, and so *a fortiori* not equivalent to any *de dicto* formula in any weaker system. It is not hard to see how to generalize the result. The key feature of the models we used is that $w_1 R w_2$ and $w_1 \neq w_2$. So any system S whose frames include at least one where this is so will have no *de dicto* wff equivalent to $\exists x L\phi x$. And in fact, as we have observed, this will include all systems S + BF, unless S is Triv or Ver or their intersection.

In the proof of theorem 13.4 a crucial role is played by the 'anti-assignment' μ^* of μ. In a model with more than two individuals there would not be a unique anti-assignment and one would have to require that μ^* be based on a permutation π of the domain, i.e. a function such that for every $u \in D$, $\pi(u) \in D$, and for every $v \in D$, there is some $u \in D$ such that $\pi(u) = v$, and where $u \neq v$ then $\pi(u) \neq \pi(v)$. For any assignment μ the μ^* based on π would have to be such that for any variable x, $\mu^*(x) = \pi(\mu(x))$. V* would be required to be such that $\langle \pi(u_1), \ldots, \pi(u_n), w \rangle \in$ V*(ϕ) iff $\langle u_1, \ldots, u_n, w \rangle \in$ V(ϕ). Fine[7] has shown that not only is a *de dicto* formula unaffected by such permutations, but that *only de dicto* formulae are unaffected, in that if any formula is unaffected then it is equivalent, in the system in question, to a *de dicto* formula.

Exercises — 13
In Part III exercises marked with * are ones for which we have not ourselves obtained a solution. Where solutions are known to us to have been obtained by others we have indicated this. Some of the remaining starred exercises may be regarded as open research problems.

13.1 (a) Derive BF from (2) on p. 245.
      (b) Prove $M\exists x\alpha \equiv \exists x M\alpha$ in K + BF.
      (c) Prove (5) and (6) on p. 246

13.2 Prove the following in S + BF, where S satisfies the conditions indicated:
    (i) $\forall x L(\alpha \supset \beta) \supset L(\exists x \alpha \supset \exists x \beta)$ (S is any normal system)
    (ii) $\exists y L M(\phi y \supset \forall x \phi x)$ (S contains B)
    (iii) $\exists x L(L\phi x \vee \psi y) \equiv L\exists x(L\phi x \vee \psi y)$ (S contains S5)
    (iv) $\exists y L \forall x(L\phi x \supset M L\phi y)$ (S contains S4.2)

13.3 S4.4 is S4 + $p \supset (MLp \supset Lp)$. Prove the following in S4.4 + BF:
    (C) $\sim L(\forall x M L\phi x \wedge \exists x \sim \phi x)$

13.4 Devise a model to show that $L\exists x\phi x \supset \exists x L\phi x$ is not valid in S5 + BF.

13.5 Show that none of the following are valid in S5 + BF:
    (a) $\exists x \sim L\phi x \supset M\forall x \sim \phi x$
    (b) $(L\exists x\phi x \wedge \forall x M\psi x) \supset M\exists x(\phi x \wedge \psi x)$
    (c) $\forall x(L\phi x \vee L\sim \phi x) \vee \forall x(M\phi x \wedge M\sim \phi x)$

13.6 Establish the validity of the wff in 13.1 and 13.2 with respect to the appropriate definition of validity.

13.7   Show that $\forall x(L\phi x \lor L\sim\phi x) \lor \exists x(M\phi x \land M\sim\phi x)$ is valid in both the models on p. 251. Then show that so is its schematic form **Pr** $\forall x(L\alpha \lor L\sim\alpha) \lor \exists x(M\alpha \land M\sim\alpha)$ provided this contains no free variables.

Notes

[1] The predicate calculus is also known as the Functional calculus. The terms 'lower' and 'first-order' are used interchangeably and refer to the fact that only individual variables appear in quantifiers. First-order logic is sometimes referred to as first-order quantification theory. Chapters 3 and 4 of Church 1956 still provide the fullest development.

[2] The definitions which follow are adapted from Kripke 1963b, though Kripke's own semantics, as we shall see in Chapter 16 differs in certain important respects. Other early semantics for modal predicate logic may be found in Kanger 1957a, 1957b, Bayart 1958, Montague 1960 and Hintikka 1961.

[3] Following the terminology of Carnap 1947 the set of n-tuples which satisfy ϕ in a world w is sometimes called the *extension* of ϕ in w, and the whole set of $n+1$-tuples which is $V(\phi)$ in a model as defined in the text is called the *intension* of ϕ. Because of their ability to distinguish between intensions and extensions modal languages are sometimes called intensional languages. In non-modal LPC the values of predicates are simply extensions, and the language of non-modal LPC is sometimes called an extensional language.

[4] The Barcan Formula appears first as axiom 11 on p. 2 of Barcan 1946, the first study of modal predicate logic, though in a slightly different form stated with $\diamond$ (*M*) and the symbol $\dashv3$ referred to on p. 245.

[5] Prior 1956 proves this when S is S5, and in 1967, p. 146 credits the first proof of BF when S is B to E.J. Lemmon.

[6] This was proved in Tichý, 1973. (The purported proof in Cresswell 1969b is defective.) On p. 184 of Hughes and Cresswell 1968 the elimination of *de re* modalities was linked to a principle due to von Wright 1951 called the *Principle of Predication*. The schematic version of the principle of predication stated on p. 185 of Hughes and Cresswell 1968 as **Pr** is too strong. From it one may derive $\forall x\forall y(M(\phi x \equiv \phi y) \supset L(\phi x \equiv \phi y))$. This is certainly strong enough for the elimination of all *de re* modalities. (Broido 1975. Broido also proves that the truth of $\exists x L\alpha \equiv L\exists x\alpha$ is a necessary and sufficient condition for the elimination of *de re* modalities in the sense of Hughes and Cresswell 1968, p. 184 – a sense attributed to Prior 1955a – though McKay, 1978, questions this sense.) If one restricts **Pr** so that it has no free variables, which is possibly what von Wright intended because $\forall x(L\phi x \lor L\sim\phi x) \lor \forall x(M\phi x \land M\sim\phi x)$ is an instance of this, then the proof given in the text shows that *de re* modalities are not eliminable, even with **Pr**. This is because both the models described there satisfy **Pr** when so restricted.

[7] Fine 1978.

255

14

THE COMPLETENESS OF
MODAL LPC

In this chapter we shall extend the canonical model technique introduced in Chapter 6 to LPC. We shall show how to define, for each modal system S, a canonical model for S + BF, relative to some language $\mathcal{L}$ of modal LPC, which will have the property that for any wff α of $\mathcal{L}$, $\vdash_S$ α iff α is valid in that model. We shall then look at the consequences of this for the completeness of systems of modal LPC. In particular we shall look at the relation between the completeness of a propositional system S and the completeness of S + BF.[1]

Canonical models for modal LPC
As in the case of a propositional modal system the worlds in the canonical model of a system of modal predicate logic will be maximal consistent sets of wff. As before we assume some system S (more strictly S + BF) to be fixed throughout the discussion and will simply say consistent rather than S-consistent. In the case of LPC we have in addition to say what the domain D of individuals is. The answer is simple: D will consist of the individual variables. It may seem strange that elements of the language, the individual variables, should themselves appear as the values over which they range, but the definition of a model did not put limits on what D could be any more than it put limits on what W could be, and the whole idea behind canonical models is to use the language itself to provide the constituents of the model.

We cannot let the worlds *just* be maximal consistent sets, they have to have another property as well. To see this recall that the 'hard' part of the canonical model theorem for modal propositional logic was to show that if $L\alpha \notin w$ then there is some w' such that wRw' and $\alpha \notin w'$. We have a similar problem in the predicate case when we have $\forall x\alpha \notin w$. Here we don't want to go to another world to make α false. But what we do need to do is to ensure that if $\forall x\alpha$ is not true in a world then there is some individual (often called a 'witness') which makes this so. If $\forall x\alpha$ is false then α should be false of something, and if the 'things' in the domain of individuals are individual variables this means that $\alpha[y/x]$ will need to be false in w for some y.

Here we run into a problem. For consider the set

$$\Omega = \{\sim\forall x\phi x,\ \phi y_1,\ \phi y_2,\ ...\}$$

I.e. Ω consists of $\sim\forall x\phi x$ together with ϕy for every individual variable y. Ω is consistent, since every finite subset obviously is, and so Ω has a maximal consistent extension. But that extension cannot have a witness to the falsity of $\forall x\phi x$, for no wff of the form $\sim\phi y$ can be consistently added to Ω.

The worlds of the canonical model must not only be maximal consistent. They must be sets which have what we call the $\forall$-property. A set Λ has the $\forall$-property iff for every wff α and every individual variable x, there is some individual variable y such that $\alpha[y/x] \supset \forall x\alpha \in \Lambda$. If Γ is maximal-consistent and has the $\forall$-property then if $\forall x\alpha \notin \Gamma$ there must be a 'witness' y such that $\alpha[y/x] \notin \Gamma$. For since Γ has the $\forall$-property there is a y such that $\alpha[y/x] \supset \forall x\alpha \in \Gamma$, and if $\alpha[y/x] \in \Gamma$ then $\forall x\alpha \in \Gamma$.

But if the worlds in the canonical model of $S + BF$ all have the $\forall$-property what are we to do about poor Ω? Clearly Ω does not have the $\forall$-property. Nor could it consistently be given it. It is consistent, and yet it seems unsatisfiable. The answer actually is quite easy. We simply extend the language by adding infinitely many new (individual) variables.

To make this precise assume that we have two languages $\mathcal{L}$ and $\mathcal{L}^+$ of modal predicate logic. They each satisfy the formation rules of p. 236 and they share the same predicates. The only difference is that $\mathcal{L}^+$ not only has all the infinitely many variables that $\mathcal{L}$ has but it has infinitely many new ones as well. It is a standard (though not entirely trivial) fact about LPC, whether modal or non-modal, that if Λ is a consistent set of wff of $\mathcal{L}$ then it remains consistent when $\mathcal{L}$ is extended to $\mathcal{L}^+$. We are now in a position to state the basic theorem about the $\forall$-property:

THEOREM 14.1   If Λ is a consistent set of wff of $\mathscr{L}$ then there is a consistent set of wff of $\mathscr{L}^+$ with the ∀-property such that $\Lambda \subseteq \Delta$.

The reason the definition of the ∀-property is given in the form it is is that once a set Δ has the ∀-property then any set (in the same language) of which Δ is a subset still has the ∀-property. In particular theorem 6.3 on p. 115 guarantees that since Δ is consistent there is a maximal-consistent set Γ such that $\Delta \subseteq \Gamma$, and so since Δ has the ∀-property Γ does also.

Proof: We assume that all wff of the form $\forall x \alpha$ for any wff α of $\mathscr{L}^+$ and any variable x are enumerated so that we can speak of the first, the second, and so on. We define a sequence of sets Δ_0, Δ_1, ... etc. as follows:

Δ_0 is Λ
Δ_{n+1} is $\Delta_n \cup \{\alpha[y/x] \supset \forall x \alpha\}$

where $\forall x \alpha$ is the $n+1$th wff in the enumeration of wff of that form and y is the first variable not in Δ_n or in α. Since Δ_0 is in $\mathscr{L}$ and Δ_n has been formed from it by the addition of only n wff there will be infinitely many variables from $\mathscr{L}^+$ left over to provide such a y.

Δ_0 is assumed consistent so we shall show that Δ_{n+1} is if Δ_n is. Suppose not. Then there will be β_1, ... ,β_n in Δ_n such that

(i) $\vdash (\beta_1 \wedge \ldots \wedge \beta_n) \supset \alpha[y/x]$ and

(ii) $\vdash (\beta_1 \wedge \ldots \wedge \beta_n) \supset \sim \forall x \alpha$.

Since y does not occur in Δ_n it is not free in $(\beta_1 \wedge \ldots \wedge \beta_n)$ and so from (ii) by ∀2

(iii) $\vdash (\beta_1 \wedge \ldots \wedge \beta_n) \supset \forall y \alpha[y/x]$.

And since y does not occur in α, $\forall y \alpha[y/x]$ is a bound alphabetic variant of $\forall x \alpha$, and so, by RBV on pp. 242,

(iv) $\vdash (\beta_1 \wedge \ldots \wedge \beta_n) \supset \forall x \alpha$.

But (ii) and (iv) give

(v) $\quad \vdash \sim (\beta_1 \wedge \ldots \wedge \beta_n)$

and (v) makes Δ_n inconsistent contrary to hypothesis. Let Δ be the union of all the Δ_ns. It is easy to see that Δ is consistent and has the $\forall$-property. This proves theorem 14.1.

As noted Δ has a maximal-consistent extension Γ in $\mathcal{L}^+$ with the $\forall$-property. Theorem 14.1 holds in any system (modal or not) which contains a standard axiomatic basis for LPC. In constructing the canonical model for S + BF our aim is to show that for any consistent set Λ of wff of a language $\mathcal{L}$ of modal predicate logic there is a world in the canonical model at which all of Λ's members are true. Because of sets like Ω the worlds in the canonical model must be maximal-consistent in the extended language $\mathcal{L}^+$. What we must now show is that where w is such a world and $L\alpha$ is false in w, then there is a world w' such that wRw' and α is false in w'. But this means showing that w' is maximal consistent (in $\mathcal{L}^+$), has the $\forall$-property, and contains $L^-(w) \cup \{\sim\alpha\}$. To do all this we need a theorem. Unlike theorem 14.1 which holds for all systems containing LPC the following theorem concerns normal modal systems, and in particular requires the Barcan Formula.[2]

THEOREM 14.2   If Γ is a maximal-consistent set of wff in some language (say $\mathcal{L}^+$) of modal predicate logic, and Γ has the $\forall$-property, and α is a wff such that $L\alpha \notin \Gamma$, then there is a consistent set Δ of wff of $\mathcal{L}^+$ with the $\forall$-property such that $L^-(\Gamma) \cup \{\sim\alpha\} \subseteq \Delta$.

Proof: We define a sequence of wff $\gamma_0, \gamma_1, \gamma_2, \ldots$ etc. γ_0 is $\sim\alpha$. Given γ_n we define γ_{n+1} as follows. Let $\forall x\delta$ be the $n+1$th wff of that form and let y be the first variable such that

(*) $L^-(\Gamma) \cup \{\gamma_n \wedge (\delta[y/x] \supset \forall x\delta)\}$ is consistent.

Let γ_{n+1} be $\gamma_n \wedge (\delta[y/x] \supset \forall x\delta)$. In order for this construction to succeed we have to be sure that there always will be a y satisfying (*). Since γ_0 is $\sim\alpha$, $L^-(\Gamma) \cup \{\gamma_0\}$ is consistent from lemma 6.4 on p. 117. We show that provided $L^-(\Gamma) \cup \{\gamma_n\}$ is consistent there will always be a y which satisfies (*).

Unlike the situation in theorem 14.1, we cannot here assume that y is a new variable, since all the variables of $\mathscr{L}^+$ will already occur in $L^-(\Gamma)$. Nevertheless we can show that there always will be an appropriate y. Suppose there were not. Then for every variable y of $\mathscr{L}^+$ there will exist some $\{L\beta_1, \ldots, L\beta_k\} \subseteq L^-(\Gamma)$ such that

$$\vdash (\beta_1 \wedge \ldots \wedge \beta_k) \supset (\gamma_n \supset \sim(\delta[y/x] \supset \forall x\delta))$$

so, by DR1 and L-distribution,

(i) $\quad \vdash (L\beta_1 \wedge \ldots \wedge L\beta_k) \supset L(\gamma_n \supset \sim(\delta[y/x] \supset \forall x\delta))$

But Γ is maximal consistent and $L\beta_1, \ldots, L\beta_n \in \Gamma$, and so $L(\gamma_n \supset \sim(\delta[y/x] \supset \forall x\delta)) \in \Gamma$.

Now this is so for *every* variable y, and Γ has the $\forall$-property. What this means is this. Let z be some variable not occurring in δ or in γ_n, and consider $\forall z L(\gamma_n \supset \sim(\delta[z/x] \supset \forall x\delta))$. Since Γ has the $\forall$-property there will be a variable y such that

(ii) $\quad L(\gamma_n \supset (\sim(\delta[y/x] \supset \forall x\delta)) \supset$
$\qquad \forall z L(\gamma_n \supset \sim(\delta[z/x] \supset \forall x\delta))$

is in Γ. But we have already noted that $L(\gamma_n \supset \sim(\delta[y/x] \supset \forall x\delta))$ is in Γ for every y. And so

(iii) $\quad \forall z L(\gamma_n \supset \sim(\delta[z/x] \supset \forall x\delta))$

is in Γ. But Γ is maximal S + BF-consistent and so, by BF,

(iv) $\quad L\forall z(\gamma_n \supset \sim(\delta[z/x] \supset \forall x\delta))$

is in Γ. Since z does not occur in γ_n or δ then by LPC2 we have in Γ

(v) $\quad L(\gamma_n \supset \forall z \sim(\delta[z/x] \supset \forall x\delta))$

But by LPC3,

$\vdash \exists z(\delta[z/x] \supset \forall x\delta)$

But then $L\sim\gamma_n \in \Gamma$ and so $\sim\gamma_n \in L^-(\Gamma)$ which would make Δ_n

inconsistent.

Let Δ be the union of $L^-(\Gamma)$ and all the γ_ns. Since each $L^-(\Gamma) \cup \{\gamma_n\}$ is consistent, and since $\vdash \gamma_m \supset \gamma_n$ for m $\geq$ n, so is their union Δ. Δ has all the required properties and so theorem 14.2 is proved.

The canonical model then for a system S + BF in a language $\mathscr{L}$ with an extension $\mathscr{L}^+$ is a quadruple $\langle W,R,D,V \rangle$ where W is the set of all maximal consistent sets with the ∀-property in $\mathscr{L}^+$; and wRw' iff for every $L\alpha \in w$, $\alpha \in w'$ (i.e. $L^-(w) \subseteq w'$). D is the set of variables in $\mathscr{L}^+$ and $\langle x_1, \ldots, x_n, w \rangle \in V(\phi)$ iff $\phi x_1 \ldots x_n \in w$. Finally take the 'canonical' value-assignment σ to be the assignment such that $\sigma(x) = x$, for every variable x in D. We prove the following theorem:

THEOREM 14.3   For any $w \in W$, and any wff $\alpha \in \mathscr{L}^+$, $V_\sigma(\alpha,w) = 1$ iff $\alpha \in w$.

The proof is by induction on the construction of wff.

(a)   First consider any atomic wff $\phi x_1 \ldots x_n$. $V_\sigma(\phi x_1 \ldots x_n, w) = 1$ iff $\langle \sigma(x_1), \ldots, \sigma(x_n), w \rangle \in V(\phi)$, iff $\langle x_1, \ldots, x_n, w \rangle \in V(\phi)$, iff $\phi x_1 \ldots x_n \in w$.

(b) $V_\sigma(\sim\alpha, w) = 1$ iff $V_\sigma(\alpha, w) = 0$, iff $\alpha \notin w$, iff $\sim\alpha \in w$.

(c) $V_\sigma(\alpha \lor \beta, w) = 1$ iff $V_\sigma(\alpha, w) = 1$ or $V_\sigma(\beta, w) = 1$ iff $\alpha \in w$ or $\beta \in w$, iff $\alpha \lor \beta \in w$.

(d)   Suppose $\forall x\alpha \in w$. Let ν be any x-alternative of σ. This means that $\nu(x) = y$ for some variable y in $\mathscr{L}^+$. Now, by $\forall 1$, $\alpha[y/x] \in w$. So $V_\sigma(\alpha[y/x], w) = 1$. So by PR, $V_\nu(\alpha, w) = 1$. Since ν is any x-alternative of σ, $V_\sigma(\forall x\alpha, w) = 1$.

(e)   Suppose $\forall x\alpha \notin w$. Then $\sim\forall x\alpha \in w$ and so, since w has the ∀-property in $\mathscr{L}^+$, there is some y in $\mathscr{L}^+$ such that $\sim\alpha[y/x] \in w$. So $\alpha[y/x] \notin w$ and so $V_\sigma(\alpha[y/x], w) = 0$. So by the validity of $\forall 1$, $V_\sigma(\forall x\alpha, w) = 0$.

(f)   Suppose $L\alpha \in w$ and wRw'. Then $\alpha \in w'$, and so $V_\sigma(\alpha, w') = 1$, and since this is so for every w' such that wRw', $V_\sigma(L\alpha, w) = 1$.

(g)   Suppose $L\alpha \notin w$. Then $\sim L\alpha \in w$. But then by theorem 14.2 there is some $w' \in w$ with the ∀-property such that $\sim\alpha \in w'$. So $\alpha \notin w'$, and so $V_\sigma(\alpha, w) = 0$. But wRw' and so $V_\sigma(L\alpha, w) = 0$.

This proves theorem 14.3.

A consequence of theorem 14.3 is the completeness of non-modal

LPC. A set of non-modal wff will be S + BF-consistent for any normal modal logic S iff it is LPC-consistent, and therefore any consistent set Λ of non-modal wff is true at some world w in S's canonical model $\langle W,R,D,V \rangle$, and w can provide an LPC interpretation $\langle D^*,V^* \rangle$ in which $V^*(\alpha) = V(\alpha,w) = 1$ for every $\alpha \in \Lambda$. Further, if every finite subset of Λ is true in some model then, by the soundness of LPC, every finite subset is consistent. (Otherwise, where α is the conjunction of all its members $\vdash \sim\alpha$, and so $\sim\alpha$ would be valid, contradicting the fact that α is true in some model.) So, by the definition of consistency, Λ is consistent, and therefore has a model. This gives us the compactness of LPC, a fact used on p. 184 in discussing propositional modal systems.

Since every theorem of S + BF is in every world in the canonical model for S + BF, theorem 14.3 means that every such theorem is valid in the canonical model. Moreover, theorem 14.1 and the definition of W show that every S + BF-consistent wff is a member of some world, and therefore, by Theorem 14.3, true in some world in the canonical model; and this in turn means that every non-theorem of S + BF is false in some world in that model. So, to parallel corollary 6.6 on p. 119, we have

COROLLARY 14.4   Any wff α is valid in the canonical model for S + BF
           iff $\vdash_{S+BF} \alpha$.

Completeness in modal LPC

On p. 249 we were able to reach a general soundness result connecting the soundness of a normal propositional modal system S with the soundness of the corresponding predicate system S + BF. In this section we shall enquire whether, and subject to what qualifications, we can obtain any analogous general results about completeness and characterization.

Our first result is that if S is incomplete (in the absolute sense explained in Chapter 9) then S + BF is incomplete too. As a preliminary to proving this, we shall introduce some new terminology and prove a lemma. Suppose that α is any wff of modal LPC, and that β is an expression which results from α by deleting all quantifiers and individual variables, and uniformly replacing each distinct predicate letter by a distinct propositional variable. Then clearly β is a wff of modal propositional logic; and we shall call it a *propositional transform* of α iff it is derived from α in this way. Next, let p_1, p_2, ... , etc., let ϕ_1, ϕ_2, ... , etc. and x_1, x_2, ... , etc. be enumerations of the propositional variables, the one-place predicate letters, and the individual variables respectively. Then we shall say that a wff γ of propositional modal logic and a wff δ of modal LPC are *mates* iff δ is the result of uniformly replacing each p_i in γ by $\phi_i x_i$. Clearly, each wff γ of propositional modal logic will have a unique mate δ, and γ will be a propositional transform of δ.

Our lemma is

LEMMA 14.5 Suppose that $\vdash_{S+BF} \alpha$ and that β is a propositional transform of α. Then $\vdash_S \beta$.

Proof: Since $\vdash_{S+BF} \alpha$, there is a proof of α in S + BF. The lemma is then proved by induction on the proof of α in S + BF. For if any wff in the proof of α is an instance of the axiom schema S, then its propositional transforms are theorems of S. If it is an instance of ∀1 or BF, then its propositional transforms are substitution-instances of $p \supset p$, and are therefore also theorems of S. The rules MP and N operate in exactly the same way in S and in S + BF. And if a wff γ' is derived from γ by ∀2, the propositional transform of γ' is simply identical with that of γ. This shows that a parallel proof of β can be given in S, and hence that $\vdash_S \beta$, which proves the lemma.

COROLLARY 14.6 If γ and δ are mates then if $\vdash_{S+BF} \delta$, $\vdash_S \gamma$.

THEOREM 14.7 Suppose that a normal propositional modal system S is incomplete. Then so is S + BF.

Proof: Since S is incomplete, there is some wff γ of propositional modal logic which is valid on every frame for S but is not a theorem of S. Let δ be the wff of modal LPC which is the mate of γ. Since δ is a substitution-instance of γ, it is also valid on every frame for S. Therefore by corollary 13.3 on p. 249, δ is valid on every frame for S + BF. But by corollary 14.6 δ is not a theorem of S + BF. So S + BF is incomplete. This completes the proof.

We know, then, that if S is not characterized by any class of frames, neither is S + BF. So the remaining question is: if S *is* characterized by some class of frames, what can we deduce from that about the characterization of S + BF? More precisely, is it the case that whenever S is characterized by the class of all the frames for S, then S + BF is also characterized by the class of all the frames for S? The answer is no – as we shall prove in the next section.

263

We proved in corollary 13.3 on p. 249, that the frames which are frames for S are precisely the frames which are frames for S + BF. But this does not of course give us completeness. Here it may help to recall again the discussion of the systems KW and KH on pp. 164-165. We were able to prove that precisely the same frames were frames for these two systems, yet it turned out that the class of these frames characterized one of them but did not characterize the other. Corollary 13.3 does, however, easily give us this conditional answer:

COROLLARY 14.8   If S + BF is complete, then it is characterized by the class of all frames for S.

The proof is simply that any complete system, i.e. any system characterized by any class of frames, is characterized by the class of all the frames for that system, and that by corollary 13.3 the frames for S + BF are precisely the frames for S. So if a system S + BF is complete, we know of at least one class of frames which characterizes it.

Our next result gives us another conditional answer.

THEOREM 14.9   Suppose that the frame of the canonical model for S + BF is a frame for S. Then S + BF is characterized by the class of all frames for S.

Proof: Suppose first that α is a theorem of S + BF. Let $\mathscr{F}$ be any frame for S. By theorem 13.1 on p. 247, $\mathscr{F}$ is also a frame for S + BF, and therefore α is valid on it. So α is valid on every frame for S. Suppose now that α is not a theorem of S + BF. Then $\sim\alpha$ is S + BF-consistent, and therefore is in some $w \in W$ in the canonical model for S + BF. So by theorem 14.3, $V(\alpha,w) = 0$. But by hypothesis the frame of the canonical model is a frame for S. Therefore α fails on some frame for S.

This means that, given the hypothesis of the theorem, any wff α of modal LPC is valid on all frames for S iff $\vdash_{S+BF} \alpha$, which is what the theorem states.

COROLLARY 14.10   If the frame of the canonical model for S + BF is a frame for S, then S + BF is characterized by any class of frames for S which contains the frame of the canonical model for S + BF.

Theorem 14.9 allows us to establish the completeness of particular systems. The completeness of K is immediate since the frame of the canonical model of K + BF is certainly a frame, and the completeness of many other systems follows exactly as in the case of propositional modal logic by proving that the frames of their canonical models are in the required class. As an example, take T + BF. By corollary 14.10, if we wish to prove that T + BF is complete with respect to the class of all reflexive frames all we need to show is that the frame of the canonical model for T + BF is reflexive. This is easily accomplished, in the same way as the parallel result for T was on p. 120. For since $Lp \supset p$ is a theorem of T, $L\alpha \supset \alpha$ is a theorem of T + BF for every wff α of modal LPC. So every such $L\alpha \supset \alpha$ is in every world w in the canonical model for T + BF, and hence whenever $L\alpha \in w$, we have $\alpha \in w$. Thus $L^-(w) \subseteq w$; i.e. wRw. We also showed on p. 249 that T + BF is sound with respect to the class of reflexive frames. It is therefore characterized by this class. Clearly, analogous results can be obtained in the same way for many of the other systems we have mentioned, including all those listed on p. 249.

Incompleteness

We shall now address the question posed on p. 263. Suppose that S is in fact complete. Does it follow that S + BF is also complete? The answer is no. Furthermore, a point worth noting is that, unlike incomplete propositional logics like KH, which often look as if they have been 'cooked up' simply to provide examples of incomplete logics, these incomplete predicate logics are based on propositional logics which have a history going back to the late fifties or early sixties. One of these is the system S4M that we discussed on pp. 131 and 175.[3] This system is characterized by the class of frames which are reflexive, transitive and final, where finality is the condition that every world can see an end world – a world that can only see itself. Further, as we noted on p. 175, *every* frame for S4M is of this kind, and so if S4M + BF were complete it would be characterized by this class of frames. Therefore, to show the incompleteness of S4M + BF it will suffice to produce a wff of modal predicate logic which is

    (I)   valid on every reflexive, transitive and final frame;

    (II) not a theorem of S4M + BF.

Such a wff is

(*) $L\exists x\phi x \supset M\exists x L\phi x$

LEMMA 14.11   (*) satisfies (I)

Proof: Let $\mathscr{F}$ be reflexive, transitive and final, and suppose that for some $w \in W$, where $\mathscr{F}$ is $\langle W,R \rangle$, and some model $\langle W,R,V \rangle$ based on $\langle W,R \rangle$ and some assignment μ to the variables of $\mathscr{L}$, $V_\mu(L\exists x\phi x,w) = 1$. Now w can see a final world w', and so $V_\mu(\exists x\phi x,w') = 1$. So there is some x-alternative ρ of μ such that $V_\rho(\phi x,w') = 1$. Since w' is final $V_\rho(L\phi x,w')$ $= 1$. So $V_\mu(\exists x L\phi x,w') = 1$ and hence $V_\mu(M\exists x L\phi x,w) = 1$, which establishes (I).

To establish (II), that (*) is not a theorem of S4M + BF, we produce a model $\langle W,R,D,V \rangle$ in which every theorem of S4M + BF is valid but (*) is not. Here is the model:

Both W and D are the set of natural numbers. I.e. where Nat = {0, 1, 2, ... etc.} then W = D = Nat. It may seem strange that worlds and individuals are the same but there is nothing in our definition of a model which prevents this. An alternative would be to index the worlds and individuals by the natural numbers and let the worlds be w_1, w_2, ... etc. and the individuals u_1, u_2, ... etc. This would not change the nature of the proof which follows but would make it a little more difficult to comprehend. R is simply $\leq$, i.e. i can see j provided j is no less than i; i.e., all numbers can see themselves and bigger numbers.

For any predicate ψ except ϕ, $V(\psi) = \varnothing$. That is any wff $\psi x_1...x_n$ will be false for any assignment when ψ is not ϕ. For ϕ, $V(\phi) = \{\langle i,i \rangle : i \in$ Nat}. What this means is that, at world i, ϕ is true of the individual i, and i alone. (If worlds and individuals are distinct one would require $V(\phi)$ to be $\{\langle w_i, u_i \rangle : i \in$ Nat}.)

We prove two things

(A)   (*) fails at 0 in $\langle W,R,D,V \rangle$;

(B)   For every wff α of modal LPC $LM\alpha \supset ML\alpha$ is valid in $\langle W,R,D,V \rangle$.

Since $\langle W,R,D,V \rangle$ is reflexive and transitive we know that all the other axioms of S4M + BF are valid in it, and since all the transformation rules of S + BF preserve validity in a model, (A) and (B) will together guarantee that (*) is not a theorem of S4M + BF.

The proof of (A) is straightforward. Let μ be any assignment to the variables. For any n $\in$ Nat, where ρ is the x-alternative of μ in which $\rho(x) = $ n, $V_\rho(\phi x, n) = 1$, and so $V_\mu(\exists x \phi x, n) = 1$ for every n $\in$ W. So $V_\mu(L\exists x \phi x, 0) = 1$. But consider any n $\in$ Nat and let ρ be any x-alternative of μ. Choose some m $\geq$ n with m $\neq \rho(x)$. Then $V_\rho(\phi x, m) = 0$, and so $V_\rho(L\phi x, n) = 0$ for every x-alternative ρ of μ. So $V_\mu(\exists x L\phi x, n) = 0$. Since this is so for every n $\in$ Nat we have $V_\mu(M\exists x L\phi x, 0) = 0$. Thus $V_\mu((*), 0) = 0$ and so (*) fails in $\langle W, R, D, V \rangle$.

The proof of (B) is more complex, although the idea behind it is really not too difficult. What $LM\alpha \supset ML\alpha$ says is that every proposition eventually settles down to a constant truth-value. If $LM\alpha$ is true this means that α is always going to be true. $ML\alpha$ says that in that case there will come a point at which it is true forever. Once a proposition has settled to a constant truth-value then *as far as that proposition is concerned* time has come to an end and if each of a finite number of propositions settles to a constant truth-value there must come a time at which they have all settled.

But in LPC it could easily happen that, although for any particular individual, the proposition that *it* is ϕ settles to a constant truth-value, there is always another individual which has not yet done so, and if there are infinitely many individuals we need never reach a world at which they have all settled, and so time need never come to an end. That is precisely what happens in this model. Each ϕi settles to the value false in worlds greater than i, but at no stage has this been settled for all individuals. So although each wff comes to have a constant value there are others which have not yet done so. First consider an atomic wff. If ψ is not ϕ then $\psi x_1...x_n$ is always false, whatever world we are in. For ϕx then if $\mu(x)$ is i, ϕx will be false at every j $> $ i. Suppose that we have two assignments μ and ρ, suppose $\mu(x) = $ n and $\rho(x) = $ m. Now consider worlds k $> $ n and h $> $ m. $V_\mu(\phi x, k) = 0$ and $V_\rho(\phi x, h) = 0$. This has the consequence that, at least for atomic formulae, and, in fact, as we shall show in a moment for *all* wff, *once we get to worlds greater than the values assigned to their free individual variables*, their truth-values become constant. It is this fact which will enable us to validate $LM\alpha \supset ML\alpha$, since if α is always going to be true, and eventually comes to have a constant truth-value, then there will come a world at which it will be necessary.

This feature of atomic wff of course has to be shown to hold of all wff. It does indeed hold of all wff, and we will be able to prove that it does by induction on the construction of wff, but the presence of quantifiers relies on an additional feature of wff in this model.

Note that $V_\mu(\phi x,n) = 1$ iff $\mu(x) = n$. Now consider some $m \leq n$, and some assignment ρ such that $\rho(x) = n-m$. Then $V_\rho(\phi x,m) = 1$ iff $\rho(x) = m$. This has the consequence that $V_\mu(\phi x,n) = V_\rho(\phi x,m)$ where $\mu(x)-\rho(x) = n-m$. In other words, given two worlds, an assignment which 'shifts' the individuals along the difference between these two worlds preserves the truth-value of the wff.

These two properties, stated for the single variable x in the case of the atomic wff ϕx generalize to an arbitrary wff α with respect to the variables free in α. This may be expressed in the following lemma.

LEMMA 14.12   Given a wff α, suppose $n \geq m$ and μ and ρ are so related that for every x free in α either

(i) $\mu(x) < n$ and $\rho(x) < m$

or

(ii) $\mu(x)-\rho(x) = n-m$

Then $V_\mu(\alpha,n) = V_\rho(\alpha,m)$.

(In this lemma (i) may hold of some variables and (ii) of others.) Given lemma 14.12 we have, for the special case where $\rho = \mu$ and (i) holds

COROLLARY 14.13   If $m > \mu(x)$ for every x free in α, and $n \geq m$ then $V_\mu(\alpha,n) = V_\mu(\alpha,m)$.

We first show that, given corollary 14.13, $LM\alpha \supset ML\alpha$ is valid in $\langle W,R,D,V \rangle$ for every wff α. Suppose $V_\mu(LM\alpha,w) = 1$. Consider some $w^* \geq w$ such that $\mu(x) < w^*$ for every x free in α. Clearly $V_\mu(M\alpha,w^*) = 1$, and so $V_\mu(\alpha, m) = 1$ for some $m \geq w^*$. Since $w^* > \mu(x)$ for every x free in α then $m > \mu(x)$ also for every such x. So by corollary 14.13 for every $n \geq m$, $V_\mu(\alpha,n) = 1$, and so $V_\mu(L\alpha,m) = 1$ and so $V_\mu(ML\alpha,w) = 1$ as required.

Now to prove lemma 14.12. The proof is by induction on the construction of α. If α is atomic then if α is $\psi x_1...x_n$ for any ψ except ϕ, $V_\mu(\alpha,w) = 0$ for every $w \in W$ and every μ, and so the lemma holds trivially. Suppose α is ϕx. If $\mu(x) < n$ and $\rho(x) < m$ then $V_\mu(\phi x,n) = 0$ and $V_\rho(\phi x,m) = 0$. So the lemma holds for atomic wff in case (i). For case (ii) suppose $\mu(x)-\rho(x) = n-m$. Then

$$V_\mu(\phi x,n) = 1 \text{ iff } \mu(x) = n$$

iff $\mu(x) - m = n - m$
iff $\mu(x) - m = \mu(x) - \rho(x)$
iff $\rho(x) = m$
iff $V_\rho(\phi x, m) = 1$

so the lemma holds for atomic wff in case (ii) also.

It should be clear that if (i) or (ii) holds of every x free in $\sim\alpha$ and of every x free in $\alpha \vee \beta$ then it holds for every x free in α and β, and so, by the induction hypothesis from (i) and (ii) we have

$$V_\mu(\alpha,n) = V_\rho(\alpha,m) \text{ and}$$

$$V_\mu(\beta,n) = V_\rho(\beta,m) \text{ and so}$$

$$V_\mu(\sim\alpha,n) = V_\rho(\sim\alpha,m) \text{ and}$$

$$V_\mu(\alpha \vee \beta,n) = V_\rho(\alpha \vee \beta,m).$$

Suppose (i) and (ii) hold for $L\alpha$. Note that any x free in $L\alpha$ is also free in α, and so (i) and (ii) also hold for α in respect of n and m.

Now suppose $V_\mu(L\alpha,n) = 1$ and suppose $k \geq n$, so that nRk. Then $V_\mu(\alpha,k) = 1$. Now every h such that $m \leq h$, i.e. every h such that mRh, will be such that for some $k \geq n$, $k - h = n - m$. (i.e. k will be as much above h as n is above m). Consider every such pair k and h and any x free in α.

(i′) If $\mu(x) < n$ and $\rho(x) < m$, then certainly $\mu(x) < k$ and $\rho(x) < h$.
(ii′) If $\mu(x) - \rho(x) = m - n$ then $\mu(x) - \rho(x) = k - h$.

This means that if (i) and (ii) hold of α in respect of n and m they also hold in respect of k and h, and so, by the induction hypothesis $V_\mu(\alpha,k) = V_\rho(\alpha,h)$. But $V_\mu(\alpha,k) = 1$ and so $V_\rho(\alpha,h) = 1$. Since there is an appropriate k for every $h \geq m$ we have $V_\rho(L\alpha,m) = 1$.

Suppose $V_\mu(L\alpha,n) = 0$. Then $V_\mu(\alpha,k) = 0$ for some $k \geq n$, and by the same argument as before, where h is the number such that $k - h = n - m$ we have $V_\rho(\alpha,h) = 0$ for some $h \geq m$, and so $V_\rho(L\alpha,m) = 0$. So the induction holds for L.

Suppose now that $V_\mu(\forall x\alpha,n) = 0$. Then $V_\nu(\alpha,n) = 0$ for some x-alternative ν of μ. We may assume that for every y free in $\forall x\alpha$, i.e. for every y free in α except possibly x, either (i) or (ii) holds.

Let σ be the x-alternative of ρ in which $\nu(x) - \sigma(x) = n - m$. Then ν and σ satisfy (i) or (ii) in respect of n and m, and so, by the induction hypothesis

$$V_\sigma(\alpha, m) = V_\nu(\alpha, n) = 0$$

so

$$V_\rho(\forall x\alpha, m) = 0.$$

If $V_\rho(\forall x\alpha, m) = 0$ then $V_\sigma(\alpha, m) = 0$ for some x-alternative σ of ρ. Let ν be the x-alternative of μ in which $\nu(x) - \sigma(x) = n - m$. As before, $V_\nu(\alpha, n) = V_\sigma(\alpha, m) = 0$, and so $V_\mu(\forall x\alpha, n) = 0$. This completes the inductive proof of lemma 14.12.

THEOREM 14.14   S4M + BF is not complete.

Proof: From lemma 14.12 we have corollary 14.13, from which we know that $LM\alpha \supset ML\alpha$ is valid in $\langle W,R,D,V \rangle$ for every wff α. Since $\langle W,R,D,V \rangle$ is reflexive and transitive this means that every theorem of S4M + BF is valid in it. But we proved at (A) above that (*) is not valid in $\langle W,R,D,V \rangle$ and so this establishes (II) that (*) is not a theorem of S4M + BF. However, by lemma 14.11, (*) is valid on every frame for S4M, and so (*) is valid on every frame for S4M + BF. So not all S4M + BF-valid wff are theorems, which is to say that S4M + BF is not complete.

Other incompleteness results

We mentioned above that incomplete predicate logics are often based on modal propositional logics with a long history. Our second example is KG1, which is K +

G1 $MLp \supset LMp$

As we mentioned on p. 134 S4 + G1 is called S4.2, and S4.2 + BF will be discussed in a moment. We shall first consider the result of adding G1 directly to K. KG1 is characterized by the class of *convergent* frames, i.e. frames satisfying

$$\forall w_0 \forall w_1 \forall w_2((w_0 R w_1 \wedge w_0 R w_2) \supset \exists w_3(w_1 R w_3 \wedge w_2 R w_3)),$$

the condition that if a world can see two worlds those two can together

270

see a world. Any frame is a frame for KG1 iff it is convergent.

KG1 + BF is formed out of KG1 in the way described on p. 244 above. From corollary 13.3 on p. 249, if KG1 + BF were complete it would be characterized by the class of convergent frames. So to establish the incompleteness of KG1 + BF it will suffice to find a non-theorem which is valid on every convergent frame – or, what comes to the same thing, a consistent wff which cannot be satisfied on any convergent frame. Such a wff is

$$M(\forall x(\phi x \supset L\phi x) \wedge L{\sim}\forall x\phi x) \wedge M\forall x(\phi x \vee L\phi x)$$
$$\wedge \ \forall x(M\phi x \supset L\phi x)$$

For S4.2 itself we have to use a different wff. S4.2 (see p. 134) is S4 + **G1**. It is characterized by frames which are reflexive, transitive and convergent, and all its frames have these properties.[4] The incompleteness of S4.2 + BF follows from the fact that

$$M(\exists x\phi x \wedge \forall x(\phi x \supset L\psi x) \wedge L{\sim}\forall x\psi x) \wedge M\forall x(\phi x \vee L\psi x)$$
$$\wedge \ \forall x(M\phi x \supset L(\exists x\phi x \supset \phi x))$$

is not satisfiable on any convergent frame but is consistent in S4.2. We shall not give the proofs of these results. The general strategy is the same as we used for S4M.

The monadic modal LPC

Non-modal LPC is not decidable. That is to say there is no effective procedure for deciding, of an arbitrarily presented wff, whether or not it is valid, or equivalently, in view of the completeness of LPC, whether or not it is a theorem. Nevertheless there are decidable fragments of which the most significant is the fragment that contains only one-place predicates.[5] By contrast the monadic modal LPC is in almost every case not decidable. Kripke has in fact proved the undecidability of the monadic fragment of any modal LPC whose class of frames contains one with a world that can see infinitely many worlds.[6] The idea is simple. Suppose $\mathscr{L}^*$ is a language of non-modal LPC with just a single two-place predicate ϕ. It is known that logical validity in this language is undecidable. Let $\mathscr{L}$ be a language of modal LPC containing just two monadic predicates ψ and χ and let S be a system which has at least one frame with a world which can see infinitely many worlds. Where α is any wff of $\mathscr{L}^*$ let its translation $\tau(\alpha)$ in $\mathscr{L}$ be obtained by replacing every atomic wff ϕxy by

$M(\psi x \wedge \chi y)$. First suppose $\tau(\alpha)$ is not valid in some model $\langle W,R,D,V \rangle$ for S. If α fails at w then let $\langle D^*,V^* \rangle$ be a model for $\mathcal{L}^*$ in which $D^* = D$ and $\langle u,v \rangle \in V^*(\phi)$ iff for some μ such that $\mu(x) = u$ and $\mu(y) = v$, $V_\mu(M(\psi x \wedge \chi y),w) = 1$. A straightforward inductive proof establishes that $V_\mu^*(\alpha) = 0$. Now suppose that $V_\mu^*(\alpha) = 0$ in some model $\langle D^*,V^* \rangle$ for $\mathcal{L}^*$ where D^* is of the same (infinite) size as the class W' of the worlds that w^* can see in a frame $\langle W,R \rangle$ for S in which w^* can see infinitely many worlds. Let π be a $1-1$ correspondence between W' and D^*, and let $\langle W,R,D^*,V \rangle$ be a model for $\mathcal{L}$ based on $\langle W,R \rangle$ in which $\langle u,w \rangle \in V(\psi)$ iff $\langle u,\pi(w) \rangle \in V^*(\phi)$ and $\langle u,w \rangle \in V(\chi)$ iff $\pi(w) = u$. Then for every $w \in W'$, $V_\mu(\psi x \wedge \chi y,w) = 1$ iff $\langle \mu(x),w \rangle \in V(\psi)$ and $\mu(y) = \pi(w)$. So $V_\mu(M(\psi x \wedge \chi y),w^*) = 1$ iff $\langle \mu(x),\mu(y) \rangle \in V^*(\phi)$, iff $V_\mu^*(\phi xy) = 1$. A straightforward induction then shows that $V_\mu^*(\alpha) = 0$. So if we could decide S + BF we could decide the dyadic LPC.

Exercises — 14

14.1   Given that S contains S4, prove that if Λ is a maximal S + BF-consistent set of wff with the $\forall$-property, then $\{L\alpha:L\alpha \in \Lambda\}$ can be extended to a consistent set with the $\forall$-property.

14.2   Prove the completeness of S4.3 + BF with respect to connected frames.

14.3   Prove that K + BF is not characterized by the class of finite frames.

*14.4   Is S4.3.1 + BF complete?

14.5   (a) Prove that KW + BF is not canonical.
        *(b) Is KW + BF complete?

14.6   Prove that the wff on p. 134 are unsatisfiable on a convergent frame.

*14.7   Axiomatize the system characterized by convergent frames.

Notes
[1] The use of maximal consistent sets to prove the completeness of non-modal LPC dates from Henkin 1949.
[2] The proof of theorem 14.2, and its use in completeness proofs for modal

predicate logic, is due in its essentials to R.H. Thomason 1970a, though Thomason considers only S4. The present method replaces the rather elaborate construction involving EM-formulae which was given in Chapter 9 of Hughes and Cresswell 1968. A somewhat different kind of completeness proof for modal predicate systems will be found in Fine 1978, pp. 131–135. Fine proves completeness by what he calls the method of 'diagrams' whereby the falsifying model for a non-theorem is obtained by forming a maximal consistent set of wff annotated by indices which become the worlds of the model. (See also Gallin 1975.) The earliest application of maximal consistent sets to proving completeness for modal predicate logic seems to have been that of Bayart 1959, though Bayart only considered S5. Kripke 1959 proves the completeness of modal predicate S5 by a different method. The method used in Hughes and Cresswell 1968 first appeared in Cresswell 1967c and is a generalization of Bayart's method.

[3] The incompleteness of S4M + BF was announced as early as 1967 in Kripke 1967. The proof we shall give is adapted from one which will appear in a forthcoming book by Kit Fine.

[4] The incompleteness of S4.2 + BF is stated in Shehtman and Skvorcov 1991, though no proof is given in their article in that volume. The incompleteness proofs of KG1 + BF and S4.2 + BF based on the wff mentioned in the text are found in Cresswell 1995b.

[5] See Kalmar 1936 and Church 1936 and 1956, pp. 272–279.

[6] Kripke 1962. Kripke's proof is in fact for all subsystems of S5, but it is not difficult, as we show, to see that his method applies to any system whose frames contain a world that can see infinitely many worlds. There are of course modal systems, such as the Alt systems mentioned on p. 142, whose frames do not include such frames.

15

EXPANDING DOMAINS

Validity without the Barcan Formula

The definition of validity which we gave for modal predicate calculi in Chapter 13 is one which makes (every instance of) the Barcan Formula come out as valid, and in Chapter 14 we showed how to define a canonical model for S + BF, whatever normal system of propositional modal logic S might be. We remarked however, although we did not prove this, that although for some choices of S, e.g. any S that contains B, BF is a theorem of LPC + S, for others it is not. The question therefore arises of how to give an account of validity for LPC + S which does not always validate the Barcan Formula.

This is not a question with a merely formal interest, for a number of objections have been brought against the validity of the formula from an intuitive point of view.[1] It is convenient here to consider the Barcan Formula as the wff

$$\forall x L\phi x \supset L\forall x\phi x$$

Under the standard interpretation what this means is that if everything necessarily possesses a certain property ϕ, then it is necessarily the case that everything possesses that property. But now, it is sometimes argued, even if everything that actually exists is necessarily ϕ, this does not preclude the possibility that there might have existed some other things which were not ϕ — and in that case it would not be a necessary truth that everything is ϕ.

This objection to the Barcan Formula depends on the assumption that in various 'possible worlds', not merely might objects have different properties from those they have in the actual world, but there might even be objects which do not exist in the actual world at all. Now it is at least plausible to think of the semantics we have given for modal predicate calculi as implicitly denying this assumption, for in each model we have had a single domain of individuals, the same for each world. The validity of the Barcan Formula is in fact connected with this feature of our semantics. And this suggests that we might obtain a semantics which does not bring the formula out as valid, by admitting models in which different domains are associated with different worlds. We shall now show how this can be done.

For systems without the Barcan Formula a model is a quintuple $\langle W,R,D,Q,V \rangle$ in which W,R and D are as before, and Q is a function from members of W to subsets of D. $Q(w)$, usually written D_w is the set of individuals which 'exist' in w. Models satisfy the *inclusion requirement*, that if wRw' then $D_w \subseteq D_{w'}$. But before we can look at the rules for assigning truth-values to wff in models for systems without BF we will have to look at the following question. In a wff like ϕx in which x is free what happens in a world w in which x is assigned as a value an individual which is not in D_w? One way of avoiding this question would be to prohibit such assignments altogether and we shall look later at what kind of semantics you get when you do. But for now we shall take it that such cases can arise. Another way, which actually turns out to be equivalent, is to say that ϕx lacks a truth-value in such worlds.[2] A third way, the way we shall choose,[3] is to say that it is either true or false, just as when x is assigned something which *is* in D_w. Which of these values it has of course is up to the model, since the value of ϕ will deliver in each world the set of things which satisfy ϕ. So [Vϕ], [V ~], [V ∨] and [VL] remain as they are, but [V∀] becomes

[V∀′] $V_\mu(\forall x\alpha, w) = 1$ if $V_\rho(\alpha, w) = 1$ for every x-alternative ρ of μ such that $\rho(x) \in D_w$ and 0 otherwise.

A wff is valid in a model $\langle W,R,D,Q,V \rangle$ iff for every world $w \in W$, $V_\mu(\alpha, w) = 1$ for every assignment μ such that $\mu(x) \in D_w$ for every variable x. α is said to be *eligible* at w with respect to μ iff $\mu(x) \in D_w$ for every x free in α. This means that another way of defining validity would be to say that a wff is true at every world at which it is eligible. The inclusion requirement guarantees that if α is eligible at w with respect to μ it remains eligible at every world w can see. Without this requirement such theorems as $L(\forall x\phi x \supset \phi y)$ need not be valid. (We shall consider such systems in the next chapter.) Both PR and PA hold in these semantics for the same reasons as they hold for the semantics which validates BF.

The proof that every theorem of LPC + S is valid in every model in which every instance of a theorem of S is valid is by induction on the proofs of theorems of LPC + S. Although straightforward it is necessary to take care at certain points. The validity of every substitution-instance of a theorem of S follows for the same reason as for systems with BF. The first hint of trouble comes with ∀1. Look first at the simplest instance of this schema

(1) $\forall x \phi x \supset \phi y$

Consider a world w and some assignment μ such that $\mu(y) \notin D_w$. Suppose that $\langle u,w \rangle \in V(\phi)$ for every $u \in D_w$, but that $\langle \mu(y),w \rangle \notin V(\phi)$. Then (1) will be false at w. However, this possibility is ruled out by defining validity as truth in every world w, with respect to every assignment *whose values are all in* D_w. And if that condition is satisfied by μ then (1) *will* be true in every w, and so will be valid. For the general case suppose that $V_\mu(\forall x \alpha, w) = 1$ and that μ gives values only from D_w. Let ρ be the x-alternative of μ such that $\rho(x) = \mu(y)$. Since $\mu(y) \in D_w$ then $\rho(x) \in D_w$, and so, by [V∀'], $V_\rho(\alpha, w) = 1$. So, by PR, $V_\mu(\alpha[y/x], w) = 1$. Thus ∀1 is valid.

MP preserves validity in a model of the present kind for the same reasons as it preserves validity in models for the systems which contain BF.

For necessitation suppose that $V_\mu(L\alpha, w) = 0$ for some $w \in W$ in some model $\langle W,R,D,Q,V \rangle$ where $\mu(x) \in D_w$ for every variable x. Then for some w' such that wRw', $V_\mu(\alpha, w') = 0$. Since wRw' the inclusion requirement ensures that $\mu(x) \in D_{w'}$ for every variable x, and so α is not valid either in $\langle W,R,D,Q,V \rangle$. (Note that it is at this point that the inclusion requirement is invoked, for if $\mu(x) \in D_w$ but $\mu(x) \notin D_{w'}$ for some x, α might be valid. In fact without the inclusion requirement, although $\forall x \phi x \supset \phi y$ is valid, $L(\forall x \phi x \supset \phi y)$ is not.)

Given PA, ∀2 is validity-preserving for the same reasons as in the semantics for systems with BF.

So every theorem of LPC + S is valid according to the present criterion. Yet it is easy to see that BF is not always a theorem of LPC + S.[4] Take S to be K and take the simplest instance of BF:

(2) $\forall x L\phi x \supset L\forall x\phi x$

Consider the following model: $W = \{w_1,w_2\}$, $w_1 R w_2$, $D = \{u_1,u_2\}$, $Q(w_1) = \{u_1\}$, $Q(w_2) = D$, $V(\phi) = \{\langle u_1,w_1\rangle, \langle u_1,w_2\rangle\}$.

This model may be pictured in the following way:

Domain

w_1 ϕu_1 $\{u_1\}$

$\downarrow$

w_2 ϕu_1 $\{u_1,u_2\}$

In this model everything in D_{w_1}, i.e. u_1, satisfies ϕ in every world and so $\forall x L\phi x$ is true there. But in w_2 $\forall x\phi x$ is false and so in w_1, $L\forall x\phi x$ is false. To show this more formally let μ be any assignment whose values are all taken from D_{w_1}. In fact $\mu(y)$ will have to be u_1 for every variable y including x. And the only x-alternative of μ whose values are all in D_{w_1} is μ itself. But by $V(\phi)$, $V_\mu(\phi x,w_1) = 1$ and $V_\mu(\phi x,w_2) = 1$, and so $V_\mu(L\phi x,w_1) = 1$, and so $V_\mu(\forall x\phi x,w_1) = 1$. So the antecedent of BF is true at w_1 in this model with respect to μ. But consider the x-alternative ρ of μ such that $\rho(x) = u_2$. Since $u_2 \in D_{w_2}$, ρ takes all its values from D_{w_2}, and so $V_\mu(\forall x\phi x,w_2) = 0$. Since $w_1 R w_2$, $V_\mu(\forall x\phi x,w_1) = 1$, and thus BF fails in this model.

The model can be made a T-model, indeed an S4-model, by requiring that $w_1 R w_1$ and $w_2 R w_2$. This would not affect the proof. In conjunction with our soundness result this shows that BF is not a theorem even of LPC + S4. However if we move to B and require that R be symmetrical we cannot preserve the inclusion requirement. For if R is symmetrical then the inclusion requirement guarantees that if wRw' then $D_w = D_{w'}$, and this is enough to validate BF. (In fact it has the consequence that in any frame which is cohesive, in the sense of p. 137, $D_w = D_{w'}$ for every w and $w' \in W$.)

Undefined formulae
We have already mentioned the problem of what to do about wff which appear to refer to non-existent objects. And we have said that an atomic

wff $\phi x_1 \ldots x_n$ is either true or false in a world w, i.e. it has a truth-value in w, *whether or not* the individuals assigned to x_1, ... , x_n are in D_w or not. Of course when we come to evaluate quantified wff in w, $\forall$ speaks of everything in D_w and $\exists$ of something in D_w. But it might be held that we ought not to be allowed even to speak of things which do not exist, so that e.g., if $\mu(x)$ is not in D_w then $V_\mu(\phi x, w)$ ought to be neither true nor false. It ought to have no value at all or to be undefined. We shall not take sides on whether this is or is not a philosophically reasonable reply, but what we shall do is show that, as far as the validity of wff of modal LPC is concerned, it makes no difference whether or not wff have truth-values at worlds where their variables are assigned elements from outside the domain of that world.

In order to prove this we need to be precise about how the values of wff are obtained when we allow undefined wff. We first note that a model for such a semantics will not differ in W, R, D, or Q from a model as defined on p. 275. Nor will an assignment V to the predicates, and nor will an assignment μ to the individual variables. What *will* differ is the way values are assigned to wff. So where $\langle W,R,D,Q,V \rangle$ is a model of the kind already defined we shall use the notation $V_\mu^*(\alpha, w)$ to mean the value assigned to α according to μ, when wff are undefined at a world w where not all their free variables are assigned values not in D_w. The rules for evaluating wff are as follows:

[V*ϕ] $V_\mu^*(\phi x_1 \ldots x_n w) = 1$ if each of $\mu(x_1)$, ... , $\mu(x_n) \in D_w$ and $\langle \mu(x_1)$, ... , $\mu(x_n), w \rangle \in V(\phi)$. $V_\mu^*(\phi x_1 \ldots x_n, w) = 0$ if each of $\mu(x_1)$, ... , $\mu(x_n) \in D_w$, but $\langle \mu(x_1)$, ... , $\mu(x_n), w \rangle \notin V(\phi)$. Otherwise $V_\mu^*(\phi x_1, \ldots, x_n, w)$ is undefined.

[V*$\sim$] For any wff α, $V_\mu^*(\sim\alpha, w) = 1$ if $V_\mu^*(\alpha, w) = 0$ and $V_\mu^*(\sim\alpha, w) = 0$ if $V_\mu^*(\alpha, w) = 1$ and is undefined otherwise.

[V*$\vee$] $V_\mu^*(\alpha \vee \beta, w)$ is defined iff both $V_\mu^*(\alpha, w)$ and $V_\mu^*(\beta, w)$ are defined and if defined, $V_\mu^*(\alpha \vee \beta, w) = 1$ if either $V_\mu^*(\alpha, w) = 1$ or $V_\mu^*(\beta, w) = 1$ and 0 otherwise.

[V*L] $V_\mu^*(L\alpha, w)$ is defined iff $V_\mu^*(\alpha, w')$ is defined for *every* w' such that wRw'. If it is defined then $V_\mu^*(L\alpha, w) = 1$ iff $V_\mu^*(\alpha, w') = 1$ for every w' such that wRw', and 0 otherwise.

[V*$\forall$] $V_\mu^*(\forall x\alpha, w) = 1$ iff $V_\rho^*(\alpha, w) = 1$ for every x-alternative ρ of μ such that $\rho(x) \in D_w$. $V_\mu^*(\forall x\alpha, w) = 0$ if $V_\rho^*(\alpha, w) = 0$ for some x-alternative ρ of μ such that $\rho(x) \in D_w$, and is undefined otherwise.

We say that α is valid* iff for every $w \in W$ and every μ, $V_\mu^*(\alpha,w) = 1$ whenever $V_\mu^*(\alpha,w)$ is defined. What we have to show is that validity* is exactly equivalent to the more 'classical' account of validity for systems without BF. So let $\langle W,R,D,Q,V \rangle$ be a model.

THEOREM 15.1 Let α be any wff, let $w \in W$ and let μ be any assignment. Then, if $\mu(x) \in D_w$ for every x free in α,
    (i) $V_\mu^*(\alpha,w)$ is defined
and
    (ii) $V_\mu(\alpha,w) = V_\mu^*(\alpha,w)$.

The proof is by induction on the construction of α. First suppose α is atomic, say $\phi x_1 \ldots x_n$. Then by $[V^*\phi]$, $V_\mu^*(\phi x_1 \ldots x_n,w)$ is defined if $\mu(x_1)$, $\ldots$, $\mu(x_n)$ are all in D_w, and so (i) holds. And by $[V\phi]$ and $[V^*\phi]$ we have $V_\mu(\phi x_1 \ldots x_n,w) = 1$ iff $\langle \mu(x_1), \ldots, \mu(x_n),w \rangle \in V(\phi)$ iff $V_\mu^*(\phi x_1 \ldots x_n,w) = 1$ and $V_\mu(\phi x_1 \ldots x_n,w) = 0$ iff $\langle \mu(x_1), \ldots ,\mu(x_n),w \rangle \notin V(\phi)$ iff $V_\mu^*(\phi x_1 \ldots x_n,w) = 0$. So the theorem holds for atomic wff.

Suppose the theorem holds for α and β in respect of a world w. Then by $[V^*\sim]$ $V_\mu^*(\sim\alpha,w)$ will be defined iff $V_\mu^*(\alpha,w)$ is, and so will be defined if $\mu(x) \in D_w$ for every x free in α. For such a μ, we have by $[V^*\sim]$ and $[V^*\vee]$, and the induction hypothesis, $V_\mu(\sim\alpha,w) = 1$ iff $V_\mu(\alpha,w) = 0$ iff $V_\mu^*(\alpha,w) = 0$ iff $V_\mu^*(\sim\alpha, w) = 1$. $V_\mu(\sim\alpha,w) = 0$ iff $V_\mu(\alpha,w) = 1$ iff $V_\mu^*(\alpha,w) = 1$ iff $V_\mu^*(\sim\alpha,w) = 0$.

For $\vee$ we have that $V_\mu^*(\alpha \vee \beta,w)$ is defined iff both $V_\mu^*(\alpha,w)$ and $V_\mu^*(\beta,w)$ are defined. By (i) for α and β this will be so if $\mu(x) \in D_w$ for every x free in α, and $\mu(x) \in D_w$ for every x free in β. Since these are precisely the xs free in $\alpha \vee \beta$ we have (i) in respect of $\alpha \vee \beta$. Given such a μ, $[V \vee]$ and $[V^* \vee]$ give the same results in a manner analogous to the case for $\sim$.

Suppose that the theorem holds for α. This means that for any $w \in W$, we may assume that it holds for α in respect of every w' such that wRw'. Now suppose that $\mu(x) \in D_w$ for every x free in $L\alpha$. Consider any w' such that wRw' and any x free in α. If x is free in α then it is free in $L\alpha$ and so $\mu(x) \in D_w$. So, by the inclusion requirement, $\mu(x) \in D_{w'}$, and so, by the induction hypothesis, $V_\mu^*(\alpha,w')$ is defined. Since this is so for every w' such that wRw', $V_\mu^*(L\alpha,w)$ is defined and so (i) holds of $L\alpha$. Further, if $V_\mu^*(\alpha,w')$ is defined for every w' such that wRw' $[VL]$ and $[V^*L]$ give the same results in a manner analogous to the case for $\sim$.

Suppose that the theorem holds for α and consider $\forall x\alpha$. Suppose that

$\mu(y) \in D_w$ for every y free in $\forall x\alpha$. Where ρ is any x-alternative of μ such that $\rho(x) \in D_w$, then $\rho(y) \in D_w$ for every y free in α, including x. So, assuming that the theorem holds for α, $V_\rho{}^*(\alpha,w)$ is defined for every such ρ, and in that case [V∀] and [V*∀] give the same result.

This means that in any model $\langle W,R,D,Q,V\rangle$ for any wff α and any $w \in W$, $V_\mu(\alpha,w) = 1$ for every μ such that $\mu(x) \in D_w$ for every x, iff $V_\mu{}^*(\alpha,w) = 1$ for every μ such that $\mu(x) \in D_w$ for every x. In other words α is valid iff α is valid*.

Canonical models without BF

For systems without BF we form the canonical model as follows. As before we assume two languages $\mathscr{L}$ and $\mathscr{L}^+$, the latter with infinitely many variables not in $\mathscr{L}$. But now we can allow the domains to vary, and we do this by letting each world w in the canonical model be a maximal consistent set of wff of a language $\mathscr{L}_w$ which contains all the variables of $\mathscr{L}$ and possibly some of the new variables of $\mathscr{L}^+$, provided that there are infinitely many variables of $\mathscr{L}^+$ not in $\mathscr{L}_w$. (From here on we shall use the following terminology. Where $A \subseteq B$ we shall say that A is an *infinitely proper* subset of B iff there are infinitely many members of B not in A. When we say that a language $\mathscr{L}$ is an infinitely proper sublanguage of a language $\mathscr{L}'$ we mean that $\mathscr{L}$ and $\mathscr{L}'$ contain the same predicates, and the variables of $\mathscr{L}$ are an infinitely proper subset of the variables of $\mathscr{L}'$.)

THEOREM 15.2 If $\sim L\alpha \in w$ then there is a maximal consistent set w' with the ∀-property in a language $\mathscr{L}_{w'}$ containing $\mathscr{L}_w$ such that $L^-(w) \cup \{\sim\alpha\} \subseteq w'$.

Proof: Let $\mathscr{L}_{w'}$ be an infinitely proper sublanguage of $\mathscr{L}^+$ such that $\mathscr{L}_w$ is an infinitely proper sublanguage of $\mathscr{L}_{w'}$ containing infinitely many of the variables of $\mathscr{L}^+$ not in $\mathscr{L}_w$. Since $w \in W$ then $\mathscr{L}_w$ lacks infinitely many variables of $\mathscr{L}^+$. Now $L^-(w) \cup \{\sim\alpha\}$ is consistent by lemma 6.4 on p. 117, and further $L^-(w) \cup \{\sim\alpha\}$ is taken from the language $\mathscr{L}_w$. Since $\mathscr{L}_{w'}$ contains infinitely many variables not in $\mathscr{L}_w$ then theorem 14.1 guarantees that $L^-(w) \cup \{\sim\alpha\}$ has a consistent extension Δ with the ∀-property in $\mathscr{L}_{w'}$. And by theorem 6.3 on p. 115, Δ has an extension w' which is maximal consistent.

The canonical model then for a system LPC + S in a language $\mathscr{L}$ with an extension $\mathscr{L}^+$ is a quintuple $\langle W,R,D,Q,V\rangle$ where W is the set of all maximal consistent sets with the ∀-property in some sublanguage of $\mathscr{L}^+$;

and wRw' iff, for every $L\alpha \in w$, $\alpha \in w'$ (i.e. $L^-(w) \subseteq w'$). D is the set of variables in $\mathcal{L}^+$ and $Q(w)$, i.e. D_w, is the set of variables in $\mathcal{L}_w$. Where $x \in D_w$ then $L(\phi x \supset \phi x) \in w$ and so where wRw', $\phi x \supset \phi x \in w'$ and thus $x \in D_{w'}$, i.e. $\mathcal{L}_w$ is a sublanguage of $\mathcal{L}_{w'}$ when wRw' and so the inclusion requirement is satisfied. $\langle x_1, \ldots, x_n, w \rangle \in V(\phi)$ iff $\phi x_1 \ldots x_n \in w$.

Finally take the 'canonical' value-assignment σ to be the assignment such that $\sigma(x) = x$, for every variable x in D. We prove the following theorem:

THEOREM 15.3 For any $w \in W$, and any wff $\alpha \in \mathcal{L}_w$, $V_\sigma(\alpha, w) = 1$ iff $\alpha \in w$.

The proof parallels that of theorem 14.3 on p. 261. However the members of W are all in different sublanguages of $\mathcal{L}^+$, and so care is needed in the various inductive steps. For that reason we shall set the proof out in full. First consider any atomic wff $\phi x_1 \ldots x_n$.

(a) $V_\sigma(\phi x_1 \ldots x_n, w) = 1$ iff $\langle \sigma(x_1), \ldots, \sigma(x_n), w \rangle \in V(\phi)$, iff $\langle x_1, \ldots, x_n, w \rangle \in V(\phi)$, iff $\phi x_1 \ldots x_n \in w$.

(b) Suppose $\sim\alpha \in \mathcal{L}_w$. Then $\alpha \in \mathcal{L}_w$, and then $V_\sigma(\sim\alpha, w) = 1$ iff $V_\sigma(\alpha, w) = 0$, iff $\alpha \notin w$, iff $\sim\alpha \in w$ iff $V_\sigma(\sim\alpha, w) = 1$.

[In (b) it is important that $\alpha \in \mathcal{L}_w$ since first, the induction hypothesis only applies to such wff, and second since w is maximal consistent only in $\mathcal{L}_w$, it is only if $\alpha \in \mathcal{L}_w$ that we can guarantee that if $\alpha \notin w$ then $\sim\alpha \in w$.]

(c) Suppose $\alpha \lor \beta \in \mathcal{L}_w$. Then $\alpha \in \mathcal{L}_w$ and $\beta \in \mathcal{L}_w$. Then, $V_\sigma(\alpha \lor \beta, w) = 1$ iff $V_\sigma(\alpha, w) = 1$ or $V_\sigma(\beta, w) = 1$ iff $\alpha \in w$ or $\beta \in w$, iff $\alpha \lor \beta \in w$. [As with (b) it is crucial that α, β and $\alpha \lor \beta$, all be in $\mathcal{L}_w$.]

(d) Suppose $\forall x\alpha \in w$. Then $\forall x\alpha \in \mathcal{L}_w$. Now let ν be any x-alternative of σ such that $\nu(x) \in D_w$. This means that $\nu(x) = y$ for some variable y in $\mathcal{L}_w$. So $\alpha[y/x] \in \mathcal{L}_w$, and so by $\forall 1$, $\alpha[y/x] \in w$. So $V_\sigma(\alpha[y/x], w) = 1$. So by PR, $V_\nu(\alpha, w) = 1$. Since ν is any x-alternative of σ, such that $\nu(x) \in D_w$, $V_\sigma(\forall x\alpha, w) \in \mathcal{L}_w$.

(e) Suppose $\forall x\alpha \in \mathcal{L}_w$ but $\forall x\alpha \notin w$. Then $\sim\forall x\alpha \in w$ and so, since w has the $\forall$-property in $\mathscr{L}_w$, there is some y in $\mathscr{L}_w$ such that $\sim\alpha[y/x] \in w$. So $\alpha[y/x] \notin w$ and since $\alpha[y/x] \in \mathscr{L}_w$, $V_o(\alpha[y/x],w) = 0$. So by the validity of $\forall 1$, $V_o(\forall x\alpha,w) = 0$.

(f)   Suppose $L\alpha \in w$ and wRw'. Then $\alpha \in w'$, and so $\alpha \in \mathscr{L}_{w'}$. So $V_o(\alpha,w') = 1$, and since this is so for every w' such that wRw', $V_o(L\alpha,w) = 1$.

(g)   Suppose $L\alpha \in \mathscr{L}_w$ but $L\alpha \notin w$. Then since w is maximal consistent in $\mathscr{L}_w$, $\sim L\alpha \in w$. But then by theorem 15.2 there is some $w' \in W$ with the $\forall$-property such that $\sim\alpha \in w'$ and wRw'. So $\alpha \notin w'$. But $\mathscr{L}_{w'}$ is an extension of $\mathscr{L}_w$ and $\alpha \in \mathscr{L}_w$, so $\alpha \in \mathscr{L}_{w'}$ and so $V_o(\alpha,w) = 0$. But wRw' and so $V_o(L\alpha,w) = 0$.

This proves theorem 15.3.

Completeness

As a result of theorem 15.3 we know that for any wff α, α is valid in the canonical model of LPC + S iff $\vdash_{\text{LPC + S}} \alpha$. This construction can be carried out for any normal modal logic. As before completeness is forthcoming for all those systems S in which the frame of the canonical model for LPC + S, constructed as in the last section, is a frame for S. It is not difficult to see that this is so for K, D, T, S4, and a number of other systems we have discussed.

The definition of R entails that if wRw' then $\mathscr{L}_w$ is a sublanguage of $\mathscr{L}_{w'}$. But also, at least some of the worlds w' such that wRw' will be in languages with additional variables, and in these cases we cannot have $w'Rw$. So R cannot be symmetrical. This means that for systems like extensions of the system B, in which the Barcan Formula is a theorem, the models produced will not be ones in which R is symmetrical, and so, although they will be *models* for these logics, they will not be based on *frames* for these logics, and so cannot be used to give completeness proofs for these systems.[5] For extensions of B, BF is provable, and so the method of Chapter 14 can be used to establish completeness. There are however systems for which neither method on its own will work. Consider the system K + $ML(p \land \sim p) \lor (q \supset LMq)$. This system is characterized by frames in which, for every world w, either w can see a dead end, or else if wRw' then $w'Rw$. In a frame whose only worlds are w_1 and w_2 where w_1Rw_2 and w_2 is a dead end BF can easily be falsified, and so the method of Chapter 14 will not work. But the method of the present chapter will not work either since the consistency of $LM(p \supset p)$ $\wedge\ p\ \wedge\ \sim Lp$ requires a pair of worlds w and w' in the canonical model with $w\ \neq\ w'$, wRw' and $w'Rw$, and that is what the method of the present chapter will not guarantee.

Incompleteness without the Barcan Formula

It is not hard to show that the analogues of theorems 13.1 on p. 247 and 13.2 on p. 248 still hold for systems without the Barcan Formula. Our soundness result on p. 276 gives 13.1, and the proof of 13.2 remains the same, since the differing domains only become relevant in the interpretation of the quantifiers, and the wff α used in that theorem is quantifier free. To establish the incompleteness of a system we show that some wff valid on all frames for S is not a theorem of LPC + S. (Or that a wff unsatisfiable on every frame for S is nevertheless consistent in LPC + S).

Our first result is that LPC + S4M is incomplete. Clearly (*) on p. 266 is not a theorem of LPC + S4M since it is not a theorem of S4M + BF. So all we have to show is that it is valid on every final frame. Look at the proof of (I) on p. 265. According to our present semantics, given that $V_\mu(\exists x\phi x, w') = 1$ for some final world w', we have that $V_\rho(\phi x, w') = 1$, where ρ is some x-alternative of μ *and* $\rho(x) \in D_{w'}$. Since w' is final $V_\rho(L\phi x, w') = 1$, and since no other world is involved $\rho(x)$ is still in $D_{w'}$. Then the proof proceeds as before. So LPC + S4M is not complete either.

The situation is different with S4.2. S4.2 + BF is, as we remarked, not complete. Yet LPC + S4.2 *is* complete,[6] and it is not hard to see why. If you look at the completeness proof of S4.2 on p. 134 you will see that it proceeds by establishing that in the canonical model for S4.2 if w_1Rw_2 and w_1Rw_3 then $L^-(w_2)\ \cup\ L^-(w_3)$ is consistent. This result still holds in predicate logic. However the problem is to give it a maximal consistent extension *with the ∀-property*, and that is what cannot be done in S4.2 + BF. But for systems without BF we can use theorem 15.2. For, since $L^-(w_2)\ \cup\ L^-(w_3)$ is consistent it will certainly have a maximal consistent extension in a language with infinitely many new variables. And that fact is all that we need for LPC + S4.2.

LPC + S4.4 (S4.9)

The systems we now go on to consider provide examples in which the predicate extension is incomplete *without* the Barcan Formula, but complete with it,[7] and include systems properly between S4.3 and S5. For definiteness we shall consider only two. One is the system S4.4[8] which is S4 +

R1 $p \supset (MLp \supset Lp)$

The other is one called S4.9.[9] This is S4.4 +

M18 $(MLp \supset p) \vee (LMq \supset MLq)$

S4.9 has the property that there is no system properly between it and S5.[10] S4.4 is characterized by reflexive and transitive frames satisfying

(1) $(w_1Rw_2 \wedge w_1 \neq w_2 \wedge w_1Rw_3) \supset w_3Rw_2$

Further, any reflexive and transitive frame is a frame for S4.4 iff it satisfies (1).

It is not difficult to show that the canonical model for S4.4 + BF, constructed in the manner described on p. 261 above satisfies (1). For if $w_1 \neq w_2$ then there must be $\alpha \in w_1$ such that $\alpha \notin w_2$, and so $\sim\alpha \in w_2$. And if not w_3Rw_2 then there must be some $L\beta \in w_3$ such that $\sim\beta \in w_2$. Since $L\beta \in w_3$, $L(\alpha \vee \beta) \in w_3$ and so $ML(\alpha \vee \beta) \in w_1$. Since $\alpha \in w_1$, $(\alpha \vee \beta) \in w_1$, and so, by R1, $L(\alpha \vee \beta) \in w_1$. But w_1Rw_2 and so $\alpha \vee \beta \in w_2$, contradicting the presence in w_2 of $\sim\alpha$ and $\sim\beta$.

For this proof to work we have to know that because $\alpha \notin w_2$ and $\beta \notin w_2$ then $\sim\alpha \in w_2$ and $\sim\beta \in w_2$. In the canonical models of systems without BF this cannot be guaranteed since, e.g., α may fail to be in w_2 because it contains a 'new' variable not in the language of w_2, and so $\sim\alpha$ may not be in w_2 either. And in fact we shall see that LPC + S4.4 is not complete, and nor is LPC + S4.9, and in fact no system properly between LPC + S4.3 and LPC + S5 is complete. To prove the incompleteness of LPC + S4.4 and LPC + S4.9 we shall show that the wff

(C) $L(\forall xML\phi x \wedge \exists x \sim \phi x)$

is consistent in LPC + S4.9 (i.e. its negation is not a theorem) yet any transitive and reflexive frame on which it is satisfiable must satisfy the condition

(2) $\exists w_0 \forall w_1(w_0Rw_1 \supset \exists w_2(w_1Rw_2 \wedge \sim w_2Rw_1))$

This will be shown in theorem 15.4. What (2) means is that in extensions of S4.3 the frame must contain an infinite chain of clusters. It is not hard to see that R1 fails on such a frame. For suppose we have even three worlds w_1, w_2 and w_3 with $w_i R w_j$ iff $i \leq j$. Then, with $V(p,w_1) = V(p,w_3) = 1$ and $V(p,w_2) = 0$ we have R1 false at w_1.[11]

THEOREM 15.4   If (C) is satisfiable on a transitive and reflexive frame $\mathcal{F}$ then $\mathcal{F}$ satisfies (2).

Proof: Suppose that for some $w_0 \in W$ in $\mathcal{F}$, $V_\mu(L(\forall x ML\phi x \wedge \exists x \sim \phi x), w_0) = 1$ and suppose that $w_0 R w_1$. Then

(3) $V_\mu(\forall x ML\phi x \wedge \exists x \sim \phi x, w_1) = 1$.

So there is an x-alternative ρ of μ such that $\rho(x) \in D_{w_1}$ and

(4) $V_\rho(\sim \phi x, w_1) = 1$. But

(5) $V_\rho(ML\phi x, w_1) = 1$

and so there is some w_2 with $w_1 R w_2$ such that

(6) $V_\rho(L\phi x, w_2) = 1$.

Now suppose $w_2 R w_1$. Then $V_\rho(\phi x, w_1) = 1$, which contradicts (4). So not $w_2 R w_1$, as required for (2).

Since no frame for R1 satisfies (2) (C) is unsatisfiable on every frame for S4.4. So the negation of (C) is valid on every frame for S4.4, and therefore also on every frame for S4.9. We now produce a model in which (C) is satisfiable, i.e., $\sim$(C) is not a theorem, and in which the theorems of S4.9 are all valid. Since R will be transitive and reflexive it will be sufficient for the latter purpose to show that R1 and M18 are true at every world. The model $\mathfrak{C}$ is defined as follows. W is a denumerable set and $w_i R w_j$ iff $i \leq j$. D consists of the natural numbers, and $Q(w_i) = \{0, \dots, i\}$. For any predicate ψ except ϕ, $V(\psi) = \emptyset$. For ϕ, $\langle u, w_n \rangle \in V(\phi)$ iff $u < n$. Thus the model looks like this:

Domain

w_0:	$\sim\phi 0$			$\{0\}$
w_1:	$\phi 0$	$\sim\phi 1$		$\{0,1\}$
w_2:	$\phi 0$	$\phi 1$	$\sim\phi 2$	$\{0,1,2\}$

.... etc

THEOREM 15.5 (C) is true in $\mathfrak{C}$ at w_0.

Proof: It should be clear that at every world $\exists x \sim\phi x$ is true, since at w_n, n is in D_{w_n} but $\langle n,w_n \rangle \notin V(\phi)$. Further, for every $u \in D_{w_n}$, for all m > n, $\langle u,w_m \rangle \in V(\phi)$ and so $\forall x ML\phi x$ is true at w_n. This means that for every μ and every $w \in W$,

(7) $V_\mu(\forall x ML\phi x \wedge \exists x \sim\phi x,w) = 1$.

So, since $w_o R w$ for every $w \in W$,

(8) $V_\mu(L(\forall x ML\phi x \wedge \exists x \sim\phi x),w_0) = 1$.

This proves theorem 15.5.

Since R is reflexive and transitive, to show that $\mathfrak{C}$ is an S4.9-model (and therefore an S4.4-model) it will suffice to show that both R1 and M18 are valid in $\mathfrak{C}$. In order to do this we note that every wff has a certain property. Recall that we say that a wff α is *ineligible* in w with respect to μ iff $\mu(x) \notin D_w$ for some x free in α. Note that if α is eligible at a world with respect to an assignment, it remains eligible at all worlds that world can see, with respect to the same assignment. With respect to any given assignment μ, any wff α gets at most one chance to change its truth-value, and that is immediately after the first world at which it becomes eligible. This may be proved by a somewhat tedious induction on the construction of wff. Given this we may conclude that R1 and M18 are valid in $\mathfrak{C}$. First consider an instance of R1, $\alpha \supset (ML\alpha \supset L\alpha)$. Suppose this is eligible at w_n with respect to some assignment μ and suppose that α is true at w_n. Then either it is true from w_n on, or it is true at w_n and false from then on. But if $ML\alpha$ is true at w_n, α cannot be false at w_m with m > n, and so α must be true from n on, making $L\alpha$ true at

w_n. For M18, if $LM\alpha$ is true at w_n then α can never become false forever and so, since it only gets one chance to change its truth-value as soon as it becomes eligible, it must eventually become true forever, and so $ML\alpha$ must also be true at w_n. This means that R1 and M18 are true in this model whenever they are eligible, and so are valid in $\mathfrak{C}$. Since (C) is satisfiable on this model its negation is not a theorem even of LPC + S4.9. Since the negation of (C) is valid in LPC + S4.4 neither LPC + S4.4 nor LPC + S4.9 is complete.

Exercises — 15

15.1 Explain why the model on p. 277 shows that BF is not a theorem of LPC + S when S is S4.9, KW, MV.

15.2 Prove the completeness of LPC + S4.2 with respect to reflexive, transitive and convergent frames.

15.3 Prove the completeness of LPC + S4.3 with respect to reflexive, transitive and connected frames. (Corsi, 1993.)

15.4 Let S be K + $ML(p \wedge \sim p) \vee (q \supset LMq)$:

(a) Show that $ML(\forall x\alpha \wedge \sim \forall x\alpha) \vee (\forall xL\alpha \supset L\forall x\alpha)$ is valid on all frames for S.

*(b) Is $ML(\forall x\alpha \wedge \sim \forall x\alpha) \vee (\forall xL\alpha \supset L\forall x\alpha)$ a theorem of LPC + S?

*(c) Prove the completeness of LPC + S + $ML(\forall x\alpha \wedge \sim \forall x\alpha) \vee (\forall xL\alpha \supset L\forall x\alpha)$ with respect to the class of frames in which for any $w \in W$, either w can see a dead end or else for every w', if wRw' then $w'Rw$.

15.5 Let S be K + $p \supset LMMp$:

(a) Show that BF is valid on all frames for LPC + S.

*(b) Is BF a theorem of LPC + S?

Notes
[1] One of the earliest of these objections is found in Prior 1957, pp. 26–28 and *passim*. There is also a discussion in Hintikka 1961. For an objection of a somewhat different kind *vide* Myhill 1958, p. 80. For a defence of the formula *vide* Barcan (Marcus) 1962, pp. 88–90 and Cresswell 1991.

[2] That was the way we proceeded in Chapter 10 of Hughes and Cresswell 1968. It is discussed below on pp. 277–280.

[3] We are following Kripke 1963b. On p. 86n Kripke points out that it might be tempting to require that if $\langle u,w \rangle \in V(\phi)$ then $u \in D_w$, but although this would make ϕx false for every atomic wff when x has a value not in D_w it would make every $\sim \phi x$ true for every such value. This requirement would have the curious consequence that, for instance, $(\phi y \wedge \forall x \alpha) \supset \alpha[y/x]$ would always be valid but $(\sim \phi y \wedge \forall x \alpha) \supset \alpha[y/x]$ would not.

[4] A proof that BF is not a theorem of LPC + S4 is found in Lemmon 1960b.

[5] Bowen 1979 contains completeness proofs for various modal systems along the lines of the present section.

[6] Corsi and Ghilardi 1989.

[7] These systems have been discussed in Ghilardi 1991 using methods from category theory. The proof summarized here appears in more detail in Cresswell 1995b. See also Corsi and Ghilardi 1992.

[8] See Hughes and Cresswell 1968, p. 263.

[9] Zeman 1973, p. 266

[10] Zeman 1973, pp. 273−275.

[11] Ghilardi 1991 shows how to extend this result to all proper extensions of S4.3 which are properly contained in S5. (This includes S4.3.1.) We shall however continue to focus on S4.4 and S4.9. In extensions of LPC + S4.3.1 weaker than S4.4 we would have axioms which would allow longer finite chains, but if a system allows finite chains of arbitrarily high length then it must be contained in LPC + S4.3.1. This shows that extensions of LPC + S4.3.1 contained in LPC + S4.9 are all incomplete since they do not contain the negation of (C). For a proof of (C) in S4.4 + BF see the solution to exercise 13.4.

16

MODALITY AND EXISTENCE

Changing domains

It is not hard to see that models for systems containing the Barcan Formula are a special case of models for systems without it. For a model will satisfy BF provided $Q(w) = D$ for every $w \in W$. So if you want the quantifiers in each world to range only over the things that exist in that world, and you don't believe that the same things exist in every world, you would probably not want the Barcan Formula. However you would probably not want its converse either. For consider

(1) $L\forall x\phi x \supset \forall xL\phi x$

It could happen that in every world everything which exists *in that world* is ϕ, but that something in our world fails to be ϕ in some other world. Of course that other world will be a world in which the object in question does not exist.

This situation does not of course satisfy the inclusion requirement, and it is the inclusion requirement which is responsible for the validity of the converse of the Barcan Formula. In terms of plausibility it might even be held that the converse of BF (BFC) is less plausible than BF itself. For it would seem not too difficult to point to something which actually exists and say *that* might not have existed. But it doesn't seem possible to point to something which *doesn't* exist and say *that* might have existed; which means that it is more plausible to suppose that an accessible world could contain *fewer* individuals rather than more, and that is exactly the reverse of what the inclusion requirement dictates. So what we must do now is examine what happens if we abandon the inclusion requirement.

The first thing we notice is that with the definition we have used up to now, abandoning the inclusion requirement means that the rule of necessitation no longer preserves validity. For although

(2) $\forall x\phi x \supset \phi y$

is valid

(3) $L(\forall x\phi x \supset \phi y)$

is not. For consider a model like this:

			Domain
w_1	ϕu_1	ϕu_2	$\{u_1, u_2\}$
↓			
w_2	ϕu_1	$\sim\phi u_2$	$\{u_1\}$

(This model is of course incompatible with the inclusion requirement.) Where $\mu(y)$ is u_2 then (2) is false at w_2, and so (3) is false at w_1. Since $\mu(y) \in D_{w_1}$ this means that (3) is not valid.

Perhaps we should insist that the variables of α should be assigned values from the domains of the evaluation world and all the worlds in the *posterity* of w, where this is defined to be the smallest set POS_w such that

(i) $w \in POS_w$.
(ii) If $w' \in POS_w$ and $w'Rw''$ then $w'' \in POS_w$.

But that will not do either since, although such a semantics validates

(4) $L\forall x\phi x \supset L\phi y$

(because if y's value is in the domain of every world accessible from w and if $\forall x\phi x$ is true in every such world then $L\phi y$ must be also), its universalized version

(5) $\forall y(L\forall x\phi x \supset L\phi y)$

is not valid, since despite (4)'s validity it can still be false when y is assigned something in D_w which is not in some accessible w' and which does not satisfy ϕ in w' even though everything in $D_{w'}$ is ϕ, and that is enough to show the invalidity of (5). Now, one can save the situation by changing the evaluation rule for the quantifier so that it reads

$[V\forall'']$ $\forall x\alpha$ is true at a world w iff α is true at w for all assignments to x which assign it some u which is in the domain of every world in the posterity of w.

The reason this works is the following. Let us define D_w^+ to be the set such that $u \in D_w^+$ iff u is in the domain of every world in the posterity of w. Then $[V\forall'']$ is just the usual rule except that D_w^+ is used as the domain instead of D_w. So although it may *look* as if D_w is the domain of things existing in w the real domain is D_w^+, and when we look at D_w^+ we notice an interesting fact. Suppose wRw'. Then if u is in the domain of every world in the posterity of w it is certainly in the domain of every world in the posterity of w'. In other words if wRw' then $D_w^+ \subseteq D_{w'}^+$. And that means that the $+$ domains satisfy the inclusion requirement and we are back to the semantics given on p. 275.

The semantics we are using at present requires all wff to be defined, i.e. to have a truth-value, at every world, even when their free variables are assigned values which do not exist in that world. We shall show that allowing undefined wff does not help when we drop the inclusion requirement. On pp. 277–280 we showed that, given the inclusion requirement, admitting undefined wff does not change the logic. We shall now show that even without the inclusion requirement the semantics given there for undefined wff validates (1).[1]

Suppose that a model satisfies $[V*\phi]-[V*\forall]$ on p. 278 and that for some $w \in W$ and assignment μ, $V_\mu*(L\forall x\phi x,w) = 1$ and $V_\mu*(\forall xL\phi x,w) = 0$. From the former, if wRw' then by $[V*L]$, $V_\mu*(\forall x\phi x,w') = 1$. From the latter by $[V*\forall]$ there is an x-alternative ρ of μ (with $\rho(x) \in D_w$) such that $V_\rho*(L\phi x,w) = 0$. So by $[V*L]$ there is some w' such that wRw' and $V_\rho*(\phi x,w') = 0$. Further, $V_\rho*(\phi x,w')$ is defined and so, by $[V*\phi]$, $\rho(x) \in D_{w'}$. So, by $[V*\forall]$, $V_\mu*(\forall x\phi x,w') = 0$, contradicting the fact that $V_\mu*(L\forall x\phi x,w) = 1$.

One might be tempted to propose an alternative evaluation rule for $\forall$ to cover the undefined cases. One might say that $\forall xL\phi x$ is true provided $L\phi x$ is *true where defined* for every value u of x taken from D_w.

However, that would have the effect of invalidating

(6) $\forall x(\phi x \land L\phi x) \supset \phi y$

This will be false in a model with wRw' and y assigned some $u \in D_w$ but $u \notin D_{w'}$. For suppose u does not satisfy ϕ in w, but every other individual satisfies ϕ both in w and in every other world. This will mean that ϕy will be false at w. But $\phi x \land L\phi x$ will be undefined at w when x is assigned u, since ϕx is undefined at w' so by [V*L], $L\phi x$ is undefined at w, so by [V*~] and [V*∨], $\phi x \land L\phi x$ is also undefined at w. But otherwise it is true, so it is true where defined for every member of D_w. So $\forall x(\phi x \land L\phi x)$ is true at w, and so (6) is false at w and so not valid. Further (for what it is worth) $\forall x(\phi x \land L\phi x) \supset \forall x\phi x$ also fails, and so the problem cannot be blamed on the presence of free variables. Admitting truth-value gaps does not therefore seem a way of avoiding the problems which arise when you drop the Barcan Formula.

The existence predicate
The reason for defining validity by putting restrictions on μ is to preserve the validity of even the simplest instance of $\forall 1$, such as (2) above. For if everything in every world is ϕ except for some $u \notin D_w$ then $V_\mu(\forall x\phi x \supset \phi y, w)$ will be false if $\mu(y) = u$. The problem with $\forall 1$ is that y might be assigned something which does not exist, while the quantifiers are restricted to things which do. This suggests that we could make the restriction explicit by adding an existence predicate, i.e., a predicate E which has the semantics:

[VE] $\langle u,w \rangle \in V(E)$ iff $u \in D_w$

What [VE] means is that Ex is true in w iff x is assigned a member of D_w. We then redefine validity to require that a valid wff be true in every world even for assignments whose values do not exist in that world. Models for these systems need not satisfy the inclusion requirement but in all other respects we shall keep the semantics set out on p. 275. For later use we note that both PR and PA are valid according to it. $\forall 1$ will then, of course, not be valid since (2) can fail in such a model. With an existence predicate however we may replace (2) by

(7) $(\forall x\phi x \land Ey) \supset \phi y$

or, schematically

∀1E $(\forall x\alpha \land Ey) \supset \alpha[y/x]$

∀1E is the standard replacement for ∀1 in what is called *free* logic (meaning, as we understand it, logic 'free' of existential assumptions) and free logic is often considered the appropriate way to deal with quantified modal logic[2]. However, care is needed in taking free logic as our model. In a non-modal free logic it is tempting to think of the variable y, in those cases when [∀1] fails, as a 'non-denoting' term. This is because in non-modal logic we don't normally have a class of things which don't happen to exist but might have. But in a modal semantics as we have been presenting it so far there are no non-denoting terms. Rather y in ∀1 denotes, but the thing it denotes does not exist in the world in which the sentence is being evaluated.

Axiomatization of systems with an existence predicate

Because we have to replace ∀1 with ∀1E we have to change other aspects of the LPC basis. In particular we cannot easily use ∀2 as it stands. For that reason we shall set out the basis explicitly. Where S is any normal system of propositional modal logic, LPCE + S is defined as follows.

S′   Any LPC substitution-instance of a theorem of S is an axiom of LPCE + S.

∀1E   Where x and y are any individual variables, and α is any wff then $(\forall x\alpha \land Ey) \supset \alpha[y/x]$ is an axiom of LPCE + S.

∀⊃ $\forall x(\alpha \supset \beta) \supset (\forall x\alpha \supset \forall x\beta)$ (where α and β are any wff and x is any variable).

VQ $\alpha \equiv \forall x\alpha$ provided x is not free in α.

UE $\forall xEx$

The transformation rules are MP, N,

UG $\vdash \alpha \rightarrow \vdash \forall x\alpha$

and

UGL∀ⁿ $\vdash \alpha_1 \supset L(\alpha_2 \supset \ldots \supset L(\alpha_n \supset L\beta)\ldots) \rightarrow \vdash \alpha_1 \supset L(\alpha_2 \supset \ldots \supset L(\alpha_n \supset L\forall x\beta)\ldots)$, where x is not free in $\alpha_1, \ldots, \alpha_n$.

293

The first thing to note is that ∀2, UG⊃, and therefore Eq (see p. 242), all follow from UG, VQ and ∀⊃. Given this basis we may prove a quantified form of ∀1 as follows:

∀1′   Where x and y are any individual variables, and α is any wff then
$\vdash \forall y(\forall x\alpha \supset \alpha[y/x])$

PROOF

∀1E × UG	(1)	$\forall y((\forall x\alpha \wedge Ey) \supset \alpha[y/x])$
(1) × PC × Eq	(2)	$\forall y(Ey \supset (\forall x\alpha \supset \alpha[y/x]))$
(2) × ∀⊃	(3)	$\forall yEy \supset \forall y(\forall x\alpha \supset \alpha[y/x])$
UE	(4)	$\forall yEy$
(3)(4) × MP	(5)	$\forall y(\forall x\alpha \supset \alpha[y/x])$ **Q.E.D.**

In the completeness proof which follows we shall need a number of other results which are standard in ordinary LPC and which in fact were appealed to in Chapter 14. Since our present basis does not contain ∀1 we can no longer take any of these results for granted and so we shall prove them explicitly now. Where appropriate we shall give them the same names as in Chapter 13.

RBV   If α and β differ only in that α has free x where and only where β has free y then

$$\vdash \forall x\alpha \equiv \forall y\beta.$$

In the proof of this we note that β is $\alpha[y/x]$ and α is $\beta[x/y]$ and that y is not free in α nor x in β.

PROOF

∀1′	(1)	$\forall y(\forall x\alpha \supset \beta)$
∀⊃	(2)	$\forall y(\forall x\alpha \supset \beta) \supset (\forall y\forall x\alpha \supset \forall y\beta)$
(1)(2) × MP	(3)	$\forall y\forall x\alpha \supset \forall y\beta$
(3) × VQ	(4)	$\forall x\alpha \supset \forall y\beta$ **Q.E.D.**

The proof of $\forall y\beta \supset \forall x\alpha$ is exactly analogous.

QR $\sim\forall y\sim(\alpha[y/x] \supset \forall x\alpha)$

PROOF

PC × UG⊃	(1)	$\forall y(\alpha[y/x] \land \sim\forall x\alpha) \supset \forall y\alpha[y/x]$	
(1) × RBV	(2)	$\forall y(\alpha[y/x] \land \sim\forall x\alpha) \supset \forall x\alpha$	
PC × UG	(3)	$\forall y(\alpha[y/x] \land \sim\forall x\alpha) \supset \forall y\sim\forall x\alpha$	
(3) × VQ	(4)	$\forall y(\alpha[y/x] \land \sim\forall x\alpha) \supset \sim\forall x\alpha$	
(2)(4) × PC × Eq	(5)	$\sim\forall y\sim(\alpha[y/x] \supset \forall x\alpha)$	Q.E.D.

In this proof we rely on the fact that VQ is an equivalence, since the form we are using is in fact $\forall x\alpha \supset \alpha$, where x is not free in α.

VQ⊃ $\quad \forall x(\alpha \supset \beta) \supset (\alpha \supset \forall x\beta)$, where x is not free in α.

PROOF

∀⊃	(1)	$\forall x(\alpha \supset \beta) \supset (\forall x\alpha \supset \beta)$	
(1) × VQ	(2)	$\forall x(\alpha \supset \beta) \supset (\alpha \supset \forall x\beta)$	Q.E.D.

It is not difficult to see that this axiomatization is sound with respect to the given definition of validity. For ∀1E suppose $V_\mu(\forall x\alpha,w) = 1$, $V_\mu(Ey,w) = 1$ but $V_\mu(\alpha[y/x],w) = 0$. Let ρ be the x-alternative of μ such that $\rho(x) = \mu(y)$. By PR, $V_\rho(\alpha,w) = 0$, and since $V_\mu(Ey,w) = 1$ then $\rho(x) \in D_w$. So by [V∀'] $V_\mu(\forall x\alpha,w) = 0$. VQ is stated as an equivalence. This assumes that each D_w is non-empty. $\forall xEx$ may equally be seen to be valid, and the other axioms are completely standard. The only non-standard transformation rule is UGL∀^{n}. Suppose that $V_\mu(\alpha_1 \supset L(\alpha_2 \supset \ldots \supset L(\alpha_n \supset L\forall x\beta)\ldots),w) = 0$. Then there is an R-chain $w_1, \ldots w_{n+1}$ with $w = w_1$ and $V_\mu(\alpha_i,w_i) = 1$ for $1 \leq i \leq n$, and $V_\mu(\forall x\beta,w_{n+1}) = 0$, and so for some x-alternative ρ of μ with $\rho(x) \in D_{w_{n+1}}$, $V_\rho(\beta,w_{n+1}) = 0$. Now x is not free in α and so, by PA, $V_\rho(\alpha_i,w_i) = V_\mu(\alpha_i,w_i) = 1$, and so $V_\rho(\alpha_1 \supset L(\alpha_2 \supset \ldots \supset L(\alpha_n \supset L\beta)\ldots),w) = 0$. Note that the fact that $\rho(x)$ may not be in D_w does not prevent $\alpha_1 \supset L(\alpha_2 \supset \ldots \supset L(\alpha_n \supset L\beta)\ldots)$ from being false in w, and therefore being invalid − since the definition of validity has now been widened to *all* assignments to the variables.

UGL∀^{n} is provable in all extensions of LPCE + B, since these all have the rule DR4 on p. 62 and its dual

DR4' $\quad \vdash \alpha \supset L\beta \;\rightarrow\; \vdash M\alpha \supset \beta$

The derivation of UGL∀^{n} is as follows: Let α_1^* be $M\alpha_1$, and let α_{i+1}^* be $M(\alpha_i^* \land \alpha_{i+1})$. Then if $\vdash \alpha_1 \supset L(\alpha_2 \supset \ldots \supset L(\alpha_n \supset L\beta)\ldots)$, by repeated applications of DR4′ we obtain $\vdash \alpha_n^* \supset \beta$, and so by ∀2 $\vdash \alpha_n^* \supset \forall x\beta$, and so by repeated applications of DR4, $\vdash \alpha_1 \supset L(\alpha_2 \supset$ ... $\supset L(\alpha_n \supset L\forall x\beta)...)$. Without DR4 the situation is less clear. Certainly UGL∀[1] is independent in at least some extensions of LPCE + S, since if we strengthen ∀1E to ∀1 (or equivalently if we add Ex as an axiom) BF follows immediately by UGL∀[1] from $\forall x L\alpha \supset L\alpha$ − but we know from p. 277 that for appropriate choices of S, BF is not a theorem of LPC + S.[3] However, derivable or not, UGL∀[n] is validity-preserving in the current semantics and so must be present in one form or another in LPCE + S.

Completeness for existence predicates

In this section we assume that we are dealing with some arbitrary but fixed system LPCE + S. For completeness[4] we proceed as in Chapter 14 and assume that Λ is a consistent set of wff of a language $\mathscr{L}$ and that $\mathscr{L}$ is an infinitely proper sublanguage of $\mathscr{L}^+$. Where Δ is a set of wff of $\mathscr{L}^+$, say that Δ has the $L\forall$-*property* in $\mathscr{L}^+$ iff,

(i) for every wff α of $\mathscr{L}^+$ and variable x there is some variable y (in $\mathscr{L}^+$) such that $Ey \wedge (\alpha[y/x] \supset \forall x\alpha) \in \Delta$..

(ii) for all wff of $\mathscr{L}^+$, $\beta_1, \ldots, \beta_n$ $(n \geq 0)$ and α, and every variable x not free in $\beta_1, \ldots, \beta_n$ there is some variable z (in $\mathscr{L}^+$) such that $L(\beta_1 \supset \ldots \supset L(\beta_n \supset L(Ez \supset \alpha[z/x]))...) \supset L(\beta_1 \supset \ldots \supset L(\beta_n \supset L\forall x\alpha)...) \in \Delta$.

THEOREM 16.1 If Λ is a consistent set of wff of $\mathscr{L}$ then there is a consistent set Δ of wff of $\mathscr{L}^+$ with the $L\forall$-property, such that $\Lambda \subseteq \Delta$.

Proof: Δ is constructed in a way similar to that used in the proof of theorem 14.1 as the union of a sequence $\Delta_0, \Delta_1, \ldots$ etc.

$$\Delta_0 = \Lambda$$

Let Y and Z be two infinite disjoint sets of variables of $\mathscr{L}^+$ not in $\mathscr{L}$, and assume the variables of Y and Z are enumerated. Assume a double enumeration of wff of $\mathscr{L}^+$, first an enumeration of all wff of $\mathscr{L}^+$ which begin with a universal quantifier, and second an enumeration of the set Θ of all wff of the form $L(\gamma_1 \supset \ldots \supset L(\gamma_h \supset L\forall x\delta)...)$ for h ≥ 0, with

x not free in $\gamma_1, \ldots , \gamma_h$. Where $\forall s\alpha$ is the $n+1$'th wff of $\mathcal{L}^+$ beginning with a universal quantifier and $L(\gamma_1 \supset \ldots \supset L(\gamma_h \supset L\forall x\delta)...)$ is the $n+1$th member of Θ and y is the first variable in Y and z is the first variable in Z not occurring in Δ_n or in α or in $\gamma_1, \ldots , \gamma_h$ or in δ then Δ_{n+1} is

$$\Delta_n \cup \{Ey, \alpha[y/s] \supset \forall s\alpha, L(\gamma_1 \supset \ldots \supset L(\gamma_h \supset L(Ez \supset \delta[z/x])) \supset L(\gamma_1 \supset \ldots \supset L(\gamma_h \supset L\forall x\delta))\}.$$

We show that Δ_{n+1} is consistent if Δ_n is. Suppose Δ_{n+1} were not consistent. Then for some $\beta_1, \ldots , \beta_k \in \Delta_n$

(i) $\vdash (\beta_1 \wedge \ldots \wedge \beta_k \wedge (Ey \wedge (\alpha[y/s] \supset \forall s\alpha)) \supset$
$\quad L(\gamma_1 \supset \ldots \supset L(\gamma_h \supset L(Ez \supset \delta[z/x])...)))$

and

(ii) $\vdash (\beta_1 \wedge \ldots \wedge \beta_k \wedge (Ey \wedge (\alpha[y/s] \supset \forall s\alpha))) \supset$
$\quad {\sim}L(\gamma_1 \supset \ldots \supset L(\gamma_h \supset L\forall x\delta)...)$

Now z does not occur free in Δ_n or in $(Ey \wedge (\alpha[y/s] \supset \forall s\alpha))$, and so from (i) by $UGL\forall^{h+1}$

(iii) $\vdash (\beta_1 \wedge \ldots \wedge \beta_k \wedge (Ey \wedge (\alpha[y/s] \supset \forall s\alpha))) \supset$
$\quad L(\gamma_1 \supset \ldots \supset L(\gamma_h \supset L\forall z(Ez \supset \delta[z/x])))$

and so by $\forall^\supset$, **K**, PC and RBV,

(iv) $\vdash L^h\forall zEz \supset ((\beta_1 \wedge \ldots \wedge \beta_k \wedge (Ey \wedge$
$\quad (\alpha[y/s] \supset \forall s\alpha)) \supset L(\gamma_1 \supset \ldots \supset L(\gamma_h \supset L\forall x\delta)))$

So by UE and N,

(v) $\vdash \quad (\beta_1 \wedge \ldots \wedge \beta_k \wedge (Ey \wedge (\alpha[y/s] \supset \forall s\alpha))) \supset L(\gamma_1 \supset \ldots$
$\quad \supset L(\gamma_h \supset L\forall x\delta))$

But (ii) and (v) give

$\vdash (\beta_1 \wedge \ldots \wedge \beta_k) \supset (Ey \supset {\sim}(\alpha[y/s] \supset \forall s\alpha))$

so by $\forall 2$

$\vdash (\beta_1 \wedge \dots \wedge \beta_k) \supset \forall y(Ey \supset {\sim}(\alpha[y/s] \supset \forall s\alpha))$

so by $\forall^\supset$

$\vdash (\beta_1 \wedge \dots \wedge \beta_k) \supset (\forall yEy \supset \forall y {\sim}(\alpha[y/s] \supset \forall s\alpha))$

and so by UE

$\vdash (\beta_1 \wedge \dots \wedge \beta_k) \supset \forall y {\sim}(\alpha[y/s] \supset \forall s\alpha)$

But y does not occur in α, and so, by QR,

$\vdash \exists y(\alpha[y/s] \supset \forall s\alpha)$

and so

$\vdash {\sim}(\beta_1 \wedge \dots \wedge \beta_k)$

contradicting the assumed consistency of Δ_n. Since each Δ_n is consistent so is Δ. And by construction Δ has the $L\forall$-property.

THEOREM 16.2   If Γ is a maximal-consistent set of wff in some language (say $\mathscr{L}^+$) of modal predicate logic, and Γ has the $L\forall$-property, and α is a wff such that $L\alpha \notin \Gamma$, then there is a consistent set Δ of wff of $\mathscr{L}^+$ with the $L\forall$-property such that $L^-(\Gamma) \cup \{{\sim}\alpha\} \subseteq \Delta$.

Proof: The proof is similar to (though a little more complicated than) that of theorem 14.2 on p. 259. Assume, as in the proof of theorem 16.1 that Θ is the set of all wff of the form $L(\theta_1 \supset \dots \supset L(\theta_h \supset L\forall x\zeta))\dots)$, where x is not free in $\theta_1, \dots, \theta_h$. We define a sequence of wff $\gamma_1, \gamma_2, \dots$ etc. as follows: γ_0 is ${\sim}\alpha$. Given γ_n we define γ_{n+1} in the following way: We first define a wff γ_n^+, and then show how to extend γ_n^+ to γ_{n+1}. Let $\forall x\delta$ be the $n+1$th wff of that form and let y be the first variable such that

(*) $L^-(\Gamma) \cup \{\gamma_n \wedge (Ey \wedge (\delta[y/x] \supset \forall x\delta))\}$ is consistent.

Let γ_n^+ be $\gamma_n \wedge Ey \wedge (\delta[y/x] \supset \forall x\delta)$. In order for this construction to succeed we have to be sure that there always will be a y satisfying (*). Since γ_0 is $\sim\alpha$, $L^-(\Gamma) \cup \{\gamma_0\}$ is consistent from lemma 6.4 on p. 117. We show that provided $L^-(\Gamma) \cup \{\gamma_n\}$ is consistent there will always be a y which satisfies (*) and thus guarantees that $L^-(\Gamma) \cup \{\gamma_n^+\}$ is consistent.

As in theorem 14.2, we cannot here assume that y is a new variable. Nevertheless we can show that there always will be an appropriate y. Suppose there were not. Then for every variable y of $\mathcal{L}^+$ there will exist some $\{L\beta_1, \ldots, L\beta_k\} \subseteq \Gamma$ such that

$$\vdash (\beta_1 \wedge \ldots \wedge \beta_k) \supset (\gamma_n \supset (Ey \supset \sim(\delta[y/x] \supset \forall x\delta)))$$

so, by DR1 and L-distribution,

(i) $\vdash (L\beta_1 \wedge \ldots \wedge L\beta_n) \supset L(\gamma_n \supset (Ey \supset \sim(\delta[y/x] \supset \forall x\delta)))$

But Γ is maximal consistent and $L\beta_1, \ldots, L\beta_n \in \Gamma$, and so $L(\gamma_n \supset \sim(\delta[y/x] \supset \forall x\delta)) \in \Gamma$. And this is so for *every* variable y.

Now Γ has the $L\forall$-property, and so there will be a variable y such that

(ii) $L(\gamma_n \supset ((Ey \supset \sim(\delta[y/x] \supset \forall x\delta))) \supset$
$\qquad L\forall z(\gamma_n \supset (Ey \supset \sim(\delta[z/x] \supset \forall x\delta)))$

is in Γ, where z is chosen so that it does not occur in γ_n or in δ. And so, since $L(\gamma_n \supset \sim(\delta[y/x] \supset \forall x\delta))$ is in Γ for every y,

(iii) $L\forall z(\gamma_n \supset (Ez \supset \sim(\delta[z/x] \supset \forall x\delta)))$

is in Γ. But Γ is maximal in LPCE + S and so,

(iv) $L\forall z Ez \supset L\forall z(\gamma_n \supset \sim(\delta[z/x] \supset \forall x\delta))$

is in Γ. And so by UE, and N we have in Γ,

(v) $L\forall z(\gamma_n \supset \sim(\delta[z/x] \supset \forall x\delta))$

But z does not occur in γ_n or δ and so by $VQ^\supset$ we have in Γ

(vi) $L(\gamma_n \supset \forall z \sim(\delta[z/x] \supset \forall x\delta))$

But by QR

$$\vdash \quad \exists z(\delta[z/x] \supset \forall x\delta)$$

and so

(vii) $\vdash L \sim \gamma_n$

But then $L \sim \gamma_n \in \Gamma$ and so $\sim\gamma_n \in L^-(\Gamma)$ which would make $L^-(\Gamma) \cup \{\gamma_n\}$ inconsistent. So $L^-(\Gamma) \cup \{\gamma_n^+\}$ is consistent if $L^-(\Gamma) \cup \{\gamma_n\}$ is.

We now show how to extend γ_n^+ to γ_{n+1}. Let $L(\theta_1 \supset ... \supset L(\theta_h \supset L\forall x\varsigma)...)$ be the nth wff in Θ and let z be the first variable such that

(†) $\quad L^-(\Gamma) \cup \{\gamma_n^+ \wedge (L(\theta_1 \supset ... \supset L(\theta_h \supset L(Ez \supset \varsigma[z/x]))...) \supset L(\theta_1 \supset ... \supset L(\theta_h \supset L\forall x\varsigma)...))\}$

is consistent. Let γ_{n+1} be

$$\gamma_n^+ \wedge (L(\theta_1 \supset ... \supset L(\theta_h \supset L(Ez \supset \varsigma[z/x]))...) \supset L(\theta_1 \supset ... \supset L(\theta_h \supset L\forall x\varsigma)...)).$$

We may assume that x is not free in γ_n^+ or in $\theta_1, ... , \theta_h$ since if it is we may choose a bound alphabetic variant of $\forall x\varsigma$ in which the variable that replaces x is not free in these wff. Suppose there were no z satisfying (†). Then for some $\beta_1, ... , \beta_k \in L^-(\Gamma)$

(i) $\quad \vdash \quad (\beta_1 \wedge ... \wedge \beta_k) \supset (\gamma_n^+ \supset \sim(L(\theta_1 \supset ... \supset L(\theta_h \supset (Ez \supset \varsigma[z/x]))...) \supset L(\theta_1 \supset ... \supset L(\theta_h \supset \forall x\varsigma)...)))$

So

(ii) $\quad \vdash \quad (\beta_1 \wedge ... \wedge \beta_k) \supset (\gamma_n^+ \supset L(\theta_1 \supset ... \supset L(\theta_h \supset L(Ez \supset \varsigma[z/x]))...))$

and

(iii) $\quad \vdash \quad (\beta_1 \wedge ... \wedge \beta_k) \supset (\gamma_n^+ \supset \sim L(\theta_1 \supset ... \supset L(\theta_h \supset \forall x\varsigma)...))$

From (ii) we have, by DR1 and L-distrib,

(iv) $\vdash$ $(L\beta_1 \wedge \ldots \wedge L\beta_k) \supset L(\gamma_n^+ \supset L(\theta_1 \supset \ldots \supset L(\theta_h \supset L(Ez \supset \S[z/x]))\ldots))$

Now $L\beta_1, \ldots, L\beta_k$ are all in Γ and so from (iv)

(v) $L(\gamma_n^+ \supset L(\theta_1 \supset \ldots \supset L(\theta_h \supset L(Ez \supset \S[z/x]))\ldots))$

is in Γ for every variable z. So, since Γ has the $L\forall$-property,

(vi) $L(\gamma_n^+ \supset L(\theta_1 \supset \ldots \supset L(\theta_h \supset L\forall x\S)\ldots))$

is also in Γ, and so

(vii) $\gamma_n^+ \supset L(\theta_1 \supset \ldots \supset L(\theta_h \supset L\forall x\S)\ldots)$

is in $L^-(\Gamma)$, which, together with (iii) would make $L^-(\Gamma) \cup \{\gamma_n^+\}$ inconsistent. So $L^-(\Gamma) \cup \{\gamma_{n+1}\}$ is consistent if $L^-(\Gamma) \cup \{\gamma_n^+\}$ is. Since $L^-(\Gamma) \cup \{\gamma_n^+\}$ is consistent if $L^-(\Gamma) \cup \{\gamma_n\}$ is then $L^-(\Gamma) \cup \{\gamma_{n+1}\}$ is consistent if $L^-(\Gamma) \cup \{\gamma_n\}$ is. So $L^-(\Gamma) \cup \{\gamma_n\}$ is consistent for every n.

Let Δ be the union of $L^-(\Gamma)$ and all the γ_ns. Since each $L^-(\Gamma) \cup \gamma_n$ is consistent, and since $\vdash \gamma_m \supset \gamma_n$ for $m \geq n$, so is their union Δ. By construction Δ has the $L\forall$-property and so theorem 16.2 is proved.

The canonical model is defined as in Chapter 14 on p. 261 except that we require that $x \in D_w$ iff $Ex \in w$.

THEOREM 16.3 For any $w \in W$ and any $\alpha \in \mathscr{L}^+$, $V_\sigma(\alpha,w) = 1$ iff $\alpha \in w$.

The proof then proceeds as in the case of theorem 14.3 on p. 261 except for the inductive step for $\forall$. If $\forall x\alpha \notin w$, then by the $\forall$-property there is some y such that $Ey \in w$ (making $y \in D_w$) and $\alpha[y/x] \notin w$. Thus $V_\sigma(\alpha[y/x],w) = 0$, and so when ν is the x-alternative of σ with $\nu(x) = \sigma(y)$, $V_\nu(\alpha,w) = 0$, and so, since $\sigma(y) \in D_w$, $V_\sigma(\forall x\alpha,w) = 0$.

Suppose $\forall x\alpha \in w$ and let ν be any x-alternative of σ such that $\nu(x) = y$ for some $y \in D_w$. Since $y \in D_w$, then $Ey \in w$. So by [$\forall$1E], $\alpha[y/x] \in w$, and so $V_\sigma(\alpha[y/x],w) = 1$, and so $V_\nu(\alpha,w) = 1$. So $V_\sigma(\forall x\alpha,w) = 1$.

From theorem 16.3 it follows that the canonical model of LPCE + S validates all and only theorems of LPCE + S. Completeness with respect to all frames for S follows as in previous chapters for all systems in which the frame of the canonical model is a frame for S. That includes all the systems mentioned on p. 249.

Incompleteness

Since LPC + S contains LPCE + S, to establish that an incompleteness result for the former applies to the latter it is sufficient to show that the frames which validate non-theorems of LPCE + S still validate those same wff when the inclusion requirement is dropped. The result for LPCE + S4M holds for the same reasons as given in the case of LPC + S4M on p. 283. Theorem 15.4 on p. 285 still holds for systems which do not satisfy the inclusion requirement, and so the incompleteness results on pp. 283−287 hold also for such systems.

Expanding languages

In Chapter 15 we were able to prove completeness for a wide range of systems of modal predicate logic without the Barcan Formula. But the technique was restricted to systems which admitted frames without any looping back. It is a feature of the canonical models defined on pp. 280−282 that when wRw', $\mathcal{L}_w$ is contained in $\mathcal{L}_{w'}$. In the models of Chapter 15 D_w is simply the class of variables in $\mathcal{L}_{w'}$ and so these models satisfy the inclusion requirement. But when we introduce an existence predicate there arises the possibility that the set of y such that $Ey \in w$ does not include all the variables of $\mathcal{L}_w$. This means that the technique used in Chapter 15 can be applied, without the need for UGL∀, to systems whose models do not satisfy the inclusion requirement.

Theorem 16.1 can be adapted in the following way. Say that Δ has the *E∀-property* iff for every wff $\forall x\alpha$ there is some variable y such that $Ey \wedge (\alpha[y/x] \supset \forall x\alpha) \in \Delta$. Clearly the *L∀*-property entails the *E∀*-property, and so theorem 16.1 guarantees that where a language $\mathcal{L}'$ extends $\mathcal{L}$ by infinitely many new variables then any consistent Λ in $\mathcal{L}$ can be extended to a set Δ of $\mathcal{L}'$ with the *E∀*-property. So if we are permitted to extend the language infinitely in passing from w to an accessible w', then if $L^-(w) \cup \{\sim\alpha\}$ is consistent in $\mathcal{L}_w$ it has a maximal consistent extension w' in $\mathcal{L}_{w'}$. However, though the models do not satisfy the inclusion requirement the languages on which they are based do, in that where wRw', $\mathcal{L}_{w'}$ is an extension of $\mathcal{L}_w$. Since some of these extensions are proper these models cannot be based on symmetrical frames.

Possibilist quantification revisited

As we said on p. 274, the philosophical plausibility of the Barcan Formula has been questioned. One way of construing it makes it look as though the validity of the BF reflects the view that the same things exist in all possible worlds. This looks like the view that everything is a necessary existent, and that makes the Barcan Formula look not only like a special case of a more general semantics, but in fact like an implausible special case. We have already mentioned (in note 1 on p. 287) that one of the earliest philosophers to get worried about BF was Arthur Prior in *Time and Modality*.[5] Prior was concerned with a temporal interpretation of the necessity operator. He read $L\alpha$ as 'it is and always will be that α' and he read BF as saying that if everything will always be ϕ then always everything will be ϕ. And he thought this was false because even if everything *now existing* will always be ϕ it does not follow that it will always be that everything *then* existing is ϕ.

But you don't have to interpret BF that way. You can interpret ∀ as ranging over all past, present or future individuals, and if every one of *them* will always be ϕ then it will always be that everything is ϕ. Similarly in the modal case. Even if each world w has its own domain D_w of the things which exist in w there is no reason why all these D_ws can't be collected into one single domain D. That at least is one way of defending BF. And if we have an existence predicate it is now easy to define a quantifier satisfying [∀∀'] on p. 275 in terms of a quantifier satisfying [∀∀]. To avoid confusion we shall temporarily (i.e. in this section) use ∀ for the 'possibilist' quantifier, that is the quantifier satisfying [∀∀] on p. 239 and ranging over the whole of D and will follow Prior's use of Łukasiewicz's symbol Π for the 'actualist' quantifier, that is the quantifier satisfying [∀∀'] and ranging over the domain of the world in question. It is then trivial to note that $\Pi x\phi x$ can be expressed as

[Def Π] $\forall x(Ex \supset \phi x)$

This means that systems without BF but which have an existence predicate emerge as subsystems of systems with BF. We can now see why ∀1 is not valid for actualist quantifiers. Consider again

(1) $\Pi x\phi x \supset \phi y$

When translated this becomes

(2) $\forall x(Ex \supset \phi x) \supset \phi y$

and if we consider an interpretation in which every member of D_w satisfies ϕ, but y is assigned something which is not in D_w and does not satisfy ϕ then (2) will be false, even in systems which contain BF for $\forall$. Of course (2) can be turned into a truth by replacing it with

Π1E $(\Pi x \phi x \wedge Ey) \supset \phi y$

or schematically

Π1E' $(\Pi x \alpha \wedge Ey) \supset \alpha[y/x]$

because, when unpacked by defining Π in terms of $\forall$ we get

(3) $(\forall x(Ex \supset \alpha) \wedge Ey) \supset \alpha[y/x]$

which is indeed a truth of S + BF. So in a way we have come full circle, since if you begin with a system containing the Barcan Formula, and you are prepared to admit an existence predicate, then you can after all have all the advantages of the simplest version of the semantics and completeness proofs for modal LPC as set out in Chapters 13 and 14, and still use quantifiers which are restricted to things which actually exist.

Kripke-style systems

In 1963 Saul Kripke[6] advocated a different way of axiomatizing systems whose semantics did not incorporate the inclusion requirement. Kripke's systems did not contain an existence predicate, so he could not respond to the problems caused by the axiom schema $\forall 1$ in the way we have done so far. Kripke's way of dealing with this situation can be expressed as follows. Although (2) on p. 290 is invalid when $\forall$ is an actualist quantifier, its universal closure, $\forall y(\forall x \phi x \supset \phi y)$ is valid. This suggests weakening $\forall 1$ along the lines of $\forall 1'$ on p. 294, though for a reason to be explained $\forall 1'$ itself will not quite do. Because these systems were first studied by Kripke we shall refer to them as 'Kripke-style' systems, and shall denote the version of LPC by LPCK, even though our axiomatization will not be exactly the same as Kripke's.[7] Where S is any normal system of propositional modal logic LPCK + S is defined as follows: S', $\forall^{\supset}$, VQ, N and MP are as on p. 293, but $\forall 1E$ is replaced by

∀1K Where x, y and z are any individual variables, and α is any wff then
$\forall y\forall z(\forall x\alpha \supset \alpha[y/x])$ is an axiom of LPCK + S.

(UGL∀ is not part of this basis, though it is in fact validity-preserving. UG, RBV, QR and VQ⊃ may be proved as on pp. 294–295.)

The semantics is as for systems with an existence predicate except that V(E) is no longer required. ∀1K may be easily seen to be valid, for suppose that for some $w \in W$, and some assignment μ,

$$V_\mu(\forall y\forall z(\forall x\alpha \supset \alpha[y/x]),w) = 0$$

Then for some y-z-alternative ρ of μ (i.e. an assignment like μ except possibly at y or z) where $\rho(y)$ and $\rho(z)$ are both in D_w,

    (1) $V_\rho(\forall x\alpha,w) = 1$ and

    (2) $V_\rho(\alpha[y/x],w) = 0$

Let ν be the x-alternative of ρ in which $\nu(x) = \rho(y)$. By PR and (2), $V_\nu(\alpha,w) = 0$, and because $\rho(y) \in D_w$ so is $\nu(x)$ and so $V_\rho(\forall x\alpha,yw) = 0$, contradicting (1).

The presence of ∀z in ∀1K may seem a little curious, but in fact it is necessary to prove a result we shall need, viz. PV ∀x∀$y\alpha \supset$ ∀y∀$x\alpha$. PV is a principle for permuting universal quantifiers.[8] ∀1′ follows from ∀1K by choosing z not free in ∀$x\alpha \supset \alpha[y/x]$. Note that ∃1K may be derived from ∀1E as ∀1′ was. We prove PV as follows

∀1K	(1)	∀y∀x(∀$y\alpha \supset \alpha$)
∀⊃	(2)	∀x(∀$y\alpha \supset \alpha$) ⊃(∀x∀$y\alpha \supset$ ∀$x\alpha$)
(2) × UG⊃	(3)	∀y∀x(∀$y\alpha \supset \alpha$) ⊃ ∀y(∀x∀$y\alpha \supset$ ∀$x\alpha$)
(1)(3) × MP	(4)	∀y(∀x∀$y\alpha \supset$ ∀$x\alpha$)
(4) × ∀⊃	(5)	∀y∀x∀$y\alpha \supset$ ∀y∀$x\alpha$
VQ	(6)	∀x∀$y\alpha \supset$ ∀y∀x∀$y\alpha$
(5)(6) × PC	(7)	∀x∀$y\alpha \supset$ ∀y∀$x\alpha$ **Q.E.D.**

We shall need the following generalization of PV:

PV′ ∀z_1...∀z_h∀y_1...∀$y_k\alpha \supset$ ∀y_1...∀y_k∀z_1...∀$z_h\alpha$

This may be proved by multiple applications of PV and UG$^\supset$. We shall also need the following generalization of ∀1K:

$$\forall 1^\wedge \quad \forall y_1 \ldots \forall y_k((\forall x_1\alpha_1 \supset \alpha_1[y_1/x_1]) \wedge \ldots \wedge (\forall x_k\alpha_k \supset \alpha_k[y_k/x_k]))$$

and the following generalization of QR:

$$\mathbf{QR}^\wedge \quad \exists y_1 \ldots \exists y_h((\alpha_1[y_1/x_1] \supset \forall x_1\alpha_1) \wedge \ldots \wedge (\alpha_h[y_h/x_h] \supset \forall x_h\alpha_h))$$

provided y_i is not free in α_j for $1 \leq j \leq i \leq h$. The proofs of $\forall 1^\wedge$ and $QR^\wedge$ are left as an exercise. They both require PV'.

Completeness of Kripke-style systems

We turn now to the problem of defining canonical models for the Kripke-style systems. In fact we shall restrict ourselves to producing models by the method of Chapter 15. It is convenient at this point to introduce an extension to the ∀-property which we shall call the extended ∀-property. Where Λ is a set of wff of a language $\mathcal{L}$ and Y is a set of variables of $\mathcal{L}$ we say that Λ has the *extended ∀-property in $\mathcal{L}$ with respect to* Y iff

(i) Λ has the ∀-property with respect to Y, i.e. for every wff α and variable x of $\mathcal{L}$, there is a variable $y \in$ Y such that, $\alpha[y/x] \supset \forall x\alpha \in \Lambda$, and

(ii)   for every wff α and variable y of Y, $\forall x\alpha \supset \alpha[y/x] \in \Lambda$.

For systems with the unquantified ∀1, maximal consistency automatically guarantees (ii), but for Kripke-style systems we don't have this axiom. We take each world w in the canonical model to be a maximal consistent set of wff of $\mathcal{L}_w$ with the extended ∀-property in $\mathcal{L}_w$ with respect to an infinitely proper subset Y of the variables of $\mathcal{L}_w$. We can then let D_w be Y, and we take wRw' iff $L^-(w) \subseteq w'$.

The principal theorem required is an analogue of theorem 14.1 on p. 258. Suppose that Λ is a consistent set of wff in a language $\mathcal{L}$ and suppose that $\mathcal{L}$ is an infinitely proper sublanguage of a language $\mathcal{L}'$. Then

THEOREM 16.4   There is an infinitely proper subset Y of the variables of $\mathcal{L}'$ and a consistent set of wff of $\mathcal{L}'$ such that $\Lambda \subseteq \Gamma$ and Γ has the extended ∀-property in $\mathcal{L}'$ with respect to

Y.

Proof: Choose Y to be an infinitely proper subset of the variables of $\mathscr{L}'$ containing infinitely many variables not in $\mathscr{L}$. Let Θ be the set of all wff of the form $\forall x\beta \supset \beta[y/x]$ where β is a wff of $\mathscr{L}'$ and $y \in$ Y. Now form a sequence $\gamma_1{}^*, \gamma_2{}^*,$ ...etc. as follows. Assume that the wff of $\mathscr{L}'$ of the form $\forall s\gamma$ have been enumerated. Where $\forall s_1\gamma_1$ is the first of these take z_1 to be the first variable in Y not in $\forall s_1\gamma_1$ and let $\gamma_1{}^*$ be $\gamma_1[z_1/s_1] \supset \forall s_1\gamma_1$. Given $\gamma_i{}^*$ let $\gamma_{i+1}{}^*$ be $(\gamma_i{}^* \wedge (\gamma_{i+1}[z_{i+1}/s_{i+1}] \supset \forall s_{i+1}\gamma_{i+1}))$, where z_{i+1} is the first variable in Y not in $\gamma_i{}^*$ or in γ_{i+1}.

Let Δ be the union of all the $\gamma_i{}^*$s. It is clear that any extension of $\Lambda \cup \Theta \cup \Delta$ in $\mathscr{L}'$ will have the extended $\forall$-property in $\mathscr{L}'$ with respect to Y, so all that is required is to show that $\Lambda \cup \Theta \cup \Delta$ is consistent. Let us first note two things about Δ:

(a)   Any finite subset of Δ will appear as the conjuncts of some $\gamma_h{}^*$.

(b)   For each h, each conjunct of $\gamma_h{}^*$ will have the form $\gamma_i[z_i/s_i] \supset \forall s_i\gamma_i$, where z_i does not appear in any wff in Λ or in any γ_j for $j \leq i$.

Now suppose that $\Lambda \cup \Theta \cup \Delta$ is not consistent. Then there must be wff $\alpha_1, ... ,\alpha_n, \beta_1, ... ,\beta_k, \gamma_h{}^*$ such that

(1) $\alpha_1, ... ,\alpha_n \in \Lambda$

(2) $\forall x_i\beta_i \supset \beta_i[y_i/x_i] \in \Theta$, for $1 \leq i \leq k$, where each $y_i \in$ Y.

(3) $\gamma_h{}^* \in \Delta$ and

(4) $\vdash \sim(\alpha_1 \wedge ... \wedge \alpha_n \wedge ((\forall x_1\beta_1 \supset \beta_1[y_1/x_1]) \wedge ... \wedge (\forall x_k\beta_k \supset \beta_k[y_k/x_k])) \wedge \gamma_h{}^*)$

It may happen for some $1 \leq i \leq k$, and for some $1 \leq j \leq h$, that y_i is z_j, but since the α_is are all in Λ they do not contain any of the y_is or any of the z_js. Let α denote $\alpha_1 \wedge ... \wedge \alpha_n$, and let β denote $((\forall x_1\beta_1 \supset \beta_1[y_1/x_1]) \wedge ... \wedge (\forall x_k\beta_k \supset \beta_k[y_k/x_k]))$. Then (4) yields

(5) $\vdash \beta \supset (\alpha \supset \sim\gamma_h{}^*)$

So by UG,

(6) $\vdash \forall y_1...\forall y_k(\beta \supset (\alpha \supset \sim\gamma_h*))$

So, by multiple applications of UG$^\supset$,

(7) $\vdash \forall y_1...\forall y_k\beta \supset \forall y_1...\forall y_k(\alpha \supset \sim\gamma_h*)$

So, by $\forall1^\wedge$ and MP,

(8) $\vdash \forall y_1...\forall y_k(\alpha \supset \sim\gamma_h*)$

From (8) by UG,

(9) $\vdash \forall z_1...\forall z_h\forall y_1...\forall y_k(\alpha \supset \sim\gamma_h*)$

and so, by PV$'$

(10) $\forall y_1...\forall y_k\forall z_1...\forall z_h(\alpha \supset \sim\gamma_h*)$

But $z_1, ... ,z_h$ are not free in α and so, by VQ$^\supset$,

(11) $\vdash \forall y_1...\forall y_k(\alpha \supset \forall z_1...\forall z_h\sim\gamma_h*)$

But z_i does not occur in γ_j for $j \le i$ and so by QR$^\wedge$,

(12) $\vdash \sim\forall z_1...\forall z_h\sim\gamma_h*$

So, from (11),

(13) $\vdash \forall y_1...\forall y_k\sim\alpha$

But $y_1, ... ,y_k$ are not free in α, and so by VQ

(14) $\vdash \sim\alpha$

which of course contradicts the supposition that Λ is consistent.

By theorem 6.3 on p. 115, any $\Lambda \cup \Theta \cup \Delta$ as defined in the present theorem can be extended to set Γ of wff which is maximal consistent in $\mathscr{L}'$ and has the extended $\forall$-property with respect to Y. We are now in a position to define canonical models for Kripke-style systems. We assume that each $\mathscr{L}_w$ is an infinitely proper sublanguage of $\mathscr{L}^+$ and that D_w is an

308

infinitely proper subset of the set of all variables of $\mathscr{L}_w$.

Then any $w \in W$ will be a set of wff maximal consistent in $\mathscr{L}_w$ and having the extended $\forall$-property with respect to D_w. Let wRw' iff $L^-(w) \subseteq w'$. Given some $\sim L\alpha \in w$ we know from lemma 6.4 on p. 117 that $L^-(w) \cup \{\sim\alpha\}$ is a consistent set of wff of $\mathscr{L}_w$. So if $\mathscr{L}_w$ is the $\mathscr{L}$ of theorem 16.1, and $L^-(w) \cup \{\sim\alpha\}$ is Λ, we know that Λ is consistent. Where $\mathscr{L}_{w'}$ extends $\mathscr{L}_w$ by the addition of infinitely many new variables, and where $D_{w'}$ is the Y of theorem 16.1, we know from that theorem that there is a maximal consistent extension of w' in $\mathscr{L}_{w'}$ of $L^-(w) \cup \{\sim\alpha\}$ which has the extended $\forall$-property in $\mathscr{L}_{w'}$ with respect to $D_{w'}$. So wRw' and $w' \in W$. V is defined as on p. 281 and the theorem to be proved is, for every $w \in W$ and every $\alpha \in \mathscr{L}_w$,

THEOREM 16.5 $V_o(\alpha,w)$ iff $\alpha \in w$.

Note that the proof is for all wff in $\mathscr{L}_w$ and follows exactly the proof of theorem 15.3 on p. 281 except for the induction step for $\forall$. Where $\forall x\alpha \in w$, in order to show that $V_o(\forall x\alpha,w) = 1$ we need merely verify that $V_\nu(\alpha,\mathrm{w}) = 1$ for every x-alternative ν of σ such that $\nu \in D_w$. This means that we need only consider $y \in D_w$, and since w has the extended $\forall$-property with respect to D_w then $\forall x\alpha \supset \alpha[y/x] \in w$ and so since $\forall x\alpha \in w$ then $\alpha[y/x] \in w$.

Completeness follows as in Chapter 15 for all those cases in which the frame of the canonical model for LPCK + S is a frame for S. Although these models do not satisfy the inclusion requirement they cannot be based on symmetrical frames for the same reasons as given on p. 282. Thus we do not have completeness results for Kripke-style systems containing B. The methods used on pp. 296−301 do not obviously apply, since there seems no way to express Ey by a finite wff. Where Ey is true we need $\forall x\alpha \supset \alpha[y/x]$ for every wff α, but that involves an infinite number of wff. As far as we are aware no completeness proofs for these systems have been published.[9]

Exercises — 16

16.1 Using $[V^*\phi]-[V^*\forall]$ on pp. 278−278, prove that if R is reflexive then if $V_\mu(\alpha,w)$ is defined and x is free in α, $\mu(x) \in D_w$.

16.2 Where S is a logic which has as one of its frames the frame $w_1 \to w_2 \to w_3$, prove that the following instance of BFC is not valid using the 'undefined' semantics: $L\forall xL\phi x \supset \forall xLL\phi x$.

16.3 Using the semantics discussed on p. 291 in which $V_\mu{}^*(\forall x\alpha,w) = 1$ provided $V_\rho(\alpha,w) = 1$ for every x-alternative of μ for which $V_\rho{}^*(\alpha,w)$ is defined, show that MP is not validity-preserving.

*16.4 Where S is K + $ML(p \wedge \sim p) \vee (q \supset LMq)$, prove the completeness of LPCE + S, without appealing to UGL$\forall$.

16.5 Show that the axiom system complete for K with possibilist quantifier and an existence predicate is K + BF if empty domains are allowed and K + BF + $\exists xEx$ if they are not.

16.6 Prove $\forall 1^\wedge$ and VQ$^\wedge$.

16.7 Where $C(\alpha)$ is α preceded by Ls and $\forall s$ for all its variables in any order and LPCK* + S has as axioms $C(\alpha)$ for every axiom α of LPCK + S, and as transformation rules UG and MP, prove that $\vdash_{\text{LPCK}+S} \alpha$ iff $\vdash_{\text{LPCK}*+S} C(\alpha)$.

*16.8 Prove the completeness of LPCK + B or LPCK + S5.

Notes

[1] For systems containing T the proof generalizes to the schematic case $L\forall x\alpha \supset \forall xL\alpha$, because of the fact that when R is reflexive if $V_\mu{}^*(\alpha,w)$ is defined then $\mu(x) \in D_w$. (Correspondence with Giovanna Corsi helped us get clear about the connection between undefined wff and BFC.)

[2] See Garson 1984, p.261. Garson's article provides a helpful overview of a number of approaches to modal predicate logic. An existence predicate is introduced in Rescher 1959, and also assumed in Fine 1978.

[3] Parsons 1975 states that this rule is not needed in proofs from closed wff. The rule comes from R.H. Thomason 1970a.

[4] The proof given here is adapted from R.H. Thomason 1970a in the same way as our proof of completeness for systems with BF was in Chapter 14. Thomason's existence predicate is defined on p.57 in terms of identity. The rules we call UGL$\forall^n$ first appear in Thomason's paper.

[5] Prior 1957, pp.26−28.

[6] Kripke 1963b.

[7] In Kripke 1963b, p.89, Kripke's own system (presented for T) is defined in terms of the closure of a wff α, meaning by that α preceded by any number of Ls and $\forall s$ in any order for all of αs free variables. If we replace all the axioms

of LPCK + S by their closures and use MP and UG as the only transformation rules then an induction on the proofs of theorems establishes that $\vdash_{\text{LPCK}+\text{S}} \alpha$ iff the closure of α is provable in the resulting axiomatization.

[8] The need for some such device is shown in Fine 1983, who points out that Kripke's basis needs amending. The problem is really one of non-modal LPC, and Fine gives an interesting history of it.

[9] Certainly none is mentioned in Garson 1984. Fine 1978, p.135, claims that the method he uses in that article for systems with an existence predicate will work for systems without one, but adds: "The construction of the canonical model is complicated rather, since it is necessary to keep an external check on which constants belong to which worlds."

17

IDENTITY AND DESCRIPTIONS

Identity in LPC

Ordinary, non-modal, LPC may be augmented by the addition of a dyadic predicate to represent identity. This predicate may be referred to as $\phi_=$, though instead of $\phi_=xy$ it is customary to write $x = y$ and to write $x \neq y$ for $\sim\phi_=xy$. (Identity is frequently referred to as Equality, especially for systems of LPC whose intended interpretation is a mathematical one. Our frequent use of $=$ as a metalogical symbol, as when we write $V_\mu(\alpha,w) = 1$ to mean that the value assigned to α by V with respect to μ is 1, should not lead to any confusion.) In order to see how to interpret $\phi_=$ consider a model $\langle D,V \rangle$ for LPC. This will be a model for identity provided that $V(\phi_=)$ consists of all and only pairs of the form $\langle u,u \rangle$ for $u \in D$. I.e. the interpretation of $\phi_=$ is the set of pairs with the same terms. A consequence of this is that for any assignment μ to the variables, and any $w \in W$,

$$V_\mu(x = y) = 1 \text{ iff } \mu(x) = \mu(y)$$

With this interpretation a complete axiomatic basis for LPC with identity may be provided by adding the axiom

I1 $x = x$

and the axiom schema

I2 $x = y \supset (\alpha \supset \beta)$

where α and β differ only in that α has free x in 0 or more places where β has free y.

I2 has to be stated as a schema, but I1 could be single formula since by UG we have $\forall x\ x = x$ and so by $\forall 1$, $y = y$, for every variable y. It is not difficult to see that both I1 and I2 are valid with this semantics. An easy consequence of I1 and I2 is

I3 $x = y \supset y = x.$

We can of course add identity to modal LPC. We shall, for simplicity, consider systems which satisfy BF. The extention of $V(\phi_=)$ to the modal case is simple. $V(\phi_=)$ is the set of triples $\langle u,u,w \rangle$ for $u \in D$, and $w \in W$. With this semantics I1 and I2 remain valid. We shall refer to S + BF with the addition of I1 and I2, as S + I. In these systems the wff α and β in I2 will now of course include wff containing modal operators.

There is however a consequence which turns out to be a matter of some controversy. That is that all identity statements are necessary. We prove this as follows:

LI $x = y \supset L\, x = y$

PROOF

I2	(1)	$x = y \supset (L\, x = x \supset L\, x = y)$
(1) × PC	(2)	$L\, x = x \supset (x = y \supset L\, x = y)$
I1 × N	(3)	$L\, x = x$
(2)(3) × MP	(4)	$x = y \supset L\, x = y$ **Q.E.D.**

(In this proof (1) is obtained by taking α as $L\, x = x$ and replacing the (free) second occurrence of x by free y.)

What LI means is that whenever x and y are the same object it is a necessary truth that they are, or that every true statement of identity is necessarily true, or that there are no true contingent statements of identity. Now it seems easy to think of counter-examples to this. E.g., the sentence:

(1) The person who lives next door is the mayor

seems to assert an identity between the person who lives next door and the mayor; and if so we could rewrite (1), semi-formally, as:

313

The person who lives next door = the mayor.

Yet surely, it may be said, this is contingent, for it is logically possible that the person who lives next door might not have been the mayor. Or, to use a classic example,[1] although the morning star is in fact the same body as the evening star, this is a contingent truth of astronomy and not a necessary truth of logic. So if we are to regard LI as valid we shall have to show that cases like these are not genuine counter-examples.

In some systems, e.g. in all extensions of B, we may derive the same principle for non-identities.

LNI $x \neq y \supset L x \neq y$

PROOF

LI × PC	(1)	$\sim L x = y \supset x \neq y$	
(1) × LMI	(2)	$M x \neq y \supset x \neq y$	
(2) × DR4	(3)	$x \neq y \supset L x \neq y$	Q.E.D.

Whatever we think of LI it is at least arguable that intuitively LI and LNI stand or fall together, and that if a satisfactory modal system is to contain LI it should contain LNI as well. We first observe that both LI and LNI are valid on the interpretation given to $\phi_=$. For suppose $\mu(x) = \mu(y)$ then $\langle \mu(x), \mu(y), w \rangle$ will be in $V(\phi_=)$ for every $w \in W$, and so $V_\mu(L x = y, w) = 1$. And if $\mu(x) \neq \mu(y)$ then there will be *no* $w \in W$ such that $\langle \mu(x), \mu(y), w \rangle \in V(\phi_=)$, and so, $V_\mu(L x \neq y, w) = 1$. Because LNI is valid according to the semantics for identity that we are using at the moment we need to ensure that it forms part of the axiomatic basis. We shall see on p. 335 that for many choices of S, LNI is not a theorem of S + I. We use S + LNI to refer to the result of adding LNI to S + I, and in this chapter these are the systems we shall consider.

Soundness and completeness

We first establish the soundness of S + LNI. That is to say we establish that if every LPC substitution-instance of a theorem of S is valid in a model $\langle W, R, D, V \rangle$ then so is every theorem of S + LNI. (Where $\langle W, R \rangle$ is a frame for S then the argument used in the proof of theorem 13.1 on p. 247 still applies, and shows that every substitution-instance of every S-theorem is valid in every model based on $\langle W, R \rangle$.) ∀1 is valid in all models $\langle W, R, D, V \rangle$ and so will still be valid in that sub-class of models which treat $\phi_=$ as identity. Further, the transformation rules preserve validity in a model, and so all that is needed for soundness is to establish that I1, I2 and LNI are valid. I1 is certainly valid since if $\mu(x) = u$, then since $\langle u,u,w \rangle \in V(\phi_=)$ we have $V_\mu(x = x,w) = 1$. We have already shown that LNI is valid. The validity of I2 may be established by induction on the construction of α and β, though because of the step for $\sim$ it is easier to prove it for

I2′ $x = y \supset (\alpha \equiv \beta)$

Intuitively it should be clear that if $\mu(x) = \mu(y)$, and α and β differ *only* in respect of x and y, then $V_\mu(\alpha,w) = V_\mu(\beta,w)$ and so $V_\mu(\alpha \equiv \beta,w) = 1$.

We now show that each system S + LNI has a canonical model, in which all and only its theorems are valid. To establish this we need to vary slightly the definition of the canonical model given in Chapter 14. The worlds are still maximal consistent sets of wff which have the ∨-property in some language $\mathcal{L}^+$ of modal LPC. And as before wRw' iff for every wff $L\alpha$ of $\mathcal{L}^+$, if $L\alpha \in w$ then $\alpha \in w'$. The change comes in the definition of D. Our earlier plan was to let D be the set of all the (individual) variables of $\mathcal{L}^+$. We then took a 'canonical' assignment $\mu(x)$ whereby $\mu(x)$ is x itself. But this plan will not work here, for if x and y are distinct variables then $\mu(x)$ and $\mu(y)$ would have to be distinct, regardless of whether or not $x = y \in w$ for some w in the canonical model.

Our way of dealing with this problem is to choose one of them, say x, as the 'representative' of both x and y so that $\mu(x) = x$ and $\mu(y) = x$. But before we describe this procedure, we need to make an observation about worlds in the canonical model. We observed on p. 137 that the frames of some canonical models for propositional systems are not cohesive, and the same is true of models for LNI systems. In proving that every S + LNI-consistent set Λ of wff is true at some world we shall restrict ourselves to the cohesive part of the canonical model to which a world containing Λ belongs.

As we said on p. 137 a cohesive part of a frame may be regarded as a complete frame in itself since the truth of wff in any world in any model based on it will not be affected by the values of wff outside that cohesive part. For this reason we shall think of the cohesive part of the canonical model of S + LNI which satisfies Λ as itself a cohesive model $\langle W,R,D,V \rangle$. The reason for this is that in a cohesive model for S + LNI every world contains exactly the same identity formulae, in the sense that for w, $w' \in$ W, and any x and y, $x = y \in w$ iff $x = y \in w'$.

It is easy to see that this is so, since consider any world w and any w' such that either wRw' or $w'Rw$. If wRw' and $x = y \in w$, then by LI, $L\, x = y \in w$ and so $x = y \in w'$. If $x = y \in w$ and $w'Rw$ then if $x = y \notin w'$, then $x \neq y \in w'$ and so by LNI $L\, x \neq y \in w'$ and so, since $w'Rw$, $x \neq y \in w$, contradicting its consistency. Now if $\langle W,R,D,V \rangle$ is cohesive and w, $w' \in$ W, then w and w' are linked by a chain of backwards or forwards R-steps, and so if $x = y \in w$ then $x = y \in w'$ and if $x = y \in w'$ then $x = y \in w$.

Given an S + LNI-consistent set Λ of wff of $\mathscr{L}$, we shall show how to construct a cohesive sub-model of the canonical model of S + LNI in which there is some world w such that $\Lambda \subseteq w$. As before the members of W are all maximal consistent sets of wff of $\mathscr{L}^+$ with the ∀-property in $\mathscr{L}^+$, and wRw' iff $L^-(w) \subseteq w'$. Given some $w*$ such that $\Lambda \subseteq w*$ we let W be the set of all and only those worlds which can be reached by a chain of forwards or backwards R-steps from $w*$. We define the domain D as follows. Assume that the individual variables of $\mathscr{L}^+$ are enumerated in some fixed order and suppose that x is any variable. Then there is some variable y, perhaps x itself, which is the earliest variable in the enumeration of variables for which $x = y \in w$. (Since exactly the same identity wff are in every $w \in$ W it makes no difference which w is selected for this purpose.) Let D consist of all variables x such that x is earlier than any other y for which $x = y \in$ W. For $x_1, \ldots ,x_n$ in D and $w \in$ W, $\langle x_1, \ldots ,x_n,w \rangle \in V(\phi)$, for n-place predicate ϕ, iff $\phi x_1 \ldots x_n \in w$.

We must first show that with this definition $V(\phi_=)$ really is the identity predicate. Suppose that $x \in$ D. Then certainly $x = x \in w$, and so $\langle x,x,w \rangle \in V(\phi_=)$. Suppose that $x \in$ D and $y \in$ D and x and y are distinct variables. Then x must be earlier than any other z (including y) for which $x = z \in w$, and y must be earlier than any z including x such that $y = z$ is in w. If $x = y$ is in w, x must be earlier than y, but by I3, $y = x$ is also in w and so y must be earlier than x. So if x and y are distinct members of D then $x = y \notin w$ and so $\langle x,y,w \rangle \notin V(\phi_=)$ as required.

We define the 'canonical' assignment μ, in such a way that $\mu(x)$ is the earliest variable y such that $x = y \in w$. By I1 we know that there always will be at least one appropriate y. In fact y will be the unique member of D for which $x = y \in w$.

THEOREM 17.1 For every wff α of $\mathcal{L}^+$ and every $w \in W$, $V_\mu(\alpha,w) = 1$ iff $\alpha \in w$.

Proof: The proof is by induction of the construction of α. Let ϕ be any n-place predicate, including $\phi_=$, let $w \in W$, and consider $\phi x_1...x_n$. Now $\mu(x_1), ... ,\mu(x_n)$ will be some $y_1, ... , y_n$, where $y_1, ... ,y_n \in D$, and $y_1 = x_1, ... ,y_n = x_n \in w$. Then

$$V_\mu(\phi x_1...x_n,w) = 1$$
$$\text{iff } \langle \mu(x_1), ... ,\mu(x_n) \rangle \in V(\phi)$$
$$\text{iff } \langle y_1, ... ,y_n \rangle \in V(\phi)$$
$$\text{iff } \phi y_1...y_n \in w.$$

But $y_1 = x_1, ... , y_n = x_n$ are all in w, and so, by repeated applications of I2

$$\phi y_1...y_n \equiv \phi x_1...x_n \in w$$

and so $\phi x_1...x_n \in w$ iff $\phi y_1...y_n \in w$, which gives us the required result. The induction for $\sim$, $\vee$ and L is as in the proof of theorem 14.3 on p. 261. For $\forall$, if $\forall x\alpha \in w$ the argument is as for case (d) on p. 261. If $\sim\forall x\alpha \in w$ then since w has the $\forall$-property there will be some $y \in \mathcal{L}^+$ such that $\sim\alpha[y/z] \in w$. So there will be some $z \in D$ such that $y = z \in w$, and so by I2, $\sim\alpha[z/x] \in w$. So $\alpha[z/x] \notin w$, so $V_\mu(\alpha[z/x],w) = 0$, and so, by the validity of $\forall 1$, $V_\mu(\forall x\alpha,w) = 0$. Completeness follows as before for all systems S + LNI whose canonical model is based on a frame for S.

These results carry over *mutatis mutandis* to systems without BF, and to systems with an existence predicate. In the case of these latter however we can now define E as[2]

$$Ex =_{df} \exists y\, x = y$$

This is because with an actualist quantifier $V_\mu(\exists y\, x = y,w) = 1$ iff there is a y-alternative ρ of μ in which $\rho(y) \in D_w$ and $V_\rho(x = y,w) = 1$. This last will be so iff $\rho(x) = \rho(y)$, i.e. iff $\mu(x) = \rho(y)$. I.e. $V_\mu(\exists x = y,w)$ is true iff there is a member of D_w that $\mu(x)$ is identical with. Which is just to say that $\mu(x) \in D_w$, or that $V_\mu(Ex,w) = 1$.

Definite descriptions

On p. 313 we used the sentence

(1)   The person next door = the mayor

to motivate the idea that the principle

LI $x = y \supset L x = y$

might be found objectionable. One way of countering this objection would be to construe (1) in such a way that it did express a necessary truth. Now it is contingent that the person who is in fact the person who lives next door is the person who lives next door, for he or she might have lived somewhere else; that is, *living next door* is a property which belongs contingently, not necessarily, to the person to whom it does belong. And similarly, it is contingent that the person who is in fact the mayor is the mayor; for someone else might have been elected instead. But if we understand (1) to mean that the object which (as a matter of contingent fact) possesses the property of being the person who lives next door is identical with the object which (as a matter of contingent fact) possesses the property of being the mayor, then we are understanding it to assert that a certain object (variously described) is identical with itself, and this we need have no qualms about regarding as a necessary truth. This would give us a way of construing identity statements which makes LI perfectly acceptable: for whenever $x = y$ is true we can take it as expressing the necessary truth that a certain object is identical with itself.

An important feature of (1) is that it is not stated using variables but is stated using complex phrases like 'the person next door' and 'the mayor'. These phrases are often called *definite descriptions* and they pose problems even in non-modal predicate logic. One of the first to see this was Bertrand Russell[3] whose celebrated example was

(2)   The present king of France is bald.

Since there is no present king of France it would seem that (2) is false. But then it would seem that

(3)   The present king of France is not bald.

is true. But (3) doesn't seem true either, for the same reason as (2).

Russell was worried about people who supposed that (2) or (3) had to be true because there was a non-existent individual who is the present king of France, about whom either baldness or non-baldness is predicated. Now we have seen that in modal logic there is no bar to having individuals which exist in some worlds but not others. And no doubt there are worlds in which there are objects which do not exist in our world, and some of them may, in their worlds, be kings of France. This is just how modal logic interprets the truth that there might have been a present king of France, and that king need not be anyone who actually exists. But *that* is not what (2) or (3) claim. For they do not speak of whether an individual who does not actually exist is or is not bald in some other world. (2), if about an individual which does not exist, would be claiming that that individual is *actually* bald, bald in the real world. And that won't do because the individual does not even exist in the real world. And (3), on at least one way of taking it, predicates lack of baldness, in other words having hair, in the real world, of a non-existent individual, and that won't do either.

Even more blatant is the sentence

(4)   The present king of France does not exist.

On Russell's view it is sheer nonsense to suppose that (4) predicates (truly) non-existence of a non-existent object. His claim was that the phrase 'the present king of France' does not function like a name at all. To see this let us go back to our example (1) of the person who lives next door, and let us use the predicate ϕ to mean 'lives next door'. Let us use ψ to mean 'is bald' and look at

(5)   The person who lives next door is bald.

If we follow Russell, (4) makes three claims

(6)   At least one person lives next door;

(7)   At most one person lives next door;

(8)   Whoever lives next door is bald.

In an LPC with identity these can be formalized as

(9) $\exists x \phi x$

(10) $\forall x \forall y ((\phi x \wedge \phi y) \supset x = y)$

(11) $\forall x (\phi x \supset \psi x)$

(9) and (10) together say that *exactly one x is* ϕ. Sometimes this is written as $\exists^1 x \phi x$ or $\exists! x \phi x$. (5) then is the conjunction of (9), (10) and (11). Now look at

(12) The person next door is not bald.

There are in fact *two* wff which can be argued to represent (12). The first is simply the negation of the conjunction of (9), (10) and (11).

(13) $\sim (\exists x \phi x \wedge \forall x \forall y ((\phi x \wedge \phi y) \supset x = y) \wedge \forall x (\phi x \supset \psi x))$

This way of negating (4) is sometimes called *external negation* because the negation sign is outside the rest of the formula. The other way of negating (4) is to regard 'not bald' as a predicate. On this interpretation (12) becomes

(14) $\exists x \phi x \wedge \forall x \forall y ((\phi x \wedge \phi y) \supset x = y) \wedge \forall x (\phi x \supset \sim \psi x)$

This is called the *internal negation* of (4) since the $\sim$ is as far in as possible, negating only the wff ψx.

Now consider the claim

(15) The person next door exists.

This can be simply represented as the conjunction of (9) and (10)

(16) $\exists x \phi x \wedge \forall x \forall y ((\phi x \wedge \phi y) \supset x = y)$

For Russell the sentence

(17) The person next door doesn't exist

would be true if there were two or more people next door as well as if there were none, since it would be

(18) $\sim(\exists x\phi x \;\wedge\; \forall x\forall y((\phi x \;\wedge\; \phi y) \supset x = y))$

though it might be argued that (17) simply means that no one lives next door:

(19) $\sim\exists x\phi x$

Finally let us return to (1) and now let us use ψ, not for 'is bald' as we have been doing, but for 'is the mayor'. On Russell's account (1) becomes the following conjunction:

(20) $\exists^1 x\phi x \;\wedge\; \exists^1 x\psi x \;\wedge\; \forall x(\phi x \supset \psi x)$

What we notice about (20) is that it does not use $=$ at all, except of course in the unpacking of $\exists^1$. We can express (20) using $=$ by replacing the last conjunct with

(21) $\forall x\forall y((\phi x \;\wedge\; \psi y) \supset x = y)$

In the presence of $\exists^1 x\phi x$ and $\exists^1 x\psi x$, (21) is equivalent to

(22) $\forall x(\phi x \supset \psi x)$

We come at last to the problem of LI, for we notice that just as in the case of $\sim$, there are two places for L to go. These are not usually called external necessity and internal necessity. The contrast is rather the *de re*/*de dicto* contrast mentioned on p. 250, since we may either put the L outside all the quantifiers, to get the *de dicto* reading, or inside, to get the *de re* reading. Now (20) is true but not necessarily true, so putting L in front of the whole conjunction gives us a false sentence. And even if we replace (22) in (20) by (21), the wff is still false when an L is put in front of the whole conjunction. But LI certainly does not license the move from (20), in either form, to its necessitated version. What LI does allow is to move from (20), using (21) as its last conjunct, to

(23) $\exists^1 x\phi x \;\wedge\; \exists^1 x\psi x \;\wedge\; \forall x\forall y((\phi x \;\wedge\; \psi y) \supset L\,x = y)$

and this gives us the interpretation we used when we defended LI on p. 318.

We even have the possibility of ambiguity in the simpler kind of wff like the conjunction we used to formalize (4). To get a more interesting case let ϕ represent

'is the number of planets'

and ψ represent 'is odd'. Then consider

(24) The number of planets is necessarily odd.

We shall assume there are nine planets. Then we may distinguish between

(25) $L(\exists^1 x \phi x \wedge \forall x(\phi x \supset \psi x))$

and

(26) $\exists^1 x \phi x \wedge \forall x(\phi x \supset L\psi x)$

(25) is the *de dicto* reading of (24) and is false, for although there happen to be nine planets this is not a necessary fact, and if there had only been eight their number would not have been odd. (26) is the *de re* reading and is true. For nine is the number of planets, and nine *is* odd by necessity, for that is a fact of arithmetic.

Another place for the L to go would be as in

(27) $\exists^1 x \phi x \wedge L\forall x(\phi x \supset \psi x)$

This is still a *de dicto* formula, and in the case of (24) the important contrast is the *de re/de dicto* contrast. However if we consider

(28) The person next door necessarily lives next door

and let ϕ mean 'lives next door' and suppose that in fact exactly one person lives next door then

(29) $\exists^1 x \phi x \wedge L\forall x(\phi x \supset \phi x)$

is true, but neither

(30) $L(\exists^1 x \phi x \wedge \forall x(\phi x \supset \phi x))$

nor

(31) $\exists^1 x \phi x \land \forall x (\phi x \supset L\phi x)$

is true.

The ambiguity between (25) and (26) in the analysis of (24) is especially significant since it still arises even though

(32) $L\exists^1 x \phi x$

is true. The significance may be seen by comparing the modal case with the non-modal case. Compare (25) and (26) as revealing the ambiguity in (24) with (13) and (14) as revealing the ambiguity in (12). Although (13) and (14) differ in meaning yet, provided that $\exists^1 x \phi x$ is true, they are equivalent. So in the modal case one might expect that since $\exists^1 x \phi x$ is not merely true but *necessarily* true, then (25) and (26) would be equivalent. Yet they are not. The importance of this lack of equivalence will be made clear in the next section.

The illustrations used so far in the chapter have involved only one-place predicates. But it is not hard to think of sentences like

(33) The height in metres of every house is necessarily odd.

We suppose that in fact the height in metres of all the relevant houses is odd. If ϕ means 'is a house', ψ means 'the height in metres of x is y' and χ means 'x is odd', then the *de dicto* and *de re* readings of (33) become respectively

(34) $L\forall x (\phi x \supset (\exists^1 y \psi yx \land \forall z (\psi zx \supset \chi z)))$

and

(35) $\forall x (\phi x \supset (\exists^1 y \psi yx \land \forall z (\psi zx \supset L\chi z)))$

(35) is true, but (34) is not.

Descriptions and scope

It is a feature of Russell's theory of descriptions that there is no expression in the analysis of (5) on p. 319 which represents the phrase 'the person next door'. What the conjunction of (9)−(11) does is provide

323

what Russell called a *contextual definition* of the phrase 'the person next door'. That is to say it shows how to take a particular sentence in which that phrase occurs and represent it by a wff of LPC. And the recipe provides a way of doing this in every case. Despite this Russell does introduce a notation for definite descriptions. If we wish to use an expression for 'the person next door' we note that, in terms of the predicate, 'lives next door' the expression we require is

(1)   the x such that x lives next door.

Russell uses the symbol ⍳ for this and with ϕ for 'lives next door' and ψ for 'is bald' would write (1) as $\imath x \phi x$ and (5) as

(2) $\psi \imath x \phi x$

(2) of course merely labels the problem. It does not solve it. For Russell, the real analysis of (5) is given in (6)−(8) on p. 319. Nevertheless (2) allows us to see a parallel between definite descriptions and quantifiers. In our analysis of (12) on p. 320 in accordance with Russell's theory of descriptions we saw that ∼ could be put in two different places in the formula. A similar ambiguity occurs in the sentence

(3)   Someone is not bald.

If the domain is people then (3) may be represented as either

(4) $\sim \exists x \psi x$ or

(5) $\exists x \sim \psi x$

(Our concern here is not with the question of which of these wff is the more natural interpretation of (3). Probably it is (4) though a sentence like

(6)   Felicity wasn't here all winter

would have to rely on such features as context or intonation to disambiguate.)

The difference between (4) and (5) is a difference in the scope of the quantifier. In (4) the quantifier has *narrow scope* with respect to ∼ since it is inside the ∼, while in (5) it has *wide scope* since ∼ is inside it. If definite descriptions *were* taken as primitive, in Russell's account they would behave like quantifiers in having scope. Taking a cue from natural language, some philosophers[4] have argued that (2) is really a quantifier-like expression, and just as $\exists x\alpha$ represents 'something satisfies α', and can be more explicitly read as 'there is an x such that α' so $\imath x\phi x\alpha$ can be read as 'the ϕ satisfies α' or more explicitly

(7)   Concerning the x which is ϕ, α.

(Strictly speaking, to accommodate cases like (33) on p. 323 we need to generalize $\imath x\phi x$ to $\imath x\beta$ to represent the unique x which satisfies some simple or complex condition β, and use $\alpha[\imath x\beta/x]$ to express the proposition that the unique x which satisfies β, satisfies α. But our illustrations will be easier to follow if we stick with $\imath x\phi x$.)

This enables us to mark the difference between

(8) $(\imath x\phi x) \sim \psi x$ and

(9) $\sim(\imath x\phi x)\psi x$

where $\imath x\phi x$ is an operator which binds any x free within its scope. Russell actually used a somewhat different notation, one which obscures the fact that $\imath x\phi x$ works like a quantifier. He treats the $\imath$ expression itself as a complex expression which replaces a variable. Such expressions are often called *terms*. He then uses the $\imath$-expression in square brackets to indicate scope. So (8) and (9) would be written

(10) $[\imath x\phi x] \sim \psi(\imath x\phi x)$ and

(11) $\sim[\imath x\phi x]\psi(\imath x\phi x)$

Using scope indicators we can recover unambiguously the original wff in the underlying LPC (without $\imath$) that analyse (10) and (11). In non-modal LPC we have the following important fact. *On the assumption that exactly one thing is ϕ* (10) and (11) are equivalent. That is to say, the following, on Russell's theory, is valid:

(12) $\exists^1 x\phi x \supset ([\imath x\phi x] \sim \psi(\imath x\phi x) \equiv \sim[\imath x\phi x]\psi(\imath x\phi x))$

When we say that (12) is valid on Russell's theory we mean that when unpacked into primitive notation in accordance with the theory of descriptions the resulting formula is valid in non-modal LPC with identity.

Because of this it is customary in non-modal LPC to restrict the use of descriptions to cases in which uniqueness is assumed, and in these cases the scope indicator [$\imath x \phi x$] can be dropped. The reason this would cause trouble in modal logic is of course that, despite Russell's notation, on Russell's theory it is really the scope indicator which marks the operator, not the occurrence of the description which replaces the variable. And this confusion, although it does no harm in non-modal LPC provided uniqueness is assumed, is what leads to problems in the modal case.

As Arthur Smullyan showed,[5] we can easily incorporate descriptions into modal LPC provided that we retain the scope indicator. If descriptions are regarded as quantifiers we can express (25) and (26) on p. 322 as

(13) $L(\imath x \phi x) \psi x$ and

(14) $(\imath x \phi x) \, L \psi x$

In Russell's terminology these would be written

(15) $L[\imath x \phi x] \psi(\imath x \phi x)$ and

(16) $[\imath x \phi x] \, L \psi(\imath x \phi x)$

In the case of a non-modal language scope does not matter provided that uniqueness is satisfied. But, as we remarked on p. 322, when ϕ means 'is the number of planets' and ψ means 'is odd', (15) and (16) are not equivalent, even though uniqueness is not merely true but is even necessarily true, it being necessary that, however many or few planets there are some unique number is their number. Given that the scope indicator cannot be dropped, if we want to retain expressions to represent definite descriptions, it seems clearer to use the (13)/(14) notation than Russell's (15)/(16) and to recognize that Russellian definite descriptions are like quantifiers, and only under certain restricted conditions, act like names. It is presumably the fact that these restricted conditions are often satisfied in non-modal LPC that has led to the assumption that definite descriptions are problematic in modal LPC.

Individual constants and function symbols

It is possible to extend the language of LPC by the addition of individual constants and function symbols. We have not done this since, provided identity is present, Russell's theory of descriptions enables them to be eliminated. We shall discuss individual constants first. Individual constants a, b, c can occur in exactly the same positions in atomic wff as individual variables can. But they do not occur in quantifiers and their values are given by V, not μ. In non-modal LPC the values of individual constants are simply members of D, so that if a is an individual constant $V(a) \in D$. Predicates are given values as before. It is convenient here to introduce explicitly the notion of a *term*. In a language with individual variables and constants a term is an individual variable or constant and where $t_1, \ldots, t_n$ are terms and ϕ is an n-place predicate then $\phi t_1 \ldots t_n$ is a wff. The value of a term differs according as it is a variable or a constant. We define $V_\mu(t)$, the value of t with respect to V and μ, as

   (i) If t is an individual constant then $V_\mu(t) = V(t)$.
   (ii) If t is an individual variable then $V_\mu(t) = \mu(t)$.
   (iii) If ϕ is an n-place predicate and $t_1, \ldots, t_n$ are terms, then $V_\mu(\phi t_1 \ldots t_n, w) = 1$ iff $\langle V_\mu(t_1), \ldots, V_\mu(t_n), w \rangle \in V(\phi)$ and 0 otherwise.

If this is to be applied to the modal case we must assume that a constant a is assigned just one member of D and that this does not change from world to world.

It is not difficult to see that individual constants are theoretically dispensable. For we may associate with each constant a a one-place predicate ϕ_a such that $\langle u, w \rangle \in V(\phi_a)$ iff $u = V(a)$. We may now define a as $\imath x \phi_a x$, and use Russell's theory of descriptions to eliminate any wff containing $\imath x \phi_a x$. In this elimination we make use of the fact that the scope distinctions embodied in (15) and (16) now make no difference. This is because not only is there a unique ϕ_a in each world, but it is the *same* ϕ, viz. $V(a)$, which is ϕ_a in each world. And when that happens the scope distinctions do indeed collapse and (15) and (16) become equivalent and so can be expressed simply as

(26) $L\psi(\imath x \phi_a x)$

Function symbols may be illustrated by the mathematical symbol $+$. In a model in which D is the natural numbers $V(+)$ is the function which takes any pair of numbers u_1 and u_2 to their sum. In the general case, where θ is an n-place function symbol and $t_1, \dots, t_n$ are terms then $(\theta t_1 \dots t_n)$ is also a term. As before constants and variables also count as terms. $V(\theta)$ will be a function from n-tuples from D into a member of D, and

$$V_\mu((\theta t_1 \dots t_n)) = V(\theta)(V_\mu(t_1), \dots, V_\mu(t_n))$$

We can represent θ by the $n+1$-place predicate ϕ_θ, where $\phi_\theta x_1 \dots x_n y$ means that y is the θ of $x_1, \dots, x_n$. For $u_1, \dots, u_n \in D$, and $w \in W$, $\langle u_1, \dots, u_n, v, w \rangle \in V(\phi_\theta)$ iff $v = V(\theta)(u_1, \dots, u_n)$. With this assignment, for any assignment μ to the variables it is the same value of y which satisfies $V_\mu(\phi_\theta x_1 \dots x_n y, w)$ for every w. Thus there is no difference between

(27) $[\imath y \phi_\theta x_1 \dots x_n y] L \psi (\imath y \phi_\theta x_1 \dots x_n y)$ and

(28) $L[\imath y \phi_\theta x_1 \dots x_n y] \psi (\imath y \phi_\theta x_1 \dots x_n y)$

For this reason the scope indicator may be removed and $\theta x_1 \dots x_n$ may be defined as $\imath y \phi_\theta x_1 \dots x_n y$.

We must however be extremely careful in interpreting this result, since in a modal language most expressions which look like function expressions actually turn out not to be. Consider for instance the expression, 'the capital of x'. Even if this expression picks out a unique individual in each world for any given value of x it need not be the same one in each world, assuming it is a contingent matter what something's capital is, so that there would be a difference between (27) and (28). Where scope makes a difference it is tempting to conclude that expressions like 'the capital of x' should not be treated as terms but should be regarded as $\imath$-expressions and analysed according to Russell's theory of descriptions. For this reason it may well be preferable to avoid altogether the use of function symbols in modal predicate logic.

Exercises — 17

17.1 Assume I2 for atomic wff only and assume LI. Prove I2 for all wff.

17.2 Prove the completeness of K + LNI but without BF.

17.3 Let ϕ = 'is a mayor of Wellington', and use Russell's theory of descriptions to distinguish two meanings for the sentence

The mayor of Wellington might not have been a mayor of Wellington

where one meaning is a logical contradiction but the other meaning is not. Represent each meaning by a wff of modal LPC, and explain why each wff has the meaning it does.

17.4 Show how the view that definite descriptions are like quantifiers brings out the parallel between the following two arguments:

(a) Every number is identical with some number
∴ If it is impossible that every number is even it is impossible that some number is even.

(b) The square of 3 is identical with the number of planets
∴ If it is impossible that the square of three is even it is impossible that the number of planets is even.

17.5 Suppose that definite descriptions are taken as primitive and that the logic contains $T + BF$ and the following two principles:

∀1 $\exists^1 x\alpha \supset (\forall x\beta \supset \beta[\imath x\alpha/x])$

DD $\exists^1 x\alpha \supset \alpha[\imath x\alpha/x]$

Show that from this we may prove $L\exists^1 x\alpha \supset \exists xL\alpha$.

17.6 Show how scope-indicating devices enable a distinction to be made between the valid principle $L\exists^1 x\phi x \supset L[\imath x\phi x]\phi(\imath x\phi x)$ and the invalid $L\exists^1 x\phi x \supset [\imath x\phi x]L\phi(\imath x\phi x)$.

Notes
[1] Although this example dates from Frege 1892 the difficulties for modal predicate logic to which it draws attention were first raised by Quine 1947. It is not our purpose to enter into a discussion of the philosophical problems with which this whole area bristles, and we shall confine any philosophical remarks we do make to those which bear directly on the interpretation of modal systems. LI is derived as a theorem in Barcan 1947.
[2] See Hintikka 1963, p. 70f.
[3] Russell 1905. The technical development of the theory discussed later in this chapter occurs in Whitehead and Russell 1910.
[4] For example Montague 1974, pp.61f. and 249. Also Cresswell 1973, p.130f.
[5] Smullyan 1948.

18

INTENSIONAL OBJECTS

The last chapter was concerned to show how the classical view of identity in modal predicate logic, according to which both LI and LNI on p. 314 are valid, can accommodate such apparent counter-examples as (1) on p. 313. In the present chapter we consider accounts of identity in which these wff are not valid.

Contingent identity

We have observed that LI and LNI might be thought unintuitive, and our next task is to see how we might adapt our semantics to avoid having them as valid. At first sight this might seem easy. For LI and LNI are surely consequences of the fact that for *any* w, $\langle u,v,w \rangle \in V(\phi_=)$ iff u and v are the very same member of D. So why not say that this may hold for some worlds, but not others?

Unfortunately this response has the consequence that it does not validate even the simplest instance of I2.

$$(2) \quad x = y \supset (\phi x \supset \phi y)$$

This will fail in a world w for which $\langle u,v,w \rangle \in V(\phi_=)$ but u and v are distinct. We might try defining validity to rule such worlds out, but then necessitation would no longer be validity-preserving since provided a world w in which $\phi_=$ *is* identity can see a world w' in which it is not then

$$(3) \quad L(x = y \supset (\phi x \supset \phi y))$$

will fail to be valid.

The upshot of this is that the problem is deeper than the question of what set of triples to assign to $V(\phi_=)$. Look again at example (1) on p. 313 (renumbered as (4)).

(4) The person next door is the mayor.

Suppose that we are in world w_1 and that there is some person u who in w_1 is both the mayor and the person next door. Since this fact is, presumably, contingent, there must be another world w_2 in which the person next door and the mayor are not one and the same person. But *that* presumably means that there are a distinct pair of people v and v' such that, in w_2, v is the person next door and v' is the mayor. And at most one of these, perhaps neither of them, will be u.

Consider now the status of LI:

LI $x = y \supset L x = y$

with respect to an assignment μ to the individual variables. In the situation envisaged the antecedent is true in w because $\mu(x) = u$ and $\mu(y) = u$, while the consequent is false because $x = y$ is false in w' when $\mu(x) = v$ and $\mu(y) = v'$. But this requires μ to give contradictory values. The situation seems to be this. We can only falsify LI if we allow μ to give the variables different values in different worlds. In the present example letting x stand for 'the person next door' would mean requiring μ to assign to x in a world w whoever it is who in w lives next door and assign to y whoever it is who is the mayor. If we think in this way then of course $\mu(x)$ and $\mu(y)$ may coincide in w_1 but not in w_2.

For such a semantics[1] a model remains a quadruple $\langle W,R,D,V \rangle$, exactly as defined on p. 243. However, an assignment μ is now world relative in that for every variable x and $w \in W$, $\mu(x,w) \in D$. The rule for evaluating atomic wff is now

$[V\phi']$ $V_\mu(\phi x_1 \ldots x_n, w) = 1$ iff $\langle \mu(x_1,w), \ldots, \mu(x_n,w), w \rangle \in V(\phi)$

$V(\phi_=)$ is as before and so we have the result that $V_\mu(x = y, w) = 1$ iff $\mu(x,w) = \mu(y,w)$. $[V\sim]$, $[V\vee]$ and $[VL]$ also remain as before. For $[V\forall]$ we need to generalize the notion of an x-alternative so that μ and ρ are x-alternatives iff for every variable y except, possibly, x, and every $w \in$

W, $\rho(y,w) = \mu(y,w)$. This semantics does not verify LI. For we need merely imagine an assignment μ such that for some $w \in$ W, $\mu(x,w) = \mu(y,w)$, while for some w' such that wRw', $\mu(x,w') \neq \mu(y,w')$. What the semantics *does* do however is validate all instances of I2, in which α and β contain no modal operators. Systems in which I2 is weakened in this way are, for obvious reasons, called *contingent identity systems*.

However, it is easy to show that the semantics so obtained would make the following schema valid:

(5) $L\exists x\alpha \supset \exists xL\alpha$

For let $\langle$W,R,D,V$\rangle$ be any model, w any world, and μ any (world relative) assignment to the variables. For every w' such that wRw', $V_\mu(\exists x\alpha,w') = 1$. This means there is some x-alternative, call it $\nu_{w'}$ of μ such that $V_{\nu_{w'}}(\alpha,w') = 1$. Define an x-alternative ρ of μ ?⁻ follows: For any w' such that wRw', let $\rho(x,w') = \nu_{w'}(x,w')$. But the $V_\rho(\alpha,w') = 1$ for every w' such that wRw' and so $V_\rho(L\alpha,w) = 1$. But ρ is an x-alternative of μ, and so $V_\mu(\exists xL\alpha,w) = 1$.

Now this formula (5) is one which we have encountered before (p. 246), and we remarked then that it is not intuitively plausible. To adapt an example given by Quine,[2] in certain games it is necessary that some player will win, but there is no individual player who is bound to win. There is, however, one way in which we could make (5) sound plausible, and that is by thinking of an expression such as 'the winner' as in a sense standing for a single 'object', though one which in a more usual sense of 'object' may be one object in a certain situation but a different one in another. For in that case, if it is necessary that someone will win then there is someone, viz. the winner, who is bound to win. Now we do often use phrases of the form 'the so-and-so' in such a way as this. Consider, for example, the expression 'the top card in the pack', as it occurs in the rules of a card game. The rules may, without ambiguity, specify that at a certain point in the play the top card is to be dealt to a certain player; yet on one occasion the top card may be the Ace of Spades and on another it may be the Queen of Hearts. Thus the phrase 'the top card in the pack' does not designate any particular card (individual piece of pasteboard), except in the context of a particular state of the pack; yet we can in one sense think of it as standing for a single object, contrasted with *the bottom card in the pack* and so forth.

Such 'objects' are often called *intensional objects* or *individual concepts*,[3] and the rules we have been considering would seem to provide a semantics for a logic in which the individual-variables range over all intensional objects. In such a logic, as the above discussion has indicated, (5) would be valid and we shall take up the question of this kind of logic on pp. 335−342 below. (Where ϕx means 'x is at the top of the pack', and x ranges over intensional objects, then (5) will be true because if it must be the case that there is a card at the top of the pack, then although no individual piece of pasteboard is bound to be at the top of the pack, yet there is something, viz. *the top card*, which is bound to be at the top of the pack. This parallels what we said about the game in which it must be the case that someone will win.)

However, (5) is not in fact a theorem of any of the contingent identity (CI) systems, since these are obtained by weakening the LNI systems and (5) is not a theorem of any of *them*. And this shows that what seemed to be the most natural semantics for the CI systems turns out not to characterize them after all.

The fault seems to be that the semantics enables us to make an 'object' out of any string of members of D whatever. E.g., suppose there are two worlds, w_1 and w_2, then where u_1 and u_2 are members of D we seem to be entitled to make up the 'object' which is u_1 in w_1 and u_2 in w_2. (Roughly, what (5) says is that any string of members of D each of which is ϕ in some world accessible to w entitles us to assume the existence of an 'object' which is ϕ in all of them.)

When we look at the matter in this way we might think of the LNI systems as requiring that the only strings of members of D which count as objects are strings consisting of the same member of D in each world (i.e., the only objects recognized in these systems are the straightforward members of D themselves). It seems therefore that an adequate semantics for the CI systems would have neither to require that only strings consisting solely of a single member of D should count as objects, nor that any string whatever of members of D should count as an object.

One way in which we might achieve such a semantics is to let the set of strings which are to count as objects be determined by each model; i.e., to let the model specify what assignments to individual-variables are to be permissible. Formally we can do this by letting the model contain a set I of 'allowable' intensional objects. An intensional object i is really a function from W into D. So if $w \in W$, then $i(w)$ is the member of D which i 'is' in w. So if i is the person next door then in world w, $i(w)$ is whoever it is who is the person next door in world w. A model then becomes a quintuple $\langle W,R,D,I,V \rangle$. An assignment μ gives a value, not in D, but in I, and where we have written $\mu(x,w)$ we shall now write

$\mu(x)(w)$, since $\mu(x)$ will be some $i \in I$, and consequently $\mu(x)(w)$, will be $i(w)$.[4] The definition of an x-alternative now becomes simple again. ρ is an x-alternative of μ iff for every y except possibly x, $\rho(y) = \mu(y)$.

For atomic wff we have

[Vϕ''] $V_\mu(\phi x_1...x_n, w) = 1$ iff $\langle \mu(x_1)(w), \ldots, \mu(x_n)(w) \rangle \in V(\phi)$

and for $\forall$

[V$\forall$] $V_\mu(\forall x\alpha, w) = 1$ iff $V_\rho(\alpha, w) = 1$ for every x-alternative ρ of μ.

Note in this definition the differing role of I and D. As far as the interpretation to the *predicates* goes, they are sets of $n+1$-tuples from D, and W, not from I. But as far as assignments to the individual variables are concerned their values come from I. We note that both PR and PA are still valid.

Contingent identity systems

In order to obtain soundness and completeness for systems of contingent identity, we need to restrict I2 so that α and β contain no modal operators.[5] In fact we can replace it by

I2″ $x = y \supset (\phi x_1...x_n \equiv \phi y_1...y_n)$

where each x_i, for $1 \leq i \leq n$ either is the very same variable as y_i, or else x_i is x and y_i is y. (In other words they are two atomic wff in which the first has (free) x in 0 or more places in which the second has (free) y.)

In non-modal LPC I2″ has the property that the full I2 may be deduced from it. (The proof is by induction on the construction of α and β.) The induction will not, however, carry through for L unless we are entitled to assume LI, and in the contingent identity systems we do not have LI. It is not difficult to see that I2″ is valid in the contingent identity semantics. For suppose that $V_\mu(x = y, w) = 1$. Then $\langle \mu(x)(w), \mu(y)(w), w \rangle \in V(\phi_=)$. So $\mu(x)(w) = \mu(y)(w)$. Now by definition of $\phi x_1...x_n$ and $\phi y_1...y_n$, for $1 \leq i \leq n$, either x_i *is* y_i, in which case $\mu(x_i)(w) = \mu(y_i)(w)$ or else x_i is x and y_i is y, in which case also $\mu(x_i)(w) = \mu(y_i)(w)$, and so $\langle \mu(x_1)(w), \ldots, \mu(x_n)(w), w \rangle$ is the very same $n+1$-tuple as $\langle \mu(y_1)(w), \ldots, \mu(y_n)(w), w \rangle$ and so $V_\mu(\phi x_1...x_n, w) = V_\mu(\phi y_1...y_n, w)$ and so $V_\mu(\phi x_1...x_n \equiv \phi y_1...y_n, w) = 1$.

This establishes the validity of I2″ in the contingent identity semantics.

By S + CI we shall denote S + BF with the addition of I1 and I2″. What we have just done is establish the soundness of S + CI. The approach to completeness will be as before, to define a canonical model. We let D be the set of all variables and define I as follows. With each variable x we associate an intensional object i_x as follows.

Assume that the variables are in some determinate order and for any world w, let $i_x(x)(w)$ be the first y in the enumeration of variables such that $x = y$ is in w. (By I1 at least $x = x$, will be in w.) Let I be the set consisting of i_x for every variable x, and let the canonical assignment μ be the assignment such that $\mu(x) = i_x$. For n-place predicate ϕ, and x_1, ... , $x_n \in$ D, put $\langle x_1, \ldots, x_n, w \rangle$ in V(ϕ) iff $\phi x_1 \ldots x_n \in w$.

THEOREM 18.1 $V_\mu(\alpha, w) = 1$ iff $\alpha \in w$.

Proof: The proof is by induction on the construction of α. Suppose α is $\phi x_1 \ldots x_n$. Then $V_\mu(\phi x_1 \ldots x_n, w) = 1$ iff $\langle \mu(x_1)(w), \ldots, \mu(x_n)(w), w \rangle \in$ V(ϕ). Now $\langle \mu(x_1)(w), \ldots, \mu(x_n)(w) \rangle$ will be some $\langle y_1, \ldots, y_n \rangle$ such that $x_1 = y_1$, ... , $x_n = y_n$ are all in w. By I2″ this means that $\phi x_1 \ldots x_n \equiv \phi y_1 \ldots y_n$ is in w and so $\phi x_1 \ldots x_n \in w$ iff $\phi y_1 \ldots y_n \in w$. Now $\langle y_1, \ldots, y_n, w \rangle \in$ V(ϕ) iff $\phi y_1 \ldots y_n \in w$. So $\langle y_1, \ldots, y_n, w \rangle \in$ V(ϕ) iff $\phi x_1, \ldots, x_n \in w$. But $\langle y_1, \ldots, y_n, w \rangle$ is $\langle \mu(x_1)(w), \ldots, \mu(x_n)(w), w \rangle$ and so $V_\mu(\phi x_1 \ldots x_n, w) = 1$ iff $\phi x_1 \ldots x_n \in w$. The remainder of the induction is as in theorem 14.3 on p. 261, since the fact that μ gives values in I rather than in D makes no difference.

If we impose the requirement that where wRw' and $i_1(w) = i_2(w)$ then $i_1(w') = i_2(w')$, then we have a semantics which will always validate LI, but need not validate LNI, though it will validate LNI in all frames in which R is symmetrical. Thus some LI systems, e.g. where S is K, T or S4, will not contain LNI, while others will, e.g. if S contains B.

Quantifying over all intensional objects

On p. 332 we showed that if I consists of *all* intensional objects − *all* functions from W into D − then certain wff, such as $L\exists x \phi x \supset \exists x L \phi x$, become valid. So the question arises of what axiomatic systems are correct for the logic of intensional objects based on an underlying propositional system S. The answer is that for most choices of S, an exception being S5, the logic of intensional objects based on S is unaxiomatizable. The unaxiomatizability result holds for such systems as B, S4.3.1 and all systems contained in either of them. In other words it includes almost every system discussed in this book except S5.[6]

To make this claim precise we consider a propositional modal logic S. For simplicity we shall confine ourselves to complete propositional logics and will consider the class $\mathscr{E}$ of frames for S. Since I is now the class of *all* functions from W into D we may omit reference to I. So we say that a wff α is $\mathscr{E}$-valid for intensional objects iff $V_\mu(\alpha,w) = 1$ for every $w \in$ W in every intensional objects model $\langle W,R,D,V \rangle$ based on some $\langle W,R \rangle$ $\in \mathscr{E}$. In what follows we shall assume that $\mathscr{E}$-valid means $\mathscr{E}$-valid for intensional objects. The claim then to be proved is that for a significant class of propositional systems S $\mathscr{E}$-validity is not axiomatizable.

We prove this by showing how to translate wff of second-order non-modal logic into wff of a fragment of modal predicate logic in such a way that validity is preserved when the modal predicate logic is interpreted as quantifying over all intensional objects. We then use the non-axiomatizability of second-order logic to establish the non-axiomatizability of intensional objects logic.

We discussed second-order logic briefly on p. 188. The fragment $\mathscr{L}$ that we shall be concerned with contains only one-place predicate variables ϕ, ψ...etc. and a two-place predicate constant R, usually written between its arguments. A model for $\mathscr{L}$ is just like a model for first-order non-modal logic except that the values of the predicate variables are given by μ and not by V. For one-place ϕ, $\mu(\phi) \subseteq$ D. Since R is the only predicate constant a model $\langle D,V \rangle$ provides a domain D and a relation $V(R)$ on D. For present purposes D is a set of worlds and $V(R)$ is just the accessibility relation R. So we shall refer to D as W, and a model for this fragment of non-modal second-order logic is simply a frame for propositional modal logic. (Note that the italicized R is the two-place predicate of $\mathscr{L}$, while the unitalicized R is the relation which is its interpretation according to V.) An assignment μ now gives values from W to all the individual variables, and subsets of W to the predicate variables. Where ϕ is a predicate variable then ρ is a ϕ-alternative of μ iff ρ and μ agree on all the individual variables and on all the predicate variables except possibly ϕ. The rule for $\forall$ is:

$[\forall\phi]$ $V_\mu(\forall\phi\alpha) = 1$ iff $V_\rho(\alpha) = 1$ for every ϕ-alternative ρ of μ.

The idea behind what we are going to do is really quite simple. Consider first a rather special kind of intensional objects model in which D contains only two objects, say 1 and 0. Then we may consider these as the two truth-values. Where W is any class of objects every subset A of

W may be coded by the intensional object i_A such that $i_A(w) = 1$ if $w \in$ A and $i_A(w) = 0$ if $w \notin$ A.

We may relax this provision in two ways. First, there is no reason why in some worlds 1 might be the 'true' value while in other worlds it is 0. All we require is that $w \in$ A iff $i_A(w)$ is the appropriate 'true' value for the world w. Second, there is nothing to prevent there being many true values and many false values. Of course many different intensional objects might then code the same subset A of W since all that is required of an i which codes A is that $i(w)$ is one of the 'true' values for w if $w \in$ A, and one of the 'false' values if $w \notin$ A.

The way we stipulate which values are the true ones and which the false ones is to translate every wff α of $\mathcal{L}$ into a wff $\tau(\alpha)$ of a language $\mathcal{L}*$ of modal predicate logic containing a single one-place predicate T, and it is those members of D which satisfy T in a world w which count as the 'true' values in w, and those which do not as the 'false' values in w. Our translation requires that the individual variables of $\mathcal{L}*$ include all those of $\mathcal{L}$ and in addition an individual variable x_ϕ for every predicate variable ϕ of $\mathcal{L}$. We show how to translate every wff of $\mathcal{L}$ into $\mathcal{L}*$ as follows:

$$\tau(\phi x) = M(Tx \wedge Tx_\phi)$$
$$\tau(xRy) = M(Tx \wedge MTy)$$
$$\tau(\sim \alpha) = \sim \tau(\alpha)$$
$$\tau(\alpha \vee \beta) = (\tau(\alpha) \vee \tau(\beta))$$
$$\tau(\forall x\alpha) = \forall x\tau(\alpha)$$
$$\tau(\forall \phi\alpha) = \forall x_\phi\tau(\alpha)$$

The atomic cases may look a little strange, and could do with some explanation. The idea is that where x in $\mathcal{L}$ is assigned a world w, then in $\mathcal{L}*$ it is assigned an intensional object true (i.e. satisfying T) only in w, and where ϕ in $\mathcal{L}$ is assigned a subset A of W then in $\mathcal{L}*$, x_ϕ is assigned an intensional object true in a world w iff w is in A. Then $M(Tx \wedge Tx_\phi)$ will be true iff there is an accessible world at which both Tx and Tx_ϕ are true. Since x is true only at the world assigned to it in $\mathcal{L}$, $Tx \wedge Tx_\phi$ will be true iff the world assigned to x in $\mathcal{L}$ is one of the worlds at which Tx_ϕ is true, which means one of the worlds assigned to ϕ in $\mathcal{L}$. $M(Tx \wedge MTy)$ will be true iff there is an accessible world at which Tx and MTy are both true. And this will be so iff MTy is true at the world assigned to x in $\mathcal{L}$, and MTy will be true at *that* world iff it can see the world assigned to y. Note that $\tau(\alpha)$ is of modal degree at most 2.

We make all this precise as follows. Where $\langle W,R \rangle$ is a frame, V (strictly $V_{\langle W,R \rangle}$) will denote the value-assignment for $\mathscr{L}$ in which $V(R) = R$. $V(\alpha)$ will then be a truth-value for α determined in accordance with the usual rules for non-modal second-order logic. Given any frame $\langle W,R \rangle$ and any intensional objects model $\langle W,R,D,V^* \rangle$ for $\mathscr{L}^*$ based on $\langle W,R \rangle$ in which, for every $w \in W$, there is some $\langle u,w \rangle \in V^*(T)$ and some $\langle v,w \rangle \notin V^*(T)$ then for any $w \in W$ and any assignment μ to the variables of $\mathscr{L}$ and μ^* to the variables of $\mathscr{L}^*$ we say that μ and μ^* *correspond* iff for every $w \in W$ and every variable x or ϕ of $\mathscr{L}$:

(i) $\langle \mu^*(x)(w),w \rangle \in V^*(T)$ iff $w = \mu(x)$;

(ii) $\langle \mu^*(x_\phi)(w),w \rangle \in V^*(T)$ iff $w \in \mu(\phi)$.

The condition that for each world w, there must be at least one member of D which satisfies T in w, and at least one which does not is needed to ensure that for every μ there will exist a corresponding μ^*.

THEOREM 18.2   Where α is any wff of $\mathscr{L}$ and $w \in W$ and $wR\mu(x)$ for every variable x, and μ and μ^* correspond, then $V_\mu(\alpha) = V_{\mu^*}^*(\tau(\alpha),w)$.

The difficult cases are in fact the atomic wff. Take first ϕx. $\tau(\phi x)$ is $M(Tx \wedge Tx_\phi)$, and $V_{\mu^*}^*(M(Tx \wedge Tx_\phi),w) = 1$ iff for some w' such that wRw'

(1) $V_{\mu^*}^*(Tx,w') = 1$

and

(2) $V_{\mu^*}^*(Tx_\phi,w') = 1$

(1) will hold iff $\langle \mu^*(x)(w'),w \rangle \in V^*(T)$, and, since μ and μ^* correspond, then by (i), (1) will hold iff

(3) $w' = \mu(x)$

and (2) will hold iff $\langle \mu^*(x_\phi)(w'),w' \rangle \in V^*(T)$. Since μ and μ^* correspond, then by (ii), (2) will hold iff

(4) $w' \in \mu(\phi)$

and clearly there will be a w' (accessible from w) for which (3) and (4) hold iff $wR\mu(x)$ and $\mu(x) \in \mu(\phi)$, i.e., given $wR\mu(x)$, iff

(5) $V_\mu(\phi x) = 1$

as required. Now consider xRy. $V_{\mu*}^*(M(Tx \wedge MTy),w) = 1$ iff there is some w' such that wRw' and

(6) $V_{\mu*}^*(Tx,w') = 1$

and

(7) $V_{\mu*}^*(MTy,w') = 1$

Now (6) holds, as before, iff

(8) $w' = \mu(x)$

And (7) will hold iff there is some w'' such that $w'Rw''$ and

(9) $V_{\mu*}^*(Ty,w'') = 1$

But (9) holds iff

(10) $w'' = \mu(y)$

And there will be a w' and w'' accessible from w and with $w'Rw''$ for which (8) and (10) hold iff $wR\mu(x)$ and $wR\mu(y)$ and $\mu(x)R\mu(y)$, i.e., given $wR\mu(x)$ and $wR\mu(y)$, iff

(11) $V_\mu(xRy) = 1$

as required.

The induction clearly holds for $\sim$ and $\vee$. For $\forall$, if $V_\mu(\forall x\alpha) = 0$ then there is an x-alternative ρ of μ such that $V_\rho(\alpha) = 0$. Let $\rho*$ be any assignment which corresponds with ρ. Then by the induction hypothesis $V_{\rho*}^*(\tau(\alpha),w) = 0$. But $\rho*$ will be an x-alternative of $\mu*$ and so

$V_{\mu*}^*(\forall x\tau(\alpha),w) = 0$. Analogously if $V_{\mu*}^*(\forall x\tau(\alpha),w) = 0$ then $V_\mu(\forall x\alpha) = 0$. If $V_\mu(\forall\phi\alpha) = 0$ then there is a ϕ-alternative ρ of μ such that $V_\rho(\alpha) = 0$. Let $\rho*$ correspond with ρ. Then $V_{\mu*}^*(\tau(\alpha),w) = 0$. But $\rho*$ will be an x_ϕ-alternative of $\mu*$ and so $V_{\mu*}^*(\forall x_\phi\tau(\alpha),w) = 0$. Analogously if $V_{\mu*}^*(\forall x_\phi\tau(\alpha),w) = 0$ then $V_\mu(\forall x\alpha) = 0$. This proves the theorem.

We must now link up validity on a frame $\langle W,R\rangle$ with validity in the corresponding model $\langle W,R,D,V*\rangle$. In doing this we notice that the variables x, y, etc. which occur also in $\mathscr{L}$ are assigned intensional objects which are true at exactly one world. So we need to be able to express the fact that a variable in effect denotes a single world.

$$Wx =_{df} MTx \wedge \forall y(L(Tx \supset Ty) \vee L(Tx \supset {\sim}Ty))$$

It might be wise to show that Wx really does mean what it is supposed to. Let $\mu*$ be an assignment to the variables of $\mathscr{L}*$ in any model $\langle W,R,D,V*\rangle$ in which in every world some members of D satisfy T and some do not and let $w* \in W$:

LEMMA 18.3 $V_{\mu*}^*(Wx,w*) = 1$ iff there is some w such that $w*Rw$ and $\langle\mu*(x)(w'),w'\rangle \in V*(T)$ iff $w' = w$.

This of course is what it takes to ensure that $\mu*(x)$ corresponds with an assignment within $\mathscr{L}$ in terms of the definition, since we may define the corresponding $\mu(x)$ as the unique w such that $\langle\mu*(x)(w),w\rangle \in V*(T)$. We prove the lemma as follows.

(a) Suppose that $w*Rw$ and $\langle\mu*(x)(w'),w'\rangle \in V*(T)$ iff $w' = w$. Then clearly $V_{\mu*}^*(MTx,w) = 1$. And if $w' \neq w$, $V_{\mu*}^*(Tx,w') = 0$ and so $V_{\mu*}^*(Tx \supset Ty,w') = 1$ and $V_{\mu*}^*(Tx \supset {\sim}Ty,w') = 1$. For w, if $\langle\mu*(y)(w),w\rangle \in V*(T)$ then $V_{\mu*}^*(Tx \supset Ty,w') = 1$ and if $\mu*(y)(w) \notin V*(T)$ then $V_{\mu*}^*(Tx \supset {\sim}Ty,w') = 1$. So either $V_{\mu*}^*(L(Tx \supset Ty),w) = 1$ or $V_{\mu*}^*(L(Tx \supset {\sim}Ty),w) = 1$.

(b) Suppose that $V_{\mu*}^*(Wx,w*) = 1$. Then since $V_{\mu*}^*(MTx,w*) = 1$ there is some w such that $w*Rw$ and $\langle\mu*(x)(w),w\rangle \in V*(T)$. So suppose there were also some $w' \neq w$ such that $w*Rw'$ and $\langle\mu*(x)(w'),w'\rangle \in V*(T)$. Let ρ be a y-alternative of $\mu*$ such that $\langle\rho(y)(w),w\rangle \notin V*(T)$ but $\langle\rho(y)(w'),w'\rangle \in V*(T)$. Then $V_\rho^*(Tx \supset Ty,w) = 0$, and so $V_\rho^*(L(Tx \supset Ty),w*) = 0$ and $V_\rho^*(Tx \supset {\sim}Ty,w') = 0$ and so $V_\rho^*(L(Tx \supset {\sim}Ty),w*) = 0$. So $V_{\mu*}^*(\forall y(L(Tx \supset Ty) \vee L(Tx \supset {\sim}Ty)),w*) = 0$. Thus

$V_{\mu*}^*(Wx,w^*) = 0$, contradicting its assumed truth. This proves the lemma.

The consequence of these results may be summed up in the following theorem; where $\langle W,R \rangle$ is any frame in which there is some w^* such that w^*Rw for every $w \in W$.

THEOREM 18.4 For any wff α of $\mathcal{L}$ and any frame $\langle W,R \rangle$, α is valid on $\langle W,R \rangle$ iff $(L(\exists xTx \wedge \exists x \sim Tx) \wedge Wx_1 \wedge \ldots \wedge Wx_n) \supset \tau(\alpha)$ is valid on every IO model $\langle W,R,D,V^* \rangle$ based on $\langle W,R \rangle$, where $x_1, \ldots, x_n$ are the individual variables free in α.

Proof: (a) Suppose $\langle W,R \rangle$ is a frame where w^*Rw for all $w \in W$, and suppose $V_\mu(\alpha) = 0$. Since w^* can see every world then it can see each $\mu(x)$. For definiteness let $\langle W,R,D,V^* \rangle$ be an IO-model based on $\langle W,R \rangle$ in which $D = \{1,0\}$ and $V^*(T) = \{\langle 1,w \rangle : w \in W\}$. Then, where μ^* is an assignment which corresponds with μ, $V_{\mu*}^*(\tau(\alpha),w^*) = 0$. But if μ^* corresponds with μ, then $V_{\mu*}^*(Wx,w^*) = 1$ for every variable x free in α. Further, for each world w, $\exists xTx$ and $\exists x \sim Tx$ must both be true in w, and so $V_{\mu*}^*(L(\exists xTx \wedge \exists x \sim Tx),w^*) = 1$. So $V_{\mu*}^*((L(\exists xTx \wedge \exists x \sim Tx) \wedge Wx_1 \wedge \ldots \wedge Wx_n) \supset \tau(\alpha),w^*) = 0$.

(b) Suppose there is some w such that $V_\mu^*(((L(\exists xTx \wedge \exists x \sim Tx) \wedge Wx_1 \wedge \ldots \wedge Wx_n) \supset \tau(\alpha)),w) = 0$. Then there are $w_1 \ldots w_n$ such that wRw_i for $1 \leq i \leq n$ and $\langle \mu^*(x_i)(w'),w' \rangle \in V^*(T)'$ iff $w' = w_i$. Let μ be an assignment to $\mathcal{L}$ such that

(i) $\mu(x_i) = w_i$.

and, for any w' such that wRw',

(ii) $w' \in \mu(\phi)$ iff $\langle \mu^*(x_\phi),w' \rangle \in V^*(T)$.

Since $V_{\mu*}^*(L(\exists xTx \wedge \exists x \sim Tx),w) = 1$ and wRw', there must be some $u \in D$ such that $\langle u,w' \rangle \in V^*(T)$ and some $v \in D$ such that $\langle v,w' \rangle \notin V^*(T)$, and so there will be a μ satisfying (ii), and since $V_\mu^*(Wx_1 \wedge \ldots \wedge Wx_n,w) = 1$, lemma 18.3 guarantees that there is a μ satisfying (i). But then μ and μ^* correspond and so since $V_{\mu*}^*(\tau(\alpha),w) = 0$ and wRw_i then $V_\mu(\alpha) = 0$.

This proves the theorem.

The unaxiomatizability of IO systems now follows from the

unaxiomatizability of the corresponding second-order logics, since if the IO systems were axiomatizable we could effectively enumerate the valid wff of $\mathcal{L}$ by generating their translations. So we will get an unaxiomatizability result for an IO system for $\mathcal{E}$-validity in any class $\mathcal{E}$ of strongly generated frames (i.e. frames where some w^* can see every world) for which the corresponding second-order logic is not axiomatizable. In particular any subsystem of S4.3.1 will be unaxiomatizable since the generated frames of such systems will include some in which R has a first member and is linear, transitive and discrete. Such frames enable a successor predicate to be defined and enable the statement of the Peano axioms for second-order arithmetic by a finite set of wff whose conjunction we may refer to as Ax. So where S is contained in S4.3.1 and $\mathcal{E}$ is the class of all frames for S, then Ax $\supset \alpha$ will be $\mathcal{E}$-valid iff α is a truth of arithmetic. Since second-order arithmetic is not axiomatizable then neither is $\mathcal{E}$-validity. Fine has also obtained this result for all systems contained in the Brouwerian system B.[7]

The unaxiomatizability result is in fact very strong since it applies to that fragment of $\mathcal{L}^*$ which contains only a single one-place predicate. (Obviously if that fragment is unaxiomatizable so is the full language.) The fragment need not even contain an identity predicate.

Intensional objects and descriptions

There is a natural connection between definite descriptions and intensional objects. Take the example of the number of planets. In each possible world there is one and only one number which is the number of planets, but in different worlds it is different numbers. In the case of the number of the planets then the intensional object corresponding to it would be the function which in each world has as its value the number which is the number of planets in that world. The problem is how to use intensional objects to bring out the difference between (13) and (14) on p. 320. Recall that intensional objects were introduced as things to be the values of the individual variables to prevent the validity of LI. So consider what happens to the wff

(1) $L\psi x$

when ψ means 'is odd' and μ assigns to x the intensional object which is the number of the planets.

$V_\mu(L\psi x, w) = 1$ iff for every w' such that wRw', $V_\mu(L\psi x, w') = 1$. And this will be so iff $\langle \mu(x)(w'), w' \rangle \in V(\phi)$. Now whether a number is odd or not does not depend on which world we are in and so $\langle \mu(w'),w' \rangle$ will be in $V(\psi)$ iff $\mu(x)(w')$ is odd. Assuming a sense of necessity in which there are accessible worlds in which there are an even number of planets there will be some worlds w' accessible to w in which $\mu(x)(w')$, the number of planets in w', is *not* odd, and so (1) is false in w. That gives us the sense represented by (13) on p. 320. To get (14) we would assign to x the number which is the number of planets in the actual world w that we begin with, say 9. Or rather we assign the function whose value in *every* world, is the number of planets in *this* world. So in every world, however many planets there are in *that* world, it is 9 which is claimed to be odd. And since 9 is odd in every world this is true.

It is not difficult to see that, as it stands, this solution is inadequate. For consider a frame $\langle W,R \rangle$ in which $W = \{w_1,w_2\}$ and $w_1 R w_2$ and $w_2 R w_1$. I.e. there are two worlds and each can see the other but neither can see itself. In such a frame the principle

LL $\alpha \equiv LL\alpha$

is valid, no matter what values are assigned to any symbols in α. In particular where $\langle W,R,D,I,V \rangle$ is any model based on $\langle W,R \rangle$ and μ is any assignment to the variables and ϕ any one-place predicate and $w \in W$,

(2) $V_\mu(\phi x,w) = V_\mu(LL\phi x,w)$

But now consider the model in which $D = \{u_1,u_2\}$ and $V(\phi) = \{\langle u_1,w_1 \rangle, \langle u_2,w_2 \rangle\}$ and consider the wff which would be expressed on the Russellian account by

(3) $L(\imath x\phi x)L\phi x$

It is clear that

(4) $(\imath x\phi x)\phi x$

is true, and true in each world. For in each world exactly one thing is ϕ, and it is indeed ϕ. But (3) is false. For in w_1 it says that in w_2 the thing which is ϕ there, in w_2, is also ϕ in w_1, and that is false. But if we try to formalize (3) as

343

(5) $LL\phi x$

and capture the ambiguity by different assignments to x the validity of **LL** will make sure that (5) is always equivalent to ϕx.

We shall describe a way out of this problem taken by Thomason and Stalnaker,[8] though we shall not present it in exactly the same form that they do. The aim is to keep $\imath x\phi x$ as a *term* expression, i.e. an expression which can replace a variable in a wff. This contrasts with the Russellian account which, at least in a modal LPC, treats definite descriptions as quantifiers (though of course defines them ultimately in terms of the resources of ordinary modal LPC with identity.) However they do not want the individual *variables* to range over intensional objects. So LI and LNI are true for variables in the form

LI $x = y \supset L\, x = y$

and

LNI $x \neq y \supset L\, x \neq y$

But we do not have

(6) $\imath x\phi x = \imath x\psi x \supset L(\imath x\phi x = \imath x\psi x)$

or the corresponding version of LNI. $\imath x\phi x$ is assigned as its value the intensional object whose value in each world is the unique individual which satisfies ϕ in that world. Where ϕ is not true of a unique individual in each world $\imath x\phi x$ can denote some arbitrary intensional object.

Given that the *variables* now range only over ordinary objects we may express the distinction between (13) and (14) on p. 320 as

(7) $L\psi(\imath x\phi x)$

and

(8) $\exists y(y = (\imath x\phi x) \wedge L\psi y)$

Intensional predicates

A feature of the CI semantics is that while the individual variables range over I, the predicates still apply to D. Given that the domain of

344

quantification is I a plausible alternative would seem to be to allow the predicates to apply to members of I. And in fact if our models admit intensional objects there would seem to be no philosophical objection to this. Members of D can then qualify as 'degenerate' intensional objects, where $i(w) = i(w')$ for every w and $w' \in W$. So let us now say that where ϕ is an n-place predicate, $V(\phi)$ is now a set of $n+1$-tuples $\langle i_1, \ldots, i_n, w \rangle$ where $i_1, \ldots, i_n$ are taken from I rather than from D.

This however raises a question as far as identity is concerned. Under what conditions do we want $x = y$ to be true in a world w? One suggestion is that $V_\mu(x = y, w) = 1$ iff $\mu(x)(w) = \mu(y)(w)$. But this has the consequence that even I2″ is no longer valid. For let i_1 and i_2 be two distinct intensional objects whose values coincide in w but not in all other worlds. Then let ϕ be a one-place predicate such that $\langle i_1, w \rangle \in V(\phi)$ but $\langle i_2, w \rangle \notin V(\phi)$. Since predicates now apply to members of I, and since i_1 and i_2 are distinct, this is a possible assignment. Now suppose that $\mu(x) = i_1$ and $\mu(y) = i_2$. Then $V_\mu(x = y, w) = 1$, $V_\mu(\phi x, w) = 1$, but $V_\mu(\phi y, w) = 0$. And this falsifies I2″ at w.

And in fact given that the predicates now apply to members of I, it seems that the identity predicate ought to also, and in that case we should let $V(\phi_=)$ be the set of all and only triples $\langle i, i, w \rangle$ for $i \in I$ and $w \in W$. This certainly validates I2″, but it also validates LI, and therefore the full I2. It also validates LNI, and in fact it is not difficult to see that with this semantics for $\phi_=$ we are back with the LNI systems. For suppose that we begin with a model $\langle W, R, D, I, V \rangle$. We define the corresponding model $\langle W', R', D', V' \rangle$ by letting $W' = W$, $R' = R$, $D' = I$, $V' = V$, and dropping all reference to D. Since an assignment μ in $\langle W, R, D, I, V \rangle$ gives values from I, and since the predicates are assigned n-tuples from I and W, we need make no other changes in moving from $\langle W, R, D, I, V \rangle$ to $\langle W, R, D', V \rangle$, and an obvious induction establishes that for all $w \in W(W')$ and all assignments μ, $V_\mu(\alpha, w) = V_\mu(\alpha, w)$.

Moving in the other direction, given a model $\langle W, R, D, V \rangle$ we may move to a model $\langle W', R', D', I, V' \rangle$ by letting $W' = W$, $R' = R$, $D' = D$, and I be the set of all functions from W into D (i.e. the set of all intensional objects based on W and D). Let $I^- \subseteq I$ be the set of constant functions i_u for $u \in D$, such that $i_u(w) = u$ for every $w \in W$. For V′ proceed as follows: Nominate some $i^* \in I^-$ and, for any $i \in I$, if $i \in I^-$ let i' be i and if $i \in I - I^-$ let i' be i^*. What this means is that i' is i if i *is* a constant function, and i' is i^* if i is *not* a constant function. The idea is that i^* will be the representative in I^- of each non-constant function in I. Each i' will therefore be i_u for some $u \in D$, and we put $\langle i_{u_1}, \ldots, i_{u_n}, w \rangle \in V'(\phi)$ iff $\langle u_1, \ldots, u_n, w \rangle \in V(\phi)$. Since each $i' \in I^-$ is i_u for some u, $V'(\phi)$ will be completely determined. For an assignment μ with $\langle W, R, D, V \rangle$ we let μ' be the corresponding assignment such that $\mu'(x)(w) = \mu(x)$ for every $w \in W$. A straightforward induction makes $V'_{\mu'}(\alpha, w) = V_\mu(\alpha, w)$ for every wff α and every $w \in W$. What this means is that a wff will be valid according to the intensional-object semantics in which predicates can apply to these objects iff it is valid according to the original LNI semantics.

This result holds for systems without identity, and even for systems with identity if $\phi_=$ is merely required to respect I1, I2 and LNI. But of course in this model $V'(\phi_=)$ need not be identity even though $V(\phi_=)$ is, and the question is whether there is an equivalent full model in which it is identity. One way of showing that there is is to adapt the completeness proof in Chapter 14 so that it applies to non-denumerable languages. For one can map the domain of all intensional objects based on D and W onto any model whose domain of individuals is the cardinality of all functions from W into D. The changes required in the proof of theorem 14.2 on p. 259 are in fact non-trivial, and lie beyond the scope of this book.

It is worth reflecting a little at this point on the philosophical interpretation of $\langle W, R, D, I, V \rangle$ models with intensional predicates. In these models the predicates apply to members of I and the assignments to the variables apply to members of I. So these models may be held to represent a philosophical or metaphysical decision to regard the 'objects' about which the predicates speak and over which we quantify as themselves made up from more basic objects. While this may be significant from a metaphysical point of view it does not affect the *logic*. The $\langle W, R, D, V \rangle$ models after all do not have anything to say about what D may be, and there is nothing at all to prevent D being a class of intensional objects based on another class of more basic primitive objects.[9]

It might be instructive to see why the proof of unaxiomatizability on pp. 335−342 does not carry over to systems with intensional predicates. Look for instance at the induction for $\forall \phi \alpha$ in the proof of theorem 18.2. It is required that there be a ρ^* in $\mathscr{L}^*$ corresponding to an assignment ρ in $\mathscr{L}$. This means that $\rho^*(x_\phi)$ is some intensional object i such that for any $w \in W$, $\langle i(w), w \rangle \in V^*(T)$ iff $w \in \rho(\phi)$. On the assumption that in every world w there is a $u \in D$ such that $\langle u, w \rangle \in V^*(T)$ and a $v \in W$ such that $\langle v, w \rangle \notin V^*(T)$ we can let $i(w)$ be u or v as appropriate. This puts no constraints whatsoever on $V^*(T)$ except that at each world it satisfy $\exists x Tx \land \exists x \sim Tx$. But consider what happens if $V^*(T)$ is an intensional predicate. Then we would need to require that $\langle i,w \rangle \in V^*(T)$ iff $w \in \mu(\phi)$, and the problem is that there may be no such i. For instance suppose there are two worlds w_1 and w_2, and two intensional objects i_1 and i_2 with $\langle i_1,w_1 \rangle \in V^*(T)$ and $\langle i_2,w_2 \rangle \in V^*(T)$, but $\langle i,w_1 \rangle \notin V^*(T)$ for every i except i_1, and $\langle i,w_2 \rangle \notin V^*(T)$ for every i except i_2. Then where $\rho(\phi) = \{w_1,w_2\}$ there is *no* i such that $\langle \rho^*(i),w \rangle \in V^*(T)$ iff $w \in \rho(\phi)$.

If we have a coincidence predicate, $\approx$, meaning by that a predicate true of a pair $\langle i_1,i_2 \rangle$ at w iff $i_1(w) = i_2(w)$ then the argument of pp. 335–342 will apply as before to yield a non-axiomatizability result, for we may nominate some variable x^* to denote the 'true' and define Tx as $x \approx x^*$.[10]

Exercises — 18

18.1 Produce a CI model in which $L\exists x \phi x \supset \exists x L \phi x$ fails.

18.2 Show that $\forall x \exists y(x = y \land \forall z(x = z \supset L(x = y \supset x = z)))$ is valid in IO-models in which I is all intensional objects.

18.3 Prove that LNI is not a theorem of S4 + I.

18.4 Show how to express arithmetic in propositional modal logic with propositional quantifiers.

*18.5 Prove that the logic of S5 with quantification over all intensional objects is S5 + CI + the two schemata $L\exists x \alpha \supset \exists x L \alpha$ and $\forall x \exists y(x = y \land \forall z(x = z \supset L(x = y \supset x = z)))$.

*18.6 Set out a semantics for the approach to definite descriptions attributed to Thomason and Stalnaker on p. 344. Provide an axiomatic system for it and prove completeness.

18.7 Show that adding intensional predicates validates LI (in its unrestricted form) and LNI.

18.8 Show that if $\langle W,R,D,V \rangle$ is a model in the sense of Chapter 13 in which D has as many members as functions from the set of variables into W then there is an IO-model $\langle W,R,D,I,V^* \rangle$ in which I is the set of all functions from D into W and any wff α is valid in $\langle W,R,D,I,V^* \rangle$ iff it is valid in $\langle W,R,D,V \rangle$.

18.9 Carry out the proof that if we have a coincidence predicate, $\approx$, meaning by that a predicate true of a pair $\langle i_1,i_2 \rangle$ at w iff $i_1(w) = i_2(w)$ then the argument of pp. 335 − 342 will yield a non-axiomatizability result for IO systems with intensional predicates.

Notes

[1] See Kanger 1957b.

[2] Quine 1953, p. 148, where however the example is used to illustrate a somewhat different point.

[3] See Carnap 1947, p. 47, and Frege 1892.

[4] Such a semantics is presented in Parks 1974. The change from $\mu(x,w)$ to $\mu(x)(w)$ is not entirely trivial. See Parks and Smith 1974.

[5] Kanger 1957b, Hintikka 1961, 1963.

[6] The history of this problem is somewhat obscure in that the result has been 'known' for some time though without making it into the literature. R.H. Thomason 1970b, p. 132 claims that David Kaplan informed him of the result but that it is unpublished and appears only in Kaplan's PhD dissertation, and Garson 1980 refers to a mimeographed report by Kamp of work by Scott and Kripke. As far as we can tell the first published proof of the unaxiomatizability of this semantics is in Garson 1984. Kripke 1992, p. 72 points out that the problem of axiomatizing quantification over intensional objects may be reduced to that of axiomatizing quantification over propositions, for which Fine 1970, p. 343 claims that an unaxiomatizability result obtains via a translation into second-order arithmetic. This is elaborated on pp. 284 − 302 of Garson 1984 where a system of arithmetic is developed by means of propositional quantifiers, and the unaxiomatizability of quantification over intensional objects is reduced to it. For S5 with a coincidence predicate Kripke 1992, p. 72 adds to S5 + CI the two schemata $L\exists x\alpha \supset \exists x L\alpha$ and $\forall x\exists y(x = y \wedge \forall z(x = z \supset L(x = y \supset x = z)))$.

[7] Fine 1970, p. 343.

[8] Thomason and Stalnaker 1968, Stalnaker and Thomason 1968.

[9] Among the intensional objects are those mentioned on p. 345 in which the value of i is a constant function whose value is the same individual in every world. Such functions are sometimes called 'individual essences'. It is also possible to follow Plantinga 1976 and take individual essences as basic. Plantinga does this because he does not believe that there are individuals in non-actual possible worlds. In place of other-worldly individuals he substitutes individual essences. What the present paragraph points out is that whatever the metaphysical importance of this distinction, it does not affect the logic.

[10] Kripke 1992, p. 73, points out that in this case, even for S5, with intensional predicates we obtain the same degree of incompleteness as full second-order logic.

19

FURTHER ISSUES

This chapter discusses some further issues in modal predicate logic. Like Chapter 12 it is not intended to be in any way complete.

First-order modal theories
In discussing the notation $\Lambda \vdash \alpha$ we observed on p. 211 that there were dangers in interpreting it as meaning that there is a proof using the members of Λ as additional axioms of α. When we move to the predicate calculus the same care is needed. In fact even more care is needed because of the use of first-order predicate logic as a language for a *first-order theory*. Consider for instance a (non-modal) theory of a predicate P which is intended to mean that x and y are causally connected, and suppose that we are working in a scientific theory in which it is assumed that there are pairs of things not causally connected. Then among the axioms might be

(1) $\exists x \exists y \sim Pxy$

Any collection Λ of axioms determines a first-order theory and, provided the axioms are all closed wff, there is no problem in defining $\Lambda \vdash \alpha$ by saying that there is a proof in LPC of α from Λ where the axioms and rules are those of LPC (PC, $\forall 1$, $\forall 2$, and MP) together with the members of Λ. When we move to the modal case the situation is more complicated. Consider a theory in which (1) is an axiom. On the assumption that (1) is true but not necessary we cannot allow N as a rule of inference, for using it we could derive the false wff $L\exists x \exists y \sim Pxy$.

For that reason the idea of a first-order theory is less useful in modal predicate logic than in non-modal predicate logic. We can of course define $\Lambda \vdash \alpha$ as on p. 211 by saying that it holds iff there are $\beta_1, \ldots, \beta_n \in \Lambda$ such that (for some given system of modal LPC)

$$\vdash (\beta_1 \wedge \ldots \wedge \beta_n) \supset \alpha$$

and then there is no problem. Or equally one could set out a natural deduction system for modal LPC.

One case in which a modal first-order theory would cause less trouble would be where the axioms *are* supposed to be necessary. For instance if P means 'is less than' such wff as $\forall x \sim Pxx$ or $\forall x \forall y \forall z((Pxy \wedge Pyx) \supset Pxz)$ are not merely true but necessary. Of course to satisfy N they must be not merely necessary but necessarily necessary and so on. For if say $\forall x \sim Pxx$ is an axiom then by N $L\forall x \sim Pxx$ is a theorem, and so is $LL\forall x \sim Pxx$, and so on.

Multiple indexing

Consider how to formalize the sentence

(1) It might have been that everyone actually happy was sad.

Use ϕ to mean 'is happy' and ψ to mean 'is sad'. Obviously we cannot represent (1) by

(2) $M\forall x(\phi x \supset \psi x)$

for that envisages a possible world in which all those happy are sad, and this can only be so if no one at all is happy. (1) speaks about another world in which those who are happy in the actual world are sad. Nor can (1) be expressed as

(3) $\forall x(\phi x \supset M\psi x)$

(3) is closer but it does not require a world in which all those actually happy are sad. For each actual happy person there is a world in which that person is sad, but it need not be a world in which the other actually happy people are sad. Consider

(4) Every loser might have won

350

which could be true even in a game which permits no more than one winner. In this case

(5) It might have been that every actual loser won

would be false. Among the ways of dealing with this problem is to introduce what is often called an 'actually' operator, A. (1) is then formalized as

(6) $M\forall x(A\phi x \supset \psi x)$

The problem with (6) is to give a semantics for A. We begin in a world w_1, and move to an accessible world w_2. But even though we are evaluating $A\phi x$ in w_2 we are interested in those who are happy in w_1. The solution is to evaluate wff at more than one index. In (6) when we come to evaluate

(7) $\forall x(A\phi x \supset \psi x)$

w_2 is called the *evaluation index* and w_1 the *reference index*. Every wff is now evaluated at a pair of worlds, though in most cases the second world (the reference index) is simply carried along as a parameter. In particular for an atomic wff the rule would be

[Vϕ2] $V_\mu(\phi x,\langle w_1,w_2\rangle) = 1$ iff $\langle \mu(x),w_1\rangle \in V(\phi)$.

As an example of how 'ordinary' operators behave look at what the rule for M becomes in a double-indexed semantics:

[VM2] $V_\mu(M\alpha,\langle w_1,w_2\rangle) = 1$ iff there is some w_3 such that w_1Rw_3 and $V_\mu(\alpha,\langle w_3,w_2\rangle) = 1$.

This means that M operates only on the evaluation world. Assume the PC operators and the quantifiers do too. A, however, has the following semantics:

[VA] $V_\mu(A\alpha,\langle w_1,w_2\rangle) = 1$ iff $V_\mu(\alpha,\langle w_2,w_2\rangle) = 1$

I.e. A turns the reference world into the evaluation world. We can illustrate this in the case of (6). We begin with a world w_1 which we assume to be both evaluation world and reference world.

(8) $V_\mu((6), \langle w_1, w_1 \rangle) = 1$

iff there is a world w_2 accessible from w_1 such that

(9) $V_\mu((7), \langle w_2, w_1 \rangle) = 1$

iff for every x-alternative ρ of μ

(10) $V_\rho(A\phi x \supset \psi x, \langle w_2, w_1 \rangle) = 1$

And (10) will hold iff either

(11) $V_\rho(A\phi x, \langle w_2, w_1 \rangle) = 0$

or

(12) $V_\rho(\psi x, \langle w_2, w_1 \rangle) = 1$

(12) will hold iff $\langle \rho(x) \rangle \in V(\psi)$, i.e. iff $\rho(x)$ is sad in w_2. By [VA] (11) will hold iff

(13) $V_\rho(\phi x, \langle w_1, w_1 \rangle) = 0$

and (13) holds iff $\rho(x)$ is not happy in w_1. So (6) does indeed hold in w_1 iff there is some accessible world w_2 such that everyone who is happy in w_1 is sad in w_2.

It is clear that corresponding to A there are a variety of other doubly indexed operators. The *locus classicus* of propositional logics of these is in a paper by Krister Segerberg.[1] Segerberg considers the following operators.

$\Box$, $\boxdot$, $\boxminus$, $\oplus$, $\ominus$, $\otimes$.

His semantics for these operators may be expressed by the following principles:

$V(\Box\alpha, \langle w_1, w_2 \rangle) = 1$ iff $V(\alpha, \langle w_3, w_4 \rangle) = 1$ for every w_3, $w_4 \in W$
$V(\boxdot\alpha, \langle w_1, w_2 \rangle) = 1$ iff $V(\alpha, \langle w, w_2 \rangle) = 1$ for every $w \in W$

$$V(\boxminus\alpha,\langle w_1,w_2\rangle) = 1 \text{ iff } V(\alpha,\langle w_1,w\rangle) = 1 \text{ for every } w \in W$$
$$V(\oplus\alpha,\langle w_1,w_2\rangle) = 1 \text{ iff } V(\alpha,\langle w_1,w_1\rangle) = 1$$
$$V(\ominus\alpha,\langle w_1,w_2\rangle) = 1 \text{ iff } V(\alpha,\langle w_2,w_2\rangle) = 1$$
$$V(\otimes\alpha,\langle w_1,w_2\rangle) = 1 \text{ iff } V(\alpha,\langle w_2,w_1\rangle) = 1$$

Segerberg then produces a system with 6 schemata which hold for various selections of wff with just one of these operators, and then a further eight principles which relate various combinations of operators. He then uses the method of canonical models to prove completeness. $\Box$ − $\boxminus$ are, as he notes, S5 modalities, while $\oplus$ − $\otimes$ are 'very strong K-modalities of rather unusual kinds'.

Doubly indexed logics can be extended to logics having even more indices, even infinitely many and have applications in the semantics of natural languages.[2]

Counterpart theory

We saw in Chapters 15 and 16 that the Barcan formula could be interpreted as expressing the view that exactly the same objects exist in all possible worlds. At the other extreme is the view, taken by David Lewis, that each world has its own domain of individuals and that these *never* overlap.[3] The semantics for modal predicate logic assumed in Chapters 13−17 makes essential use of the fact that the same individual can exist in more than one world and so the question arises of how to incorporate Lewis's view in a modal LPC.

One way to incorporate it is to use intensional objects, for then the domain of quantification is functions from W into D, and that domain can remain constant even if the value of an intensional object in one world is never the same as the value of an intensional object in another world. In this case we would use a $\langle W,R,D,I,V\rangle$ model, or rather a $\langle W,R,D,Q,I,V\rangle$ model since we want each world to have its own domain of individuals. We should require that when $w \neq w'$ then $D_w \cap D_{w'} = \varnothing$. If we use this technique we can see that it will make no difference to the logic since the domain of quantification is not D but I, and we may define an equivalent model $\langle W',R',D',V'\rangle$, by letting $D' = I$ and omitting both D and Q. As we remarked on p. 346 the nature of D' in $\langle W',R',D',V'\rangle$, however important it may be in metaphysics, has no effect on the logic. Looked at in this way Lewis's metaphysical views can be incorporated into modal systems with both LNI and BF.

However, this is not the approach Lewis takes. Lewis himself only provides a semantics for modal LPC indirectly, by giving a translation procedure for converting every wff of modal LPC into an extensional non-modal LPC in which there are variables for possible worlds and accessibility is represented by a two-place predicate. But this translation trivially induces a direct interpretation to a language of modal LPC.

One feature of Lewis's semantics is worth commenting on since it affects the interpretation of the predicates. Let us consider a one-place predicate ϕ. So far $V(\phi)$ has been a set of pairs of the form $\langle u,w \rangle$ with $u \in D$ and $w \in W$. But if u can exist only in one world *and we restrict our predicates to things which exist in that world* then we can assign to ϕ simply a set of individuals. Where $V^*(\phi)$ is a set of individuals then $V(\phi)$ will be the set of pairs $\langle u,w \rangle$ such that $u \in D_w$ and $u \in V^*(\phi)$. Conversely we put $u \in V^*(\phi)$ iff $\langle u,w \rangle \in V(\phi)$, where w is the unique world such that $u \in D_w$. Obviously this procedure would not work if u could be in more than one world, since it might be ϕ in w but not in w'. The $[V\phi]$, $[V\sim]$, $[V\vee]$ and $[V\forall']$ which are induced by Lewis's translation all remain the same, but $[VL]$ requires modification. A model for interpreting Lewis's theory may be defined as a 6-tuple $\langle W,R,D,Q,C,V \rangle$ in which $\langle W,R,D,Q,V \rangle$ is a model as for the systems in Chapter 16, but with the restriction that the domains of distinct worlds have no common members. C is a relation on D, where uCu' means that u' is a *counterpart* of u in another world. C satisfies the constraint that if u and u' are both in D_w then uCu' iff $u = u'$. Lewis's idea is that when we talk about what happens to an individual u in some other world, as we might when we say for instance that a particular table might have looked better nearer the window, we are not really referring to the very same individual in that other world, but are referring to its *counterpart*, to the thing in that other world which corresponds most closely with the thing in this world. The rule then is

[VL'] $V_\mu(L\alpha,w) = 1$ iff $V_\rho(\alpha,w') = 1$ for every w' such that wRw' and for every assignment ρ such that for every x free in α $\mu(x)C\rho(x)$ and $\rho(x) \in D_{w'}$.

We say that α is *valid* in such a model if it is true in every world for every assignment taken from the domain of that world.

What modal logic do we get with this semantics? Well, that depends on what conditions the counterpart relation C satisfies. The most stringent condition is that C is an equivalence relation, and that every individual has one and only one counterpart in every world. With this requirement it turns out that we get precisely the same semantics as for the LNI systems. For suppose that we have a model $\langle W,R,D,Q,C,V\rangle$. We define an equivalent model $\langle W',R',D',V'\rangle$ as follows. $W' = W$ and $R' = R$. For D' proceed as follows. Choose some world w^* in W, and let D' be D_{w^*} (i.e. $Q(w^*)$). For $u_1, \ldots ,u_n \in D'$ and $w \in W$ let $\langle u_1, \ldots ,u_n,w\rangle \in V'(\phi)$ iff, where $v_1, \ldots ,v_n$ are the unique members of D_w such that u_iCv_i for $1 \le i \le n$, $\langle v_1, \ldots ,v_n\rangle \in V(\phi)$. What this means is that we take the individuals of the new model to be the members of some selected world w^*, and stipulate that *they* are to do in another world w what their counterparts in w do in the original model.

In what follows we shall use μ and v for assignments within $\langle W,R,D,Q,C,V\rangle$ and ρ and σ for assignments within $\langle W',R',V'\rangle$. Given any $w \in W$ we shall say that ρ *corresponds* with μ in w provided that for every variable x, $\rho(x)$ is the unique $v \in D_w$ such that $\mu(x)Cv$.

LEMMA 19.1 Where α is any wff and $w \in W$, and μ and ρ are any assignments which correspond in w, then $V_\mu(\alpha,w) = V'_\rho(\alpha,w)$.

Suppose α is $\phi x_1...x_n$. Then $V'_\rho(\phi x_1...x_n,w) = 1$ iff

(i) $\langle \mu(x_1), \ldots ,\mu(x_n),w\rangle \in V'(\phi)$

Now if μ and ρ correspond in w, each $\rho(x_i)$, for $1 \le i \le n$, will be the unique v_i such that $\mu(x_i)Cv_i$. But then (i) will hold iff

(ii) $\langle \rho(x_1), \ldots ,\rho(x_n)\rangle \in V(\phi)$

and (ii) holds if $V_\mu(\phi x_1...x_n,w) = 1$.

So the lemma is proved for atomic wff. The induction for $\sim$ and $\lor$ is straightforward. So consider $\forall$ and suppose that ρ corresponds with μ in w.

Suppose $V_\mu(\forall x\alpha,w) = 0$. Then there is some x-alternative v of μ such that $V_v(\alpha,w) = 0$. Let σ be the x-alternative of ρ such that $\sigma(x)$ is the unique $u \in w^*$ (where w^* is the arbitrarily chosen member of W whose domain is D') such that $uCv(x)$. Since $v(x) \in D_w$ this means that v corresponds with σ in w, and so $V_\sigma(\alpha,w) = 0$. But σ is an x-alternative of ρ, and so $V'_\rho(\forall x\alpha,w) = 0$.

Suppose $V'_\rho(\forall x\alpha,w) = 0$. Then there is some x-alternative σ of ρ such that $V'_\sigma(\alpha,w) = 0$. Let v be the x-alternative of σ such that $v(x)$ is the unique $v \in D_w$ such that $\sigma(x)Cv$. Then v corresponds with σ in w and so $V_v(\alpha,w) = 0$. But v is an x-alternative of μ and so $V_\mu(\forall x\alpha,w) = 0$.

Suppose $V_\mu(L\alpha,w) = 0$. Then there is some w' such that wRw' and $V_v(\alpha,w') = 0$ where v corresponds with μ in w'. Now μ corresponds with ρ in w, and since C is transitive and v corresponds with μ in w' then v corresponds with ρ in w'. So $V'_\rho(\alpha,w') = 0$ and so $V'_\rho(L\alpha,w) = 0$. Suppose $V'_\rho(L\alpha,w) = 0$. Then there is some w' such that wRw' and $V_{\rho'}(\alpha,w) = 0$. Where v is an assignment which corresponds with ρ in w', then, by the induction hypothesis $V_v(\alpha,w') = 0$. Now μ corresponds with ρ in w, and so, since C is an equivalence relation, v corresponds with μ in w'. But then by [VL'], $V_\mu(L\alpha,w) = 0$.

Now it is clear, first that where $\langle W,R,D,Q,C,V\rangle$ and $\langle W',R',D',V'\rangle$ correspond in the way described the lemma entails that any wff α is valid in one iff it is valid in the other. Second, as we have seen, given a $\langle W,R,D,Q,C,V\rangle$ you can define a $\langle W',R',D',V'\rangle$, but also given a $\langle W',R',D',V'\rangle$ you can define an equivalent $\langle W,R,D,Q,C,V\rangle$ by taking D' and letting D_w be the set of pairs $\langle u,w\rangle$ for each $u \in D$, and letting $\langle u,w\rangle C\langle v,w'\rangle$ iff $u = v$.

This is in fact the way Lewis himself imagined someone claiming that counterpart theory is just ordinary modal predicate logic in disguise. For what we have shown is that if C is an equivalence relation and every individual has a counterpart in every world then the modal predicate logic of counterpart theory is just that of ordinary modal logic with the Barcan Formula. Lewis's reply is that C need not be an equivalence relation.[4] He wants it to be reflexive since everything is its own counterpart in its own world, and nothing else is its counterpart in its own world. If C is required to be reflexive but nothing else then, although **T** is valid, even such simple K-theorems as

(1) $L(\phi x \land \forall x\phi x) \supset L\forall x\phi x$

fail.[5] For consider the following model $\langle W,R,D,Q,C,V\rangle$:

$$W = \{w_1,w_2\}, R = W^2, D = \{u_1,u_2\}, D_{w_1} = \{u_1\}, D_{w_2} = \{u_2\}$$
$$C = \{\langle u_1,u_1\rangle, \langle u_2,u_2\rangle\}, V(\phi) = \{u_1\}$$

I.e., there are two worlds, each with one individual and no trans-world counterparts, and ϕ is only true of u_1 in w_1. Let μ be an assignment such that $\mu(x) \in D_{w_1}$, and consider any assignment ρ such that $\mu(y)C\rho(y)$ and

$\rho(y) \in D_{w_2}$ for every y free in $\phi x \land \forall x \phi x$. In fact there is no such ρ, and so, by [VL'], $V_\mu(L(\phi x \land \forall x \phi x), w_1) = 1$. But where $\sigma(y) = u_2$ for every y then $V_\sigma(\forall x \phi x, w_2) = 0$, and (trivially) $\mu(y) C \sigma(y)$ and $\sigma(y) \in D_{w_2}$ for every y free in $\forall x \phi x$. So $V_\mu(L \forall x \phi x, w_1) = 0$, and thus $V_\mu(L(\phi x \land \forall x \phi x) \supset L \forall x \phi x, w_1) = 0$ in this model.

The matter is different for closed formulae. In the case of a closed formula [VL'] reduces to [VL] since PA still holds in counterpart-theoretic semantics and the assignment to the variables does not affect the truth of closed wff.

Counterparts or intensional objects?

In counterpart theory the values assigned to individuals may change from world to world. Another way of realizing this possibility is by the assignment of intensional objects, and we shall now compare this with Lewis's semantics. We have seen that counterpart theory only becomes significant when the counterpart relation is not an equivalence relation, and then the rule for L requires that x be necessarily ϕ only if in every accessible world *all* its counterparts in that world are ϕ.

When we look at the semantics for intensional objects we see that although each particular intensional object has just one counterpart in each world there is nothing to stop distinct intensional objects coinciding in one world but differing in another. Suppose then that $i(w)$ and $i'(w)$ are the same object, say u. Then if $i(w') \neq i'(w')$ and $i(w')$ is v and $i'(w')$ is v' then we can say that v and v' are counterparts in w' of u.

Suppose that $\mu(x)$ is i and $\mu(y)$ is i' in the intensional objects semantics. Then $V_\mu(L\phi x, w) = 1$ iff ϕx is true in all accessible worlds, and in w' this will be so if v satisfies ϕ in w', while $V_\mu(L\phi y, w) = 1$ iff ϕy is true in all accessible worlds, and in w' this will be so if v' satisfies ϕ in w'. This feature of the intensional objects semantics embodies the assumption that it is the intensional object itself which determines what its counterparts are. For Lewis the range of the quantifier in each world is just the ordinary things in this world, and it is part of the model (and one might even say frame if you think that all but V should be part of the frame) to say what the counterpart relation is.

On the assumption that the counterpart relation is symmetrical, though not necessarily transitive, one can express counterpart theory in CI systems as follows. Wherever Lewis has $L\phi x$ this should be replaced by

(1) $\forall y(x = y \supset L\phi y)$

357

This translation is of course under the proviso that the domain I of intensional objects is so restricted that all the D_ws are disjoint and that where $u \in D_w$ and $v \in D_{w'}$ then uCv iff there is some $i \in$ I such that $i(w) = u$ and $i(w') = v$.

Lewis does not accept that C is in general symmetrical, but in the cases where it is this translation has the advantage that, being in a CI system with no extra logical symbols, all the principles of the propositional modal systems on which it is based carry over S+CI. By varying the translation we can also express what it would be for *some* counterpart of x to be ϕ in every world, viz.,

(2) $\exists y(x = y \land L\phi y)$

In order to express this in the modal logic of counterpart theory, we would need a different symbol, say L', satisfying

[VL''] $V_\mu(L\alpha,w) = 1$ iff for every w' such that wRw', there is some assignment ρ such that for every x in α, $\rho(x) \in D_{w'}$, and $\mu(x)C$ $\rho(x)$.

Notes

[1] Segerberg 1973b. Other work on multiply indexed logic has been done by Åqvist 1973 and Crossley and Humberstone 1977, Kuhn 1989 and others. The phenomenon was noticed for tense logic by Prior 1968 and discussed by Kamp 1971, Vlach 1973 and Gabbay and Rohrer 1979 and, more recently, Venema 1992. Theorems to the effect that 'actually' operators cannot be defined in ordinary modal predicate logic have been proved by Hazen 1976. See also Hodes 1984a and 1984b and Hazen 1990.

[2] Kuhn 1979 shows how to use multiple indexing to express the predicate calculus as a normal (multi-) modal propositional logic. Applications in the philosophy of language are discussed in Forbes 1989 and Cresswell 1990.

[3] The view was originally put forward in D.K. Lewis 1968. A more recent defence of the metaphysics underlying it is found in D.K. Lewis 1986.

[4] D.K. Lewis 1968 p.115. We read this passage as an acknowledgement that if the counterpart relation is an equivalence relation then there may be no more than a terminological difference between counterpart theory and the more standard semantics.

[5] We owe this point to Lin Woollaston, who is attempting to come up with a revision of [VL'] which would validate all of K and yet be acceptable to counterpart theorists. A discussion of counterpart-theoretic semantics for modal logic may also be found in Hazen 1979.

AXIOMS, RULES AND SYSTEMS

In this book, we have discussed many modal systems. These systems have often been introduced to illustrate various properties that modal systems possess. Our aim in this appendix is to list the axioms and rules which define these systems and present them together all in one place. This will show the wide range of modal systems which have been studied, and will enable readers to see at a glance the place each system occupies in a map of modal systems.

Axioms for normal systems

We shall first list the axioms which define the normal systems we have discussed, and give them the names they have been given in the text. In a few cases (mainly in exercises) axioms or systems have been introduced without giving them names, and in these cases a name has been supplied here. In other cases the axiom has been referred to by name in the notes, but without identifying it. Such axioms also will be listed here. And finally there are a few axioms discussed in other works but not in our text. Where an axiom is not discussed in the text a work is cited in which it is discussed. We do not pretend to provide a complete survey of axioms which have been suggested for modal systems.

Some axioms have alternative names. Mostly these derive from Lemmon and Scott 1977 and are used in Segerberg 1971, Chellas 1980 and by other authors. These names have been given in parentheses. We are assuming a language of modal propositional logic as defined on p. 16 in which L is taken as the primitive modal operator, and M is defined as $\sim L \sim$. Axioms are listed in order of introduction except for a few cases in which the first mention does not give adequate information.

K	$L(p \supset q) \supset (Lp \supset Lq)$	(p. 25)
T	$Lp \supset p$	(p. 42)
D	$Lp \supset Mp$	(p. 43)
4	$Lp \supset LLp$	(p. 53)
E	$Mp \supset LMp$	(**5**, p. 58)
B	$p \supset LMp$	(p. 62)
T$_c$	$p \supset Lp$	(p. 66)
Triv	$p \equiv Lp$	(p. 65)
Ver	Lp	(p. 67)
E$_1$	$LMLp \supset p$	(p. 69)
E$_2$	$MLp \supset LMLLp$	(p. 69)
D$_c$	$Mp \supset Lp$	(p. 123)
D1	$L(Lp \supset q) \vee L(Lq \supset p)$	(**Lem**, p. 128)
F	$(LMp \wedge LMq) \supset M(p \wedge q)$	(p. 131)
M	$LMp \supset MLp$	(p. 131)
G1	$MLp \supset LMp$	(p. 134)
W	$L(Lp \supset p) \supset Lp$	(p. 139)
MV	$MLp \vee Lp$	(p. 141)
R1	$MLp \supset (p \supset Lp)$	(p. 141)
BM	$p \supset LMMp$	(p. 141)
TM	$MLp \supset Mp$	(p. 141)
BV	$ML(p \wedge \sim p) \vee (q \supset LMq)$	(p. 141)
Lem$_0$	$L((p \wedge Lp) \supset q) \vee L((q \wedge Lq) \supset p)$	(p. 141)
H1	$p \supset L(Mp \supset p)$	(p. 142)
G$_0$	$M(p \wedge Lq) \supset L(p \wedge Mq)$	(p. 142)
Alt$_n$	$Lp_1 \vee L(p_1 \supset p_2) \vee \ldots \vee L((p_1 \wedge \ldots \wedge p_n) \supset p_{n+1})$	(p. 142)
4$_t$	$(Lp \wedge p) \supset LLp$	(p. 142)
J1	$L(L(p \supset Lp) \supset p) \supset p$	(**Grz**, p. 142)
Mk	$L(LLp \supset Lq) \supset (Lp \supset q)$	(p. 154)
Mk*	$L(LLp \supset LLLp) \supset (Lp \supset LLp)$	(p. 156)
Seg$_n$	$(MMp_1 \wedge \ldots \wedge MMp_n) \supset M(Mp_1 \wedge \ldots \wedge Mp_n)$	(p. 158)
H	$L(Lp \equiv p) \supset Lp$	(p. 160)
VB	$MLp \vee L(L(Lq \supset q) \supset q)$	(p. 169)
KH$_n$	$L^n(L(Lp \equiv p) \supset Lp)$	(p. 170)
N1	$L(L(p \supset Lp) \supset p) \supset (MLp \supset p)$	(**Dum**, p. 180)
G'	$M^m L^n p \supset L^j M^k p$	(p. 182)
MT$_n$	$M((Lp_1 \supset p_1) \wedge \ldots \wedge (Lp_n \supset p_n))$	(p. 185)

B⁺	$Lp \supset (Mq \supset L(Lp \vee Mq))$	(p. 219)
Z	$L(Lp \supset p) \supset (MLp \supset Lp)$	(Segerberg 1971, p.84)
P	$MLMp \supset (p \supset Lp)$	(Segerberg 1971, p.152)
Zem	$LMLp \supset (p \supset Lp)$	(Segerberg 1971, p.152)
Sch	$L(MLp \supset Lp) \vee Lq \vee L(q \supset r)$	(Segerberg 1971, p.159)
M18	$(MLp \supset p) \vee (LMq \supset MLq)$	(p. 284)

Some normal systems

We define a system S as a class of wff whose members are called its
theorems. We write $\vdash_s \alpha$ for $\alpha \in S$. A normal system of modal
propositional logic (see p. 111) is a class S of wff of modal propositional
logic which contains all PC-valid wff and **K**, $(L(p \supset q) \supset (Lp \supset Lq)$,
p. 25); and has the property that if α and β are in S then so is anything
obtainable from them by the use of the following rules:

US: $\vdash \alpha \rightarrow \vdash \alpha[\beta_1/p_1, \ldots, \beta_n/p_n]$.

MP: $\vdash \alpha, \alpha \supset \beta \rightarrow \vdash \beta$.

N: $\vdash \alpha \rightarrow \vdash L\alpha$.

The weakest normal modal system is called K (p. 24) and every normal
system S may be expressed as $K + \Lambda$ (see pp. 39, 111) where Λ is the
set of proper axioms of S. Where Λ contains just a single wff α then S
may be expressed as $K + \alpha$. Where S is a system of modal logic we shall
use the notations $S + \Lambda$ or $S + \alpha$ analogously with $K + \Lambda$ and $K + \alpha$
to denote the system obtained from S by adding the members of Λ as
additional axioms.

The following list identifies most of the normal modal systems which
have been given names in the text, and a number of others as well. In
addition, any normal modal system may be defined by means of a list of
axioms. Thus, although this system has not, to the best of our knowledge,
been studied, KHLem$_0$ would denote $K + H + Lem_0$. In some cases,
e.g. $T + W$, the resulting system will be inconsistent in the sense of
containing all wff. (We shall denote the inconsistent system by $\mathscr{L}$.) Note
that the same system can easily result from different combinations of
axioms. Thus $T + E = T + 4 + B$. Where a system is characterized by
a simple semantics this has been mentioned.

T	K + **T**	(M, p. 41, reflexive frames)
D	K + **D**	(p. 43, serial frames)
S4	T + **4**	(KT4, p. 53, reflexive transitive frames)
S5	T + **E**	(KTE, KT5, p. 58, equivalence frames)
B	T + **B**	(KTB, p. 62, reflexive symmetrical frames)

K4	K + **4**	(p. 64, transitive frames)
KB	K + **B**	(p. 64, symmetrical frames)
KD4	D + **4**	(p. 64, serial reflexive frames)
KDB	D + **B**	(p. 64, serial symmetrical frames)
Triv	K + **Triv**	(pp. 65, 108, one reflexive world)
Ver	K + **Ver**	(pp. 66, 108, one dead end)
KE	K + **E**	(p. 69, euclidian frames)
KBE	K + **B** + **E**	(symmetrical euclidian frames)
T_c	K + T_c	(p. 70, one-world frames)
$S4_n$	K + 4_n	(p. 70, If $wR^{n+1}w'$ then wR^nw')
KD_c	K + D_c	(p. 123, every world can see at most one world)
KW	K + **W**	(p. 139, finite irreflexive transitive frames)
$KAlt_n$	K + Alt_n	(p. 142, every world can see at most n-worlds)
BSeg	B + Seg_n $(1 \le n)$	(p. 158)
KH	K + **H**	(p. 160, incomplete, KH frames characterize KW)
B^+	B + B^+	(p. 219)

An area of modal logic which was singled out for special study in earlier days was extensions of S4. Not all of the following are discussed in the present text. Details may be found in Sobociński, 1964a–c.

S4.1	S4 + **N1**	
S4.2	S4 + **G1**	(p. 134, convergent S4 frames)
S4.2.1	S4.2 + **N1**	
S4.3	S4 + **D1**	(KT4Lem, p. 128, connected S4 frames)
S4.3.1	S4.3 + **N1**	(D, p. 180, discrete time)
S4.4	S4 + **R1**	(p. 284, $(w_1Rw_2 \land w_1 \ne w_2 \land w_1Rw_3) \supset w_3Rw_2$)
S4.9	S4.4 + **M18**	(p. 284)
S4M	S4 + **M**	(K1, S4.1, p. 131, reflexive final frames)

(K1 is Sobociński's name for S4M)

K1.1	S4 + **J1**	(p. 142, finite partial orderings)
K1.2	K1 + **H1**	
K2	S4.2 + **M**	
K2.1	K2 + **J1**	
K3.1	S4.3 + **J1**	(D*, p. 191, finite reflexive linear frames)
K4′	K2 + **R1**	(K4, S4.2MR1)

(K4 is Sobociński's name, see Hughes and Cresswell 1968, p. 266; K4′ should not be confused with the K4 of p. 64.)

Another area of study has been extensions of K4 not containing S4. (K4 here is K + $Lp \supset LLp$, not the system Sobociński calls K4, which we have called K4'.) In many cases these systems are characterized by transitive irreflexive frames which correspond with the reflexive frames which characterize extensions of S4. Thus, for instance, where S4.3 is characterized by reflexive connected frames K4.3 (K + **Lem₀**) is characterized by transitive irreflexive frames in which for $w \neq w'$, either wRw' or $w'Rw$, and so on. These systems are discussed in Volume 2 of Segerberg 1971. Despite their names, they are not extensions of the K1−K3.1 mentioned in the previous list.

K4Z   K4 + **Z**
K4.2   K4 + **G₀**
K4.2Z   K4.2 + **Z**
K4.2W   K4.2 + **W**
K4.3   K4 + **Lem₀**
K4.3Z   K4.3 + **Z**
K4.3W   K4.3 + **W**

A diagram showing most of the normal modal systems listed here apears in Table I on p. 367.

Non-normal systems

Non-normal systems are systems which lack the rule of necessitation. In all other respects the ones that concern us are like normal systems. As described in Chapter 11 the earliest modal systems were in fact non-normal. We shall follow Segerberg 1971 in dividing non-normal systems into 'quasi-normal', 'regular' and 'quasi-regular'. Quasi-normal systems are systems which contain all theorems of K, so that N applies to those wff, but contain extra axioms as well, to which N need not apply. Semantically these systems are studied by assuming a subset of 'normal' worlds and defining validity in terms of truth only in those worlds. In this book we have not been concerned with quasi-normal systems. (But see p. 208, n25.)

Regular systems are like normal systems except that N is replaced by the rule R* $\vdash \alpha \supset \beta \rightarrow \vdash L\alpha \supset L\beta$. The weakest regular system may be called E2⁰, and its basis consists simply in replacing N by R*. Semantically its frames are as described on p. 208, n25, in which in addition to normal worlds there may be non-normal worlds in which $L\alpha$ is false for every wff. If we insist that there *must* be such worlds we validate $MM\alpha$ (or $\sim LL\alpha$), and obtain a system we might call E6⁰ by adding MMp as an additional axiom. If we insist that *all* worlds be non-normal then we add Mp. E2 results from E2^0 by the addition of **T** and its frames are those in which R is reflexive over normal worlds. E3^0 is E2^0 + $L(p \supset q) \supset L(Lp \supset Lq)$ and E3 is E2^0 + **T**. In E3 frames R is transitive in normal worlds.

Quasi-regular systems are those whose semantics involves regular frames in which validity is defined as truth in all normal worlds in all models based on the frame, and include the 'Lewis' systems S2 and S3 described on pp. 200−202. For every regular system E there is a corresponding quasi-regular system E* defined as $\{L\alpha: \alpha \in E\}$. Thus S2^0 is E2^0*, S2 is E2*, etc. Axiomatic bases for these systems are described in Chapter 11. As before we may require that there be at least one non-normal world by adding MMp as an axiom.

All these systems may be listed as follows beginning from E2^0.

E2	E2^0 + **T**
E3^0	E2^0 + $L(p \supset q) \supset L(Lp \supset Lq)$
E3	E3^0 + **T**
E6^0	E2^0 + MMp
E6	E6^0 + **T**
E7^0	E3^0 + MMp
E7	E7^0 + **T**
E$^+$	E2^0 + Mp

S2^0	E2^0* (i.e. $\{L\alpha : \alpha \in E2^0\}$)
S2	E2*
S3^0	E3^0*
S3	E3*
S3.5	S3 + $Mp \supset LMp$
S6^0	S2^0 + MMp
S6	S2 + MMp
S7^0	S3^0 + MMp
S7	S3 + MMp
S8	S3 + $LMMp$
S9	S3.5 + MMp

No non-normal system contains any normal system since they all lack $LL(p \supset p)$. A diagram of non-normal modal systems appears in Table II on p. 368.

Modal predicate logic

In this section we summarize the bases of the various systems we discuss in Part III. The formation rules for predicate logic are given on p. 236 and for modal predicate logic on p. 243. Where S is a (normal) system of modal predicate logic LPC + S may be defined as on p. 244:

S'   If α is an LPC substitution-instance of a theorem of S then α is an axiom of LPC + S.

∀1 If α is any wff and x and y any variables and $\alpha[y/x]$ is α with free y replacing every free x, then $\forall x\alpha \supset \alpha[y/x]$ is an axiom of LPC + S.

N   If α is a theorem of LPC + S then so is $L\alpha$.

MP If α and $\alpha \supset \beta$ are theorems of LPC + S then so is β.

∀2 If $\alpha \supset \beta$ is a theorem of LPC + S and x is not free in α then $\alpha \supset \forall x\beta$ is a theorem of LPC + S.

Where **BF** is the schema $\forall x L\alpha \supset L\forall x\alpha$ (p. 244) then S + BF is LPC + S + **BF**. Validity for BF systems is defined on p. 243. Its key feature is that there is a single domain of individuals for all worlds. A canonical model may be defined for S + BF as described in Chapter 14. If S + BF is complete it will be characterized by the class of all frames for S. The completeness of S + BF will follow in all cases where the frame of the canonical model for S + BF is a frame for S. In particular, where S is K, D, T, K4, D4, B, KB, DB, DE or S5 completeness follows immediately with respect to the class of frames for the propositional system. It is not automatic however and does not hold for S4M + BF, KG1 + BF or S4.2 + BF. For LPC + S domains are allowed to vary provided that if wRw', $D_w \subseteq D_w'$. (This is called the 'inclusion' requirement, p. 275.) For systems with an existence predicate E, LPCE + S may be axiomatized as on p. 293:

S'   Any LPC substitution-instance of a theorem of S is an axiom of LPCE + S.

∀1E Where x and y are any individual variables, and α is any wff then $(\forall x\alpha \wedge Ey) \supset \alpha[y/x]$ is an axiom of LPCE + S.

∀⊃ $\forall x(\alpha \supset \beta) \supset (\forall x\alpha \supset \forall x\beta)$ (where α and β are any wff and x is any variable.)

VQ $\alpha \equiv \forall x\alpha$ provided x is not free in α.

UE $\forall x Ex$

The transformation rules are MP, N,

UG $\vdash \alpha \rightarrow \vdash \forall x\alpha$, and

UGL∀ⁿ $\vdash \alpha_1 \supset L(\alpha_2 \supset ... \supset L(\alpha_n \supset L\beta)...) \rightarrow \vdash \alpha_1 \supset L(\alpha_2 \supset ...$
$\supset L(\alpha_n \supset L\forall x\beta)...)$, where x is not free in $\alpha_1, ... , \alpha_n$.

In the semantics for LPCE + S the inclusion requirement is not assumed. LPCE + S is contained in LPC + S. Without an existence predicate such systems may be axiomatized (as LPCK + S, p. 305) with S', $\forall^\supset$, VQ, N and MP as before, but ∀1E is replaced by

∀1K Where x, y and z are any individual variables, and α is any wff then $\forall y \forall z(\forall x\alpha \supset \alpha[y/x])$ is an axiom of LPCK + S.

(UGL∀ is not part of this basis.) The converse of **BF** is not in general a theorem of any LPCE + S or LPCK + S.

For identity add to S + BF the axiom **I1** $x = x$ and the axiom schema **I2** $x = y \supset (\alpha \supset \beta)$ (p. 312) to obtain S + I. For S + LN1 add **LNI** $x \neq y \supset L x \neq y$ (p. 314). I1 and I2 can also be added to systems without BF. For contingent identity weaken I2 to **I2″** $x = y \supset (\phi x_1...x_n \equiv \phi y_1...y_n)$ (p. 334). In such systems the variables range over 'intensional objects', functions from W to D. Where they range over all such objects the logic is in most cases unaxiomatizable.

Table I: Normal Modal Systems

The following diagram provides a map of most of the normal systems we have discussed. An arrow indicates (proper) containment in the sense that the system above the arrow contains all the theorems of the system below, but not vice versa. The inconsistent system is denoted by $\mathcal{L}$. Systems to the left of the line --- contain D and systems to the right of the line — • — • — are not contained in Triv. Systems between these lines are contained in both Triv and Ver.

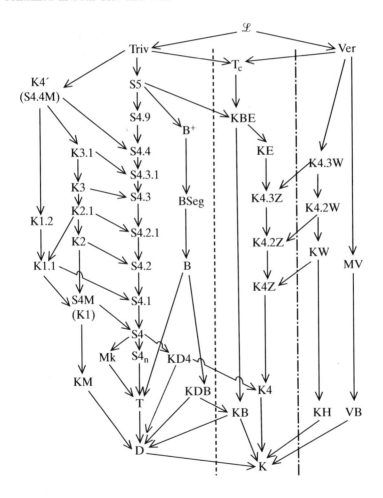

Table II: Non-normal Modal Systems

The non-normal systems referred to in this appendix may be listed in the following chart. We have also included S1, S1⁰, S0.5 and S0.5⁰ which are mentioned on pp. 198, 199 and 207. Systems to the left of the line --- contain N. Systems with a numerical index 6 or above would become inconsistent if N were added.

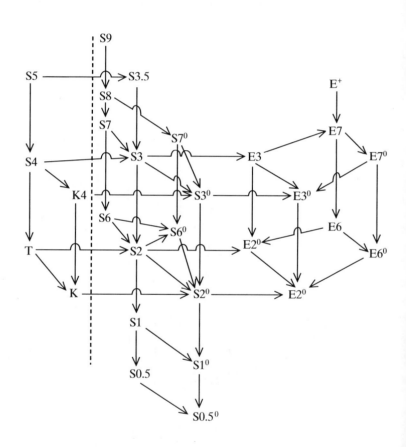

SOLUTIONS TO SELECTED EXERCISES

Some solutions (mostly in Part I) are given in full, some are merely sketched or hinted at, and some are not given at all.

Exercises — 1 (p. 21)

1.1 (c) It is sufficient to show that the implication is valid in both directions. If A's hand is raised for $L(p \land q)$ but not for $Lp \land Lq$ then it must be kept down for Lp or for Lq. So A must be able to see a player B whose hand is kept down for p or for q. So B's hand is kept down for $p \land q$, contradicting the fact that A can see B and A's hand is raised for $L(p \land q)$. If A's hand is raised for Lp and Lq but not for $L(p \land q)$ then A must be able to see a player B whose hand is down for $p \land q$. But if A can see B and A's hand is raised for Lp and for Lq then B's hand must be raised for p and for q, and so for $p \land q$

1.2 Suppose A cannot see A. Let p be on every player's sheet *except* A's. Show that A's hand is kept down for $Lp \supset p$.

1.3 (c) There are two players, A and B. Each can see both. p is on B's sheet but not on A's. q is on neither sheet.

(d) A can see B, B can see C, but A cannot see C. p is on A's sheet and on B's but not on C's.

1.4 (b) Suppose A can see B and C. Let p be on B's sheet but not on C's.

Exercises — 2 (p. 48)

2.1 (a) PC, DR1,K2

(b) $K[\sim q/p, \sim p/q]$, Transp, Eq, Def M

(d) DR3, K8, K7, Eq

(e)   DR3, K7

(f)   PROOF

K	(1)	$L(p \supset q) \supset (Lp \supset Lq)$
(1) × PC	(2)	$(L(p \supset q) \wedge Lp) \supset (Lp \wedge Lq)$
(2) × K3 × Eq	(3)	$(L(p \supset q) \wedge Lp) \supset L(p \wedge q)$
PC	(4)	$(p \wedge q) \supset ((q \supset r) \supset (p \wedge r))$
(4) × DR1	(5)	$L(p \wedge q) \supset L((q \supset r) \supset (p \wedge r))$
(b)$[q \supset r/p, p \wedge r/q]$		
	(6)	$L((q \supset r) \supset (p \wedge r)) \supset (M(q \supset r) \supset M(p \wedge r))$
(3)(5)(6) × PC	(7)	$(Lp \wedge M(q \supset r)) \supset (L(p \supset q) \supset M(p \wedge r))$

Q.E.D.

The PC principle used in getting from (1) to (2) is $(p \supset (q \supset r)) \supset ((p \wedge q) \supset (q \wedge r))$ $[L(p \supset q)/p, Lp/q, Lq/r]$ and in getting from (3), (5) and (6) to (7) is $((p \wedge q) \supset r) \supset ((r \supset s) \supset ((s \supset (t \supset v)) \supset ((p \wedge t) \supset (q \supset v))))$ $[L(p \supset q)/p, Lp/q, L(p \wedge q)/r, L((q \supset r) \supset (p \wedge r))/s, M(q \supset r)/t, M(p \wedge r)/v]$. Three applications of MP are then required. The PC steps could have been done in several stages. For instance, (3), (5) and (6) could have been combined by Syll to get $(L(p \supset q) \wedge Lp) \supset (M(p \supset q) \supset M(p \wedge r))$. Imp would give $(L(p \supset q) \wedge Lp \wedge M(p \supset q)) \supset M(p \wedge r)$, and Exp would give $(Lp \wedge M(q \supset r)) \supset (L(p \supset q) \supset M(p \wedge r))$.

2.3   It is sufficient to derive the basis of each system in the other. The basis of T* is contained in K except for **K*** and R*. **K*** is obtained in T from **K** by N, and R* is DR1. To obtain the basis of T in T* it is sufficient to prove **K** and N.

Proof of K in T*:
$\mathbf{T}[L(p \supset q) \supset (Lp \supset Lq)/p]$

	(1)	$L(L(p \supset q) \supset (Lp \supset Lq)) \supset$
		$(L(p \supset q) \supset (Lp \supset Lq))$
(1)K* × MP	(2)	$L(p \supset q) \supset (Lp \supset Lq)$

Q.E.D.

Proof of N:

Given	(1)	α
(1) × PC	(2)	$(L(p \supset q) \supset (Lp \supset Lq)) \supset \alpha$
(2) × R*	(3)	$L(L(p \supset q) \supset (Lp \supset Lq)) \supset L\alpha$

(3) **K*** × MP (4) *L*α   **Q.E.D.**

2.6 (a)   N, K9
  (b)   Where α and β are each $p \supset p$ this rule allows the derivation of
$M(p \supset p)$, and therefore of **D**. But **D** was shown on p. 45 not to be a
theorem of K.

2.7 (a)   PC, N, D1, K6
  (b)   Prove $M(M \sim p \lor Mp)$ and use LMI.

2.8 A falsifying model may be constructed as follows. W has two
worlds w_1 and w_2. Each can see the other but neither can see itself. If p
is true at w_1 and false at w_2 then $M(p \supset Lp)$ is false at w_1.

2.9 Show that if α is not D-valid then neither is Mα. If $V(\alpha,w) = 0$ in
some D-model define a new model exactly like the old one except that
it has an extra world w^* which can see w and w alone. Show that this is
a D-model in which $V(M\alpha,w^*) = 0$.

2.11 See Williamson 1988

Exercises — 3 (p. 68)
3.1 (a)
PROOF
K   (1) $L(p \supset q) \supset (Lp \supset Lq)$
(1) × N   (2) $L(L(p \supset q) \supset (Lp \supset Lq))$
(1)[$L(p \supset q)/p, Lp \supset Lq/q$]
                         (3) $L(L(p \supset q) \supset (Lp \supset Lq))$
                               $\supset (LL(p \supset q) \supset L(Lp \supset Lq))$
(2)(3) × MP   (4) $LL(p \supset q) \supset L(Lp \supset Lq)$
4   (5) $Lp \supset LLp$
(5)[$p \supset p/p$]   (6) $L(p \supset q) \supset LL(p \supset q)$
(6)(4) × MP   (7) $L(p \supset q) \supset L(Lp \supset Lq)$ **Q.E.D.**

[The PC principle used in getting from (6) and (4) to (7) is $(p \supset q) \supset$
$((q \supset r) \supset (p \supset r))$ with $L(p \supset q)/p, LL(p \supset q)/q$, and $L(Lp \supset Lq)/r$.]

(b)   PC9, PC10, DR1, **4**.

(c)

PROOF

T2[Mp/p]	(1)	$M(Mp \supset LMp)$
S4(2)[Mp/p]	(2)	$LMp \equiv LLMp$
(1)(2) × Eq	(3)	$M(Mp \supset LLMp)$
(3) Def $\supset$ × LMI	(4)	$M(L\sim p \lor LLMp)$
K4[$\sim p/p\ LMp/q$]	(5)	$(L\sim p \lor LLMp) \supset L(\sim p \lor LMp)$
(5) × DR3	(6)	$M(L\sim p \lor LLMp) \supset ML(\sim p \lor LMp)$
(4)(6) × MP	(7)	$ML(\sim p \lor LMp)$
(7) Def $\supset$	(8)	$ML(p \supset LMp)$ **Q.E.D.**

(d)   S4(1) [$p \supset q/p$], K7, Eq.

3.2   Show that it holds for the case where A is just L or M. Then show that if it holds for A it holds for LA and for MA. Explain why this gives the result.

3.3   Let **K*** denote the wff: $L(p \supset q) \supset L(Lp \supset Lq)$ and call T with **K*** in place of **K**, S4*. It will be sufficient to prove **K** and the S4 axiom **4** ($Lp \supset LLp$) in S4*, and to prove **K*** in S4. The proof of K* in S4 is exercise 3.1(a).

Proof of K in S4*:

K*	(1)	$L(p \supset q) \supset L(Lp \supset Lq)$
T	(2)	$Lp \supset p$
(2)[$Lp \supset Lq/p$]	(3)	$L(Lp \supset Lq) \supset (Lp \supset Lq)$
(1)(3) × PC	(4)	$L(p \supset q) \supset (Lp \supset Lq)$ **Q.E.D.**

[The PC principle used in getting from (2) and (4) to (5) is $(p \supset q) \supset ((q \supset r) \supset (p \supset r))$ with $L(p \supset q)/p$, $L(Lp \supset Lq)/q$ and $(Lp \supset Lq)/r$.]

Proof of 4 in S4*:

PC	(1)	$p \supset ((p \supset p) \supset p)$
(1) × DR1	(2)	$Lp \supset L((p \supset p) \supset p)$
K*[$p \supset p/p,p/q$]	(3)	$L((p \supset p) \supset p) \supset L(L(p \supset p) \supset Lp)$
(2)(3) × PC	(5)	$Lp \supset L(L(p \supset p) \supset Lp)$
K[$L(p \supset p)/p,Lp/q$]	(6)	
		$L(L(p \supset p) \supset Lp) \supset (LL(p \supset p) \supset LLp)$
(3)(6) × PC	(7)	$LL(p \supset p) \supset (Lp \supset LLp)$

PC	(8) $p \supset p$	
(8) × N twice	(9) $LL(p \supset p)$	
(7)(9) × MP	(10) $Lp \supset LLp$	Q.E.D.

[The PC principle used in getting from (3) and (4) to (5) is $(p \supset q) \supset ((q \supset r) \supset (p \supset r))$ with Lp/p, $L((p \supset p) \supset p)/q$ and $L((p \supset p) \supset Lp/r$. The PC principle used in getting from (5) and (7) to (8) is $(p \supset q) \supset ((q \supset (r \supset s)) \supset (r \supset (p \supset s)))$ with Lp/p, $L(L(p \supset p) \supset Lp)/q$, $LL(p \supset p)/r$ and LLp/s. The PC wff used at (9) is $p \supset p$.]

3.4 To show that Lp is stronger than $LMLp$ use a two world frame where the first world can see both worlds but the second world can see only itself. Put p true at the second and false at the first. To show that $MLMp$ is stronger than Mp put p true at the first and false at the second. For the remainder it is sufficient to show that neither MLp nor LMp imply each other, since then neither could imply $LMLp$ or be implied by $MLMp$. To show that MLp does not imply LMp use a three world frame in which the first world can see all worlds but each of the other two can only see itself. Put p true at one of these and false at the other. To show that LMp does not imply MLp use a two-world frame in which both worlds can see both worlds and put p true in one but not in the other.

3.5 It is sufficient to show that $L^n p \supset L^{n+1} p$ is not a theorem of T. For suppose n ≠ m. If n < m then repeated applications of **T** (or of PC for the case m = n + 1) give $\vdash_T L^m p \supset L^{n+1} p$, and so if $\vdash_T L^n p \equiv L^m p$ then $\vdash_T L^n p \supset L^{n+1} p$. If m < n the same argument yields $\vdash_T L^m p \supset L^{m+1} p$. To prove that $L^n p \supset L^{n+1} p$ is never a theorem of T choose a frame with n + 2 worlds, $w_1, \ldots, w_{n+2}$, and for $1 \le i \le j \le n + 2$, let $w_i R w_j$. Put p true at every world but w^{n+2}, and show that $L^n \supset L^{n+1} p$ is false at w_1. Then use the soundness of T.

3.7 (a) Prove $L(Lp \supset Lq) \equiv (Lp \supset Lq)$ from S5(5) and then use $(p \supset q) \lor (q \supset p)$.

(b) First prove $L(Mp \supset Lq) \supset L(p \supset Lq)$ (T1, DR1, PC) and then prove $L(Mp \supset q) \supset L(Mp \supset Lq)$ (S5(4) Def $\supset$). For the converse implication prove $L(p \supset Lq) \supset L(Mp \supset Lq)$.

3.10

S5(4)[Mp/p, $\sim p/q$]	(1)	$L(Mp \lor L\sim p) \supset (LMp \lor L\sim p)$
PC	(2)	$\sim p \lor p$
(2)[$L\sim p/p$] Def M	(3)	$Mp \lor L\sim p$
(3) $\times$ N	(4)	$L(Mp \lor L\sim p)$
(1)(4) $\times$ MP	(5)	$LMp \lor L\sim p$
(5) $\times$ PC	(6)	$\sim L\sim p \supset LMp$
(6) Def M	(7)	$Mp \supset LMp$ **Q.E.D.**

So **E** can be derived from S5(4) using only principles in T. Thus S5(4) added to T gives S5.

3.12 (b)

B	(1)	$p \supset LMp$
(1) [$\sim p/p$]	(2)	$\sim p \supset LM\sim p$
(2) $\times$ LMI	(3)	$\sim p \supset \sim MLp$
(1)(3) $\times$ PC	(4)	$MLp \supset LMp$ **Q.E.D.**

The PC principle used in getting from (1) and (3) to (4) is $(p \supset q) \supset ((\sim p \supset \sim r) \supset (r \supset q))$ with LMp/q and MLp/r.

3.14 Let α be $M(p \supset p)$

3.15 It is sufficient to show that the addition to T of
   (*) $(Lp \supset Lq) \supset L(p \supset q)$
would cause the resulting system to collapse into PC.

PC	(1)	$(p \supset \sim p) \supset \sim p$
(1) $\times$ DR1	(2)	$L(p \supset \sim p) \supset L\sim p$
(*) [$\sim p/q$]	(3)	$(Lp \supset L\sim p) \supset L(p \supset \sim p)$
(2)(3) $\times$ Syll	(4)	$(Lp \supset L\sim p) \supset L\sim p$
PC	(5)	$((p \supset q) \supset q) \supset (\sim q \supset p)$
(5)[$Lp/p, L\sim p/q$]	(6)	(4) $\supset$ (7)
(4)(6) $\times$ MP	(7)	$\sim L\sim p \supset Lp$
(7) Def M	(8)	$Mp \supset Lp$
(8) T1 $\times$ Syll	(9)	$p \supset Lp$ **Q.E.D.**

3.10 It is sufficient to prove $p \supset Lp$.

Given	(1)	$LMp \supset MLp$	
S5(1)	(2)	$MLp \supset Lp$	
(1)(2) × Syll	(3)	$LMp \supset Lp$	
E	(4)	$Mp \supset LMp$	
T1	(5)	$p \supset Mp$	
(3)(4)(5) × Syll	(6)	$p \supset Lp$	Q.E.D.

Exercises — 4 (p. 92)

4.1 (a)   K-valid.

   (b)   Invalid in K, D-valid.

   (c)   K-valid.

   (d)   Invalid in K, D-valid.

   (e)   K-valid.

   (f)   Invalid in D, T-valid.

   (h)   Invalid in D, valid in T.

   (i)   Invalid in T

4.3 (b)   See p. 129. Since the diagram ends without contradiction the wff is not T-valid.   A falsifying model is: $W = \{w_1, w_2, w_3\}$, $w_1Rw_1, w_1Rw_2,\ w_2Rw_2, w_2Rw_3,\ w_3Rw_3$

    $V(p,w_1) = 1^*$ $V(q,w_1) = 1^*$

    $V(p,w_2) = 1$ $V(q,w_2) = 0$

    $V(p,w_3) = 0$ $V(q,w_3) = 1$

    * optional values

4.4(a)

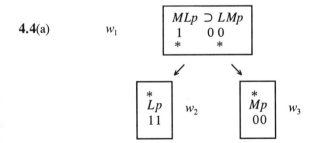

Wff is not S4-valid.   Falsifying S4-model is: $W = \{w_1, w_2, w_3\}$, w_1Rw_1, w_1Rw_2, w_2Rw_2, w_1Rw_3, w_3Rw_3. $V(p,w_1) = 1$ (optional), $V(p,w_2) = 1$, $V(p,w_3) = 0$

(b)   Consider the diagram in (a) and suppose that we were to add a world w_4 which could be seen by both w_2 and w_3. Then the truth of Lp in w_2 would require that $p = 1$ in w_4 and the falsity of Mp in w_3 would require that $p = 0$ in w_4, which is contradictory. [This also shows that the wff is S5-valid since all S5-models satisfy this condition, though not all models satisfying the condition are S5-models.]

Exercises — 5 (p. 110)

5.1 (a) $L(p \lor q) \land (L(p \lor r) \lor Ls)$ Invalid.

(b) $(Lp \lor L\sim(p \land q) \lor Mq) \land L\sim(p \land q) \lor M(\sim q \lor q))$ Valid.

(c) $(L(\sim p \lor q) \lor L(\sim p \lor \sim q) \lor M(p \land q)) \land$
      $(L(\sim p \lor q) \lor L(\sim p \lor \sim q) \lor M(p \land \sim q))$ Valid.

(d) $(Lr \lor M(p \lor q) \lor M\sim(p \lor q)) \land$
      $(\sim r \lor L(p \supset p) \lor M(p \lor q))$ Valid.

(e) $(L\sim p \lor Lp \lor M(q \lor (p \land \sim q)) \land$
      $(L\sim p \lor Lp \lor L\sim p \lor Lp \lor M(p \land \sim q)$ Invalid.

(f) $(\sim q \lor L(p \supset r) \lor Mp) \land (\sim q \lor L(p \supset r) \lor M\sim(q \supset r))$
                                                Invalid.

(h) $(L\sim p \lor Lp \lor Lp \lor M\sim p) \land (Lp \lor M(\sim p \lor \sim p))$,
                                                Valid.

(i) $(L(L(p \supset q) \supset q) \supset p) \supset M(Lq \supset p)$
    $\sim(\sim L(\sim L(p \supset q) \lor q) \lor p) \lor M(\sim Lq \lor p)$ [Def $\supset$]
    $(L(\sim L(p \supset q) \lor q) \land \sim p) \lor M(\sim Lq \lor p)$ [De M]
    $(L(M\sim(p \supset q) \lor q) \land \sim p) \lor M(M\sim q \lor p)$ [LMI]
    $((M\sim(p \supset q) \lor Lq) \land \sim p) \lor (M\sim q \lor Mp)$
          $[L(Mp \lor q) \equiv (Mp \lor Lq), M(Mp \lor q) \equiv (Mp \lor Mq)]$
    $(M\sim(p \supset q) \lor Lq \lor M\sim q \lor Mp)$
       $\land (\sim p \lor M\sim q \lor Mp)$ [Distrib]

Wff now in MCNF. To test for S5-validity first obtain an ordered MCNF. We use the principle $M(p \lor q) \equiv (Mp \lor Mq)$ and PC re-ordering principles to obtain

    $(Lq \lor M(\sim(p \supset q) \lor \sim q \lor p)) \land (\sim p \lor M(\sim q \lor p))$.

The wff will be valid iff each conjunct is. The first conjunct is valid because $q \lor \sim(p \supset q) \lor \sim q \lor p$ is PC-valid; and the second conjunct is valid because $\sim p \lor \sim q \lor p$ is PC-valid.

(j) $L(L(Lp \supset Lq) \supset L(p \supset q))$
    $L(\sim L(\sim Lp \lor Lq) \lor L(p \supset q))$ [Def $\supset$]

$L(M \sim (\sim Lp \lor Lq) \lor L(p \supset q))$ [LMI]
$L(M(Lp \land \sim Lq) \lor L(p \supset q))$ [DeM]
$L(M(Lp \land M \sim q) \lor L(p \supset q))$ [LMI]
$M(Lp \land M \sim q) \lor L(p \supset q)$ $[L(Mp \lor Lq) \equiv (Mp \lor Lq)]$
$(Lp \land M \sim q) \lor L(p \supset q)$ $[M(Lp \land Mq) \equiv (Lp \land Mq)]$
$(Lp \lor L(p \supset q)) \land (M \sim q \lor L(p \supset q))$ [Distrib]
$(Lp \lor L(p \supset q)) \land (L(p \supset q) \lor M \sim q)$ [Com]

Wff now in (ordered) MCNF. The original wff will be S5-valid iff the MCNF is, and the MCNF will be valid iff each conjunct is. Consider the first conjunct. This will be S5-valid iff either p or $p \supset q$ is PC-valid. But neither is, so the conjunct is not S5-valid, and so the whole wff is not either. The following PC assignments may be used.

$V_1(p) = 0$ $V_1(q) = 1$ (optional)
$V_2(p) = 1$ $V_2(q) = 0$

Define an S5-model on this basis by letting $W = \{w_1, w_2\}$.

$V(p,w_1) = V_1(p) = 0, V(q,w_1) = V_1(q) = 1$
$V(p,w_2) = V_2(p) = 1, V(q,w_2) = V_2(q) = 0$

Since $V(p,w_1) = 0$ then $V(Lp,w_1) = 0$ and since $V(p,w_2) = 1$ and $V(q,w_2) = 0$, then $V(p \supset q,w_2) = 0$, and so $V(L(p \supset q),w_2) = 0$. So $V(Lp \lor L(p \supset q),w_1) = 0$, showing that the conjunct, and therefore the whole wff is not S5 valid.

5.2 Consider two models, each with the same set of three worlds, w_1, w_2, w_3. w_1 can see both w_2 and w_3, and all worlds can see themselves. In the first model w_2 can see w_3, but in the second model it cannot. In both models p is true only at w_2. Thus:

$\langle W_1, R_1, V_1 \rangle$ $\langle W_2, R_2, V_2 \rangle$

w_1 $p = 0$ w_1 $p = 0$
$\swarrow$ $\searrow$ $\swarrow$ $\searrow$
w_2 $\rightarrow$ w_3 w_2 w_3
$p = 1$ $p = 0$ $p = 1$ $p = 0$

Let every other variable be true in all worlds in both models. Both models are S4 models so if $M(p \land M \sim p)$ is equivalent in S4 to a first-degree wff α, then $V_1(M(p \land M \sim p),w_1) = V_1(\alpha,w_1)$ and $V_2(M(p \land M \sim p),w_1) = V_2(\alpha,w_1)$. Now if α is of first degree then $V_1(\alpha,w_1) = V_2(\alpha,w_1)$. (The proof relies on the fact that if β is any wff of degree 0 then $V_1(\beta,w) = V_2(\beta,w)$ for every $w \in W$.) So $V_1(M(p \wedge M\sim p),w_1) = V_2(M(p \wedge M\sim p)$. But $V_1(M(p \wedge M\sim p),w_1) = 1$ and $V_2(M(p \wedge M\sim p),w_1) = 0$. So $M(p \wedge M\sim p)$ is not equivalent in S4 to any first degree formula.

Exercises — 6 (p. 122)

6.1 First suppose that Γ is maximal consistent and suppose that $\Gamma \cup \{\alpha\}$ is consistent. Now if $\alpha \notin \Gamma$ then, by maximal consistency $\sim\alpha \in \Gamma$. But in that case $\Gamma \cup \{\alpha\}$ is not consistent. So if $\Gamma \cup \{\alpha\}$ is consistent then $\alpha \in \Gamma$, and this is enough to make Γ maximal consistent*. Now suppose that Γ is maximal consistent* and suppose that there is some wff α such that neither α nor $\sim\alpha$ is in Γ. Then both $\Gamma \cup \{\alpha\}$ and $\Gamma \cup \{\sim\alpha\}$ are inconsistent. But then Γ would be inconsistent by the argument on p. 115.

6.2 Suppose $\alpha \supset \beta \in \Gamma$. Then, if we don't have either $\alpha \notin \Gamma$ or $\beta \in \Gamma$, we have $\alpha \in \Gamma$ and $\beta \notin \Gamma$. But since Γ is maximal consistent, we have $\alpha \in \Gamma$ and $\sim\beta \in \Gamma$. But $\{\alpha, \sim\beta, \alpha \supset \beta\}$ is inconsistent. For the converse, suppose $\sim\alpha \in \Gamma$. Then since $\vdash \sim\alpha \supset (\alpha \supset \beta)$, $\alpha \supset \beta \in \Gamma$ by lemma 6.2b on p. 114. And suppose $\beta \in \Gamma$. Then, since $\vdash \beta \supset (\alpha \supset \beta)$, $\alpha \supset \beta \in \Gamma$, also by lemma 6.2b.

6.3 Suppose $\Lambda \subseteq \Gamma$ but $\Delta \neq \Gamma$. Then there exists $\alpha \in \Gamma$ but $\alpha \notin \Lambda$. Since Λ is maximal then by lemma 6.1a on p. 114 $\sim\alpha \in \Lambda$ and so $\sim\alpha \in \Gamma$. But then Γ would be inconsistent.

6.4 Suppose $\{M\alpha: \alpha \in \Lambda\} \not\subseteq \Gamma$. Then there exists $\alpha \in \Lambda$ with $M\alpha \notin \Gamma$. But Γ is maximal, so $\sim M\alpha \in \Gamma$, and so $L\sim\alpha \in \Gamma$. And Λ is consistent so $\sim\alpha \notin \Lambda$, and so $\{\alpha: L\alpha \in \Gamma\} \not\subseteq \Lambda$. Suppose $\{\alpha: L\alpha \in \Gamma\} \not\subseteq \Lambda$. Then there exists $L\alpha \in \Gamma$ with $\alpha \notin \Lambda$. So $\sim\alpha \in \Lambda$. But Γ is consistent and $L\alpha \in \Gamma$ so $\sim L\alpha \notin \Gamma$ so $M\sim\alpha \notin \Gamma$, so $\{M\alpha: \alpha \in \Lambda\} \not\subseteq \Gamma$.

6.7 Suppose $\{L\gamma_1, \dots ,L\gamma_n\}$ is not consistent. Then (as in the proof of lemma 6.4 on p. 117)
$$\vdash_S (L\gamma_1 \wedge \dots \wedge L\gamma_n) \supset \beta$$
so
$$\vdash_S (LL\gamma_1 \wedge \dots \wedge LL\gamma_n) \supset L\beta.$$
Since S contains S4 then $\vdash L\gamma_1 \supset LL\gamma_1, \dots, \vdash L\gamma_n \supset LL\gamma_n$ and so
$$\vdash_S (L\gamma_1 \wedge \dots \wedge L\gamma_n) \supset L\beta.$$

So $\{L\gamma_1, \ldots ,L\gamma_n, \sim L\beta\}$ is not S-consistent.

6.8 Suppose w_1 can see two distinct worlds, w_2 and w_3. Since $w_2 \neq w_3$ there is some $\alpha \in w_2$ with $\sim\alpha \in w_3$. So $M\alpha \in w_1$. So by $Mp \supset Lp$, $L\alpha \in w_1$, and so $\alpha \in w_3$ contradicting w_3's consistency.

6.9 It is sufficient to show that where $\langle W,R,V \rangle$ is the canonical model of W2 then R satisfies the condition. Suppose there is some $w_1 \in W$ such that w_1Rw_2, w_1Rw_3 and $w_1 \neq w_2$, $w_1 \neq w_3$ and $w_2 \neq w_3$. Since $w_2 \neq w_3$ there is some $\alpha \in w_2$ such that $\sim\alpha \in w_3$. Since $w_1 \neq w_2$ there is some $\beta \in w_1$ with $\sim\beta \in w_2$. Since $w_1 \neq w_3$ there is some $\gamma \in w_1$ with $\sim\gamma \in w_3$. So

   (a) $\gamma \in w_1$, $\beta \in w_1$

   (b) $\alpha \in w_2$, $\sim\beta \in w_2$

   (c) $\sim\alpha \in w_3$, $\sim\gamma \in w_3$.

From (b) $((\alpha \vee \gamma) \wedge \sim\beta) \in w_2$, and since w_1Rw_2, $M((\alpha \vee \gamma) \wedge \sim\beta) \in w_1$. From (a) $\alpha \vee \gamma \in w_1$ and so

   (d) $((\alpha \vee \gamma) \wedge \beta \wedge M((\alpha \vee \gamma) \wedge \sim\beta)) \in w_1$.

So by **W2** $L(\alpha \vee \gamma) \in w_1$. But w_1Rw_3 and so $\alpha \vee \beta \in w_3$. But then $\{\alpha \vee \gamma, \sim\alpha, \sim\gamma\} \subseteq w_3$, which contradicts its consistency.

6.11 If w is not a dead end and can see a world besides itself then there is a world w' with $w \neq w'$ and wRw'. So there is some $\alpha \in w$ with $\sim\alpha \in w'$. But $L\alpha \in w$ and so $\alpha \in w'$, which contradicts its consistency.

Exercises — 7 (p. 141)

7.1(b) See p. 284 (S4.4 + BF)

7.2 For completeness establish the consistency in Mk of

   (Λ) $L^-(w) \cup \{\sim L\beta : \sim\beta \in w\} \cup \{LL\gamma : L\gamma \in w\}$

for any $w \in W$, and explain why this is sufficient.

7.6 First note that the canonical model of any normal extension of KB will be symmetrical, and that in a cohesive symmetrical frame, for any $w, w' \in W$, there is some $n \geq 0$ such that wR^nw'. Consider the set $\Lambda = \{L^np:n \geq 0\}$. Λ is clearly consistent for if not then

$$\vdash_S \sim(p \wedge Lp \wedge \ldots \wedge L^kp)$$

for some k. But with $p \supset p/p$ we then obtain

$$\vdash_S \sim((p \supset p) \wedge L(p \supset p) \wedge \ldots \wedge L^k(p \supset p))$$

379

making S inconsistent. So let w^* be a world in the canonical model at which all members of Λ are true. If the frame of this model is cohesive then any $w \in W$ will be such that for some n, w^*R^nw and so $V(p,w) = 1$. So p will be valid in S's canonical model, and so $\vdash_S p$, making S inconsistent.

7.8 For (ii), given any non-theorem α, let w^* be a world in the canonical model of the system in which α is false. Let $\langle W^*, R^*, V^* \rangle$ be that part of the canonical model generated (see p. 143) by w^* (i.e. its worlds are those to which there is an R-chain from w^*) and let R^* be $\neq$. Let $V^*(p,w) = V(p,w)$ for $w \in W^*$. Use the fact that R satisfies (i) to shew that $V^*(\alpha,w^*) = V(\alpha,w^*) = 0$ and that $\langle W^*, R^*, V^* \rangle$ is a model for the system.

7.8 Show that if S provides RD then $\{\sim L\alpha : \dashv_S \alpha\}$ is S-consistent. Explain why this gives the result.

7.9 Suppose none of $\alpha_1, \ldots, \alpha_n$ is a theorem of S. Then $\{\sim L\alpha_1, \ldots \sim L\alpha_n\} \subseteq \{\sim L\beta : \dashv_S \beta\}$. So if $\{\sim L\beta : \dashv_S \beta\}$ is consistent so is $\{\sim L\alpha_1, \ldots \sim L\alpha_n\}$, and so $\dashv_S L\alpha_1 \vee \ldots \vee L\alpha_n$. We proved on p. 139 that $\{\sim L\beta : \dashv_S\}$ is consistent where S is T or K, and on p. 140 where S is KW. The case of S4 is similar.

7.10 Use the fact that $LM \sim p \vee Lp$, $LM \sim p \vee LMp$ and $LM \sim p \vee Lp$ are theorems of, respectively, B, S4.2 and S5.

7.11 Prove that K1.1 provides the rule of disjunction in the following form: where $\alpha_1, \ldots, \alpha_n$ are any wff and β is a wff of PC then if $\vdash L\alpha_1 \vee \ldots \vee L\alpha_n \vee \beta$ then either $\vdash \alpha_i$ for some $1 \leq i \leq n$ or $\vdash \beta$. Then shew that the canonical model of K.1. can see a pair of distinct worlds that can see each other, but that no frame for K1.1 contains such a pair.

Exercises — 8 (p. 156)
8.2 Base the mini-canonical model on the set Φ_α^{M+} of all wff of modal degree no more than one greater than the degree of α which are made up from the variables of α. Let wRw' iff for all $L\beta \in w$, $L\beta \in w'$ and prove the analogue of theorem 8.4 for all $\gamma \in \Phi_\alpha$. Then shew how to adapt the completeness proofs given for these systems in Chapter 7.

8.3 Show that the completeness proof for KW still holds when Φ_α^+ is replaced by Φ_α^{M+}, and shew that **Lem$_0$** imposes linearity. Then shew that any finite irreflexive transitive linear frame can be mapped onto an initial segment of the natural numbers with R as $>$.

8.4 Base the mini-canonical model on the set of all wff of modal degree no more than two greater than the degree of α which are made up from the variables of α. Let wRw' iff either $w = w'$ or else
    (i) If $L\beta \in w$ then $L\beta \in w'$
    (ii) There is some $L\gamma \in w'$ such that $L\gamma \notin w$.

8.5 Show that each generated sub-frame of the finite canonical model based on Φ_α^{M+} consistes of a finite sequence of clusters. Arbitrarily order the members of each cluster and let $\langle n,m \rangle$ denote the n'th world in the m'th cluster. Show that R, as defined in the exercise, is equivalent to R in the original finite model.

Exercises — 9 (p. 169)

9.2 (This solution is amplified in Chapter 4 of Hughes and Cresswell 1984.) For (A) first shew that a frame is a frame for **MV** iff every world either is or can see a dead end. Then suppose a frame in which this is not so and let w^* be a world which is not a dead end and cannot see one. Let v^* be a world that w^* can see. Put p false everywhere and q false at v^* but true everywhere else. Show that this falsifies **VB**. For (B) use a frame in which W is all the finite natural numbers together with the two infinite numbers ω and $\omega + 1$. $\omega + 1$ can see ω and ω alone. ω and all the natural numbers can see numbers less than themselves. Every variable is false everywhere. This falsifies **MV** but validates every instance of **VB**. (Use the fact that $|\alpha|$ for any wff α is finite without ω or cofinite with ω.)

9.3 Derive **VB** from the two axioms given. Then use exercise 9.2 to establish (A). For (B) shew that the frame used in 9.2 validates (i) and (ii).

Exercises — 10 (p. 189)

10.2 Suppose w_1Rw_2, w_2Rw_3 but not w_1Rw_3. Put p false at w_1 and w_3 but true everywhere else.

In Part III exercises marked with * are ones for which we have not ourselves obtained a solution. Where solutions are known to us to have been obtained by others we have indicated this. Some of the remaining starred exercises may be regarded as open research problems. The few solutions which follow are mostly proofs of wff in systems of modal LPC in an abbreviated form. The full proofs will need to be reconstructed from these.

Exercises — 13 (p. 254)
13.1 (a) Use (2) in the form $\forall x L((\alpha \supset \alpha) \supset \alpha) \supset L(\forall x(\alpha \supset \alpha) \supset \forall x\alpha)$.

13.2 (ii) $\exists y(\phi y \supset \forall x\phi x)$
$(\phi y \supset \forall x\phi x) \supset LM(\phi y \supset \forall x\phi x)$
$\exists y(\phi y \supset \forall x\phi x) \supset \exists yLM(\phi y \supset \forall x\phi x)$
$\exists yLM(\phi y \supset \forall x\phi x)$

13.3 Proof of $\sim$(C) in S4.4 + BF.
Choose y to be a variable distinct from x.
$\forall x\forall y((\phi x \supset \phi y) \supset (ML(\phi x \supset \phi y) \supset L(\phi x \supset \phi y)))$ [R1 × UG]
$\sim\exists x\exists y((\phi x \supset \phi y) \wedge \sim L(\phi x \supset \phi y) \wedge ML(\phi x \supset \phi y))$
$\sim\exists x\exists y(\sim\phi x \wedge M(\phi x \wedge \sim\phi y) \wedge ML\phi y)$
$\sim\exists x(\sim\phi x \wedge \exists yM(\phi x \wedge \sim\phi y) \wedge \forall yML\phi y)$
$\sim\exists x\sim\phi x \wedge \forall x\exists yM(\phi x \wedge \sim\phi y) \wedge \forall yML\phi y$
$\sim\exists x\sim\phi x \wedge \forall xM\exists y(\phi x \wedge \sim\phi y) \wedge \forall yML\phi y$ [× BF]
$\sim\exists x\sim\phi x \wedge \forall xM(\phi x \wedge \exists x\sim\phi x) \wedge \forall xML\phi x$
$\sim\exists x\sim\phi x \wedge \forall x(M\phi x \wedge L\exists x\sim\phi x) \wedge \forall xML\phi x$
$\sim L(\forall xML\phi x \wedge \exists x\sim\phi x)$

13.5 (b) and (c):   Show that the wff fail in the following models $\langle W,R,V\rangle$, $\langle W,R,V'\rangle$ where $W = \{w_1,w_2\}$, R is universal and $D = \{u_1,u_2\}$:
(b) $V(\phi) = \{\langle u_1,w_1\rangle,\langle u_2,w_2\rangle\}$, $V(\psi) = \{\langle u_2,w_1\rangle,\langle u_1,w_2\rangle\}$
(c) $V(\phi) = \{\langle u_1,w_1\rangle\}$

Exercises — 14 (p. 272)
14.5(b) Montagna 1984 proves that for systems without BF the wff $\exists xM\phi x \wedge \forall x\exists yL(\phi x \supset M\phi y)$ is unsatisfiable on all KW frames but is consistent in (i.e. its negation is not a theorem of) LPC + KW. He leaves it as an open question whether the result still holds in KW + BF.

Exercises — 17 (p. 328)

17.3 The first of the two meanings may be expressed by the wff: $M\exists x(\phi x \wedge \forall y(\phi y \supset x = y) \wedge \sim\phi x)$. This wff says that it might have been that there be exactly one thing which is a mayor of Wellington and not a mayor of Wellington. This meaning is contradictory. The second meaning may be expressed by $\exists x((\phi x \wedge \forall y(\phi y \supset x = y)) \wedge M\sim\phi x)$. This wff says that there is exactly one thing which is a mayor of Wellington and, concerning that thing, it is possible that it might not have been a mayor of Wellington. This wff is not contradictory.

17.5
$$\exists^1 x\alpha \supset (\forall x\sim L\alpha \supset \sim L\alpha[\imath x\alpha/x]) \qquad [\forall 1\imath, \text{ where } \beta \text{ is } \sim L\alpha]$$
$$\exists^1 x\alpha \supset (L\alpha[\imath x\alpha/x] \supset \exists x L\alpha)$$
$$L\exists^1 x\alpha \supset (L\alpha[\imath x\alpha/x] \supset \exists x L\alpha) \qquad [\times \mathbf{T}]$$
$$L\exists^1 x\alpha \supset L\alpha[\imath x\alpha/x] \qquad [\mathbf{DD} \times \mathbf{DR1}]$$
$$L\exists^1 x\alpha \supset \exists x L\alpha$$

Exercises — 18 (p. 347)

18.1 Take I to be the set of constant functions (i.e. for $i \in$ I there is some $u \in$ D such that $i(w) = u$ for all $w \in$ W) and then use the fact that $L\exists x\phi x \supset \exists x L\phi x$ fails in ordinary modal LPC.

18.2 Where $\mu(x) = i$, choose $\mu(y)$ to be a function such that $\mu(y)(w) = i(w)$ but $\mu(y)(w') \neq i(w')$ for all $w \neq w'$. Show that this choice of $\mu(y)$ satisfies the formula provided there are at least two individuals. (Explain why the formula is also true if there is only one individual.)

BIBLIOGRAPHY

Each item is followed by a list of numbers of the notes in which it is referred to. Thus **(4.3)** indicates note 3 to Chapter 4 and so on.

Alban, M.J., 1943, 'Independence of the primitive symbols of Lewis' calculi of propositions', *The Journal of Symbolic Logic*, 8, 24–6 **(11.24)**.

Anderson, A.R., 1954, 'Improved decision procedures for Lewis's calculus S4 and Von Wright's calculus M', *The Journal of Symbolic Logic*, 19, 201–14 (Correction in ibid 20, 150) **(4.1)**.

Åqvist, L., 1964, 'Results concerning some modal systems that contain S2', *The Journal of Symbolic Logic*, 29, 79–87 **(11.27)**.

1973, 'Modal logic with subjunctive conditionals and dispositional predicates', *Journal of Philosophical Logic*, 2, 1–76 **(12.16, 19.1)**.

Aristotle, BC350, *Prior Analytics* (tr. R.Smith, Indianapolis, Hackett Publishing Co, 1989) **(11.1)**.

Barcan, (Marcus) R.C., 1946, 'A functional calculus of first order based on strict implication', *The Journal of Symbolic Logic*, 11, 1–16 **(1.2, 14.3)**.

1947, 'The identity of individuals in a strict functional calculus of second order', *The Journal of Symbolic Logic*, 12, 12–5 **(17.1)**.

1962, 'Interpreting quantification', *Inquiry*, 5, 252–9 **(15.1)**.

Bayart, A., 1958, 'La correction de la logique modale du premier et second ordre S5' *Logique et Analyse*, 1, 28–44 **(1.3, 13.2)**.

Bayart, A., 1959, 'Quasi-adéquation de la logique modale de second ordre S5 et adéquation de la logique modale de premier ordre S5', *Logique et Analyse*, 2, 99–121 **(6.1, 14.2)**.

Becker, O., 1930, 'Zur Logik der Modalitäten', *Jahrbuch für Philosophie und Phänomenologische Forschung*, 11, 497–548 **(1.3, 3.3, 3.5, 11.10, 11.20, 12.18)**.

Bellissima, F., 1989, 'Infinite sets of non-equivalent modalities', *Notre Dame Journal of Formal Logic*, 30, 574–82 **(3.1)**.

Bellissima, F., and M. Mirolli, 1983, 'On the axiomatization of finite K-frames', *Studia Logica*, 383–8 **(8.3)**.

Benthem, J.F.A.K. van, 1975, 'A note on modal formulae and relational properties', *The Journal of Symbolic Logic*, 40, 55–8 **(10.12)**.

1978, 'Two simple incomplete logics', *Theoria*, 44, 25–37 **(8.9, 9.1, 9.6)**.

1979a, 'Canonical modal logics and ultrafilter extensions', *The Journal of*

Symbolic Logic, 44, 1–8 **(7.12)**.

1979b, 'Syntactic aspects of modal incompleteness theorems', *Theoria*, 45, 63–77 **(9.1)**.

1980, 'Some kinds of modal completeness', *Studia Logica*, 39, 125–41 **(10.6)**.

1983, *Modal Logic and Classical Logic*, Naples, Bibliopolis **(10.9)**.

1984, 'Correspondence theory', *Handbook of Philosophical Logic*, ed. D.M. Gabbay and F. Guenthner, Dordrecht, Reidel, Vol. II, Ch. 4, 167–247 **(10.9)**.

Benthem, J.F.A.K. van, and W.J. Blok, 1978, 'Transitivity follows from Dummett's axiom', *Theoria*, 44, 117f **(10.6)**.

Bergmann, G., 1949a, 'The finite representations of S5', *Methodos*, 1, 217–19 **(8.1)**.

Blackburn, P, 1993, 'Nominal tense logic', *Notre Dame Journal of Formal Logic*, 34, 56–83 **(12.9)**.

Blok, W.J., 1979, 'An axiomatization of the veiled recession frame', *Studia Logica*, 38, 37–47 **(8.9)**.

1980, 'The lattice of modal logics: an algebraic investigation', *The Journal of Symbolic Logic*, 44, 221–36 **(9.1)**.

Bocheński, I.M., 1961, *A History of Formal Logic*, (Translated and edited by Ivo Thomas) Notre Dame, University of Notre Dame Press **(11.1)**.

Boolos, G., 1979, *The Unprovability of Consistency*, Cambridge, Cambridge University Press **(7.13, 8.4)**.

1980, 'On systems of modal logic with provability interpretations', *Theoria*, 46, 7–18 **(9.1)**.

Boolos, G., and G. Sambin, 1985, 'An incomplete system of modal logic', *Journal of Philosophical Logic*, 14, 351–8 **(9.1)**.

1990, 'Provability: the emergence of a mathematical modality', *Studia Logica*, 50, 1–23 **(7.12)**.

Bowen, K.A., 1979, *Model Theory of Modal Logic*, Dordrecht, Reidel **(15.5)**.

Broido, J., 1975, 'von Wright's principle of predication – some clarifications', *Journal of Philosophical Logic*, 4, 6–16 **(13.6)**.

Bull, R.A., 1964, 'A note on the modal calculi S4.2 and S4.3', *Zeitschrift für mathematische Logik und Grundlagen der Mathematik*, 10, 53–5 **(8.1)**.

1965a, 'An algebraic study of Diodorean modal systems', *The Journal of Symbolic Logic*, 30, 58–64 **(7.4, 10.7)**.

1965b, 'A class of extensions of the modal system S4 with the finite model property', *Zeitschrift für mathematische Logik und Grundlagen der Mathematik*, 11, 127–32 **(8.1)**.

1966, 'That all normal extensions of S4.3 have the finite model property', *Zeitschrift für mathematische Logik und Grundlagen der Mathematik*, 12, 341–4 **(8.3)**.

1970 'An approach to tense logic', *Theoria*, 36, 282–300 **(12.9)**.

Bull, R.A., and K. Segerberg, 1984, 'Basic modal logic', *Handbook of*

Philosophical Logic, ed. D.M. Gabbay and F. Guenthner, Dordrecht, Reidel, Vol. II, Ch. 1, 1–88 **(12.17)**.

Burgess, J.P., 1984, 'Basic tense logic', *Handbook of Philosophical Logic*, ed. D.M. Gabbay and F. Guenthner, Dordrecht, Reidel, Vol. II, Ch. 1 89–133 **(12.5)**.

Byrd, M., 1978, 'The extensions of BAlt₃ – revisited', *Journal of Philosophical Logic*, 7, 407–13 **(7.10)**.

Carnap, R, 1946, 'Modalities and quantification', *The Journal of Symbolic Logic*, 11, 33–64 **(1.3, 5.1)**.

1947, *Meaning and necessity*, Chicago, University of Chicago Press **(13.6)**.

Chellas, B.F., 1980, *Modal Logic: An Introduction*, Cambridge, Cambridge University Press **(Exercise 2.10, 2.7, 3.4, 3.6, 8.1, 10.10)**.

Chellas, B.F., and K. Segerberg, 1994, 'Modal Logics with the MacIntosh Rule', *Journal of Philosophical Logic*, 23, 67–86 **(3.6)**.

Church, A., 1936, 'A note on the *Entscheidungsproblem*', *The Journal of Symbolic Logic*, 1, 40–1 (correction in *ibid* 101–2) **(14.5)**.

1956, *Introduction to mathematical logic Vol. I*, Princeton, Princeton University Press **(1.1, 13.1, 14.5)**.

Churchman, C.W., 1938, 'On finite and infinite modal systems', *The Journal of Symbolic Logic*, 3, 77–82 **(11.20)**.

Corsi, G., 1993, 'Quantified modal logics of positive rational numbers and some related systems', *Notre Dame Journal of Formal Logic*, 34, 263–283 **(Exercise 15.3)**.

Corsi, G., and S. Ghilardi, 1989, 'Directed frames', *Archive for Mathematical Logic*, 29, 53–67 **(15.6)**.

1992, 'Semantical aspects of quantified modal logic', *Knowledge, Belief and Strategic Action*, Ed. C. Bicchieri and M.L. Dalla Chiara, Cambridge, Cambridge University Press, 167–95 **(15.7)**.

Cresswell, M.J., 1967a, 'Note on a system of Åqvist', *The Journal of Symbolic Logic*, 32, 58–60 **(11.27)**.

1967b, 'The interpretation of some Lewis systems of modal logic', *Australasian Journal of Philosophy*, 45, 198–206 **(11.23)**.

1967c, 'A Henkin completeness theorem for T', *Notre Dame Journal of Formal Logic*, 8 186–90 **(14.2)**.

1969a, 'A conjunctive normal form for S3.5', *The Journal of Symbolic Logic*, 34 253–5 **(11.27)**.

1969b, 'The elimination of *de re* modalities', *The Journal of Symbolic Logic*, 34 329–30 **(13.6)**.

1973, *Logics and Languages*, London, Methuen **(17.4)**.

1979, 'BSeg has the finite model property', *Bulletin of the Section of Logic, Polish Academy of Sciences*, 8, 154–60 **(8.7)**.

1982, 'A canonical model for S2', *Logique et Analyse*, 97, 3 **(11.23)**.

1983a, 'KM and the finite model property', *Notre Dame Journal of Formal*

Logic, 24, 323–7 **(8.1)**.

1983b, 'The completeness of KW and K1.1', *Logique et Analyse*, No 102, 123–7 **(8.2)**.

1984, 'An incomplete decidable modal logic', *The Journal of Symbolic Logic*, 49, 520–7 **(8.10)**.

1985, 'We are all children of God', *Analytical Philosophy in Comparative Perspective* (ed. B.K. Matilal and J.L. Shaw), Dordrecht, Redel **(10.20)**.

1987, 'Magari's theorem via the recession frame', *Journal of Philosophical Logic*, 16, 13–5 **(9.1)**.

1988, 'Necessity and contingency', *Studia Logica*, 47, 146–9 **(1.2)**.

1990, *Entities and Indices*, Dordrecht, Kluwer **(19.2)**.

1991, 'In defence of the Barcan Formula', *Logique et Analyse*, No 135–6, 271–82 **(15.1)**.

1995a, 'S1 is not so simple', *Modality, Morality, and Belief*, Cambridge, Cambridge University Press, 29–40 **(11.28, 12.13)**.

1995b, 'Incompleteness and the Barcan Formula', *Journal of Philosophical Logic* 24, 379-403 **(14.4, 15.7)**.

Cross, C.B., 1993, 'From worlds to probabilities: a probabilistic semantics for modal logic', *Journal of Philosophical Logic*, 22, 169–92 **(12.25)**.

Crossley, J.N., and I.L. Humberstone, 1977, 'The logic of "Actually"', *Reports on Mathematical Logic*, No 8, 11–29 **(19.1)**.

Dalen, D. van, 1986, 'Intuitionistic logic', *Handbook of Philosophical Logic*, ed. D.M. Gabbay and F. Guenthner, Dordrecht, Reidel, Vol. III, Ch. 4, 225–39 **(12.18)**.

Dugundji, J., 1940, 'Note on a property of matrices for Lewis and Langford's calculi of propositions', *The Journal of Symbolic Logic*, 5, 150–1 **(8.1)**.

Dummett, M.A.E. and E.J. Lemmon, 1959, 'Modal logics between S4 and S5', *Zeitschrift für mathematische Logik und Grundlagen der Mathematik*, 5, 250–64 **(7.4, 7.9, 10.6, 12.9)**.

Dunn, J.M., 1986, 'Relevance logic and entailment', *Handbook of Philosophical Logic*, ed. D.M. Gabbay and F. Guenthner, Dordrecht, Reidel, Vol. III, Ch. 3, 117–224 **(11.34)**.

Emch, A.F., 1936, 'Implication and deducibility', *The Journal of Symbolic Logic*, 1, 26–35, and 58 **(11.31)**.

Feys, R., 1937, 'Les logiques nouvelles des modalités', *Revue Néoscholastique de Philosophie*, 40, 517–53, and 41, 217–52 **(2.7)**.

1950, 'Les systèmes formalisés Aristotéliciennes', *Revue Philosophique de Louvain*, 48, 478–509 **(1.2, 11.27)**.

1965, *Modal Logics*, Louvain, E. Nauwelaerts **(11.11, 11.17, 11.27)**.

Fine, K., 1970, 'Propositional quantifiers in modal logic', *Theoria*, 36, 336–46 **(18.6, 18.7)**.

1971, 'The logics containing S4.3', *Zeitschrift für mathematische Logik und Grundlagen der Mathematik*, 17, 371–6 **(8.3)**.

1972, 'Logics containing S4 without the finite model property', in Hodges, W. (ed), *Conference in Mathematical Logic – London '70*, Berlin, Springer-Verlag, 98–102 **(8.8)**.

1974a, 'Logics containing K4, Part I', *The Journal of Symbolic Logic*, 39, 31–42 **(10.4, 10.8)**.

1974b, 'An incomplete logic containing S4', *Theoria*, 40, 23–9 **(9.1)**.

1974c, 'An ascending chain of S4 logics', *Theoria*, 40, 110–6 **(9.1)**.

1975a, 'Some connections between elementary and modal logic', in Kanger, S. (ed), *Proceedings of the Third Scandinavian Logic Symposium*, Amsterdam, North Holland, 15–39 **(7.14, 10.14)**.

1975b, 'Normal frames in modal logic', *Notre Dame Journal of Formal Logic*, 16, 229–37 **(8.1)**.

1978, 'Model theory for modal logic, Part I, the *de re/de dicto* distinction', *Journal of Philosophical Logic*, 7, 125–56. (Part II 277–306) **(13.714.2, 16.2, 16.9)**.

1983, 'The permutation principle in quantificational logic', *Journal of Philosophical Logic*, 12, 33–7 **(16.9)**.

Fitch, F.B., 1952, *Sympolic Logic; An Introduction*, New York, Ronald Press Co **(12.3)**.

Fitting, M.C., 1983, *Proof Methods for Modal and Intuitionistic Logics*, Dordrect, Reidel, 1983 **(12.3, 12.18)**.

Forbes, G., 1989, *Languages of Possibility*, Oxford, Basil Blackwell **(19.2)**.

Frege, G., 1892, 'Über Sinn und Bedeutung', *Zeitschrift für Philosophie und Philosophische Kritik*, 100, 25–50 (English translation: 'On sense and reference', *Translations from the writings of Gottlob Frege*, P.T. Geach and M Black, Oxford, Basil Blackwell, 1952) **(17.1)**.

Gabbay, D.M., 1975, 'A normal logic that is complete for neighbourhood frames but not for Kripke frames', *Theoria*, 41, 148–53 **(12.17)**.

1976, *Investigations in Modal and Tense Logics with Applications to Problems in Philosophy and Linguistics*, Dordrecht, Reidel **(8.1, 8.3, 8.10)**.

1981, 'An irreflexivity lemma with applications to axiomatizations of conditions on tense frames', *Aspects of Philosophical Logic*, ed. U. Mönnich, Dordrecht, Reidel, 67–89 **(10.2, 10.3)**.

Gabbay, D.M., and F. Guenthner, 1984, *Handbook of Philosophical Logic*, Dordrecht, Reidel (four volumes) **(12.1)**.

Gabbay, D.M., and Ch. Rohrer, 1979, 'Do we really need tenses other than future and past?', *Semantics From Different Points of View*, (ed. R. Bäuerle *et al.*), Berlin, Springer, 15–20 **(19.1)**.

Gallin, D, 1975, *Intensional and Higher-Order Modal Logic*, Amsterdam, North Holland **(14.2)**.

Gargov, G., and V. Goranko, 1993, 'Modal logic with names', *Journal of Philosophical Logic*, 22, 607–36 **(12.9)**.

Garson, J.W., 1980, 'The unaxiomatizability of a quantified intensional logic',

Journal of Philosophical Logic, 9, 59–72 **(18.6)**.

1984, 'Quantification in modal logic', *Handbook of Philosophical Logic*, ed. D.M. Gabbay and F. Guenthner, Dordrecht, Reidel, Vol. II, Ch. 5, 249–307 **(16.2, 16.9, 18.6)**.

Gentzen, G., 1934, 'Untersuchungen über das logische Schliessen', *Mathematische Zeitschrift*, 39, 176–210, 405–13 **(12.3)**.

Gerson, M. 1975, 'The inadequacy of the neighbourhood semantics for modal logic', *The Journal of Symbolic Logic*, 40, 141–8 **(12.17)**.

1975a, 'An extension of S4 complete for the neighbourhood semantics but incomplete for the relational semantics', *Studia Logica*, 34, 333–342 **(12.17)**.

Ghilardi, G., 1991, 'Incompleteness results in Kripke semantics', *The Journal of Symbolic Logic*, 56, 517–38 **(15.7, 15.11)**.

Gödel, K., 1933, 'Eine Interpretation des intuitionistischen Aussagenkalküls', *Ergebnisse eines mathematischen Kolloquims* 4, 34–40 **(2.7, 11.15, 12.18)**.

Goldblatt, R.I., 1973, 'A model-theoretic study of some systems containing S3', *Zeitschrift für mathematische Logik und Grundlagen der Mathematik*, 19, 75–82 **(11.21)**.

1975a, 'First-order definability in modal logic', *The Journal of Symbolic Logic*, 40, 35–40 **(10.12)**.

1975b, 'Solution to a completeness problem of Lemmon and Scott', *Notre Dame Journal of Formal Logic*, 16, 405–8 **(10.11)**.

1976, 'Metamathematics of modal logic', *Reports on Mathematical Logic*, 6, 41–77 (part I); 7, 21–52 (part II) **(10.12)**.

1987, *Logics of Time and Computation*, Stanford, CSLI **(12.10, 12.11)**.

1991, 'The McKinsey axiom is not canonical', *The Journal of Symbolic Logic*, 56, 554–62 **(10.12)**.

Goranko, V., 1990, 'Modal definability in enriched languages', *Notre Dame Journal of Formal Logic*, Vol. 31, 81–105 **(12.7, 12.8)**.

Halldén, S., 1949a, 'Results concerning the decision problem of Lewis's calculi S3 and S6', *The Journal of Symbolic Logic*, 14, 230–6 **(11.24)**.

1949b, 'A reduction of the primitive symbols of the Lewis calculi', *Portugaliae Mathematica*, 8, 85–8 **(1.2)**.

Hanson, W.H., 1966, 'On some alleged decision procedures for S4', *The Journal of Symbolic Logic*, 31, 641–3 **(4.1)**.

Hawthorn, J., 1990, 'Natural deduction in normal modal logic', *Notre Dame Journal of Formal Logic*, 31, 263–73 **(12.3)**.

Hazen, A., 1976, 'Expressive incompleteness in modal logic', *Journal of Philosophical Logic*, 5, 25–46 **(19.1)**.

1979, 'Counterpart-theoretic semantics for modal logic', *The Journal of Philosophy*, 76, 319–38 **(19.5)**.

1990, 'Actuality and quantification', *Notre Dame Journal of Formal Logic*, 31, 498–508 **(19.1)**.

Henkin, L., 1949, 'The completeness of the first-order functional calculus', *The*

Journal of Symbolic Logic, 14, 159–66 **(6.2, 14.1)**.

1950, 'Completeness in the theory of types', *The Journal of Symbolic Logic*, 15, 81–91 **(9.6)**.

Heyting, A., 1930, 'Die formalen Regeln der intuitionistischen Logik', *Sitzungsberichte der Preussischen Akademie der Wissenschaften, Physikalische-mathematische Klasse*, 42–56 **(12.18)**.

Hintikka, K.J.J., 1961, 'Modality and quantification', *Theoria*, 27, 110–28 **(13.2, 15.1)**.

1963, 'The modes of modality', *Acta Philosophica Fennica – Modal and Many-valued Logics*, 65–81 **(17.2)**.

Hodes, H.T., 1984a, 'Some theorems on the expressive limitations of modal languages', *Journal of Philosophical Logic*, 13, 13–26 **(19.1)**.

1984b, 'Axioms for actuality', *Journal of Philosophical Logic*, 13, 27–34 **(19.1)**.

Hughes, G.E., 1975, 'B(S4.3,S4) unveiled', *Theoria*, 41, 85–8 **(12.6)**.

1980, 'Equivalence relations and S5', *Notre Dame Journal of Formal Logic*, 21, 577–84 **(Exercise 3.8)**.

1982, 'Some strong omnitemporal logics', *Synthese*, 53, 19–42 **(12.6)**.

1990, 'Every world can see a reflexive world', *Studia Logica*, 49, 175–81 **(10.13)**.

Hughes, G.E. and M.J. Cresswell, 1968, *An Introduction to Modal Logic*, London, Methuen, (reprinted with corrections, 1972) **(7.7, 10.6, 10.8, 11.11, 11.24, 11.25, 12.2, 12.6, 13.6, 14.2, 15.2, 15.8)**.

1975, 'Omnitemporal logic and converging time', *Theoria*, 41, 11–34 **(8.7)**.

1982, 'K1.1 is not canonical', *Bulletin of the Section of Logic, Polish Academy of Sciences*, 11, 109–13 **(Exercise 7.12)**.

1984, *A Companion to Modal Logic*, London, Methuen **(4.2, 7.11, 7.12, 8.1, 9.1, 10.1)**.

1986, 'A Companion to Modal Logic – some corrections', *Logique et Analyse*, No 112, 41–51 **(8.1)**.

Humberstone, I.L., 1983, 'Inaccessible worlds', *Notre Dame Journal of Formal Logic*, 24, 346–52 **(12.7, 12.14)**.

1987, 'The modal logic of "all and only"', *Notre Dame Journal of Formal Logic*, 28, 177–88 **(12.14)**.

Isard, S., 1977, 'A finitely axiomatizable undecidable extension of K', *Theoria*, 43, 195–202 **(8.6)**.

Jansana, R., 1994, 'Some logics related to von Wright's logic of place', *Notre Dame Journal of Formal Logic*, 35, 88–98 **(7.10)**.

Jennings, R.E., 1981, 'A note on the axiomatisation of Brouweresche modal logic', *Journal of Philosophical Logic*, 10, 341–3 **(Exercise 3.13)**.

Jónsson, B, and A Tarski, 1951, 'Boolean algebras with operators', *American Journal of Mathematics*, 73, 891–939 **(1.3, 12.26)**.

Kalmar, L., 1936, 'Zurückführung des Entscheidungsproblems auf den Fall von

Formeln mit einer einzigenbinaren Funktionsvariablen', *Compositio Mathematica*, 4, 137–44 **(14.5)**.

Kamp, J.A.W., 1971, 'Formal properties of "now"', *Theoria*, 40, 76–109 **(19.1)**.

Kanger, S., 1957a, *Provability in Logic*, Stockholm, Almqvist & Wiksell **(1.3, 13.2)**.

1957b, 'The morning star paradox', *Theoria*, 23, 1–11 **(18.1, 18.5)**.

Kaplan, D., 1966, 'Review of Kripke', *The Journal of Symbolic Logic*, 31, 120–2 **(6.1)**.

Kneale, W.C., 1956, 'The province of logic', *Contemporary British Philosophy*, (ed. H.D.Lewis), London, George Allen and Unwin, 237–61 **(11.33)**.

Kneale, W.C. and M. Kneale, 1962, *The development of logic*, Oxford, Clarendon Press **(11.1, 11.33)**.

Kracht, M, 1991, 'A solution to a problem of Urquhart', *Journal of Philosophical Logic*, 20, 285–6 **(8.6)**.

Kripke, S.A., 1959, 'A completeness theorem in modal logic', *The Journal of Symbolic Logic*, 24, 1–14 **(1.3, 6.1, 12.20, 14.2)**.

1962, 'The undecidability of monadic modal quantification theory', *Zeitschrift für mathematische Logik und Grundlagen der Mathematik*, 8, 113–6 **(14.6)**.

1963a, 'Semantical analysis of modal logic I, normal propositional calculi', *Zeitschrift für mathematische Logik und Grundlagen der Mathematik*, 9, 67–96 **(1.3, 2.3, 4.2, 6.1, 7.4)**.

1963b, 'Semantical considerations on modal logics', *Acta Philosophica Fennica – Modal and Many-valued Logics*, 83–94 **(13.2, 15.3, 16.6, 16.7)**.

1965a, 'Semantical analysis of intuitionistic logic I', *Formal Systems and Recursive Functions* (ed. J.N. Crossley, M.A.E. Dummett), Amsterdam, North Holland Publishing Co., 92–129 **(12.18)**.

1965b, 'Semantical analysis of modal logic II, non-normal modal propositional calculi', *The Theory of Models* (ed. J.W. Addison, L. Henkin, A. Tarski), Amsterdam, North Holland Publishing Co., 206–20 **(11.23, 11.26)**.

1967, 'Review of E.J. Lemmon; Algebraic semantics for modal logics II', *Mathematical Reviews* 34, 1022 (Review no. 5662.) **(14.3)**.

1992, 'Individual concepts, their logic, philosophy, and some of their uses', (abstract) *American Philosophical Association, Eastern Division, Eighty second Annual Meeting, December 27–30 1992*, 70–3 **(18.6, 18.10)**.

Kuhn, S.T., 1979, 'Quantifiers as modal operators', *Studia Logica*, 39, 145–58 **(19.1, 19.2)**.

1989, 'The domino relation: Flattening a two-dimensional modal logic', *Journal of Philosophical Logic*, 18, 173–95 **(19.1)**.

Langholm, T, 1987, 'H.B. Smith on modality', *Journal of Philosophical Logic*, 16, 337–46 **(11.25)**.

Lemmon, E.J., 1956, 'Alternative postulate sets for Lewis's S5', *The Journal of Symbolic Logic*, 21, 347–49 **(Exercise 3.9)**.

1957, 'New foundations for Lewis modal systems', *The Journal of Symbolic*

Logic, 22, 176–86 **(11.19, 11.27)**.

1959, 'Is there only one correct system of modal logic?', *Aristotelian Society Supplementary Volume XXXIII*, 23–40 **(11.19)**.

1960a, 'An extension algebra and the modal system T', *Notre Dame Journal of Formal Logic*, 1, 2–12 **(12.26)**.

1960b, 'Quantified S4 and the Barcan formula', (Abstract), *The Journal of Symbolic Logic*, 24, 391–2 **(15.4)**.

1965a, 'Some results on finite axiomatizability in modal logic', *Notre Dame Journal of Formal Logic*, 6, 301–7 **(10.15)**.

1965b, *Beginning Logic*, London, Van Nostrand **(12.3, 12.4)**.

1966a, 'Algebraic semantics for modal logics I', *The Journal of Symbolic Logic*, 31, 46–65 **(12.26)**.

1966b, 'Algebraic semantics for modal logics II', *ibid.*, 191–218 **(12.26)**.

Lemmon, E.J., and D.S. Scott, 1977, *The 'Lemmon Notes': An Introduction to Modal Logic*, ed. K. Segerberg, Oxford, Basil Blackwell **(2.1, 2.3, 2.7, 2.8, 3.4, 6.1, 7.8, 9.1, 10.10, 10.12)**.

Lewis, C.I., 1912, 'Implication and the algebra of logic', *Mind*, N.S. 21, 522–31 **(11.6, 11.7)**.

1913, 'Interesting theorems in symbolic logic', *Journal of Philosophy*, 10, 239–42 **(11.6)**.

1914a, 'A new algebra of strict implication', *Mind* N.S. 23, 240–7 **(11.6, 11.33)**.

1914b, 'The matrix algebra for implication', *Journal of Philosophy*, 11, 589–600 **(11.6)**.

1918, *A Survey of Symbolic Logic*, Berkeley, University of California Press, (N.B. The chapter on strict implication is not included in the 1961 Dover reprint) **(11.6, 11.7, 11.9, 11.11)**.

1920, 'Strict implication. An emendation', *Journal of Philosophy*, 17, 300–2 **(11.9)**.

Lewis, C.I., and C.H. Langford, 1932, *Symbolic Logic*, New York, Dover publications **(1.2, 3.2, 3.5, 11.6, 11.11, 11.14, 11.21, 11.22, 11.32, 11.33)**.

Lewis, D.K., 1968, 'Counterpart theory and quantified modal logic', *The Journal of Philosophy*, 65, 113–26 **(19.3, 19.4)**.

1973, *Counterfactuals*, Oxford, Basil Blackwell **(12.16)**.

1974, 'Intensional logics without iterative axioms', *Journal of Philosophical Logic*, 3, 457–66 **(9.2)**.

1986, *On the Plurality of Worlds*, Oxford, Basil Blackwell **(19.3)**.

Löb, M.H., 1966, 'Extensional interpretations of modal logics', *The Journal of Symbolic Logic*, 31, 23–45 **(7.13)**.

Loux, M.J., 1979, *The Possible and the Actual: Readings in the Metaphysics of Modality*, Ithaca, Cornell University Press **(1.4)**.

McCall, S., 1963, *Aristotle's Modal Syllogisms*, Amsterdam, North Holland Publishing Co **(11.1)**.

MacColl, H., 1880, 'Symbolical reasoning', *Mind*, 5, 45–60 **(11.2)**.

1903, 'Symbolic reasoning V', *Mind* (N.S.) 12, 355–64 **(11.3)**.

1906a, *Symbolic logic and its applications*, London **(11.3, 11.4)**.

1906b, 'Symbolic reasoning VIII', *Mind* (N.S.) 15, 504–18 **(11.3, 11.4, 11.30)**.

McKay, T.J., 1975, 'Essentialism in quantified modal logic', *Journal of Philosophical Logic*, 4, 423–38 **(13.6)**.

1978, 'The principle of predication', *Journal of Philosophical Logic*, 7, 19–26 **(13.6)**.

McKinsey, J.C.C., 1934, 'A reduction in the number of postulates for C.I. Lewis' system of strict implication', *Bulletin of the American Mathematical Society*, 40, 425–7**(11.14)**.

1941, 'A solution of the decision problem for the Lewis systems S2 and S4 with an application to topology', *The Journal of Symbolic Logic*, 6, 117–34 **(8.1, 12.26)**.

1944, 'On the number of complete extensions of the Lewis systems of sentential calculus', *The Journal of Symbolic Logic*, 9, 41–5 **(3.7)**.

1945, 'On the syntactical construction of systems of modal logic', *The Journal of Symbolic Logic*, 10, 83–96 **(1.3, 7.7, 12.20)**.

McKinsey, J.C.C., and A. Tarski, 1944, 'The algebra of topology', *Annals of Mathematics*, 45, 141–91 **(12.26)**.

1948, 'Some theorems about the sentential calculi of Lewis and Heyting', *The Journal of Symbolic Logic*, 13, 1–15 **(12.18)**.

Makinson, D.C., 1966a, 'There are infinitely many Diodorean modal functions', *The Journal of Symbolic Logic*, 31, 406–8 **(5.2)**.

1966, 'On some completeness theorems in modal logic', *Zeitschrift für mathematische Logik und Grundlagen der Mathematik*, 12, 379–84 **(6.1)**.

1969, 'A normal modal calculus between T and S4 without the finite model property', *The Journal of Symbolic Logic*, 34, 35–8 **(8.8)**.

1970, 'A generalisation of the concept of a relational frame for modal logic', *Theoria*, 36, 331–5 **(9.6)**.

1971, 'Some embedding theorems in modal logic', *Notre Dame Journal of Formal Logic*, 12, 252–4 **(3.7)**.

Marcus, Mrs J.A., *vide* Barcan, R.C.

Meredith, C.A., 1956, *Interpretations of Different Modal Logics in the 'Property Calculus'*, (cyclostyled) Christchurch, Philosophy Department, Canterbury University College (recorded and expanded by A.N. Prior) **(1.3)**.

Ming Xu, 1991, 'Some descending chains of incomplete logics', *Journal of Philosophical Logic*, 20, 265–83 **(9.1)**.

Moh Shaw-Kwei, 1950, 'The deduction theorems and two new logical systems', *Methodos*, 2, 56–75 **(11.33)**.

Montagna, F., 1984, 'The predicate modal logic of provability', *Notre Dame Journal of Formal Logic*, 25, 179–89 **(Exercise 14.5)**.

Montague, R.M., 1960, 'Logical necessity, physical necessity, ethics and quantifiers', *Inquiry*, 4, 259–269. (reprinted in Montague 1974 71–83) **(1.3, 13.2)**.

1963, 'Syntactical treatments of modality', *Acta Philosophica Fennica – Modal and Many-valued Logics*, 153–66 (reprinted in Montague 1974, 286–302) **(12.22)**.

1974, *Formal Philosophy*, New Haven, Yale University Press **(17.4)**.

Montgomery, H.A., and F.R. Routley, 1966, 'Contingency and non-contingency bases for normal modal logics', *Logique et Analyse*, 9, 318–28 **(1.2)**.

Moore, G.E., 1919, 'External and internal relations', *Proceedings of the Aristotelian Society* (reprinted in *Philosophical Studies*, London, Kegan Paul, Trench, Trubner & Co., (subsequent reprints, Routledge and Kegan Paul) 276–309 **(11.29)**.

Morgan, C.G., 1982, 'Simple probabilistic semantics for propositional K, T, B, S4 and S5', *Journal of Philosophical Logic*, 11, 443–58 **(12.23, 12.24)**.

Myhill, J.R., 1958, 'Problems arising in the formalization of intensional logic', *Logique et Analyse*, 1, (No.2) 74–83 **(15.1)**.

Ōhama, S. 1982, 'Conjunctive normal forms and weak modal logics without the axiom of necessity', *Notre Dame Journal of Formal Logic*, 25, 141–51 **(5.1)**.

Parks, Z., 1974, 'Semantics for contingent identity systems', *Notre Dame Journal of Formal Logic*, 15, 333–4 **(18.4)**.

Parks, Z, and T.L. Smith, 1974, 'The inadequacy of Hughes and Cresswell's semantics for the CI systems', *Notre Dame Journal of Formal Logic*, 15, 331–2 **(18.4)**.

Parry, W.T., 1939, 'Modalities in the *Survey* system of strict implication', *The Journal of Symbolic Logic*, 4, 131–54 **(3.3, 5.3, 11.21)**.

Parsons, C.D., 1975, 'On modal quantifier theory with contingent domains' (abstract), *The Journal of Symbolic Logic*, 40, 302 **(16.3)**.

Plantinga, A, 1976, 'Actualism and possible worlds', *Theoria*, 42, 139–60 (reprinted in Loux 1979, 253–73) **(18.9)**.

Pledger, K.E., 1972, 'Modalities of systems containing S3', *Zeitschrift für mathematische Logik und Grundlagen der Mathematik*, 18, 267–83 **(11.21)**.

Pollock, J.L., 1966, 'The paradoxes of strict implication', *Logique et Analyse*, 34, (Vol. 9) 180–96 **(11.32)**.

Prior, A.N., 1955a, *Formal logic*, Oxford University Press, Second Edition, 1962 **(Exercise 3.9, 13.9)**.

1955b, 'Diodoran modalities', *The Philosophical Quarterly*, 5, 205–13 **(7.2)**.

1956, 'Modality and quantification in S5', *The Journal of Symbolic Logic*, 21, 60–2 **(13.5)**.

1957, *Time and Modality*, Oxford University Press **(3.3, 7.1, 7.2, 7.3, 15.1, 16.5)**.

1958, 'Diodorus and modal logic, a correction', *The Philosophical Quarterly*, 8, 226–30 (a correction to Prior 1955b) **(7.3)**.

1962, 'Possible worlds', *The Philosophical Quarterly*, 12, 36–43 **(7.4)**.

1967, *Past, Present and Future*, Oxford University Press **(7.1, 13.5)**.

1968, 'Now', *Noûs*, 12, 191–207 **(19.1)**.

Quine, W.V., 1947, 'The problem of interpreting modal logic', *The Journal of Symbolic Logic*, 12, 43–8 **(17.1)**.

1953, 'Reference and modality', *From a Logical Point of View*, Cambridge, Mass, Harvard University Press, 139–59 **(18.2)**.

Rescher, N., 1959, 'On the logic of existence and denotation', *The Philosophical Review*, 58, 157–80 **(16.2)**.

Russell, B.A.W., 1905, 'On denoting', *Mind*, 14, 479–93 **(17.3)**.

Sahlqvist, H., 1975, 'Completeness and correspondence in first and second-order semantics for modal logic', in Kanger, S. (ed), *Proceedings of the Third Scandinavian Logic Symposium*, Amsterdam, North Holland, 110–43 **(10.1, 10.11)**.

Schotch, P.K., and R.E. Jennings, 1980, 'Modal logic and the theory of modal aggregation', *Philosophia*, 9, 265–78 **(12.15)**.

Schumm, G.F., 1975, 'Wajsberg normal forms for S5', *Journal of Philosophical Logic*, 4, 357–60 **(5.1)**.

1987 'Some noncompactness results for modal logic', *Notre Dame Journal of Formal Logic*, 30, 285–90 **(10.8)**.

Schweizer, P., 1992, 'A syntactical approach to modality', *Journal of Philosophical Logic*, 22, 1–31 **(12.20)**.

1993, 'Quantified Quinean S5', *Journal of Philosophical Logic*, 22, 589–605 **(12.20)**.

Scroggs, S.J., 1951, 'Extensions of the Lewis system S5', *The Journal of Symbolic Logic*, 16, 112–20 **(8.1)**.

Segerberg, K, 1968a, 'Decidability of S4.1', *Theoria*, 34, 7–20 **(8.1, 9.5)**.

1968b, *Results in Non-classical Logic*, Lund, Berlingska Boktryckeriet **(2.3)**.

1970, 'Modal logics with linear alternative relations', *Theoria*, 36, 301–22 **(7.6, 10.7)**.

1971, *An Essay in Classical Modal Logic* (3 vols), Uppsala, Filosofiska studier **(2.9, 7.5, 7.10, 7.13, 8.1, 8.4, 8.5, 9.3, 9.4, 12.12)**.

1972, 'Post completeness in modal logic', *The Journal of Symbolic Logic*, 37, 711–15 **(3.7)**.

1973a, 'Franzén's proof of Bull's theorem', *Ajatus*, 35, 216–21 **(8.2)**.

1973b, 'Two-dimensional modal logic', *Journal of Philosophical Logic*, 2, 77–96 **(19.1)**.

1975, 'That every extension of S4.3 is normal', in Kanger, S. (ed), *Proceedings of the Third Scandinavian Logic Symposium*, Amsterdam, North Holland, 194–6 **(8.3)**.

1980 'A note on the logic of elsewhere', *Theoria*, 46, 183–7 **(7.11)**.

Shehtman, V.B., and D.P. Skvorcov, 1991, 'Semantics of non-classical first-order predicate logics', *Mathematical Logic, Proceedings of Heyting 88 at Chajka (Bulgaria) 1988*, New York, Plenum Press **(14.4)**.

Skyrms, B., 1978, 'An immaculate conception of modality', *The Journal of Philosophy*, 75, 368–87 **(12.20, 12.21, 12.22)**.

Smith, H.B., 1936, 'The algebra of propositions', *Philosophy of Science*, 2, 551–78 **(11.25)**.

Smullyan, A.F., 1948, 'Modality and description', *The Journal of Symbolic Logic*, 13, 31–7 **(17.5)**.

Sobociński, B., 1953, 'Note on a modal system of Feys-von Wright', *The Journal of Computing Systems*, 1, 171–8 **(2.7)**.

— 1964a, 'Remarks about the axiomatizations of certain modal systems', *Notre Dame Journal of Formal Logic*, 5, 71–80 **(7.7)**.

— 1964b, 'Modal system S4.4', *Notre Dame Journal of Formal Logic*, 5, 305–12 **(7.6)**.

— 1964c, 'Family K of the non-Lewis modal systems', *Notre Dame Journal of Formal Logic*, 5, 313–8 **(7.1)**.

Stalnaker, R.C. 1968, 'A theory of conditionals', *Studies in Logical Theory* (ed. N. Rescher), Oxford, Basil Blackwell, 98–112 **(12.16)**.

Stalnaker, R.C., and R.H. Thomason, 1968, 'Abstraction in first-order modal logic', *Theoria*, 34, 203–7 **(18.8)**.

Sugihara, T., 1962, 'The number of modalities in T supplemented by the axiom CL^2pL^3p', *The Journal of Symbolic Logic*, 27, 407–8 **(3.1)**.

Thomas, I, 1962, 'Solutions of five modal problems of Sobociński', *Notre Dame Journal of Formal Logic*, 3 199–200. **(1.3)**.

— 1964, 'Modal systems in the neighbourhood of T', *Notre Dame Journal of Formal Logic*, 5, 59–61 **(3.1)**.

Thomason, R.H., 1970a, 'Some completeness results for modal predicate calculi', *Philosophical Problems in Logic* (ed K. Lambert), Dordrecht, Reidel, 56–76 **(14.2, 16.3, 16.4)**.

— 1970b, 'Modality and metaphysics', *The Logical Way of Doing Things* (ed. K. Lambert), New Haven, Yale University Press **(18.6)**.

Thomason, R.H., and R.C. Stalnaker, 1968, 'Modality and reference', *Noûs*, 2, 359–72 **(18.8)**.

Thomason, S.K., 1972a, 'Semantic analysis of tense logics', *The Journal of Symbolic Logic*, 37, 150–8 **(9.6, 9.7)**.

— 1972b, 'Noncompactness in propositional modal logic', *The Journal of Symbolic Logic*, 37, 716–20 **(10.8)**.

— 1974a, 'An incompleteness theorem in modal logic', *The Journal of Symbolic Logic*, 40, 30–4 **(9.1)**.

— 1974b, 'Reduction of tense logic to modal logic', *The Journal of Symbolic Logic*, 39, 549–51 **(10.16)**.

— 1975a, 'The logical consequence relation of propositional tense logic', *Zeitschrift für mathematische Logik und Grundlagen der Mathematik*, 21, 29–40 **(10.16)**.

— 1975b, 'Reduction of second-order logic to modal logic', *Zeitschrift für mathematische Logik und Grundlagen der Mathematik*, 21, 107–14 **(10.16)**.

Tichý, P., 1973, 'On *de dicto* modalities in quantified S5', *Journal of Philosophical Logic*, 2, 687–92 **(13.6)**.

Ullrich, D., and M. Byrd, 1977, 'The extensions of BAlt₃', *Journal of Philosophical Logic*, 6, 109–117 **(7.10)**.

Urquhart, A., 1981, 'Decidability and the finite model property', *Journal of Philosophical Logic*, 10, 367–70 **(8.5)**.

Venema, Y., 1992, 'A note on the tense logic of dominoes', *Journal of Philosophical Logic*, 21, 173–82 **(19.1)**.

Vlach, F., 1973, '"Now" and "then". A formal study in the logic of tense anaphora', PhD dissertation, UCLA. **(19.1)**.

Vredenduin, P.G.J, 1939, 'A system of strict implication', *The Journal of Symbolic Logic*, 4, 73–76 **(11.31)**.

Wajsberg, M., 1933, 'Ein erweiteter Klassenkalkül', *Monatshefte für Mathematik und Physik*, Vol. 40, 113–26 **(1.3, 5.1)**.

Wang, X., 1992, 'The McKinsey axiom is not compact', *The Journal of Symbolic Logic*, 57, 1230–8 **(10.12)**.

Whitehead, A.N., and B.A.W. Russell, 1910, *Principia mathematica*, Cambridge, Cambridge University Press, 3 vols., First edition 1910-1913, Second edition 1923-1927 **(11.5, 12.2, 17.3)**.

Williamson, T, 1988, 'Assertion, denial and some cancellation rules in modal logic', *Journal of Philosophical Logic*, 17, 299–318 **(3.6)**.

1992, 'An alternative rule of disjunction in modal logic', *Notre Dame Journal of Formal Logic*, 33, 89–100 **(3.6)**.

1994, 'Non-genuine MacIntosh Logics', *Journal of Philosophical Logic*, 23, 87–101 **(3.6)**.

Wright, G.H. Von, 1951, *An Essay in Modal Logic*, Amsterdam, North Holland Publishing Co **(2.7, 4.1, 13.6)**.

1979, 'A modal logic of place', *The Philosophy of Nicholas Rescher* (ed. E. Sosa), Dordrecht, Reidel, 63–73 **(7.11)**.

Yonemitzu, N., 1955, 'A note on the modal systems, von Wright's and Lewis's S1', *Memoirs of the Osaka University of the Liberal Arts and Education Bulletin of Natural Science*, no.4, 45 **(11.18)**.

Zeman, J.J., 1973, *Modal Logic: The Lewis Systems*, Oxford, Clarendon Press **(11.11, 15.9, 15.10)**.

INDEX

418